窪薗晴夫教授近影

音韻研究の新展開
窪薗晴夫教授還暦記念論文集

音韻研究の新展開

窪薗晴夫教授還暦記念論文集

[編]
田中真一・ピンテール=ガーボル
小川晋史・儀利古幹雄・竹安 大

開拓社

#　まえがき

　本書は，2017年3月に還暦を迎えられる，窪薗晴夫教授をお祝いするために編纂された論文集である．先生と数十年に渡って親交のある音韻論・音声学の研究者，そして，先生が神戸大学，大阪外国語大学（現大阪大学外国語学部）で教鞭を執られた時期の教え子が執筆し，合わせて22組29名による論考が収められている．

　所収論文は，それぞれ関連するテーマをもとに「音韻理論と音韻現象」，「語形成と音韻現象」，「日本語アクセントと形態論」，「音声知覚・生成とL1獲得」，「借用語音韻論とL2習得・知覚」の5部により構成されている．

　編纂にあたり，執筆者には，記念論文集としては比較的多めの分量でご寄稿頂くようお願いした．これは，本書が通常の研究書と変わらず，多くの研究者に参照される水準を目指したためである．この点については窪薗先生もきっと喜んでいただけるものと自負している．

　論文以外の部分では，窪薗先生の履歴，業績，そして先生への祝辞の頁を設けた．履歴・業績からは，これまでの軌跡が年代を追って確認でき，2016年12月時点における，すべての著書，論文が網羅されている．

　先生のご研究の特徴として多くの方の認めることとして，何より明晰で分かりやすいことがあげられる．複雑に見える，あるいは，そもそも気付かれていないような事象に対し，独自の切り口によって，そこに秩序の存在を鮮やかに指し示す．また，身近な例と的確な説明によって，誰もが納得させられる．こういった，学界にインパクトを与えた数々の著作が確認できる．

　還暦の年に日本言語学会会長である窪薗先生は，言語学各分野の多くの方々と親交がある．先生ととくに関係の深い研究者が，祝辞という形でご寄稿下さった．留学先での指導教員であるBob Ladd教授（エジンバラ大学），神戸大学時代の同僚としても特別なつながりのある，柴谷方良（ライス大学教授），西光義弘（神戸大学名誉教授），松本曜（神戸大学教授），岸本秀樹（神戸大学教授）の各先生，また，音声学・音韻論の分野で長年懇意にされている上野善道先生（東京大学名誉教授）に，執筆をご快諾いただいた．窪

蘭先生とのエピソードが，お祝いの言葉とともに披露されている．

　本書に掲載された以外の面について，簡単に触れておきたい．
　窪薗先生は，研究はもちろん，教育であれ組織運営であれ，一貫して的確かつ分かりやすい形で，多くのものやことを産み出して来られた．それは，先生の座右の銘である 'What is true is simple' や「真理は人を自由にする」の実践にほかならない．そういった姿勢に多くの人が引きつけられ，つねに大きな輪が作られてきた．
　音韻研究では，1993年に関西音韻論研究会（PAIK）を創設され，大学の垣根を超えた，風通しのよい研究交流が行われるようになった．1996年には音韻論研究会（現日本音韻論学会）の第1回音韻論フォーラムを神戸大学で開催された．それ以降，国内外の著名な音韻論研究者が各会場を訪れ，音韻研究にますますの活性化をもたらした．2002年には，関東・関西の音韻論研究会の交流を目的として（その後は音韻論研究者の交流を目的として），音韻論フェスタを立ち上げられた．いずれの会も，現在に至るまで途切れることなく発展を続けている．本書の執筆者の大半が上記と何らかの関わりを持ち，教え子全員は，それらの会を通して，外部の研究者と交流する大切さを教えられながら育てられた．
　このように，著作以外の面においても，窪薗先生が国内外の音韻研究に与えた恩恵は計り知れない．
　研究以外の面においても，「真理は人を自由にする」という姿勢は一貫している．神戸大学文学部にサバティカル制度を導入（第1号として権利を行使）されたのをはじめ，多くのことを提案され，周囲を情理両面において納得させた．赴任間もない時期に，紫煙の充満していた当時の教授会から，それを一掃させたという逸話も残っている（同時期に，言語学専修でのバーベキューを行事化し，別の形で煙を充満させた）．
　教育の面においても窪薗先生は，常に的確に本質を捉え，学生に道を照らして下さる理想の指導者であった．また，厳しい先生でもあった．
　学部・大学院の演習や発表会では，教え子の誰もが，自身のよく理解していない部分や，あいまいな部分，矛盾等を先生から的確な形で指摘され，不明を実感した．また，頂いたコメントによって，自分では意識に上っていなかった事柄が，にわかに明示化されたという瞬間を何度も経験している．

厳しい先生であるのと同時に，思いやりに満ちた，とても面倒見のよい教師というのが，教え子誰もの窪薗先生に対する見方である．学生時代も，また修了後も，研究や進路，状況について気に掛けて下さっていることが，直接間接の別を問わず，さまざまな形で知られることになり，その都度，有り難さを実感する．

　いったん学問を離れると，コンパなどの場では，得意の自虐ネタで周囲を笑わせ，先生のこよなく愛する，血液型，寅さん，相撲などの話題で場を和ませる．こういった，随所に滲み出るお人柄のよさが明晰さと相まって，事を進める上で多くの人を納得させることにつながっているように思う．教え子も例外なく，こういった先生の教えを空気のように享受してきた．

　本書の完成までに，多くの方々からご協力をいただいた．記して御礼を申し上げたい．各論文の書式チェックに関して，後藤さやか氏，黄賢暻氏にご協力頂いた．御礼を申し上げたい．また，論文執筆者には，製作費の一部についてもご協力賜った。さらに，論文の執筆は辞退されたものの，寄付を申し出て下さった方々にも，御礼を申し上げたい．出版事情の厳しい中，記念論文集の出版を引き受けて下さった開拓社，とくに，企画の段階からさまざまな形でご協力と助言を下さった川田賢氏に御礼を申し上げたい．

　最後に，本論文集を，これまで育てて下さった窪薗先生に，心からの感謝とともに捧げる．

2017 年 1 月

編者一同

Congratulations, Haruo!
Bob Ladd

It was the middle of January 1985. I had arrived at the University of Edinburgh only a few weeks earlier to take up my position as a lecturer in linguistics. The low mid-morning sun shone through the window of my new office as I sat thinking about the undergraduate courses I was already teaching. Then there came a knock at the door, and a young man came in and introduced himself as Haruo Kubozono. He was, he said, a PhD student in the department and was interested in accent, rhythm, and intonation in Japanese. He asked me if he could tell me a little about his work. Before long he was describing to me things like how the accent patterns differ in the Japanese versions of the American baseball team names *New York Yankees* and *Boston Red Sox,* and how the difference can be explained with reference to the different internal branching structure of the two names. We talked for at least an hour.

This turned out to be the first of many conversations I had with Haruo, and it was typical of most of them. I was soon officially assigned as his supervisor, and for the remaining year and a half of his residence in Edinburgh we met regularly to talk about theories of prosodic structure, and phonetic details of specific cases in Japanese, and experimental ways to test his ideas. He was the first PhD student I had ever supervised, and (as I have said half-jokingly to many people since then) I thought that my experience with him was typical of doctoral supervision. It was not long before I realised that his combination of seriousness, determination, and linguistic insight is rare, and that I was lucky to have someone like him as a regular discussion partner. It is no coincidence that some of my own papers from the late 1980s deal with hierarchical prosodic structure and other topics related to Haruo's work.

Although the distance between Japan and Scotland makes it difficult to have regular discussions of the sort we had during my first years in Edinburgh, Haruo and I have managed to stay in touch. Our connection is not just professional: somewhere I have pictures from twenty years ago of his children and mine playing in a big park in the Netherlands, and more recently he and Keiko befriended one of my nephews who spent a few years teaching English in Japan. As both friend and teacher, I have followed his success with delight and perhaps even a small measure of pride. I am happy to join the scholars assembled in this volume to mark his sixtieth birthday and to recognise his thirty years (so far!) of contributions to the field.

 Congratulations, Haruo!

Bob Ladd
Edinburgh, December 2016

(エジンバラ大学)

祝　辞

柴谷　方良

　窪薗晴夫さんが還暦を迎えられたとのこと，先ずはお目出とうございますと，お祝いの言葉をお贈りします．

　窪薗さんと私が親しく仕事を一緒にすることになったのは，1996年に窪薗さんを神戸大学文学部にお迎えしてからであった．その前年あたりに，ちょうど彼がサンタクルーズで，私がUCLAで研究生活を送っていた時に，ロサンゼルスに立ち寄っていただき，懇願して実現した人事であった．言語学講座を拡充していく上で，音声学・音韻論を専攻する教員・研究者が必要であったからの人事であるが，窪薗さんは持ち前の研究への熱意と実行力の強さによって，神戸大の言語学講座を大いに盛り立ててくださった．

　研究者としての窪薗さんの功績については，いまさらここで述べるまでもないことであるが，優れた伝統をもつ日本の音声学・音韻論の領域において，さまざまな角度からの新しい研究方法を開発し，輝かしい成果を積み上げてこられた．最近の，ベルリン・ムートン社からの *Handbook of Japanese Phonetics and Phonology* (2015) に見られるように，ご自身の研究を通して，また本記念論文集の寄稿者によって代表される研究仲間とともに，日本の音声学・音韻論の研究成果を海外にも浸透させ，この分野における日本の学術水準の高さを内外に明確な形で示した点も大いに評価されるべき功績である．

　ますますのご健勝を祈念しながら，これでもってお祝いの言葉とさせていただきます．

（ライス大学）

窪薗晴夫さんの還暦を祝って

上野　善道

　あの窪薗さんが還暦を迎えるとの知らせを受け取って驚いた．10歳違いなので頭の中では分かっているつもりであるが，なにしろ，私がその歳のときはすでに周りから「お年寄り」扱いされて席を替わられたり，自分でも物忘れが増えたりして衰えを自覚せざるを得なかったのに対して，窪薗さんは最初のころの印象と変わりなく，はるかに若いと思っていたからである．

　その窪薗晴夫さんと知り合ったのが日本言語学会の大会会場だったことは覚えている．ただ，それがいつであったかは定かでなくなっているが，それから間もなくして『語形成と音韻構造』（1995，くろしお出版）を入手したような気がするので，その少し前ぐらいだったのかもしれない．ともあれ，早速その本を大学の演習テキストとして使ったが，それまで扱われて来なかった分野まで広く考察の対象に入れていて，とても刺激的であった．特に目を引いたのが第3章「混成語形成と音韻構造」であった．もっとも，一般常識に欠ける私には初めて見る混成語例が多く，特にその練習問題は学生に教えてもらうばかりで，「演習」にならなかった記憶がある．学生も興味を持ち，それをテーマに卒業論文を書いた者も出たほどである．

　窪薗さんの魅力は，その卓越した組織力と国際発信力にあり，新制かつ新生の国立国語研究所に呼ばれたのは当然のことであった．赴任するや，いくつものプロジェクトを立ち上げ，傍から見る限り何の苦労もなさそうに予算を獲得し，チームを引っ張って次々に成果をあげている．また，国内に留まりがちであった日本語の音研究の蓄積を海外に積極的に発信しようとしていることも注目される．ここでも，自ら先頭に立って実践するのみならず，関連のある研究者を集めて国際誌への投稿や英語論文集の出版の形で公表するように働きかけている．これにより，日本における研究がさらに進むとともに，これまでの日本語の研究成果も広く世界に知られるようになってきている．

　このたび，その還暦を祝って記念論文集が出るという．これもまた，間接的な形ではあるが，斯界に対する窪薗さんの貢献であるに違いない．その息のかかった寄稿者の論考を読むのが今から楽しみである．

（東京大学名誉教授）

窪薗晴夫氏の研究スタイルを考える

西光　義弘

　自分自身の還暦からほぼ10年たった立場から，窪薗晴夫氏の研究態度等に関する私なりの考えを書きとどめておきたいと思う．

　人に対してどのように呼ぶかについてはなかなか難しい問題がある．対人関係が時と共に変化して，それにつれて調整し，変えていく必要がある．学部生のころに後輩たちを集めて，言語学研究会を大阪外大で始めたころは後輩たちを何々君と呼んでいた．この状態はそれぞれが大学に就職してしばらくは続いたが，10年くらいたったころから，それが難しくなって，他の人にその人のことを言う時には何々氏と言うようになっていった．今でもあまりしっくり来るとは思わないが，何々君というとすでに名を成している後輩のことを見下したような響きを与え，それも使いにくい．やむなく何々氏という言い方をしている．窪薗氏は神戸大学で同僚になって初めて親しく付き合うようになったので，上に述べたようなことは起こらなかった．残念ながら窪薗氏が大阪外大で学部時代を過ごしたころ私はすでに在籍しておらず，上述の研究会に窪薗氏を誘うということも起こらなかった．したがってもっぱら他の人たちに氏のことを話すときは一貫して窪薗氏という関係であった．少々よそよそしい感じがするが，後輩たちを何々君と言っていた時代から何々氏というようになった経緯の後では窪薗氏という形を選ぶことになってしまうのである．

　窪薗氏と初めて会ったのは私が神戸大学教養部に所属していて，彼が名古屋大学の大学院生であったころであった．大阪外大での同級生で同じく名古屋大学の大学院に在籍していた鈴木誠一氏と一緒に研究室に訪ねてきたのであった．私が持っている音韻関係の欧米の Working Papers を借りたいということであった．ただ残念なことはそのうちにいくつかは名古屋大学の大学院生たちがコピーをとっている間に行方不明になったことであった．

　窪薗氏のことを次に聞いたのは大阪外大の日本語学科にいた三原健一氏（三原君）から窪薗という優秀な音韻論学者を採用することになったという話を聞いた時である．もちろんその前に活躍ぶりはどこかで耳にしたりしたとは思うが，はっきりと意識したのはそのときである．

　窪薗氏が書いたものによると「日本語の研究に関心を持ったのも大阪外大

時代でした．当時留学生別科というところで日本語を教えていらした寺村秀夫先生の講義を受講してからです．寺村先生が日本語文法の大家であることは当時全く知りませんでしたが，日本語について素朴な疑問を投げかけるスタイルの授業が実に新鮮でした．」(「言語学との出会い」言語学出版社フォーラム）と述べている．先日ネット上で寺村秀夫先生の筑波大学から大阪大学に移動する際の最終講義のビデオを見て，寺村先生の在りし日の姿および声を思い出し懐かしく思ったのである．もちろんいろいろな点で私と窪薗氏の研究スタイルは異なっているのであるが，日本語についての素朴な疑問を出発点とするという点はおそらくは寺村先生の薫陶によるものであることは間違いのないところだと思われる．

　人文系の学問の価値があまり認められない風潮が強くなっているが，それには人文系の個々の学問分野があまりにも蛸壺的に孤立していて，外国関係の学問分野ではともすれば，本国の研究を後追いする傾向が強く，日本関係の学問分野ではともすれば，独特の伝統に固執するガラパゴス化の傾向が強いということもあって，関連分野との連携があまりにも少ないということが放置されて孤立化したことに原因があるように思われてならない．たとえば，英語学者はあくまでも研究対象を英語に絞るべきで，日本語に手を出すことはあってはならないことだと一部の英語学者は考えていることを漏れ聞くことが多々ある．確かに英語学者が行う日本語の分析には欧米の言語理論を無理やりあてはめたものや，表面的な観察で終わっているものがよくみられるのであるが，それは学部大学院時代に英語学と日本語学の交流が行われていれば，防げることである．その意味で寺村先生の教えを受けた英語学専攻の研究者は幸せであったといえる．窪薗氏および教え子の研究者たちが興味深いデータを発掘し，細かい観察と一般化によって学界に寄与することによってあるべき姿を示していると思われる．

　私と窪薗氏の研究スタイルの違いとしては私はどちらかというと言語学以外の隣接分野の成果に興味を持ち，言語学に持ち込んで大胆な仮説を立てたがるところがあり，窪薗氏は用意周到な性格の反映もあってか，綿密な手順で手堅く組み立てていく着実な方法をとることである．神戸大学の言語学教室では教員全員で卒論および修論を集団的に週一回指導するゼミを行うようになって，お互いの研究スタイルを意識することとなった．特に私は時にとてつもない仮説を提示したりしたので，窪薗氏の着実な研究スタイルにふ

れ，もう少し着実性を身につけねばと反省したものであった．なかなかこのスタイルのバランスをとるのは難しく，どちらかに傾きがちである．

　窪薗氏の教え子の研究者たちも恩師の教えを守り，着実な手順を守るという態度がちゃんと身についた研究者として独り立ちしてきている．ただ時には大胆な仮説も立てることによってお釈迦様の掌の中を筋斗雲で飛んでいる孫悟空から卒業し，新しいものの見方ができる人たちが出てくるようになってほしいと願うこの頃である．

（神戸大学名誉教授）

祝　辞

　　　　　　　　　　　　　　　　　　　　　　　　　松本　曜

　窪薗先生，還暦のお祝いを申し上げます．
　窪薗先生とは，2004年から2010年まで神戸大学人文学研究科でご一緒させていただきました．言語学専修の様々な打合せや会議で共に議論し，また窪薗先生の指導する学生の論文審査にも加わらせていただき，私自身いろいろ学ぶことができました．窪薗先生の一番の印象は，徹底した合理主義者だということです．無駄を一切省き一般的な規則に帰着させるという考え方は，音韻論の考察のみならず，大学の運営に関しても適用されていました．教授会で「まずルールを決めましょう」という発言を何度も聞いた覚えがあります．
　私のような意味論を専攻しているものからすると，窪薗先生の音韻論は，何か固いもの，触れるものを研究対象にしているように感じられます．意味の世界にも音韻のようなはっきりとした規則性があればいいのにと，うらやましく思うこともあります．
　窪薗先生には年齢は関係ないと思います．これからも言語学の世界で大きな働きをされることを期待しています．

　　　　　　　　　　　　　　　　　　　　　　　　　（神戸大学）

お祝いのことば

岸本　秀樹

　窪薗先生が還暦を迎えられるということで，すこし信じられない気がします．私が神戸大学に赴任してから，先生が国立国語研究所（国語研）に移られるまで窪薗先生とは同僚でした．窪薗先生と言ってすぐに思い出すのは，先生が学生の心をつかむのがとても上手であったということです．いつも，聞いて「あっ，なるほど」と思うような例をあげて，学生の関心を引き，学生を音の世界へ導かれていました．たとえば，日本語で「じじ」「ばば」の前や後ろの音節を長くして，「じ〜じ」「ば〜ば」と言えば親しみがこもるのに，「じじい」「ばばあ」と言えば逆に悪いニュアンスをもつようになるというような例です（もっとも，学会の発表などシリアスな場面でもいつもおもしろい例をあげられますが）．そのためか，窪薗先生はいつも多くの指導学生を抱えておられました．窪薗先生の研究に触発され，音を研究する専門家になった学生もたくさんいます．国語研に移られてからは学生を指導する機会は減ったと想像しますが，いつも興味深い例で説得的に論を展開する研究のスタイルが依然として健在なことは，先生のお話を聞くたびに再認識させられます．窪薗先生は，還暦を迎えて人生の1つの節目を迎えられたのではありますが，もちろんこれで終わりというわけではなく，むしろ新たな始まりであると言えます．窪薗先生には，これからも人々を魅了する研究を精力的に続けていただきたいことをここに記して，還暦の祝辞といたします．

（神戸大学）

窪薗晴夫教授　履歴

1957 年 3 月 17 日　鹿児島県川内市（現薩摩川内市）生まれ

【学位】
Ph. D.（言語学）（エジンバラ大学，1988 年）

【学歴】
1972 年 4 月　　鹿児島県立川内高等学校入学（1975 年 3 月卒業）
1975 年 4 月　　大阪外国語大学外国語学部（現大阪大学外国語学部）英語学科入学（1979 年 3 月卒業）
1979 年 4 月　　名古屋大学大学院文学研究科博士前期課程英語学専攻入学（1981 年 3 月卒業）
1981 年 4 月　　名古屋大学大学院文学研究科博士後期課程英語学専攻入学（1982 年 3 月中途退学）
1983 年 9 月　　イギリス・エジンバラ大学大学院博士課程言語学科言語学専攻入学（1988 年 7 月修了）

【職歴】
1982 年 4 月　　南山大学外国語学部英米科・助手（〜1984 年 3 月）
1984 年 4 月　　南山大学外国語学部英米科・講師（〜1990 年 3 月）
1990 年 4 月　　南山大学外国語学部英米科・助教授（〜1992 年 3 月）
1992 年 4 月　　大阪外国語大学外国語学部日本語学科・助教授（〜1996 年 3 月）
1994 年 8 月　　カリフォルニア大学サンタクルズ校・客員研究員（フルブライト若手研究員）（〜1995 年 6 月）
1995 年 7 月　　マックスプランク心理言語学研究所・客員研究員（〜1995 年 8 月）
1996 年 4 月　　神戸大学文学部・助教授（〜2001 年 12 月）
2002 年 1 月　　神戸大学文学部・教授（〜2007 年 3 月）
2007 年 4 月　　神戸大学大学院人文学研究科・教授（改組により）（〜2010 年 9 月）
2010 年 10 月　大学共同利用機関法人人間文化研究機構国立国語研究所理論・構造研究系 教授，研究系長（現在に至る）

【専門領域】　言語学，日本語学，音声学，音韻論，危機方言

【所属学会】　日本言語学会，日本音声学会，日本音韻論学会，日本語学会，関西言語学会，日本音響学会，Association for Laboratory Phonology, International Phonetic Association

【学会等の役員・委員（主なもの）】
・日本言語学会会長（2015年4月〜現在），編集委員長（2009年4月〜2012年3月）
・日本音声学会編集委員長（2001年4月〜2004年3月），理事（2001年4月〜2007年3月，企画委員長：2013年4月〜2016年3月）
・日本音韻論学会会長（2005年4月〜2009年3月），副会長（2001年4月〜2005年3月），顧問（2009年4月〜現在），理事（1997年4月〜2000年3月）
・日本学術会議連携会員（2011年10月〜現在）
・関西言語学会運営委員
・理化学研究所脳科学研究センター　客員研究員
・市河三喜賞　審査委員・幹事
・東京言語研究所　運営委員
・The Association for Laboratory Phonology, Executive Committee member
・Oxford Studies in Phonology and Phonetics Series (OUP), Advisory Editor
・International Congress of Phonetic Sciences (ICPhS), Permanent Council member
・*Lingua*, Editorial Board member.

【受賞歴】
1985年　イギリス政府 Overseas Research Student Award
1988年　名古屋大学英文学会 IVY Award
1995年　市河三喜賞
1997年　金田一京助博士記念賞
2010年　国立国語研究所第1回所長賞
2013年　国立国語研究所第6回所長賞
2015年　国立国語研究所第10回所長賞

窪薗晴夫教授　業績

1. 著書

1. 1991『英語の発音と英詩の韻律』英潮社，溝越彰氏と共著．
2. 1993 *The Organization of Japanese Prosody.* くろしお出版，単著［学位論文改稿版］．
3. 1995『語形成と音韻構造』くろしお出版，単著．
4. 1997『日英語対照による英語学概論』くろしお出版，西光義弘氏他と共著．
5. 1998『音韻構造とアクセント』研究社，太田聡氏と共著．
6. 1998『音声』（岩波講座「言語の科学」第2巻）岩波書店，田窪行則氏等と共著．
7. 1998『音声学・音韻論』くろしお出版，単著．
8. 1999『日本語の発音教室——理論と練習』くろしお出版，田中真一氏と共著．
9. 1999『日本語の音声』岩波書店，単著．
10. 2002『音節とモーラ』研究社，本間猛氏と共著．
11. 2002『新語はこうして作られる』岩波書店，単著．
12. 2006『アクセントの法則』（岩波科学ライブラリー118）岩波書店，単著．
13. 2008『ことばの力を育む』慶應義塾大学出版会，大津由紀雄氏と共著．
14. 2008『ネーミングの言語学』（言語・文化選書）開拓社，単著．
15. 2011『ことばワークショップ——言語を再発見する』開拓社，大津由紀雄（編），池上嘉彦氏ら3名と共著．
16. 2011『数字とことばの不思議な話』（岩波ジュニア新書684）岩波書店，単著．
17. 2013『日英対照 英語学の基礎』くろしお出版，三原健一・高見健一（編）並木崇康氏ら4名と共著．

2. 編著書

1. 2008. *Asymmetries in Phonology: An East-Asian Perspective.* くろしお出版．
2. 2012. *Lingua* 12, Issue 13, *Special Issue: Varieties of Pitch Accent Sys-*

3. 2013. *Journal of East Asian Linguistics* 22(4) *Special Issue: Japanese Geminate Obstruents*. Springer.
  4. 2015. 窪薗晴夫（監修）, 森勇太・平塚雄亮・黒木邦彦（編）『甑島里方言記述文法書』東京：国立国語研究所.
  5. 2015. *The Handbook of Japanese Phonetics and Phonology*. De Gruyter Mouton.
  6. Kubozono, Haruo, Maekawa, Kikuo and Timothy Vance (eds.). 2015. *Laboratory Phonology* 6, Issue 3-4, *Special Issue: Corpus-Based Approaches to the Phonological Analysis of Speech*. De Gruyter Mouton.

3. 論文

  1. 1980. The English Great Vowel Shift reconsidered. *IVY* 16, 27-41. 名古屋大学英文学会.
  2. 1982. The genesis of the English Great Vowel Shift: A new hypothesis. *Studies in Linguistic Change*, 39-52. 研究社.
  3. 1983. Explanatory formalism: GVS metarule schema revisited. 『アカデミア』34, 1-23. 南山大学.
  4. 1983「英語に於ける等時化の歴史について」『英文学研究』LX1, 133-147. 日本英文学会.
  5. 1983. Particle phonology and the mechanism of sound change. 『アカデミア』35, 1-31. 南山大学.
  6. 1985. On the syntax of Japanese compounds. *Work in Progress* 18, 60-89. Edinburgh University.
  7. 1985. Speech errors and syllable structure. *Linguistics and Philology* 6, 220-243. 名古屋大学英語学談話会.
  8. 1987. On the phonetics and phonology of the accent-induced F0 fall in Japanese. *Linguistics and Philology* 7, 1-21. 名古屋大学英語学談話会.
  9. 1987.「日本語複合語の意味構造と韻律構造」『アカデミア』43, 25-62. 南山大学.
  10. 1988.「等時化の条件とそのメカニズム：音量対立の史的研究」*IVY* XXI, 231-247. 名古屋大学英文学会.
  11. 1988. Constraints on phonological compound formation. *English Linguistics* 5, 150-169. 日本英語学会.
  12. 1989. The mora and syllable structure in Japanese: Evidence from

speech errors, *Language and Speech* 32-3, 249-278. SAGE Publications.
13. 1989. Syntactic and rhythmic effects on downstep in Japanese. *Phonology* 6-1, 39-67. Cambridge University Press.
14. 1990. Phonological constraints on blending in English and Japanese as a case for phonology-morphology interface. *Yearbook of Morphology* 3, 1-20. Foris Publications.
15. 1991. Modeling syntactic effects on downstep in Japanese. *Papers in Laboratory Phonology II*, 368-387. Cambridge University Press.
16. 1991. The phonology of tongue twisters in English.『言語の構造と歴史』3-19. 英潮社.
17. 1991.「音節構造と言語文化」『アカデミア』51, 65-99. 南山大学.
18. 1992. On the metrical structure of Japanese downstep. *Phonologica 1988*, 368-387. Cambridge University Press.
19. 1993.「日本語複合語における平板化形態素の作用域について」『日本語・日本文化研究』9-18. 大阪外国語大学.
20. 1994.「日本語の音節量について」『国語学』178, 7-17. 国語学会.
21. 1994. Prosodic categories and hierarchy in Japanese. *Dokkyo International Review* 7, 91-110. 獨協大学.
22. 1994. Temporal regulation of phonological prominence.『ことばの音と形』3-22. こびあん書房.
23. 1995. Perceptual evidence for the mora in Japanese. In *Phonology and Phonetic Evidence: Papers in Laboratory Phonology IV*, 141-156. Cambridge University Press.
24. 1995. Constraint interaction in Japanese phonology: Evidence from compound accent. *Phonology at Santa Cruz* (PASC) 4, 21-38. University of California at Santa Cruz.
25. 1995「音韻部門と統語部門・意味部門のインタフェース」『認知心理学3 言語』47-61. 東京大学出版会.
26. 1996. Syllable and accent in Japanese: Evidence from loanword accentuation, *Bulletin* 211, 71-82. 日本音声学会.
27. 1996. Speech segmentation and phonological structure. In Takashi Otake and Anne Cutler (eds.), *Phonological Structure and Language Processing: Cross-linguistic Studies*, 77-94. Mouton de Gruyter.
28. 1996.「英語の複合語強勢について」『言語の深層を探ねて』3-17. 英潮社.
29. 1997.(伊藤順子, アーミン・メスター氏と共著)「音韻構造からみた語と句の境界」『文法と音声』147-166. くろしお出版.

30. 1997. Lexical markedness and variation: A nonderivational account of Japanese compound accent, *Proceedings of The West Coast Conference on Formal Linguistics* 15, 273-287. CSLI Publications.
31. 1997.「日本語の韻律構造とその獲得」『音声言語医学』38, 281-286. 日本音声言語医学会.
32. 1997.「アクセント・イントネーションの構造と文法」『日本語音声 2』203-229. 三省堂.
33. 1998.「金太郎と桃太郎のアクセント構造」『神戸言語学論叢』1, 35-49. 神戸大学.
34. 1998.「モーラと音節の普遍性」『音声研究』2(1), 5-15. 日本音声学会.
35. 1999. Mora and Syllable. In Natsuko Tsujimura (ed.), *The Handbook of Japanese Linguistics*, 31-61. Blackwell.
36. 1999.「歌謡におけるモーラと音節」『文法と音声 II』241-260. くろしお出版.
37. 2000.「子供のしりとりとモーラの獲得」『五十周年記念論集』587-602. 神戸大学文学部.
38. 2000.「日本語の語彙と音節構造」『日本語研究』20, 1-18. 東京都立大学.
39. 2001. Epenthetic vowels and accent in Japanese: Facts and paradoxes. In Jaroen van de Weijer and Tetsuo Nishihara (eds.), *Issues in Japanese Phonology and Morphology*, 111-140. Mouton de Gruyter.
40. 2001. On the markedness of diphthongs.『神戸言語学論叢』3, 60-73. 神戸大学.
41. 2001.「語順と音韻構造――事実と仮説――」『文法と音声 III』107-140. くろしお出版.
42. 2002. Temporal neutralization in Japanese. In Carlos Gussenhoven and Natasha Warner (eds.), *Papers in Laboratory Phonology* 7, 171-201. Mouton de Gruyter.
43. 2002. Prosodic structure of loanwords in Japanese: Syllable structure, accent and morphology.『音声研究』6(1), 79-97. 日本音声学会.
44. 2003. The syllable as a unit of prosodic organization in Japanese. In Caroline Féry and Ruben van der Vijver (eds.), *The Syllable in Optimality Theory*, 99-122. Cambridge University Press.
45. 2003. Accent of alphabetic acronyms in Tokyo Japanese. In Takeru Honma, Masao Okazaki, Toshiyuki Tabata, and Shin-ichi Tanaka (eds.), *A New Century of Phonology and Phonological Theory*, 356-370. 開拓社.
46. 2003.「鹿児島方言におけるアクセントの変化」『國文學』48(4), 46-52.

學燈社.

47. 2003.「日本語の頭文字語アクセントについて」『音韻研究』6, 31-38. 日本音韻論学会.
48. 2003.「音韻の獲得と言語の普遍性」『音声研究』7(2), 5-17. 日本音声学会.
49. 2003.「日本語プロソディーの構造とその教育——アクセントとイントネーションを中心に」*BATJ Journal* 4, 1-9. The British Association for Teaching Japanese as a Foreign Language.
50. 2004.「音韻構造から見た単純語と合成語の境界」『文法と音声 IV』123-143. くろしお出版.
51. 2004.（Yayoi Fujiura 氏と共著）Morpheme-dependent nature of compound accent in Japanese: An analysis of 'short' compounds.『音韻研究』7, 9-16. 日本音韻論学会.
52. 2004. What does Kagoshima Japanese tell us about Japanese syllables?『日本語の分析と言語類型』75-92. くろしお出版.
53. 2004. Weight neutralization in Japanese. *Journal of Japanese Linguistics* 20, 51-70. Institute for Japanese Studies, The Ohio State University.
54. 2004. Tone and syllable in Kagoshima Japanese.『神戸言語学論叢』4, 69-84. 神戸大学.
55. 2004.「音韻論概説」西原哲雄・那須川訓也共編『音韻理論ハンドブック』3-14. 英宝社.
56. 2005.(小川晋史氏と共著)「ストライキ」はなぜ「スト」か？——短縮と単語分節のメカニズム」『現代形態論の潮流』155-174. くろしお出版.
57. 2005.「日本語音韻論に見られる非対称性」『音声研究』9(1), 5-19. 日本音声学会.
58. 2005.(Mikio Giriko 氏と共著)Vowel quality and emotion in Japanese.『音韻研究』8, 33-40. 日本音韻論学会.
59. 2005. [ai]-[au] asymmetry in English and Japanese. *English Linguistics* 22(1), 1-22. 日本英語学会.
60. 2005.「音韻論」中島平三（編）『言語の事典』20-40. 朝倉書店.
61. 2005. *Rendaku*: Its domain and linguistic conditions. In Jeroen van de Weijer, Kensuke Nanjo, Tetsuo Nishihara (eds.), *Voicing in Japanese*, 5-24. Mouton de Gruyter.
62. 2006.「日本語のリズムと時間制御」広瀬啓吉（編著）『韻律と音声言語情報処理』34-43. 丸善.
63. 2006. Where does loanword prosody come from? A case study of Japa-

nese loanword accent. *Lingua* 116, 1140-1170. Elsevier.
64. 2006.「方言アクセントの変容」明治書院『日本語学』25(8), 6-17. 明治書院.
65. 2006. (with Misa Fukui) Phonological structure and unaccented nouns in Tokyo and Osaka Japanese. In Timothy J. Vance and Kimberly Jones (eds.), *Japanese/Korean Linguistics 14*, 39-50. CSLI Publications and SLI.
66. 2006. The phonetic and phonological organization of speech in Japanese. In Mineharu Nakayama, Reiko Mazuka and Yasuhiro Shirai (eds.), *The Handbook of East Asian Psycholinguistics. Volume II Japanese*, 191-200. Cambridge University Press.
67. 2007.「レキシコンとアクセント指定」『レキシコンフォーラム』3, 1-32. ひつじ書房.
68. 2007. Focus and intonation in Japanese: Does focus trigger pitch reset? In Ishihara, S. (ed.) *Working Papers of the SFB632, Interdisciplinary Studies on Information Structure* (ISIS) 9, 1-27. University Potsdam.
69. 2007. Tonal change in language contact: Evidence from Kagoshima Japanese. In Tomas Riad and Carlos Gussenhoven (eds.), *Tones and Tunes. Volume 1: Typological Studies in Word and Sentence Prosody*, 323-351. de Gruyter Mouton.
70. 2007.「鹿児島方言のアクセント変化──複合法則の崩壊──」『神戸言語学論叢』5, 111-123. 神戸大学.
71. 2008. [ai]-[au] asymmetry: A phonetic account. In Haruo Kubozono (ed.) *Asymmetries in Phonology: An East-Asian Perspective*, 147-163. くろしお出版.
72. 2008.「プロソディーの基礎研究と日本語教育」『日本語教育と音声』101-116. くろしお出版.
73. 2008. Japanese Accent. In Shigeru Miyagawa and Mamoru Saito (eds.), *The Oxford Handbook of Japanese Linguistics*, 163-189. Oxford University Press.
74. 2009.「音韻規則の実在性について」由本陽子・岸本秀樹（編）『語彙の意味と文法』11-23. くろしお出版.
75. 2009.「音韻論」中島平三（編）『言語学の領域 (I)』46-72. 朝倉書店.
76. 2009.「数字の世界と言葉の法則」『理大 科学フォーラム』26(6), 9-14. 東京理科大学.
77. 2009.「発音の仕組みをさぐる」大津由紀雄（編著）『はじめて学ぶ言語学：

ことばの世界をさぐる17章』16-33. ミネルヴァ書房.
78. 2009.「言葉のあいまい性と日本語の発音」『日本語学』28(15), 13-19. 明治書院.
79. 2009. Accent and the lexicon in Japanese. In Shunji Inagaki, Makiko Hirakawa, Setsuko Arita, Yahiro Hirakawa, Hiromi Morikawa, Mineharu Nakayama, Hidetosi Sirai, and Jessika Tsubakita (eds.), *Studies in Language and Sciences 8*, 31–42. Kurosio.
80. 2010.「アルファベット頭文字語のアクセントと音節構造」岸本秀樹（編）『ことばの対照』257-270. くろしお出版.
81. 2010. Accentuation of alphabetic acronyms in varieties of Japanese. *Lingua* 120, 2323-2335. Elsevier.
82. 2010.「語形成と音韻構造——短縮語形成のメカニズム——」『国語研プロジェクトレビュー』1(3), 17-34.
83. 2011. Japanese pitch accent. In Marc van Oostendorp, Colin Ewen, Elizabeth Hume and Keren Rice (eds.), *The Blackwell Companion to Phonology* 5, 2879-2907. Wiley-Blackwell.
84. 2011.「喜界島南部・中部地域のアクセント」木部暢子他（編）『消滅危機方言の調査・保存のための総合的研究——喜界島方言調査報告書』（国立国語研究所共同研究報告 11(01)）51-70. 国立国語研究所.
85. 2011.「日本語の促音とアクセント」『国語研プロジェクトレビュー』6, 3-15. 国立国語研究所.
86. 2012. Word-level vs. Sentence-level Prosody in Koshikijima Japanese. *The Linguistic Review* 29, 109-130. de Gruyter Mouton.
87. 2012.「鹿児島県甑島方言のアクセント」『音声研究』16(1), 93-104. 日本音声学会.
88. 2012. Varieties of pitch accent systems in Japanese. *Lingua* 122, 1395-1414. Elsevier.
89. 2012. Introduction : Special issue on varieties of pitch accent systems. *Lingua* 122, 1325-1334. Elsevier.
90. 2013. Japanese word accent. In Mark Aronoff (ed), *Oxford Bibliographies in Linguistics*. Oxford University Press. http://www.oxfordbibliographies.com/view/document/obo-9780199772810/obo-9780199772810-0103. xml?rskey=jotgCZ&result=41&q=
91. 2013. Introduction to the special issue on Japanese geminate obstruents. *Journal of East Asian Linguistics* 22(4), 303-306. Springer.
92. 2013. (with Hajime Takeyasu and Mikio Giriko) On the positional

asymmetry of consonant gemination in Japanese loanwords. *Journal of East Asian Linguistics* 22(4), 339-371. Springer.
93. 2013「自然条件とことばの変化——甑島方言を例に」木部暢子, 小松和彦, 佐藤洋一郎 (編)『アジアの人びとの自然観をたどる』157-183. 勉誠出版.
94. 2015. Introduction to Japanese phonetics and phonology. In Haruo Kubozono (ed.), *Handbook of Japanese Phonetics and Phonology*, 1-40. De Gruyter Mouton.
95. 2015. Diphthongs and vowel coalescence. In Haruo Kubozono (ed.), *Handbook of Japanese Phonetics and Phonology*, 215-249. De Gruyter Mouton.
96. 2015. Loanword phonology, In Haruo Kubozono (ed), *Handbook of Japanese Phonetics and Phonology*, 313-361. De Gruyter Mouton.
97. 2015.「音韻論における'drift'」『日本エドワード・サピア協会研究年報』29, 1-11. 日本エドワード・サピア協会.
98. 2015. Japanese dialects and general linguistics. *Gengo Kenkyu* 148, 1-31.
99. 2016「日本語の方言と一般言語学——「音節量」による一般化——」『文化情報学』12(2), 112-126. 同志社大学.
100. 2016. Diversity of pitch accent systems in Koshikijima Japanese. *Gengo Kenkyu* 150, 1-31.
101. 2016. Accent in Japanese phonology. In Mark Aronoff (ed.), *Oxford Research Encyclopedia of Linguitics* (online encyclopedia).
102. 2016. Diphthongs and word accent in Japanese. *KLS* (*Proceedings of the 40th Annual Meeting of the Kansai Linguistic Society*), 195-206.

4. 解説論文 (2000 年～)

1. 2000.「最適性理論の課題」『音声研究』4(3), 36-39. 日本音声学会.
2. 2001.「制約はいくつあるのか」『言語』30(10), 45-49. 大修館.
3. 2002.「音声知覚と音韻理論」『英語青年』148(2), 62-63. 研究社.
4. 2002.「最適性理論と忠実性制約」『英語青年』148(8), 36-37. 研究社.
5. 2002.「日本語の音声研究と一般音声学・音韻論」『日本の言語学』(言語 30 周年記念別冊) 136-147. 大修館.
6. 2003.「言葉遊びの言語学」『言語』32(2), 26-35. 大修館.
7. 2005.「名前の言語構造」『言語』34(3), 58-65. 大修館.
8. 2005.「音韻論研究の動向」『日本音響学会誌』61(9), 550-556. 日本音響

学会.
9. 2005.「ちょっとマクっていいですか」『文藝春秋』臨時増刊「言葉の力」112-113. 文藝春秋.
10. 2006.「若者言葉の言語構造」『言語』35(3), 52-59. 大修館.
11. 2006.「幼児語の音韻構造」『言語』35(9), 28-35. 大修館.
12. 2007.「外来語の音韻構造」『言語』36(6), 60-67. 大修館.
13. 2008.「神様の手帳をのぞく」大津由紀雄（編）『ことばの宇宙への旅立ち』73-109. ひつじ書房.
14. 2009.「最適性理論の位置づけ」深澤はるか（訳）『最適性理論』369-373. 岩波書店.
15. 2009.「私が勧めるこの一冊 最適性理論：生成文法における制約相互作用」『日本語学』28(12), 82-91. 明治書院.
16. 2009.「次世代の音声研究」『言語』38(12), 38-43. 大修館.
17. 2010.「英語らしい発音の正体は何か」「英語の命名にはどんな法則があるか」『英語教育』9月号. 大修館.
18. 2010.「Smoke Free と婉曲表現」『語学ジャーナル』9月号. 語学教育研究所.
19. 2011.「アクセントとイントネーション――日本語の多様性」『人間文化』13, 11-16. 人間文化研究機構.
20. 2011.「音の法則」『人と自然』2, 14-15. 人間文化研究機構.
21. 2011.「音声研究の新たな展開」『日本語学』11月臨時増刊号, 21-28. 明治書院.
22. 2011.(論文紹介)「Accentuation of alphabetic acronyms in varieties of Japanese. *Lingua* 120, 2323-2335. (2010)」『国語研プロジェクトレビュー』6, 51-54. 国立国語研究所.
23. 2016.「日本語音声の謎と難問」『日本語学』35(5), 特集「日本語の難問」2-12. 明治書院.

5. 辞典，事典項目執筆

1. 1993.『現代英文法辞典』"English dialects" など約30項目執筆及び索引作成, 三省堂.
2. 1994. *The Encyclopedia of Language and Linguistics* "pitch accent" の項執筆, Pergamon Press.
3. 2016. 中島平三（編）『ことばのおもしろ事典』4 (「ママは昔パパだったのか？――五十音図の秘密――」112-118,「「むっつ」と「みっつ」の関係とは？」119-125.) 朝倉書店.

目　次

まえがき　v
祝辞　ix
窪薗晴夫教授　履歴　xix
窪薗晴夫教授　業績　xxi

Part I　音韻理論と音韻現象

Ancient Greek Pitch Accent: Anti-Lapse and Tonal Antepenultimacy
　……………………………………Junko Ito and Armin Mester　2

Rendaku Following a Moraic Nasal
　………………………………………………Timothy J. Vance　19

Containment Eradicates Opacity and Revives OT in Parallel:
　Some Consequences of Turbid Optimality Theory
　…………Shin-ichi Tanaka, Clemens Poppe, and Daiki Hashimoto　40

三重県志摩和具方言における前鼻子音
　……………………………………………………高山　知明　70

Part II　語形成と音韻現象

日本語の名詞形成接尾辞「-さ」と「-み」について
　…………………………………………………………太田　聡　84

Motorola は，混成か接尾辞付加か
.... 本間　猛　98

キラキラネームは音韻的にキラキラしているのか？
　──名前と一般語の頻度分布比較による予備的考察──
.... 北原　真冬　112

英語の形容詞の比較級の語形とフット構造について
.... 山本　武史　126

Part III　日本語アクセントと形態論

ピッチ・アクセント言語に於ける無アクセントとは
.... 吉田　優子　144

日本語複合動詞のアクセント特性について
.... 田端　敏幸　156

ナガラ節における音調の形成と変異
.... 那須　昭夫　169

擬似形態素境界が複数挿入される可能性について
.... 小川晋史・儀利古幹雄　184

Part IV　音声知覚・生成と L1 獲得

"Good Infant-directed Words" Do Not Sound like "Good Japanese Words."
.... Reiko Mazuka, Akiko Hayashi and Tadahisa Kondo　202

言語共通の音韻発達遅滞評価をめぐって
 ………………………………………………………… 上田　功　220

日本語分節音の音韻要素表現とその内部構造
 ………………………………………………………… 松井　理直　231

語末 F0 上昇が母音の長短判断に及ぼす影響：
　Takiguchi et al. (2010) の再検証
 ………………………………………………………… 竹安　大　249

アクセント型と位置の視点から見る長母音の知覚
 ………………………………………………………… 薛　晋陽　264

Part V　借用語音韻論と L2 習得・知覚

What Neural Measures Reveal about Foreign Language Learning
　of Japanese Vowel Length Contrasts with Hand Gestures
 ………………………………… Spencer D. Kelly and Yukari Hirata　278

Effects of Pitch Height on L2 Learners' Identification
　of Japanese Phonological Vowel Length
 ………………………………………………… Izumi Takiguchi　295

学習者の作文エラーに見る日本語のリズム
 ………………………………………………………… 権　延姝　312

英語および仏語由来の借用語における促音分布
 ………………………………………………………… 竹村　亜紀子　325

パドヴァとヴェローナの韻律構造：
　イタリア語由来の借用語における音節量・強勢の受入と音韻構造
　　……………………………………………………………田中　真一　342

執筆者一覧…………………………………………………………………　357

Part I

音韻理論と音韻現象

Ancient Greek Pitch Accent: Anti-Lapse and Tonal Antepenultimacy*

Junko Ito and Armin Mester
University of California, Santa Cruz

1. Introduction

Modern phonological theory advanced our understanding of so-called pitch accent languages such as Lithuanian, Northern Bizkaian Basque, or Somali by recognizing that they do not constitute a separate third type of languages besides stress languages and tone languages, but result from the overlay of metrical and tonal factors (Prince (1983: 88), Hyman (2006)). While the broad picture is clear in its general outlines, the exact distribution of labor between metrical and tonal constraints is by no means easy to determine in individual cases, and widely different approaches have been pursued, with success, for specific languages. In the case of Japanese, for example, Shosuke Haraguchi has at different points advocated both purely tonal and purely metrical types of analysis (Haraguchi (1977, 1991)). More recently, a whole dissertation (Poppe (2015)) addresses the difficult task of sorting out the relative roles of tonal and metrical constraints in the analysis of Japanese and its dialects. While many questions of detail are still unsettled, some basic points have become clear. In an important series of papers, Haruo Kubozono has established the fact that

---

* Part of this research was supported by COR grants from UC Santa Cruz and by NINJAL (National Institute for Japanese Language and Linguistics, Tachikawa, Tokyo, Japan). We would like to take this opportunity to thank Professor Haruo Kobozono for his support, encouragement, and friendship for almost 30 years. His insightful work on many aspects of Japanese phonology has been a source of inspiration for us throughout this time.

the (bimoraic trochaic) foot plays an irreducible role in the accent pattern of Japanese (Kubozono (1988, 1989, 1995, 2009)). In this short note, we would like to make a small contribution to the establishment of a complementary point, namely, that some features of particular pitch accent systems are irreducibly tonal in nature. Focusing on tonal anti-lapse constraints, we will briefly review the main results of our earlier study of Japanese minor phrasing (Ito and Mester (2013)), and will then devote the main part of this paper to the lexical pitch accent pattern of Ancient Greek. Our main finding is that the antepenultimacy characterizing recessive accent, which never fit well into standard foot-based antepenultimacy, follows in its entirety from the tonal pattern: the basic word melody and the constraints governing it, crucially including a tonal anti-lapse constraint.

2. No-Lapse in Japanese

Anti-lapse constraints militate against stretches of low-toned material exceeding a certain limit, typically at the ends of words and phrases. Ito and Mester (2013) develop an analysis of the way Japanese utterances are parsed into phonological phrases where NoLapse plays a central role in forcing the accentual fall to occur late in the word.

The facts at issue are well-known since Kubozono's (1988, 1989) ground-breaking work, we illustrate them with phrases consisting of two content words (after Vance (2008: 181)). The parses assigned to these examples by the theory proposed in Ito and Mester (2013) appear in the second column in (1), where (1cd) crucially involve recursive phrasing, as first recognized by Kubozono.[1]

(1)   Syntactic   Prosodic   Schematic tonal
             phrasing: phrasing: profile:
          a.   [$_{XP}$ [$_{XP}$ u   ]   u   ]
             [[Hiroshima-no] sakana-to]   ($_\phi$ u u)   (u   u)
             'Hiroshima fish and ...'

---

[1] Notation: ϕ = "phonological phrase", ω = "phonological word", a = "accented ω", u =

b. [$_{XP}$ [$_{XP}$ u   ] a   ]
   [[Hiroshima-no] tamágo-to]   ($_\phi$ u a)   (u   a)
   'Hiroshima eggs and …'

c. [$_{XP}$ [$_{XP}$ a   ] a   ]
   [[Okáyama-no] tamágo-to]   ($_\phi$ ($_\phi$ a) ($_\phi$ a))   ((a) (a))
   'Okayama eggs and …'

d. [$_{XP}$ [$_{XP}$ a   ] u   ]
   [[Okáyama-no] sakana-to]   ($_\phi$ ($_\phi$ a) ($_\phi$ u))   ((a) (u))
   'Okayama fish and …'

The differences between these parses—flat prosodic phrasing in (1ab), recursive phrasing in (1cd), but never exactly mirroring the syntax—are entirely due to the locations of accented and unaccented words within the two-word phrase. As shown in the schematic tonal profiles (where the main tonal events are indicated with schematic pitch arrows), the beginning of a phonological phrase in Japanese is cued by a tonal rise ($_\%$LH-), and accented words contain a steep tonal fall following the accented syllable (H*L).[2]

While two *a*'s are each parsed as a separate phrase (1c) (because each accent has to be the head of a minimal phrase), *u* is typically phrased together with an adjacent *a* or *u* (1ab) (because one-word phrases violate binarity). This is where Kubozono (1988: 150–154) discovered a directional asymmetry: *u* is only phrased together with a following *u* (1a) (*uu*) or *a* (1b) (*ua*), not with a preceding *a* (1d) ((*a*) (*u*)). So the results are (*uu*) and ((*a*) (*a*)), but ((*a*) (*u*)) with an initial rise at the beginning of the second word and (*ua*) without such a rise. In Ito and Mester (2013), we argue that this asymmetry is caused by the anti-lapse constraint in (2).

(2) N$_O$L$_{APSE}$-L/ω   No tonal lapses. Violated by each fully L-toned ω in φ

The tonal profiles of the words in (3) contain no violations of the anti-

---

"unaccented ω", "[…]" indicates syntactic phrasing, "(…)" phonological phrasing.

[2] It is always possible, in careful pronunciation, to parse each word as a separate φ, with its own initial rise, but we here focus on the usual default pattern.

lapse constraint, since no ω is fully L-toned.

(3) NoLapse-L/ω observed:

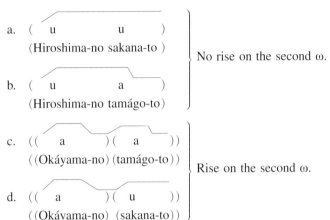

a. (u   u)
   (Hiroshima-no sakana-to)   No rise on the second ω.

b. (u   a)
   (Hiroshima-no tamágo-to)

c. ((a)(a))
   ((Okáyama-no) (tamágo-to))   Rise on the second ω.

d. ((a)(u))
   ((Okáyama-no) (sakana-to))

A fully L-toned ω arises after an accentual fall unless it is in its own φ (thereby receiving the tonal rise on its own). In (3c, d), this is exactly what happens, leading to a rise on the second ω. The directional asymmetry (singly-phrased (*ua*) is acceptable but *(*au*) is not) is illustrated in (4), where the competing candidate (*au*) with a single phrase has a fatal NoLapse-L/ω violation.

(4) Directional asymmetry

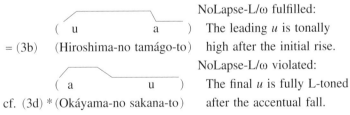

                                     NoLapse-L/ω fulfilled:
       (u   a)   The leading *u* is tonally
= (3b) (Hiroshima-no tamágo-to)   high after the initial rise.
                                     NoLapse-L/ω violated:
       (a   u)   The final *u* is fully L-toned
cf. (3d) *(Okáyama-no sakana-to)   after the accentual fall.

In this analysis, the directional asymmetry has an explanation rooted in the very shape of the tonal melody of (Tokyo) Japanese (unaccented $_{\%}$LH- and accented $_{\%}$LH-H*L). A virtue of this approach is that the orientation of the accent towards the end is not accounted for by means of a right alignment constraint, a strictly formal device, but rather by substantive tonal factors. In other words, explaining the right-alignment of the accent as a way of avoiding a long final tonal lapse is more principled and more revealing than explaining it by a statement that blandly says that the accent is right-aligned.

3. Ancient Greek Accent: Tonal Antepenultimacy and NoLapse[3]

NoLapse-L/ω is part of a family of tonal anti-lapse constraints that also includes the constraint operative in Ancient Greek against more than one low-toned vocalic mora at the end of the word. As is well known, the accent of Ancient Greek is governed by what is traditionally called the "three-syllable law". The accent can only fall on one of the last three syllables of the word, and on the antepenult only when the final contains no more than one vocalic mora: Antepenult accent is possible in a word like *Hɛɛrákleitos* 'Heraclitus' with short /o/ in the last syllable, but not in *Sɔɔkrátɛɛs* 'Sokrates' (*Sɔɔ́kratɛɛs*) with long /ɛɛ/.[4] When the antepenult has a long vowel or diphthong, accent can only fall on its second mora (acute, not circumflex, in the standard terminology): *beboúleust^{h}e* 'you have deliberated' (*bebóuleust^{h}e*), and the same is true for penult accent when the final has two vocalic moras: *epeít^{h}ou* 'you were obeying' (*epéit^{h}ou*). The complexity of the rule stems from the intricate way it depends on the weight of the final syllable, and has given rise to a number of different analyses. Building on earlier work including Misteli (1868), Allen (1966, 1973, 1987), Steriade (1988), Sauzet (1989), Golston (1990), Kiparsky (2003), and Probert (2003, 2006), we interpret the accentual melody of a Greek word as arising out of a combination of two things: a HL pitch accent (the "contonation", in Allen's terminlogy) and a word-final boundary tone $L_\%$. The overall word melody is thus $HL + L_\%$, and the law of limitation is in our analysis essentially reduced to the constraint on $L_\%$ in (5).

---

[3] We are indebted to Alan Prince for helpful discussion of the antepenultimacy syndrome.

[4] The location of stress in the English versions of these names follows the Latin stress rule, which is sensitive to the weight of the penult, not of the final.

(5) NoLapse-$L_\%/\mu$: Boundary $L_\%$ occupies no more than one mora.

NOLAPSE-$L_\%/\mu$ rules out a boundary tone $L_\%$ stretched out over more than the prosodic minimum: one mora.[5] Such a restriction seems eminently natural, given the very role of $L_\%$ as a boundary tone. We follow Allen (1966: 10) in assuming that the contonation is a tonal [HL] complex: a high pitch on the accented mora followed by a low tone, probably realized as a falling glide—Misteli's (1868) *Mittelton* 'mid tone'. Kiparsky (1967: 75) conjectures in a similar way that the post-tonic string of moras was "probablement réalisée phonétiquement comme un contour accentuel descendant".

(6) Word melody: $HL + L_\%$

If H is linked to the first mora of a syllable with two vocalic moras, the L of the accent is linked to its second mora, otherwise it is linked to the subsequent syllable. It is followed by boundary $L_\%$ occupying no more than one mora. This yields the window in (7) for licit accentuations.

(7) H L $L_\%$
    | ⟍ |
    μ μ (μ) $μ_\%$

To forestall misunderstandings sometimes encountered in linguistic writings, it might be useful to point out that three-syllable windows, including the one in Greek, are not basic principles of grammar to be taken at face value, whose rationale would remain mysterious, but rather emerge out of the interactions of more basic constraints, as recognized in classical metrical phonology (see Hayes 1982 and work cited there).

That the accent is "recessive" in certain word classes means that the H of the accent associates as far to the left as compatible with (7). More formally, H is aligned as closely as possible with the left word edge (8e), provided (8a–d) are satisfied.

---

[5] An empirically almost equivalent statement was proposed by Jakobson (1962: 263) ("the vocalic morae between the accented vocalic mora and the final one cannot belong to different syllables. In other words, the span between the accented and the final mora cannot exceed one syllable.")

(8) a. ALIGNRIGHT-L_%/ω   L_% is a word-final boundary tone.
    b. NOLAPSE-L_%/μ   L_% occupies no more than one mora.
    c. CONTIGUITY-T   Tone domains are contiguous.[6] One violation for every pair of adjacent tone domains in a word that are not contiguous (i.e., separated by one or more toneless vocalic moras).
    d. CRISPEDGE-σ/T   Multiple linking of tones between syllables is prohibited. One violation for every tone associated to two syllables.[7]
    e. ALIGNLEFT-H/ω_i   H is leftmost in ω. One violation for every vocalic mora intervening between the left edge of H and the left edge of the prosodic word. The subscript *i* indicates that this constraint is indexed to specific lexical classes designated to carry recessive accent.

These constraints give rise to alternations between antepenult and penult accent throughout the language, as between the different case forms in (9).

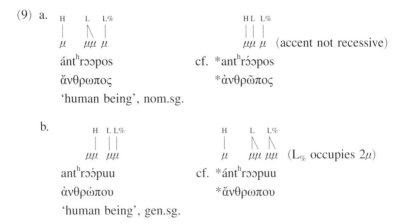

---
[6] This is part of Goldsmith's (1976: 27) "Wellformedness Condition".
[7] For such CRISPEDGE constraints, see Ito and Mester (1999).

Recessive accent is illustrated in (9a): Here the last syllable contains only a single vocalic mora carrying the $L_%$, the L of the accent can fill the penult, and the H can (and therefore must, when the accent is recessive) associate to the antepenult. On the other hand, when the final syllable has two vocalic moras (9b), antepenult accent is not possible: If H is associated to the antepenult, the trailing $L_%$ stretches out over more than the prosodic minimum, one mora. The ranking of the constraints given in tableau (10) accounts for these facts. A final syllable with a single vocalic mora gives rise to antepenult accent, as in (10a), where all constraints are satisfied. On the other hand, when the final syllable has two vocalic moras, the accent not only has to be on the penult, it also has to be the acute (10c), with H on the second mora of the penult, not the circumflex (10d), with H on the first vocalic mora. The antepenult can thus carry the accent (10a), or the penult the circumflex (10c), only when the final has a short vowel.[8]

(10)

/anthrɔɔpos/$_i$ HLL$_%$			ALIGNRIGHT-L$_%$	CONTIGUITY-T	CRISPEDGE-σ/T	NOLAPSE-L$_%$/μ	ALIGNLEFT-H/ω$_i$
	a. ▶	H L L% | \| ánt^{h}rɔɔpos					
	b.	HL L% || | ant^{h}rɔ́ɔpos					*W

---

[8] The tableaux below are violation tableaux with added comparative markings (Prince (2000)), with W's and L's appearing in the rows of losing candidates. "W" in a constraint column indicates the winner is favored by the constraint, "L" indicates the loser is favored, and no entry indicates a tie (i.e., the violation marks for the winner equal those of the loser). In order for a ranking tableau to be consistent, each L has to be preceded by a W in its row (in order to win, the winner needs to do better than each loser on the highest-ranked constraint that distinguishes the two, in Jane Grimshaw's succinct phrasing).

	candidate				
/anthrɔɔpuu/ᵢ HLL%	c. ▶ H L L% | | | antʰrɔɔpuu				**
	d. HL L% || ∧ antʰrɔɔpuu			*W	*L
	e. H L L% | ∧ ∧ ántʰrɔɔpuu			*W	L
	f. H L L% | ∧ | antʰrɔ́ɔpuu		*W		*L
	g. H L L% | ∧ | ántʰrɔɔpuu		*W		L
	h. H L L% | ∧ | ántʰrɔɔpuu	*W			L

When an antepenult with two vocalic moras carries the accent, it can only be the acute (11a), not the circumflex (11b). Pre-antepenult accent is never a possibility (11c).

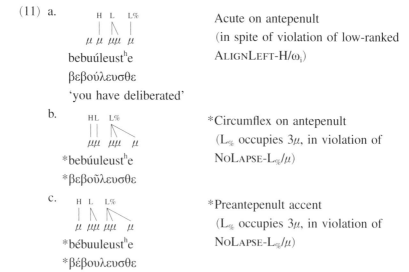

(11) a.   H L   L%
         \| ∧   \|
         μ μ μμ μ
         bebuúleustʰe
         βεβoύλευσθε
         'you have deliberated'

   Acute on antepenult
   (in spite of violation of low-ranked
   ALIGNLEFT-H/ωᵢ)

   b.   HL   L%
        \|\| ∧
        μμ μμ μ
        *bebúuleustʰe
        *βεβoῦλευσθε

   *Circumflex on antepenult
   ($L_\%$ occupies 3μ, in violation of
   NOLAPSE-$L_\%/\mu$)

   c.   H L   L%
        \| ∧ ∧
        μ μμ μμ μ
        *bébuuleustʰe
        *βέβoυλευσθε

   *Preantepenult accent
   ($L_\%$ occupies 3μ, in violation of
   NOLAPSE-$L_\%/\mu$)

This is the Misteli-Allen "Law of Limitation", and what we see here is a pattern of antepenultimacy which follows entirely from the tonal melody and its alignment, crucially including a NoLapse constraint, there is no influence of metrical structure. One could do worse than quote Misteli's characterization of tonal antepenultimacy in detail:

> Die beschränkung des tones innert der drei letzten moren oder wenigstens silben folgt daraus, dass die Griechen den ton nicht weiter vom ende zurückziehen wollten, als es überhaupt sprachaccente gab; denn weil mit jeder auf den hauptton folgenden silbe der ton schwächer wird, unter der tieftonigen silbe aber sich nichts mehr findet, musste der hauptton höchstens der dritten silbe vom ende weg zufallen, so dass die zweite den mittelton, die dritte den tieftonerhielt […] (Misteli (1868: 92)).[9]

As long as it stays within the limits of tonal antepenultimacy, the Greek word accent is in the general case free, i.e., subject to lexical marking. Thus we find accentual contrasts due to lexical marking as in (12), where recessive accent would entail accent on the penult (*híppeus*, *híppeu*).

(12)   hippeús 'horseman',   hippéu 'horseman',
              nominative   vocative

Crucially, no such lexical accents are found earlier in the word, outside of the tonal antepenultimacy window. This follows from the constraint ranking in (13), where NoFlop-H protects lexical accent against the general imperative for accent to be left-aligned, modulo NoLapse-L$_\%$/μ.

(13)   NoLapse-L$_\%$/μ >> NoFlop-H >> AlignLeft-H/ω

Certain word classes, including finite verbs, neuter nouns, and exocentric

---

[9] 'The limitation of the tone within the last three moras or at least syllables follows from the fact that the Greeks did not want to pull the tone further away from the end than there were linguistic accents; given that with every syllable following the main tone the tone is getting weaker, and that there is no room left below the low-toned syllable, the main tone had to fall maximally on the third syllable from the end, so that the second syllable received the mid tone, and the third one the low tone […]' (our translation).

compounds, have recessive accent and have been illustrated above in (9)-(11), meaning that here the accent must appear as far to the left as possible within the accent window, overriding any lexical specifications.[10] Recessive accent is due to a higher-ranked specific ALIGNLEFT-H/ω_i constraint indexed to these lexical classes (see Wackernagel (1877) for an idea of how to understand recession in a more principled way). The overall ranking is as in (14).

(14)　NOLAPSE-L$_{\%}$/μ ≫ ALIGNLEFT-H/ω_i ≫ NOFLOP-H ≫ ALIGNLEFT-H/ω

Up to this point, we have assumed that NOLAPSE-L$_{\%}$/μ scrutinizes only vocalic moras. Things change once we consider words ending in underlying clusters. The empirical observation is that such word-final consonant clusters, whose first consonant carries weight (single final consonants are not moraic), always limit the accent to the penult. This restriction, clearly stated in the works of 19th century accentologists (Misteli (1868: 107), Chandler (1881: 176), see Probert (2006: 60)), was in the generative tradition rediscovered by Steriade (1988: 273-275). For example, in compounds known to have recessive accent, such as bahuvrihis like *polú-naos* 'with many temples' or synthetic compounds like *p^{h}iló-ksenos* 'hospitable', a word-final cluster implies penult accent and excludes antepenult accent: *polu-ánt^{h}raks* 'with much coal', not **polú-ant^{h}raks*, *p^{h}ilo-spéɛlunks* 'fond of grottoes', not **p^{h}iló-spɛɛlunks*. It would be possible to follow earlier generative approaches starting with Steriade (1988) and interpret this as the place where foot structure makes itself felt within this system. But in the approach pursued here, a simpler and more tantalizing idea suggests itself. We can assume that in these cases L$_{\%}$ is forced to link to the word-final intrametrical consonantal mora, so the L of the accent links to the vowel of the last syllable, and H ends up on the last (or only) vocalic mora of the penult. This is shown in (15) (where consonantal moras

---

[10] Probert (2006: 128-148) makes a strong case that recessive accentuation is in fact the default.

(15)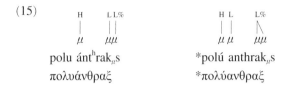

polu ánt^hrak$_\mu$s   *polú anthrak$_\mu$s
πολυάνθραξ   *πολύανθραξ

Steriade-type accentuation holds even when the cluster is merely an underlying one and has undergone simplification in the output, resulting in opacity, as in *et^hélon* (**et^helon*) 'want', part.pres.nom./acc. (from /et^hélont/, cf. *et^hélontos* gen.neut.). Such underlying clusters attract the accent only when they are supported by synchronic alternations, not when they are merely reconstructible on historical grounds. So we find antepenult accent in *et^héleesan* 'want', 3.pl.aorist (historically from *et^héleesant*) because no alternation supports an underlying cluster.[12]

If the accent of Ancient Greek is truly a case of antepenultimacy completely determined by the tonal melody and its alignment conditions, not by foot structure and NONFINALITY, as in standard cases of antepenulti-

---

[11] In this context, another ingredient of Greek accent needs to be considered, the so-called σωτῆρα (sotera) Law, which allows only circumflex (H on first μ), not acute (H on second μ), on a penult with two vocalic moras preceding a final with one vocalic mora (the mnemonic example is σωτῆρα *sɔɔtéera* 'savior' (acc.sg.), not *σωτήρα *sɔɔtεéra). The σωτῆρα Law counts only vocalic moras, so the final counts as monomoraic for σωτῆρα in *p^hilo-spéelunks* (i.e., with circumflex). Such cases require the accentual H to first be assigned immediately before the last syllable as an acute, i.e., to the second vowel mora of the penult in *p^hilo-spεélunks*. It is then, perhaps at a later stratum, retracted by σωτῆρα. A stratal account, with early accent assignment, has been motivated for Ancient Greek accentuation by Kiparsky (2003) for situations where the accent has to be assigned before vowel contraction. No workable alternative to such a stratal analysis, e.g. by means of OO-constraints, is known to us.

[12] Sauzet (1989: 101) points to some complications: Underlying *-id-s,* well supported by alternations, sometimes attracts the accent to the penult, sometimes not. Thus we see the effect in *hikétis* 'female supplicant' (from /hikétid-s/), but not in *áleksis* (from /áleksid-s/) (proper name), or in *artópɔɔlis* 'baker' fem.nom.sg. and in all other words in *-pɔɔlis,* whose other case forms (such as *artopɔɔ́lid-a* acc. sg.) clearly require underlying *-id-s.* We assume that L$_%$ is linked to the final consonantal mora in cases like *hikétis* but not, for reasons unknown, in cases like *áleksis.*

mate stress (Prince and Smolensky (1993)) and also antepenultimate pitch accent, as in Japanese (see Ito and Mester (2016)), this might be the reason why the Greek rule has been so recalcitrant to metrical approaches within the generative tradition. Since the tones associate to vowel moras, a tonal melody counts moras in ways somewhat similar to feet, so it is not surprising that analyses in terms of foot structure can approximate the pattern quite closely without actually capturing its real nature.

Two main lines of approach to a foot-based treatment of Greek accent have been pursued in the past. The first sticks to the standard idea that the H tone of the accent has to coincide with a foothead, its foremost implementation is the one proposed by Steriade (1988). With final light syllables declared extrametrical, the challenge is to reach across a heavy penult with two vocalic moras and plant a foothead on the antepenult, as in *ánt^{h}rɔɔpos* 'human being'—something unthinkable in a quantitative trochaic system like Latin or English. Steriade's answer is to instead build a quantity-insensitive syllabic trochee: (*ánt^{h}rɔɔ*) ⟨*pos*⟩. This is descriptively successful, but Sauzet (1989) points out a deep problem with this kind of quantity-insensitive footing within an otherwise thoroughly quantitative system, whose quantity-sensitivity is even recognized within the same analysis (which declares final syllables extrametrical only when they are light). Sauzet (1989, 105) argues that metrical theory should not allow this kind of discrepancy between the quantity conditions governing the metrical structures of a language in general, determining which kinds of syllables can occupy weak positions of feet, and the quantity conditions on extrametrical material: "Une séquence extramétrique pour un niveau doit être définie dans les mêmes termes que les constituants de ce niveau".[13] His general conclusion sees the standard approach locating the H tone in the foothead at a dead end: "Les representations organisées en constituants que permet de construire la théorie métrique n'apparaissent pas capables de caractériser directement la place de l'accent en grec an-

---

[13] 'An extrametrical sequence at a given level must be defined in the same terms as the constituents of that level' (our translation).

cient" (Sauzet (1989: 81)).[14] This leads to his own proposal, the second main line of analysis, which divorces H tone from foothead, and places it instead before it "[...] par une règle assignant un ton haut à la syllable precedent le pied final [...]"[15] (Sauzet (1989: 105)): *án(tʰrɔɔ)* ⟨*pos*⟩. This is further rationalized by understanding the accentual melody as HL*, where it is the designated low tone that associates to the foothead. Now the trochee can be quantity-sensitive, as seems required, but at a cost: The cross-linguistically solid link between H tones and footheads (de Lacy (2002)) is severed, *contra naturam*. There are certainly intonational pitch accents whose designated tone is L, but we are here not dealing with special intonational markers with specific meanings, but with the basic word prominence marker of a language.

Golston (1990) and Kiparsky (2003) have developed Sauzet's approach further, the latter using a tonal faithfulness constraint in stratal OT to prevent any accentuation or deaccentuation within the final trochaic foot, and then aligning the H tone as far to the right as possible, effectively to the immediate left of the foot declared inaccessible in this way. Besides the problematic aspects of Sauzet's analysis already outlined, this approach incurs a further liability in that it not only necessitates a non-parallel version of OT to be formalized, but also makes the implausible prediction that accent assignments as in Greek should only be possible at non-initial strata (since the foot that rejects the H tone must already have been established at an earlier stratum before H can then be aligned to its immediate left). This is unlikely to withstand typological scrutiny.

All these various solutions along two different paths are ingenious ways of trying to reconcile the recalcitrant Greek accent with the foot structure which is supposed to be its anchor, but as often in linguistics, their very ingenuity is also their liability. In contrast, the rather straightforward analysis in terms of tonal antepenultimacy developed here, based on

---

[14] 'The representations organized into constituents that metrical theory allows us to build seem unable to characterize the place of the Ancient Greek accent in direct terms' (our translation).

[15] '[...] by a rule assigning a high tone to the syllable preceding the final foot' (our translation).

Misteli's (1868) insight, associates the H tone of the accent to the correct mora/syllable by simply lining up the three tones of the melody (HL+ L$_{\%}$) at the right word edge, with very mundane conditions on their alignment with syllables and moras—including NoLapse-L$_{\%}$ as a crucial ingredient. In a more general perspective, both the directional asymmetry in Japanese discovered by Kubozono and the unusual antepenultimacy pattern of recessive Greek accent find a direct explanation in the shape of the tonal word melodies involved and the general constraints governing them. The next step should be a further exploration of the factorial typology of the constraint system, which might yield unexpected and surprising results.

References

Allen, W. S. (1966) "A Problem of Greek Accentuation," *In Memory of J. R. Firth*, ed. by C. E. Bazell, J. C. Catford, M. A. K. Halliday and R. H. Robins, 8–14, Longmans, London.

Allen, W. S. (1973) *Accent and Rhythm*, Cambridge University Press, Cambridge.

Allen, W. S. (1987) *Vox Graeca*, Cambridge University Press, Cambridge.

Chandler, Henry W. (1881) *A Practical Introduction to Greek Accentuation*, Clarendon Press, Oxford.

de Lacy, Paul (2002) "The Interaction of Tone and Stress in Optimality Theory," *Phonology* 19, 1–32.

Goldsmith, John (1976) *Autosegmental Phonology*, Doctoral dissertation, MIT. [Published by Garland Press, New York, 1979.]

Golston, Chris (1990) "Floating H (and L*) Tones in Ancient Greek," *Proceedings of the Arizona Phonology Conference*, ed. by James Myers and Patricia E. Pérez, 66–82, Department of Linguistics, University of Arizona, Tucson.

Haraguchi, Shosuke (1977) *The Tone Pattern of Japanese: An Autosegmental Theory of Tonology*, Kaitakusha, Tokyo.

Haraguchi, Shosuke (1991) *A Theory of Stress and Accent*, Foris, Dordrecht.

Hayes, Bruce (1982) "Extrametricality and English Stress," *Linguistic Inquiry* 13, 227–276.

Hyman, Larry M. (2006) "Word-prosodic Typology," *Phonology* 23, 225–257.

Ito, Junko and Armin Mester (1999) "Realignment," *Proceedings of the Utrecht Workshop on Prosodic Morphology*, ed. by René Kager, Harry van der Hulst

and W. Zonneveld, 188-217, Cambridge University Press, Cambridge.
Ito, Junko and Armin Mester (2013) "Prosodic Subcategories in Japanese," *Lingua* 124, 20-40.
Ito, Junko and Armin Mester (2016) "Unaccentedness in Japanese," *Linguistic Inquiry* 47, 471-526.
Jakobson, Roman (1962) *Selected Writings, vol. 1: Phonological Studies*, Mouton, 'S-Gravenhage.
Kiparsky, Paul (1967) "A propos de l'histoire de l'accentuation grecque," *Languages* 2, 73-93.
Kiparsky, Paul (2003) "Accent, Syllable Structure, and Morphology in Ancient Greek," *Selected Papers from the 15th International Symposium on Theoretical and Applied Linguistics*, ed. by Elizabeth Mela-Athanasopoulou, 81-106, Thessaloniki.
Kubozono, Haruo (1988) *The Organization of Japanese Prosody*, Doctoral dissertation, University of Edinburgh. [Published by Kurosio, Tokyo, 1993.]
Kubozono, Haruo (1989) "Syntactic and Rhythmic Effects on Downstep in Japanese," *Phonology* 6, 39-67.
Kubozono, Haruo (1995) "Constraint Interaction in Japanese Phonology: Evidence from Compound Accent," *Phonology at Santa Cruz.* Vol. 4, 21-38.
Kubozono, Haruo (2009) "Japanese Accent," *Handbook of Japanese Linguistics*, ed. by Shigeru Miyagawa and Mamoru Saito, 165-191, Oxford University Press, Oxford.
Misteli, Franz (1868) "Über die Accentuation des Griechischen," *Zeitschrift für vergleichende Sprachforschung* 17, 81-134, 161-194.
Poppe, Clemens Pieter (2015) *Word-prosodic Structure in Japanese: A Cross-dialectal Perspective*, Doctoral dissertation, Tokyo University.
Prince, Alan S. (1983) "Relating to the Grid," *Linguistic Inquiry* 14, 9-100.
Prince, Alan S. (2000) "Comparative Tableaux," Rutgers Optimality Archive. ROA-376. http://roa.rutgers.edu/. (Retrieved 8/15/2015).
Prince, Alan S. and Paul Smolensky (1993) *Optimality Theory: Constraint Interaction in Generative Grammar*, RuCCS-TR-2, Rutgers University and University of Colorado. [Published 2004, Blackwell, Malden, MA.]
Probert, Philomen (2003) *A New Short Guide to the Accentuation of Ancient Greek*, Bristol Classical Press, London.
Probert, Philomen (2006) *Ancient Greek Accentuation. Synchronic Patterns, Frequency Effects, and Prehistory*, Oxford University Press, Oxford.
Sauzet, Patrick (1989) "L'accent du grec ancien et les relations entre structure métrique et représentation autosegmentale," *Languages* 95, 81-113.

Steriade, Donca (1988) "Greek Accent: A Case for Preserving Structure," *Linguistic Inquiry* 19, 271–314.

Vance, Timothy J. (2008) *The Sounds of Japanese*, Cambridge University Press, Cambridge.

Wackernagel, Jacob (1877) "Der griechische Verbalaccent," *Zeitschrift für vergleichende Sprachforschung* 23, 457–470.

Rendaku Following a Moraic Nasal*

Timothy J. Vance
National Institute for Japanese Language and Linguistics

1. Introduction

The term *rendaku* 連濁 denotes a well-known set of morphophonemic alternations in Japanese. The phenomenon is now so widely known among phonologists all over the world that no English translation is necessary, and I will use the Japanese term hereafter without italicization.

Rendaku can be described as a process that replaces a morpheme-initial voiceless obstruent with voiced obstruent. The prototypical environment for this replacement is immediately following the primary boundary in a two-element compound (E1 + E2). For example, the E2 in /kami + bukuro/ 紙袋, 'paper bag' appears as a word on its own as /fukuro/ 袋 'bag'.

Two important characteristics of rendaku are often treated as uninteresting or disregarded entirely. First, because of historical changes, the voiced and voiceless obstruents paired by rendaku differ in many cases by more than just the presence vs. absence of voicing (Vance (2014: 139-141, 2015a: 397-398)). Second, rendaku is irregular to a significant degree, often failing to apply to an eligible E2 even when no known inhibiting factor is at work (Vance (2015a: 408)).

---

* The research reported here was carried out as part of the NINJAL project headed by the author ("The Japanese Lexicon: A *Rendaku* Encyclopedia"), which ran from December of 2010 until March of 2016. Some of the material in this paper was presented on March 4, 2016, at Lexicon Festa 4, the last annual conference of NINJAL's Department of Linguistic Theory and Structure.

The goal of this paper is to assess the claim that a moraic nasal (transcribed phonemically as /N/) at the end of E1 promotes rendaku. The conclusion will be that there is no convincing evidence for this claim.

2. Sino-Japanese Binoms and Postnasal Voicing

Lyman (1894: 3-4) cited mostly Sino-Japanese binoms such as /hoN·goku/ 本国 'native country' (cf. /koku·boH/ 国防 'national defense') in support of the suggestion that rendaku is frequent in Sino-Japanese elements immediately following /N/. Okumura (1955: 962) made the same suggestion, after identifying rendaku with what Japanese language scholars traditionally call *shindaku* 新濁 'new voicing'.

Most instances of binom-medial new voicing can be attributed to a process known as postnasal voicing (PNV), which was active in the Early Middle Japanese (EMJ) period (800-1200) but, according to Frellesvig (2010: 307-308), "ceased to apply as an automatic phonological rule" during the Late Middle Japanese (LMJ) period (1200-1600). In terms of type frequency, most /N/+obstruent sequences in EMJ were in Sino-Japanese words, but it should be kept in mind that, outside of elite circles, this stratum of the vocabulary played a much smaller role than it does in modern Japanese.

For reasons that have been explained in detail elsewhere (Vance (2011)), new voicing in Sino-Japanese binoms is highly problematic for a synchronic analysis of rendaku in modern Japanese. The position adopted here is that Sino-Japanese binoms are not ordinary compounds and that instances of binom-internal voicing are not instances of rendaku (Vance and Asai (2016: 124)).[1] When such instances are excluded from consideration, it is not easy to find examples that are relevant to the question of whether a moraic nasal at the end of E1 promotes rendaku in an E1+E2 compound.

---

[1] Ito and Mester (2003: 80) take the same position, treating Sino-Japanese binoms as instances of "root compounding" rather than "word compounding" and noting that only the latter "is the locus of *rendaku* voicing."

3. Postnasal Voicing and Rendaku in Modern Japanese

PNV was not restricted to Sino-Japanese vocabulary items in EMJ. /N/ + obstruent sequences also arose in native words, including some inflectional forms, because of some of the reduction processes known as *onbin* 音便 'euphonic changes' (Frellesvig (1995), Satō (2007)). A typical example that preserves the effects of reduction and PNV is /yoN-de/ 読んで 'reading' (<Old Japanese /yomi-te/). There are also examples that developed in compounds and frozen phrases, such as /yuN+de/ 弓手 'bow hand; left hand' (cf. /yumi/ 'bow', /te/ 'hand') and /saki+N+zu-ru/ 先んずる 'to precede' (cf. /saki/ 'ahead', /ni/ 'to', /su-ru/ 'to do'). Many hybrid compounds consisting of a single Sino-Japanese morpheme followed by the native verb /su-ru/ 'to do' also preserve the outcome of PNV (Vance and Asai (2016: 125–129)), as in /eN+zu-ru/ 演ずる 'to perform' (cf. Sino-Japanese /eN/ 'performing').

Some phonologists claim that PNV is still active in modern Japanese but that it applies exclusively or mainly to native Japanese elements (Ito and Mester (2003a: 130–131), Tabata (2010: 98), Labrune (2012: 128–130)). It is usually assumed without comment that PNV does not simply add voicing to a voiceless obstruent; instead, PNV replaces a voiceless obstruent with the same voiced obstruent that would result from rendaku. Even if the domain of PNV is restricted to morpheme-internal position, its status as a synchronically active process is highly dubious, but if PNV is assumed to apply across the boundary between E1 and E2 in compounds, rendaku and PNV are indistinguishable following /N/ (Labrune (2012: 129)). Thus, any investigation of the influence of E1-final /N/ on rendaku, this paper included, presupposes that examples like /giN+gicune/ 銀狐 'silver fox' (cf. /giN/ 'silver', /kicune/ 'fox') are instances of rendaku, not PNV (Vance (2015a: 421)).

4. Individual Element Behavior

Sakurai (1966: 41–42), like other Japanese language scholars, identifies rendaku with new voicing (see §2 above), but he does not cite Sino-Japanese binoms to support the claim that an E1-final /N/ makes rendaku more likely. Instead, he cites the examples in (1), each of which has a native E2.

(1) a. /kaN + buna/ 寒鮒 'crucian carp caught in winter'
cf. /kaN/ 'cold', /funa/ 'crucian carp'
b. /saN + zuke/ さん付け 'addressing as -*san*'
cf. /saN/ 'Mr/Ms', /cuke-ru/ 'to attach'
c. /baN + gasa/ 番傘 'oil-paper umbrella'
cf. /baN/ 'number', /kasa/ 'umbrella'
d. /haN + gi/ 版木 'wooden printing block'
cf. /haN/ 'printing plate', /ki/ 'wood'

The E1 in (1b) is etymologically a contraction of native /sama/, while the other three E1s in (1) are Sino-Japanese. Since the examples in (1) are clearly compounds, the E2-initial voiced obstruent in each case is considered an instance of rendaku here. In short, these are precisely the sort of examples that bear on the question of whether E1-final /N/ promotes rendaku.

To be relevant, however, a compound must have an E2 that is not immune to rendaku but also does not undergo rendaku consistently. The absence of rendaku in /keN + saki/ 剣先 'sword point' (cf. /keN/ 'sword', /saki/ 'tip') is a consequence of the fact that this E2 is idiosyncratically immune.[2] In the case of /hoN + bako/ 本箱 'bookcase' (cf. /hoN/ 'book', /hako/ 'box'), on the other hand, the E2-initial /b/ is uninformative because this E2 consistently shows rendaku regardless of the last segment of E1 (Irwin (2016a: 104)).[3] Thus, the rendaku rate when E1 ends in /N/ cannot be any higher. Examples (1a) and (1c) should probably be set aside too for this same reason.

---

[2] The only apparent exception is /saki + zaki/ 先々 'destinations', but this kind of reduplication strongly favors rendaku (Vance (2015a: 417-419)), and reduplication trumps immunity (Nishimura (2007: 22-23)).

[3] Although /hito + hako/ 一箱 'one box' lacks rendaku, it is not really an exception, since the bound numeral /hito/ 'one' consistently inhibits rendaku when it appears as E1 (Nakagawa (1966: 314), Irwin (2012: 31-32)).

Only a few compounds contain /funa/∼/buna/ 'crucian carp' as E2. One comprehensive dictionary (Matsumura (1995); referred to hereafter as *Daijirin*) lists 18 as headwords, and most are obscure, except perhaps to fishermen.[4] Only one of these compounds is listed as a headword in a popular medium-size Japanese-English dictionary (Kondō and Takano (1986); referred to hereafter as *Progressive*): /hera+buna/ 箆鮒 'deep-bodied crucian carp' (cf. /hera/ 'spatula'). Of the 18 headwords in *Daijirin*, all have rendaku except /cuka+funa/ 束鮒 'hand-size crucian carp' (cf. /cuka/ 'handbreadth').[5] Since this compound without rendaku is very unlikely to be in the vocabulary of an ordinary speaker, and since all the other attested compounds have rendaku, the rendaku in example (1a) (/kaN+buna/) cannot be construed evidence for the influence of E1-final /N/.[6]

Compounds containing /kasa/∼/gasa/ 'umbrella' as E2 are only slightly more numerous, with 29 appearing as headwords in *Daijirin*, but eight of these are common enough to be listed in *Progressive*, including example (1c) (/baN+gasa/). The only one without rendaku is /kara+kasa/ 唐傘 'Chinese umbrella', which appears in both dictionaries. Since rendaku is strongly disfavored in compounds with this E1 (Irwin (2012: 29-30)), this example should probably be excluded from consideration, but even if it is not excluded, the rendaku rate is 97% (28/29) for compounds listed in *Daijirin* and 88% (7/8) for those listed in *Progressive*. These rates are so high that the rendaku in /baN+gasa/ cannot realistically be attributed to the influence of /N/.[7]

The E2 in example (1b) (/saN+zuke/) is deverbal, and the likelihood of rendaku in compounds of this type (N+V=N compounds) is influ-

---

[4] A reverse-lookup dictionary (Sanseidō Henshū-jo (1997)) based on *Daijirin* (Muramatsu (1995)) makes it possible to do exhaustive searches for compound headwords that are listed in the latter and share an E2.

[5] The headword in *Daijirin* is actually the longer compound /mo+fuši+cuka+funa/ 藻臥束鮒 'waterweed-lying hand-size crucian carp', in which /cuka+funa/ is E2.

[6] The names of the eight varieties of crucian carp listed on the Japanese Wikipedia page for /funa/ (https://ja.wikipedia.org/wiki/フナ) all have rendaku.

[7] The rendaku rate for etymologically identical /kasa/ 笠 'conical straw hat' is also very high, but most native speakers today probably do not identify this /kasa/ as the same morpheme as /kasa/ 'umbrella'.

enced by a semantic factor that is not relevant in prototypical compound nouns (N + N = N compounds). Specifically, if E1 is semantically the direct object of the verb underlying E2, rendaku seems to be disfavored (Sugioka (2002: 500-501, 2005: 218), Yamaguchi (2011), Vance (2014: 143-149, 2015a: 429-431)). Rendaku should thus be disfavored in example (1b), since the literal meaning is 'attaching (the honorific title) -san', that is, E1 is the direct object of the underlying verb /cuke-ru/ 'to attach'. A small database of commonly used N + V = N compounds (Nakamura, Takemura and Vance (2012)) contains 18 examples ending in /cuke/∼/zuke/. In 15 of these 18 compounds, E1 is a semantic direct object, and a majority of these 15 have rendaku (10/15 = 67%). Rendaku occurs in all three of the compounds in which E1 has some other relationship to the underlying verb. Given the rather high rendaku rate in the 15 direct-object examples, none of which has an E1 ending in /N/, it is hardly persuasive to attribute the rendaku in (1b) to the E1-final /N/.

The last example in (1) is the best, since /ki/∼/gi/ 'wood; tree' occurs as E2 in a large number of compounds and has a rendaku rate that is not very high. Thus, there is some hope of finding sufficient examples to allow a meaningful comparison of compounds with and without /N/ at the end of E1. One potential complication is the polysemy of this E2. Most content morphemes are polysemous in some way or other, and it is well known that different senses of the same morpheme can have very different rendaku rates (Vance (2015a: 433); Irwin (2016a: 104)).[8] Before considering the behavior of /ki/∼/gi/ in more detail, another confounding factor that must be taken into account is explained just below in §5.

5. Element Length and Rosen's Rule

To be relevant for assessing the influence of E1-final /N/, a compound must consist of an E1 and an E2 that are both shorter than three moras,

---

[8] Irwin (2016a: 105) treats /ki/ 'wood' and /ki/ 'tree' separately but classifies both as "waverers" (i.e., having a rendaku rate between 33% and 67%) in the Rendaku Database (Irwin and Miyashita (2016)). For a description of the Rendaku Database, see §6 below.

because the rendaku behavior of compounds in which at least one element is long (three or more moras) is much more regular than the behavior of compounds in which both E1 and E2 are short (one or two moras). This strong tendency has been dubbed "Rosen's Rule" in recent years (Vance (2015b), Irwin (2016b)) because it was first proposed by Rosen (2001, 2003). Rosen's Rule has two parts. The first part says that if E1 is long, E2 always undergoes rendaku unless it is immune. The second part says that if E2 is long, it always undergoes rendaku unless it is immune.

Since /tori/∼/dori/ 'bird' as an E2 often shows rendaku and often does not, it is tempting to consider examples like /guN·kaN + dori/ 軍艦鳥 'frigate bird' (cf. /guN·kaN/ 'frigate') as evidence for the influence of E1-final /N/. But /guN·kaN/ is four moras long, so the first part of Rosen's Rule predicts that /dori/, not /tori/, will appear regardless of the final segment of E1. In the case of /kaN + zakura/ 寒桜 'Chinese primrose', since E2 (/sakura/∼/zakura/ 'cherry blossom') is three moras long, the second part of Rosen's Rule predicts that /zakura/, not /sakura/, will appear regardless of the final segment of E1. In both cases, if Rosen's Rule is correct, the E1-final /N/ is irrelevant. Rosen himself restricted his claim to compounds in which both E1 and E2 are native nouns, and /guN·kaN/ is a Sino-Japanese binom, but the etymological stratum of E1 does not actually seem to make any difference (Vance (2015b: 211)). On the other hand, E2 does have to be a non-deverbal noun (Vance (2015b: 211)). There are exceptions to Rosen's Rule in the existing vocabulary (Irwin (2005: 130)), but they seem to be very rare, even when non-native elements are involved (Vance (2015a: 410-412)).[9] The upshot is that any assessment of the effect of an E1-final moraic nasal has to consider only compounds in which both E1 and E2 are short.

Returning now to the behavior of /ki/∼/gi/ 木 'wood; tree' as an E2, the results of a careful check have already been reported (Vance (2015b:

---

[9] The long E1 in /hidari + te/ 左手 'left hand' makes it an exception to the first part of Rosen's rule (Kubozono (2005: 16)), and the long E2 in /kita + kicune/ 北狐 'northern fox' makes it an exception to the second part (Irwin (2005: 130)), since neither E2 is immune (cf. /uširo + de/ 後ろ手 'hands behind one's back' and /širo + gicune/ 白狐 'white fox').

209–210)). Among 30 commonly used compounds in which E2 is /ki/ ~ /gi/ 木 and E1 is short and ends in a segment other than /N/, 11 (37%) have rendaku. Separated into those that denote a kind of wood and those that denote a kind of tree, the rendaku rate is 50% for 'wood' and 25% for 'tree'.[10] Even if we assume that this difference is salient enough that native speakers are sensitive to it, example (1d) in §4, /haN+gi/ 版木 'wooden printing block', is in the 'wood' category. In any case, the most one can say is that this single example is consistent with the idea that E1-final /N/ promotes rendaku in this E2.

6. The Rendaku Database

To carry out a rigorous test of the claim that E1-final /N/ promotes rendaku, it is necessary to examine as many relevant compounds as possible. The recently created Rendaku Database (Irwin and Miyashita (2016)) makes it feasible to search systematically for compounds that meet the criteria of interest here. Each entry in the Rendaku Database is a compound that appears as a headword in one or both of two large dictionaries (Watanabe et al. (2003), Shinmura (2008)). Each compound is tagged for a number of properties that can serve as search parameters (for details, see Irwin (2016a)).

For the reasons given above, Sino-Japanese binoms (§2) and compounds containing an element longer than two moras (§5) are excluded from consideration. Consequently, given the restrictive phonotactics of Japanese, all the relevant compounds have an E1 of the form (C)(/y/)V /N/ and an E2 of the form CV((C)V).[11]

Proper nouns are excluded for two reasons. First, many are written

---

[10] One compound with rendaku and one without rendaku are themselves polysemous: /dai+gi/ 台木 'parent stock (tree); wooden block'; /nama+ki/ 生木 'live tree; unseasoned wood'. Leaving these two examples aside, rendaku occurs in 6/12 'wood' compounds and 4/16 'tree' compounds.

[11] C/y/V moras are rare in the native vocabulary except in mimetic words, which are normally treated as a separate stratum. None of the E2s in the sample extracted from the Rendaku Database contains a C/y/V mora.

with kanji that are morphologically misleading. Second, some E2s appear to behave differently in proper nouns and common nouns with respect to rendaku. Thus, proper nouns should be treated as a separate category from common nouns in assessing the influence of E1-final /N/.

In addition, compounds with an E2 containing a medial voiced obstruent are excluded from consideration because a well-known constraint called Lyman's Law blocks rendaku in such E2s (Vance (2007: 157–159, 2015a: 402–408)). Thus, the absence of rendaku in examples such as /paN+kuzu/ パン屑 'breadcrumb' (cf. /kuzu/ 'crumb') and /haN+sode/ 半袖 'short sleeve' (cf. /sode/ 'sleeve') is beside the point, and compounds like these are not even entered in the Rendaku Database (Irwin (2016a: 80)).[12]

Finally, most compounds that involve verb or adjective elements are not considered. N+V=N compounds like /eN+kiri/ 縁切り 'severing relations' (cf. /eN/ 'connection', /kir-u/ 'to cut'), in which E2 is deverbal, were discussed briefly above in §4, and some other compound types involving verb (or deverbal) and/or adjective (or deadjectival) elements have also been investigated to some degree (Vance (2005, 2015b: 426–431)). Indications are that each type needs to be considered separately, and it would therefore be ill-advised in most cases to lump them together with the prototypical N+N=N compounds that make up the bulk of the examples considered below in §7. On the other hand, compounds with a deverbal or deadjectival E1 and a noun E2 do not seem to require special treatment. Thus, some of the examples examined (although not mentioned explicitly) in §7 are V+N=N (e.g., /age+zoko/ 上げ底 'raised bottom'; cf. /age-ru/ 'to raise', /soko/ 'bottom') or A+N=N (e.g., /ama+

---

[12] The Rendaku Database does include a very small number of compounds that are exceptions to Lyman's Law (Irwin (2016a: 82)), all containing E2s that three moras or longer. Most of these compounds do not have an E1 ending in /N/. Both of the dictionaries used to create the database list /daN+bašigo/ 段梯子 'staircase' (cf. /daN/ 'step', /hašigo/ 'ladder, stairs'), but this example provides no evidence for the influence of /N/. One of the two dictionaries (Shinmura (2008)) also lists 17 other compounds with the same E2 following an E1-final vowel, and all 17 have rendaku (e.g., /nawa+bašigo/ 縄梯子 'rope ladder'). The behavior of /saburoH/∼/zaburoH/ 三郎, a conventional name for a third son, is more interesting and will be taken up below in §8.

zake/ 甘酒 'sweet saké'; cf. /ama-i/ 'sweet', /sake/ 'saké').

7. Relevant Examples Extracted from the Rendaku Database

The Rendaku Database makes it easy to extract all the compounds that have an E1 ending in /N/ and then set aside those that need to be excluded for any of the reasons listed above in §6. There are only 295 examples that meet all the criteria (assuming the examples are correctly tagged), and the four in (2) are typical.

(2) a. /teN+gusa/ 天草 'agar weed'
cf. /teN/ 'heaven', /kusa/ 'grass'
b. /kiN+ba/ 金歯 'gold tooth'
cf. /kiN/ 'gold', /ha/ 'tooth'
c. /šiN+soko/ 心底 'bottom of one's heart'
cf. /šiN/ 'heart', /soko/ 'bottom'
d. /guN+te/ 軍手 'cotton work gloves'
cf. /guN/ 'military', /te/ 'hand'

Each example in (2) is a common noun with a two-mora E1 ending in /N/ and a one- or two-mora noun E2.[13]

Needless to say, large dictionaries like the two used to build the Rendaku Database (Watanabe et al. (2003), Shinmura (2008)) list many words that are obsolete or obscure. The goal of the present paper is to assess

---

[13] Compounds with a Sino-Japanese or recently borrowed E2 that at least sometimes shows rendaku are included in the Rendaku Database (Irwin (2015a: 80)). Only one with a Sino-Japanese E2 meets the other criteria adopted here: /noN+ki/ 呑気 'easygoing' (cf. /ki/~/gi/ 気 'spirit'). This word is etymologically a Sino-Japanese binom, written 暖気, with the first kanji representing a very rare morpheme meaning 'warm', but it seems clear that native speakers now analyze /noN/ as something else. The kanji 呑 suggests a folk etymology, with /noN/ identified as a reduced form of native deverbal /nomi/ 呑み 'swallowing'. Whether native speakers really think of /noN+ki/ this way or not, as long as they do not see it as a Sino-Japanese binom, it qualifies for inclusion in the present dataset. No example with a recently borrowed E2 qualifies. The E1 (< English *ten*) in /teN+kiH/ テンキー 'numeric key' ends in /N/, but the recently borrowed E2 (< English *key*), like most recently borrowed morphemes, never shows rendaku.

the influence of E1-final /N/, and it is certainly preferable for such an assessment to be based on the linguistic knowledge of ordinary native speakers. In order to limit the dataset to compounds that are reasonably likely to be in the active vocabularies of most such speakers, the medium-size Japanese-English dictionary mentioned above in §4 (*Progressive*; Kondō and Takano (1986)) was employed. Of the 295 relevant example extracted from the Rendaku Database, only 68 are listed as headwords in this smaller dictionary. This method is crude, and it causes some obvious problems that will be pointed out below, but on balance it makes the assessment more realistic.[14]

Many of the 68 remaining compounds must be set aside for various reasons. Three have the E2 /gawa/ 側 'side' and one has the E2 /gara/ 柄 'pattern', and while these are historically instances of rendaku, these E2s appear in isolation as /gawa/ (not /kawa/) and /gara/ (not /kara/) in modern Japanese. Four others have an etymologically deverbal or deadjectival E2, although they are not tagged this way in the Rendaku Database.[15]

Eight of the 68 compounds have E2s that are immune to rendaku, and another 20 have E2s that consistently undergo rendaku (see the discussion of /keN+saki/ 剣先 'sword point' and /hoN+bako/ 本箱 'bookcase' in §4).[16] There is no reason to consider these examples any further, since an

---

[14] To give the flavor of what has been excluded, among the compounds not listed in *Progressive* are /boN+bune/ 盆舟 'small boat used during O-bon to send off ancestral spirits' and /saN+zuna/ 産綱 'rope that a mother grabs while giving birth'.

[15] In the case of /baN+gumi/ 番組 'program', one could certainly argue that /kumi/ 'group' is basically a noun, despite its connection to /kum-u/ 'to put together', but such judgments are difficult to make consistently. As for /boN+kure/ 盆暮れ 'the O-bon and year-end periods', the related verb is /kure-ru/ 'to come to an end', and this example would have to set aside anyway because the absence of rendaku can be attributed to its coordinate meaning (Vance (2015a: 425-426)). The E2 in /kiN+daka/ 金高 'amount of money' and /zaN+daka/ 残高 '(account) balance' is related to the adjective /taka-i/ 'high' but occurs on its own as the noun /taka/ 'amount'. In any case these last two examples would have to be set aside later in this section, since this /taka/ always undergoes rendaku as an E2 (Vance (2015a: 428)).

[16] Some of the E2s that are categorized here as consistently undergoing rendaku are attested without rendaku in a small number of obsolete or obscure words or in combination with an E1 that inhibits rendaku (see the discussion of /kasa/∼/gasa/ 傘 'umbrella' in

E1-final /N/ has no effect on the rendaku rate of such E2s.

At this point, only 32 compounds remain to be considered. Nine of these have E2s that do not always undergo rendaku but nonetheless strongly favor rendaku. Each of these nine E2s appears in only one of the compounds still under consideration, one of which is /hoN+goši/ 本腰 'strenuous effort' (cf. /hoN/ 'full', /koši/ 'hips, lower back'). This compound is typical of the group. The comprehensive dictionary mentioned above in §4 (*Daijirin*; Matsumura (1995)) lists 37 relevant compounds consisting of an E1 that does not end in /N/ followed by this E2 (/koši/~/goši/), 35 with rendaku and two without.[17] *Progressive* (the smaller Japanese-English dictionary) lists 16 of these 37 compounds, all with rendaku. If the rendaku rate for /koši/~/goši/ were extremely low when immediately preceded by a segment other than /N/, the rendaku in /hoN+goši/ would be noteworthy, but in fact the rate is very high. Thus, the rendaku in /hoN+goši/ is no more significant than the rendaku in /hoN+bako/ 'bookshelf'. Neither can be construed as evidence that an E1-final /N/ makes rendaku more likely.

Excluding the nine compounds with E2s that strongly favor rendaku leaves 23 compounds still to consider, but 12 of these have an E2 that appears in only a single compound. Such a single example is evidence for the influence of E1-final /N/ only if (1) the E2 has rendaku in that isolated example, and (2) the E2 never or almost never has rendaku in com-

---

§4). One of the E2s treated as immune is /ko/ in /meN+ko/ 面子 'card-throwing game' and /haN+ko/ 判子 'signature seal'. Although etymologically the same as /ko/ 'child', which sometimes undergoes rendaku, the /ko/ in these two compounds means something vague like 'thing'. In this meaning, /ko/ seems to resist rendaku consistently. Incidentally, /haN+ko/ originated as the Sino-Japanese binom /haN·koH/ 判行, but it has lost the vowel length in its final syllable and been reanalyzed.

[17] *Daijirin* lists four others without rendaku that have been excluded from consideration here. The absence of rendaku in /hito+koši/ 一腰 'one sword' can be attributed to the E1, as explained in note 3 above (§4). Although /futa/ 'two' does not inhibit rendaku as consistently as /hito/ 'one' (Irwin (2012: 31-32)), /futa+koši/ 二腰 'two swords' has also been excluded. Both /aši+koši/ 足腰 'legs and lower back' and /šiQ+koši/ 尻腰 'courage' are excluded because they are coordinate (Vance (2015a: 425-426)), and the moraic obstruent /Q/ in the latter preempts rendaku regardless of meaning (Vance and Asai (2016: 132-133)).

pounds with an E1 ending in something other than /N/. Of these 12 isolated examples in the dataset under consideration here, six have rendaku. Four of these can probably be set aside because their E2s often undergo rendaku, even though it would be an exaggeration to say that any of these E2s strongly favors rendaku. Among these four E2s, the one with the lowest rendaku rate is /kusa/~/gusa/ 草 'grass'.[18] Of the relevant headwords listed in *Progressive* that have an E1 ending in something other than /N/ followed by /kusa/~/gusa/, 24% (5/21) have rendaku. The isolated example with this E2 following /N/ is /teN + gusa/ 天草 'agar weed', which appeared above as example (2a). This compound is certainly consistent with the notion that E1-final /N/ promotes rendaku, but it would take many similar examples to make a convincing case.

The other two isolated examples with rendaku are suggestive but not easy to evaluate. One is semantically opaque /daN + bira/ 段平 'broadsword' (cf. /daN/ 'step; layer', /hira/ 'flat'), which appears to be the result of a folk etymology. Even on the assumption that present-day native speakers see it as a compound of the two morphemes suggested by the kanji, it is not clear that a rendaku rate can be calculated in any meaningful way for /hira/~/bira/ not preceded by /N/. Although *Daijirin* lists five such examples, two with rendaku and three without, none of these is common enough to appear as a headword in *Progressive*.

The last isolated example is /maN + zara/ 満更 'wholly', a negative polarity item with an E2 that occurs independently in the adverbial phrase /sara ni/ 更に 'moreover; even more'. This E2 appears in very few other compounds. Six are listed in *Daijirin*, all without rendaku, and four of these appear as headwords in *Progressive*: /ima + sara/ 今更 'at this (late) point', /nao + sara/ 尚更 'all the more', /koto + sara/ 殊更 'intentionally', and reduplicated /sara + sara/ 更々 'in the least (negative polarity)'. If it were not for /maN + zara/, /sara/~/zara/ would be classified as immune. This is precisely the sort of behavior that would corroborate the hypothesis that an E1-final /N/ promotes rendaku, but /sara/~/zara/ is the only E2

---

[18] The other three are /kawa/~/gawa/ 革 'leather' (Irwin (2016b: 104)), /ki/~/gi/ 木 'wood' (see §5 above), /haši/~/baši/ 橋 'bridge'.

in the dataset that clearly behaves this way.

Only 11 compounds now remain to be considered. Each contains one of four E2s, and each of these E2s appears in at least two of the 11 compounds. To assess the behavior of these four E2s, the rendaku rate is provided for compounds with the same E2 in which E1 does not end in /N/. To save space, the two types of compounds will be referred to hereafter as "/N/ compounds" (those with E1-final /N/) and "non-/N/ compounds" (those without E1-final /N/). To limit the comparison to common words, the non-/N/ compounds are restricted to those that appear as headwords in *Progressive*.

Two of the 11 remaining /N/ compounds have /soko/∼/zoko/ 'bottom' as E2: /doN+zoko/ どん底 'rock bottom' (with rendaku) and /šiN+soko/ 心底 'bottom of one's heart' (without rendaku). The rendaku rate for the non-/N/ compounds with this E2 is high: 80% (8/10). Of course, these numbers are far too small to take very seriously.

Another two of the 11 remaining /N/ compounds have /tori/∼/dori/ 'bird' as E2, and both have rendaku: /oN+dori/ 雄鳥 'rooster' and /meN+dori/ 雌鳥 'hen'. The rendaku rate for the non-/N/ compounds with this E2 is 68% (13/19).[19] Here again, the numbers are very small, and not much can be read into the difference between 100% and 68%.

The are also two examples in the 11 remaining /N/ compounds that have /tama/∼/dama/ 'ball' as E2: /keN+dama/ 剣玉 'cup-and-ball toy' and /zeN+dama/ 善玉 'good guy', both with rendaku. Since the meaning of /tama/∼/dama/ is literal in the former and figurative in the latter, it would seem advisable to separate the non-/N/ compounds with this E2 by meaning (see §5 above). Some of the many senses of this morpheme can

---

[19] One of the 19 non-/N/ compounds listed in *Progressive* is /mizu+tori/ 水鳥 'water bird', but this word is variable in modern Japanese (/mizu+tori/∼/mizu+dori/), and the form with rendaku seems to be ousting the form without (Shioda (2001: 102)). Surprisingly, the common compound /ji+dori/ 地鶏 'locally-produced chicken' is not listed in *Progressive*. These examples show that using a smaller dictionary is a far from perfect method for surveying relevant compounds in common use. The sample of non-/N/ compounds used here also includes two words normally written with single kanji, which might obscure their compound status for some speakers: /hiyo+dori/ 鵯 'bulbul' (cf. /hiyo/ 'bulbul') and /niwa+tori/ 鶏 'chicken' (cf. /niwa/ 'yard').

be distinguished orthographically by using different kanji, although this is not done consistently.[20] However, the rendaku rate for the non-/N/ compounds with this E2 in any of its senses is 92% (22/24), which is so high that it would be hard to argue that an E1-final /N/ elevates the rate significantly, no matter which sense is involved.[21]

Furthermore, there is an /N/ compound without rendaku that is not listed in *Progressive* but is familiar to virtually all native speakers: /kiN + tama/ 金玉 'testicle'. The dictionary editors presumably felt that this word might offend some users, and their decision not to list it reveals one drawback to the method adopted here for sampling compounds in common use. If this compound had been considered along with the two mentioned in the preceding paragraph (/keN + dama/ and /zeN + dama/), the rendaku rate for /N/ compounds ending in /tama/~/dama/ would be 67% (2/3) instead of 100%. What this drastic difference shows, of course, is just that the number of relevant examples is much too small for quantitative analysis.

The other five examples in the 11 remaining /N/ compounds have /te/~/de/ 'hand, arm' as E2, and these five are shown below in (3).

(3) a. /guN + te/ 軍手 'cotton work gloves' (cf. /guN/ 'military')
 b. /seN + te/ 先手 'first move' (cf. /seN/ 'ahead, first')
 c. /baN + te/ 番手 '(thread) count' (cf. /baN/ 'number')
 d. /hoN + te/ 本手 'true ability; proper way' (cf. /hoN/ 'real; proper')
 e. /yuN + de/ 弓手 'bow hand; left hand' (cf. /yumi/ 'bow')

Since only one of the five examples in (3) has rendaku, it is tempting

---

[20] For example, /tama/~/dama/ can be written 弾 when it it means 'bullet', 珠 when it means 'bead, jewel', and 球 when it means 'ball used in a game or sport'. It is normally written 玉 when it means 'drop(let)', 'lens', 'coin', or 'guy'.

[21] The two non-/N/ compounds without rendaku are /mizu + tama/ 水玉 'water droplet' and /šira + tama/ 白玉 'rice-flour dumpling'. Examples like /kani + tama/ 蟹玉 'crab omelette' are not considered because E2 is a clipping of /tama + go/ 卵 (sometimes written 玉子) 'egg'. Truncated E2s are generally immune to rendaku (Haraguchi (2001: 12), Irwin (2016a: 83)).

simply to conclude that an E1-final /N/ has no rendaku-promoting effect on this E2, but the polysemy of /te/∼/de/ is much more problematic than that of /ki/∼/gi/ 木 'wood; tree' (see §5) or /tama/∼/dama/ 玉 'ball; bullet; guy; etc.' (see note 20). The many senses of /te/∼/de/ are hard to distinguish in any consistent way, and as an independent word, this morpheme occurs in a bewildering variety of idioms and conventional collocations. For example, it is not clear whether or not the figurative use in (3a) and the literal use in (3e) should be treated as the same sense. No attempt will be made here to sort out all these problems, since this paper is not a lexicographical study. Consequently, rendaku rates for non-/N/ compounds with most senses of /te/∼/de/ cannot be calculated in any meaningful way.[22]

By focusing only on example (3e), however, a reasonable comparison is possible. A set of 18 relevant non-/N/ compounds was extracted systematically from *Progressive* by limiting the search to those in which E1 is shorter than two moras and E2 is /te/∼/de/ with an arguably literal meaning. The set includes examples like /su+de/ 素手 'bare hands' and /hira+te/ 平手 'open hand' but not examples like /kuma+de/ 熊手 'bamboo rake' (cf. /kuma/ 'bear') and /ko+te/ 籠手 'fencing glove' (cf. /ko/ 'basket'; obsolete as an independent word). Obviously polysemous examples were included as long as one sense involved the literal meaning of /te/∼de/, as in /uwa+te/ 上手 'arm on top; higher position; superior ability'. The rendaku rate for these 18 compounds is 17% (3/18), which means that the rendaku in example (3e) /yuN+de/ is roughly as persuasive (or unpersuasive) as the rendaku in example (2a) /teN+gusa/ 天草

---

[22] One sense that can be isolated quite easily is /te/ combined with a verb E1 to form a noun denoting a human agent, as in /kiki+te/ 聞き手 'listener' (cf. /kik-u/ 'to listen') and /uri+te/ 売り手 'seller' (cf. /ur-u/ 'to sell'). This pattern is highly productive, and /te/ in this use is often described as a dervational suffix (Irwin (2016a: 83)). It is no simple matter to decide what counts as an affix, but agent nouns of this type never have rendaku, and even if they are considered compounds, it makes sense to say that /te/ in this meaning is rendaku-immune. In any case, examples with long E1s, such as /kasegi+te/ 稼ぎ手 'breadwinner' (cf. /kaseg-u/ 'to earn') would violate Rosen's Rule (see §5 above) if this sense of /te/ were lumped together with the literal sense (Kubozono (2005: 16)), since /te/∼/de/ meaning 'hand, arm' is not immune.

'agar weed' as evidence for the rendaku-promoting effect of E1-final /N/.

8. Vocabulary Sectors Where E1-Final /N/ Does Promote Rendaku

In a preliminary assessment of compounds like those treated above in §7, Vance and Asai (2016: 125) say, "It seems unlikely that there are enough such examples to make a convincing case for the claim that an E1-final moraic nasal promotes rendaku." It appears that this prediction is correct. There are, however, two small sectors of the Japanese vocabulary in which an E1-final /N/ clearly does increase the likelihood of rendaku, and this section will discuss these sectors briefly.

First, in compounds consisting of a single Sino-Japanese morpheme followed by the native verb /su-ru/ 'to do' (see §3), there is no question that the rendaku rate is markedly higher for Sino-Japanese morphemes ending in /N/ than for those ending in something else. Typical examples are /šiN+zu-ru/ 信ずる 'to believe' and /sei+su-ru/ 制する 'to control'. There are complications, but compounds of this type are treated in detail by Vance and Asai (2016: 125-129), and there is no reason to repeat the details here.

Second, in given names ending in /saburoH/∼/zaburoH/ 三郎 , a stereotypical name for a third son, /zaburoH/ is much more likely to appear following /N/ than following something else.[23] As a quick method of estimating the distribution of the two allomorphs, the reverse-lookup function of an electronic version of a comprehensive dictionary (Shinmura (2008)) was used to extract all the names ending in this element. This is not really a random sample of course, since only the names of people who happen to be famous are listed in this dictionary, but the sample is reasonably representative. There are 43 relevant given names (some shared by more than one person), 12 with an E1 ending in /N/ (e.g., /geN+zaburoH/ 源三

---

[23] As mentioned in note 12 above, /saburoH/ contains a medial voiced obstruent, so it is one of the rare E2s that undergoes rendaku in violation of Lyman's Law (§6). Although /saburoH/ is etymologically a Sino-Japanese binom, the first morph /sabu/ is phonologically anomalous (Vance (2015a: 405)), and no morpheme boundary is marked in the examples cited here.

郎) and 31 with an E1 ending in a vowel (e.g., /gi + saburoH/ 義三郎). The rendaku rate is 100% (12/12) for the former group but only 32% (10/31) for the latter group.[24]

9. Conclusion

This paper has taken a careful look at the idea that an E1-final moraic nasal makes E2 more likely to undergo rendaku in an E1 + E2 compound. When potential confounding factors are controlled to a reasonable extent, this idea does not stand up to scrutiny, except in the small sectors of the vocabulary described just above in §8. There may well be other such sectors, but there is little doubt that the hypothesized trend does not hold in the overall vocabulary.

Attempting to control for confounding factors is a tedious but necessary process. When element length (see §5) and the idiosyncrasies of individual E2s (see §7) are not taken into account, compounds in the Rendaku Database (see §6) with an E2-final /N/, grouped all together, show an elevated rendaku rate (Irwin (2016a: 96-97)).

In closing, it must be noted that the absence of an overall trend in the existing vocabulary does not necessarily imply that E1-final /N/ will have no effect on native speakers' responses in psycholinguistic experiments. Recent research indicates that "identity avoidance" is a psychologically active factor that influences the likelihood of applying rendaku in nonce compounds (Kawahara and Sano (2016)), despite the fact that there does not appear to be any evidence for such a preference in existing compounds (Irwin (2014)). In one experiment reported by Tamaoka et al. (2009: 28-31), the test items were compounds consisting of a real, two-mora E1 and a made-up E2, and the responses showed a higher rendaku rate for the E1s ending in /N/ than for E1s ending in a vowel. The number of test items was small, but these results are certainly suggestive, and

---

[24] Since /saburoH/~/zaburoH/ is three moras long, it violates the second part of Rosen' Rule (see §5), which says that a three-mora element must undergo rendaku always or never as an E2.

it would not be at all surprising to see the same effect of E1-final /N/ emerge in other experiments.

References

Frellesvig, Bjarke (1995) *A Case Study in Diachronic Phonology: The Japanese Onbin Sound Changes*, Aarhus University Press, Aarhus.
Frellesvig, Bjarke (2010) *A History of the Japanese Language*, Cambridge University Press, Cambridge.
Haraguchi, Shosuke (2001) "On Rendaku," *Phonological Studies* 4, 9-32.
Irwin, Mark (2012) "Rendaku Dampening and Prefixes," *NINJAL Research Papers* 4, 27-36.
Irwin, Mark (2014) "Rendaku Across Duplicate Moras," *NINJAL Research Papers* 7, 93-109.
Irwin, Mark (2016a) "The Rendaku Database," *Sequential Voicing in Japanese Compounds: Papers from the NINJAL Rendaku Project*, ed. by Timothy J. Vance and Mark Irwin, 79-106, John Benjamins, Amsterdam.
Irwin, Mark (2016b) "Rosen's Rule," *Sequential Voicing in Japanese Compounds: Papers from the NINJAL Rendaku Project*, ed. by Timothy J. Vance and Mark Irwin, 107-117, John Benjamins, Amsterdam.
Irwin, Mark and Mizuki Miyashita (2016) "The Rendaku Database," version 2.7 (http://www-h.yamagata-u.ac.jp/~irwin/site/Rendaku_Database.html).
Ito, Junko and Armin Mester (2003) *Japanese Morphophonemics: Markedness and Word Structure*, MIT Press, Cambridge, MA.
Kawahara, Shigeto and Shin-ichiro Sano (2016) "Rendaku and Identity Avoidance: Consonantal Identity and Moraic Identity," *Sequential Voicing in Japanese Compounds: Papers from the NINJAL Rendaku Project*, ed. by Timothy J. Vance and Mark Irwin, 47-55, John Benjamins, Amsterdam.
Kondō, Ineko and Fumi Takano, eds. (1986) *Shogakukan Progressive Japanese-English Dictionary*, Shogakukan, Tokyo.
Kubozono, Haruo (2005) "*Rendaku*: Its Domain and Linguistic Conditions," *Voicing in Japanese*, ed. by Jeroen van de Weijer, Kensuke Nanjo and Tetsuo Nishihara, 5-24, de Gruyter Mouton, Berlin.
Lyman, Benjamin Smith (1894) *The Change from Surd to Sonant in Japanese Compounds*, Oriental Club of Philadelphia, Philadelphia.
Matsumura, Akira, ed. (1995) *Daijirin*, 2nd edition, Sanseido, Tokyo.

Nakagawa, Yoshio (1966) "Rendaku, Rensei (Kashō) no Keifu," *Kokugo Kokubun* 35(6), 302–314.

Nakamura, Kumiko, Akiko Takemura and Timothy J. Vance (2012) "N + V = N Rendaku Database" (http://pj.ninjal.ac.jp/rendaku/en/database/).

Nishimura, Kohei (2007) "Rendaku and Morphological Correspondence," *Phonological Studies* 10, 21–30.

Okumura, Mitsuo (1955) "Rendaku," *Kokugo-gaku Jiten*, ed. by Kokugo Gakkai, 961–962, Tokyodo, Tokyo.

Rosen, Eric Robert (2001) *Phonological Processes Interacting with the Lexicon: Variable and Non-regular Effects in Japanese Phonology*, Doctoral dissertation, University of British Columbia.

Rosen, Eric (2003) "Systematic Irregularity in Japanese *Rendaku*: How the Grammar Mediates Patterned Lexical Exceptions," *Canadian Journal of Linguistics* 48, 1–37.

Sakurai, Shigeharu (1966) "Kyōtsugo no Hatsuon de Chūi subeki Kotogara," *Nihongo Hatsuon Akusento Jiten*, ed. by Nihon Hōsō Kyōkai, 31–43, Nihon Hōsō Shuppan Kyōkai, Tokyo.

Sanseido Henshu-jo, ed. (1997) *Kanji-biki Gyakubiki Daijirin*, Sanseido, Tokyo.

Satō, Nobuo (2007) "Onbin," *Nihongo-gaku Kenkyū Jiten*, ed. by Yoshifumi Hida et al., 353–354, Meiji Shoin, Tokyo.

Shinmura, Izuru, ed. (2008) *Kōjien*, 6th edition, Iwanami Shoten, Tokyo.

Shioda, Takehiro (2001) "Yōgo no Kettei," *Hōsō Kenkyū to Chōsa* (April), 94–97.

Sugioka, Yoko (2002) "Incorporation vs. Modification in Deverbal Compounds," *Japanese/Korean Linguistics 10*, ed. by Noriko M. Akatsuka and Susan Strauss, 495–508, CSLI Publications, Stanford.

Sugioka, Yoko (2005) "Mechanisms Underlying Morphological Productivity," *Polymorphous Linguistics: Jim McCawley's Legacy*, ed. by Salikoko S. Mufwene, Elaine J. Francis and Rebecca S. Wheeler, 203–223, MIT Press, Cambridge, MA.

Tabata, Toshiyuki (2010) "Sūshi 'San' to 'Yon' ni tsuite," *Kango no Gengogaku*, ed. by Hiroko Ōshima, Akiko Nakajima and Raoul Blin, 91–106, Kurosio, Tokyo.

Tamaoka, Katsuo, Mutsuko Ihara, Tadao Murata and Hyunjung Lim (2009) "Effects of First-Element Phonological-Length and Etymological-Type Features on Sequential Voicing (*Rendaku*) of Second Elements," *Journal of Japanese Linguistics* 25, 17–38.

Vance, Timothy J. (2005) "Rendaku in Inflected Words," *Voicing in Japanese*, ed. by Jeroen van de Weijer, Kensuke Nanjo and Tetsuo Nishihara, 89–103, de

Gruyter Mouton, Berlin.

Vance, Timothy J. (2007) "Have We Learned Anything about *Rendaku* that Lyman Didn't Already Know?" *Current Issues in the History and Structure of Japanese*, ed. by Bjarke Frellesvig, Masayoshi Shibatani and John Charles Smith, 153-170, Kurosio, Tokyo.

Vance, Timothy J. (2011) "*Rendaku* in Sino-Japanese: Reduplication and Coordination," *Japanese/Korean Linguistics* 19, ed. by Ho-Min Sohn et al., 465-482, CSLI Publications, Stanford.

Vance, Timothy J. (2014) "If Rendaku Isn't a Rule, What in the World Is It?" *Usage-Based Approaches to Japanese Grammar*, ed. by Kaori Kabata and Tsuyoshi Ono, 137-152, John Benjamins, Amsterdam.

Vance, Timothy J. (2015a) "Rendaku," *The Handbook of Japanese Phonetics and Phonology*, ed. by Haruo Kubozono, 397-441, De Gruyter Mouton, Berlin.

Vance, Timothy J. (2015b) "Rendaku no Fu-kisoku-sei to Rōzen no Hōsoku," *NINJAL Research Papers* 9, 207-214.

Vance, Timothy J. and Atsushi Asai (2016) "Rendaku and Individual Segments," *Sequential Voicing in Japanese Compounds: Papers from the NINJAL Rendaku Project*, ed. by Timothy J. Vance and Mark Irwin, 119-137, John Benjamins, Amsterdam.

Watanabe, Toshirō, Edmund R. Skrzypczak and Paul Snowden, eds. (2003) *Kenkyusha's New Japanese-English Dictionary*, 5th edition, Kenkyusha, Tokyo.

Yamaguchi, Kyoko (2011) "Accentedness and *Rendaku* in Japanese Deverbal Compounds," *Gengo Kenkyu* 140, 117-134.

Containment Eradicates Opacity and Revives OT in Parallel: Some Consequences of Turbid Optimality Theory

Shin-ichi Tanaka[1], Clemens Poppe[2], and Daiki Hashimoto[3]
University of Tokyo[1], *NINJAL*[2], and *University of Canterbury*[3]

1. Introduction: The Culprit behind Opacity

The history of OT can be characterized partially as one in which various correspondence relations in phonology and morphology have been understood by using faithfulness constraints, such as input-output identity, base-reduplicant, output-output identity, transderivational identity, paradigm uniformity, antifaithfulness, and so on. The birth of Correspondence Theory circa 1995 was precisely a landmark in the OT history and ignited lots of studies about correspondence thereafter. On the other hand, the history of OT can also be characterized partially as one of repeated trials and revisions in order to overcome opacity. The advent of Sympathy Theory circa 1997 was no doubt a critical point in the OT history and instigated various works on solving opacity thereafter. But these two historic events are neither unrelated nor a coincidence. In fact, they are cause and effect, and the latter is even an inevitable chain reaction to the former. Thus, overcoming opacity has become an urgent mission for OT in parallel with uncovering correspondence.

The schema in (1) shows an idea of how they are in a cause-effect relation, or how correspondence causes an opacity effect. Correspondence Theory, unlike Containment Theory with Parse/Fill faithfulness constraints, has lost important information in the output representation on behalf of correspondences with Max/Dep faithfulness constraints.

(1) Correspondence and Opacity

Theory	Deletion	No Change	Epenthesis	No Change
Correspondence Theory	/ABC/ ↓ AB	/AB/ ↓ AB	/AB/ ↓ ABC	/ABC/ ↓ ABC
Containment Theory	/ABC/ ↓ AB\<C\>	/AB/ ↓ AB	/AB/ ↓ AB[C]	/ABC/ ↓ ABC

The crucial point is whether output representations contain information on how outputs are derived. In Correspondence Theory, AB after C-deletion is no different from underlying AB; likewise, ABC after C-epenthesis is no different from underlying ABC. In short, the derivational history cannot be read off solely from output forms, and the underlying contrasts between /AB/ and /ABC/ are lost in the cases of both deletion and epenthesis. This is exactly where opacity lies, or the culprit of the problem. In contrast, Containment Theory literally contains the derivational history, and the underlying contrasts between /AB/ and /ABC/ are reflected in the output representations of AB\<C\> vs. AB and of AB[C] vs. ABC, although each pair has the same pronunciation on the surface. In other words, the outputs of AB\<C\>, AB, AB[C], and ABC show that their corresponding inputs are uniquely /ABC/, /AB/, /AB/, and /ABC/, respectively. The 'hidden properties' at the core are known completely from the representations on the surface. This is why the original OT with containment was called 'output-oriented'.[1]

The situation is just like a game to 'spot the difference' as in (2).

---

[1] For the definition of containment, McCarthy and Prince (1993: 21) state that "[n]o element may be literally removed from the input form and that [t]he input is thus contained in every candidate form."

(2) Spot the Difference

(Adopted from Copyright ⓒ www.ActivityVillage.co.uk-Keeping Kids Busy)

If you are shown an original and its corresponding manipulated pictures, you have to search both of them for the differences again and again. However, if the manipulated picture is shown in a contained manner, you do not have to look back at the original one. In fact, the answers are obvious from the manipulated one as it contains all information about how the original one is changed, and the game does not stand up at all. That is, a contained representation makes a question out of the question and a before/after relation self-evident in a single picture. To answer it is to represent it in contained fashion.

In the following sections, we will present a principled way based on this insight to solve opacity, but the Zeitgeist in the 1990s required correspondence to be substituted for containment. So specific mechanisms were proposed that make up for the 'missed properties' in correspondence, such as local conjunction (Kirchner (1996) et seq.), sympathy (McCarthy (1999) et seq.), OO-correspondence (Benua (1997/2000) et seq.), Stratal OT (Bermúdez-Otero (1999) et seq.), turbid representations (Goldrick (2001) et seq.), targeted constraints (Wilson (2001) et seq.), PC theory (Łubowicz (2003) et seq.), comparative markedness (McCarthy (2003) et seq.), OT-CC (McCarthy (2007) et seq.), Harmonic Serialism (McCarthy (2008a) et seq.), and so on, although they were used for other purposes as well. Attractive as these proposals might seem, it has turned out that any of them lacks a finishing stroke or a decisive blow strong enough to clinch its case against the culprit of opacity: some are empirically impoverished or superfluous, others are theoretically too complicated in their mechanics, and still others demand radical revisions of such basic architectural assumptions in OT as GEN and EVAL. In fact, recent developments in OT have focused on the last resort, Harmonic Serialism (HS),[2] and this may be one way to prove a breakthrough in the fight to conquer opacity by revising the assumptions in GEN and EVAL. But another way is Turbid OT as Tanaka (2014a, b, c, 2015, 2016) proposes, which is a parallel but not classic OT framework for tackling opacity while keeping the assumptions in GEN and EVAL as they are. We will offer an array of arguments for the latter theory in the subsequent sections, and there are several reasons for us to avoid taking the former way in the first place.

First, according to McCarthy (2006, 2008a, 2009), HS, or serial OT, is said to have some advantages over parallel OT with respect to typological predictions (including a solution to the so-called too-many-repairs problem), but typological restrictiveness may prove to be just a *theoretical illusion* in OT. Blaho and Rice (2014: 8-10) state that "[s]ince the overwhelming majority of existing languages are still undescribed, and most other languages only received impressionistic descriptions, our understanding of what is impossible is tentative at best," that "[i]n fact, many language types thought to be impossible have recently been shown to exist," and hence that "proposing a theoretical tool *solely* for the purpose of excluding a non-existing pattern decreases the coherence of the theory. ... [T]heoretical innovations should always be based on existing patterns, not motivated by trying to exclude unattested patters." So it is true that typology is important in theory construction as ever, but not a sole source in evaluation metric.

Second, according to McCarthy (2010: 1015), "OT is hard, but HS makes it even harder. In parallel OT, typology follows from hypotheses about the constraint set. In HS, typology follows from a combination of hypotheses about GEN and the constraint set." This point, i.e., *hypotheses about GEN in HS*, is too hard a nut to crack, as the definitions of 'gradualness' are still unclear and far from unanimous among analysts. What does it actually mean that GEN is limited to making just 'one change' at

---

[2] This tendency is clear from a collection of papers in McCarthy and Pater eds. (2016) whose publication appears to be a grand project mainly of UMass researchers.

a time? What change counts as 'one'? The change of a segment or a feature value? What if the change of a feature value redundantly entails that of another? Are there any differences between oral and laryngeal features or between place and manner features? What about the deletion or epenthesis of a segment comprising multiple feature values? Or what about operations on prosodic features such as stress and tone? All these issues are still under dispute and virtually have no consensus, and proponents of HS might say that these unknown factors make it all the more interesting. However, changing hypotheses about GEN along these lines might amount to overdoing or underdoing the desirable typological predictions. So a possibility of tampering with the basic architecture in OT might lead to a double-edged sword for typological restrictiveness.

Third, from the viewpoint of analysts, taking into account hypotheses about CON and GEN requires much *heavier load* than simply those about CON. In addition to the number of components to be considered, the nature of serial vs. parallel also matters here. In electric circuits consisting of one battery and three components (i.e., resistors), the same amount of electrons must flow equally at each of the three components of a series circuit, while only one third of electrons must flow dispersively at each of the three of a parallel circuit. This means that the consumption or exhaustion of electric power is heavier in a series circuit than in a parallel circuit. In the same way, analysts in HS must devote their energy equally to each of the three components CON, GEN, and EVAL at every path/trial of local optimality and it repeats until harmonic ascent reaches convergence. However, analysts in parallel OT have only to focus their saved energy dispersively on the three, actually on CON, in the single system of global optimality. Economy and simplicity are essential factors in theory as well as in analysis.

Fourth, OT should be *a theory of the content and interaction of constraints in CON*, not a theory of GEN or EVAL, because the latter two are part of the mechanical primitives in the established platform. Tampering with them (just like Harmonic Grammar) is possible but not probable theorizing in OT any more than abandoning hypotheses about the violability of constraints or the richness of the base. In fact, as McCarthy (2008b:

27) himself originally stated, "research in OT is primarily focused on developing and improving hypotheses about the constraints in CON in order to understand and eventually solve specific empirical problems." To put differently, "[a]ny OT analysis is a partial theory of CON as well as a description of some facts. The ultimate goal of the analysis is to support claims about the universal properties of CON." (McCarthy (2008b: 31)). This is because the universal properties of GEN and EVAL are axiomatic or even trivial. If so, why not go back to the original claim in order to solve opacity problems, instead of changing the basic architecture of GEN and EVAL?

These are the reasons why we explore here how containment eradicates opacity and revives OT in parallel, instead of doing it in HS-like serial fashion. If parallel OT can overcome opacity, it has significant advantages in terms of economy and simplicity.

2. The Building Blocks of Turbid Optimality Theory

Turbidity is one of the notions that concerns containment and was originally defined by Goldrick (2001: 13) as "a single complex representation which incorporates covert, structural relationships (projection) and audible, surface relationships (pronunciation)" (emphasis by us). He interprets it as denoting some *underlying-surface relations* between prosodic structure and segmental material in autosegmental fashion and successfully showed a specific case for solving opacity. See also van Oostendorp (2006), Trommer (2011), and Zimmerman (2017) for related proposals to revive containment.

But we propose to apply it very differently and extend the notion to more general affairs: we simply apply it to the *parsed/unparsed and filled/unfilled relations* (and even to the *identical/unidentical relation* as we will see below) in the output representations. For example, in (1), the contrasting pairs of AB<C> vs. AB and of AB□ vs. ABC are different in covert, structural projection, but are the same in audible, surface pronunciation, respectively. Note also that this view is radically different from the original notion of containment proposed in Prince and Smolensky

(1993/2004) as well, since, for example, the segmental material is undetermined when elements in the output are not filled with those in the input, e.g., /AB/ → AB☐ in the original conception. So the crucial point of our proposal is that *the segmental material is contained even within a Fill-violating element* X̄ and that *this epenthetic* X̄ *is pronounceable or phonetically implemented*. As for the mapping /ABC/ → AB<C>, in which elements in the input are not parsed in the output, Prince and Smolensky (1993/2004) consider <C> as unpronounceable because it is not incorporated into the whole prosodic structure. However, we propose that *even a Parse-violating deleted element <X> is incorporated into the prosodic structure and is viable in its structural projection* even though it is not pronounceable or phonetically implemented. This is also a crucial difference from the original notion of containment. This new conception of projection/pronunciation in the output representations makes it possible for us to extend Goldrick's idea to fairly general cases and develop a novel theory called Turbid Optimality Theory (hereafter, Turbid OT).

The following assumptions are building blocks in Turbid OT (cf. Tanaka (2014a, b, c, 2015, 2016)). First, constraints are categorized into the four types given in (3), based on the sensitivity of the output representations. Each of the three types in (3b-d) has an entailment relation between X and its turbid element, by definition, as shown in (4b-d).

(3) Turbidity-Sensitive Constraints[3]

    a. X-Sensitive Con = constraints that are sensitive only to <u>an element X (segment, stress, tone, association line, etc.) present in both the input and the output, or to a feature value αX identical between both the input and the output.</u>

    b. X̄-Sensitive Con = constraints that are sensitive to an element X, and <u>its epenthesized counterpart X̄ that is absent in the in-</u>

---

[3] Here again, X̄, |X|, and <X> indicate an epenthesized element, a changed feature value, and a deleted element, respectively. A constraint is "sensitive" to a certain element if its violability is influenced by the derivational history the element has. The sensitivity has an entailment relation, as (4) shows. Specifically, the sensitivity of X̄ entails that of X; the sensitivity of $|-\alpha X|$ entails that of αX; and the sensitivity of <X> entails that of X and X̄.

put but emergent in the output.
c. |X|-Sensitive Con = constraints that are sensitive to a feature value αX, and its opposite value |−αX| that is changed from the input to the output.
d. <X>-Sensitive Con = constraints that are sensitive to an element X, X̄, and its deleted counterpart <X> that is present in the input but lost in the output.

(4) Entailment Relation for Sensitivity[3]
  a. X-Sensitive = sensitive to X or to αX only
  b. X̄-Sensitive = sensitive to both X and X̄
  c. |X|-Sensitive = sensitive to both αX and |−αX|
  d. <X>-Sensitive = sensitive to any of X, X̄, and <X>

Given these turbidity-sensitive constraints and their entailment relations of sensitivity, we can make it possible to predict when and where the basic cases of opacity (underapplication and overapplication) occur. Underapplication occurs when an element X or a feature value αX in the input that *is not* a trigger/target of a certain process changes into the trigger/target-*matching* X̄ or |−αX| in the output. This is true for 'counterfeeding on environment and on focus.' Conversely, overapplication occurs when an element X or a feature value αX in the input that *is* a trigger/target of a certain process changes into the trigger/target-*non-matching* X̄ or |−αX| in the output. This is true for 'counterbleeding on environment or and focus.' In addition, overapplication also occurs when an element X in the input that *is* a trigger of a certain process changes into <X> that is *phonetically empty* in the output, which counts as 'counterbleeding on environment.'

In this theory, containment and correspondence can stand together. Parse and Fill, instead of Max and Dep, prohibit deletion and epenthesis, ruling out any outputs including <X> and X̄, while Ident forbids any feature change involving |−αX|. In the OT history, Ident was a crucial advantage of Correspondence Theory over Containment Theory, but one of the novel aspects of Turbid OT is that it succeeds in incorporating the Ident constraint into Containment Theory. This new idea of devising the representation $|-\alpha X|$ for an Ident violation is also a crucial difference from the classic version of Containment Theory, and in this way, various findings uncovered so far in Correspondence Theory survive in Turbid OT.[4]

3. Applications

3.1. Underapplication and Overapplication

Now let us show some model cases of underapplication and overapplication, focusing on what McCarthy (1999) calls 'counterfeeding on environment' and 'counterbleeding on environment', respectively. They can be observed when so-called Canadian raising interacts with final devoicing and flapping, respectively. Raising and flapping are widely seen in Canadian English, while final devoicing may only be seen in one particular dialect, i.e., Dutchified English, spoken in the southwestern part of Ontario where German immigrants live.

Canadian raising is a rule which raises underlying /ai/ and /au/ to [ʌi] and [ʌu] before voiceless consonants, as shown in (5a, b) (Harris (1951/1960), Chomsky (1964), et seq.).

(5) Canadian Raising
 a. ride [raid] live [laiv] (adj.) house [hauz] (v.) owl [aul]
 b. write [rʌit] life [lʌif] house [hʌus] out [ʌut]

(6) Interaction with Final Devoicing
 a. ride [rait] hide [hait] house [haus] (v.) cloud [klaut]
 b. write [rʌit] height [hʌit] house [hʌus] clout [klʌut]

(7) Interaction with Flapping
 a. rider [raiɾɚ] cider [saiɾɚ] louder [lauɾɚ] powder [pauɾɚ]
 b. writer [rʌiɾɚ] citer [sʌiɾɚ] shouter [ʃʌuɾɚ] outer [ʌuɾɚ]

Interestingly enough, when some processes apply *after* this rule, they may

---

[4] Incorporating containment into correspondence does not violate Ockham's razor, because their scopes and empirical consequences are entirely different from each other.

create or erase the relevant environments for raising and cause opacity, because *the underlying contrast in the environments is neutralized and lost.* That is, raising and final devoicing in (6a) are in counterfeeding order (i.e., raising *(n.a.)* → devoicing), leading to the apparent underapplication of raising on account of the following *voiceless* environment, while raising and flapping in (7b) are in counterbleeding order (i.e., raising → flapping), resulting in the apparent overapplication of raising due to the following *voiced* environment.

In a case involving opacity, a 'straight' OT analysis necessarily results in a ranking paradox among the two paradigms in (8a), or makes an opaque output ☹ harmonically-bounded by a transparent unwanted one as in (8b), so the desired optimal output never comes out in either case.

(8) Straight Analyses
   a. ride /raid/ → *[rʌit], not [rait]

	*[ai, au]/__[−voi]	*[+voi/__$]	Ident [voi, low]
ride /raid/			
raid		*!	
rʌid		*!	*
☹ rait	*!		*
☞! rʌit	✓		**
write /rait/			
rait	*!		
☞ rʌit	✓		*

   b. writer /raitɚ/ → *[rairɚ], not [rʌirɚ]

	*[ai, au]/__[−voi]	*[t, d]/v__v	Ident [voi, low]
rider /raidɚ/			
raidɚ		*!	
rʌidɚ		*!	*
☞ rairɚ	✓		
rʌirɚ			*!

writer /raitɚ/			
raitɚ	*!	*!	
rʌitɚ		*!	*
☞! raiɾɚ	✓		*
☹ rʌiɾɚ			**!

However, Turbid OT, which carries over underlying contrasts in the paradigm to the surface, wipes out such problems and makes the desired output win out in an analysis of either case, as shown in (9a,b). Here, L and V indicate the features [low] and [voice], respectively.

(9) Turbid OT Analyses
    a. Interaction with Final Devoicing

Input	Output	*+L/__|+V|	*+V/__$	Ident−L/V
ride /raid/ | | +L+V	raid | | +L+V		*!	
	rʌid | | |−L|+V		*!	*
	☞ rait | | +L|−V|	✓		*
	rʌit | | |−L||−V|			**!
write /rait/ | | +L−V	rait | | +L−V	*!		
	☞ rʌit | | |−L|−V			*

b. Interaction with Flapping

Input	Output	*+L/__ |+V|	*[t,d]/v__v	Ident – L/V
rider /raidɚ/ | | +L +V	raidɚ | | +L + V		*!	
	rʌidɚ | | |–L|+V		*!	*
	☞ rairɚ | | +L + V			
	rʌirɚ | | |–L| +V	✓		*!
writer /raitɚ/ | | +L –V	raitɚ | | +L – V	*!	*!	
	rʌitɚ | | |–L|–V		*!	*
	rairɚ | | +L |+V|	*!		*
	☞ rʌirɚ | | |–L||+V|	✓		**

The constraint *+L/__ |+V| is a |X|-Sensitive Con, so it excludes *+L/__ –V as well as *+L/__ |+V| as a result of the entailment relation in (4c). In (9a), the surface coda consonant crucially preserves the underlying contrast of |–V| and –V depending on whether it was originally /d/ or /t/, and |–V| does not trigger raising even though it is *voiceless on the surface*. This is why underapplication or 'counterfeeding on environment' occurs here. On the other hand, in (9b), the crucial point is that the surface flap [ɾ] preserves the underlying contrast of +V and |+V| depending on whether it was originally /d/ or /t/, and |+V| does trigger raising precisely because it was *voiceless underlyingly*. Hence, overapplication or 'counterbleeding on environment' is observed here. Note also that demoting *+L/__ |+V| in (9a, b) below Ident correctly results in optimal forms with devoicing in Pennsylvania Dutchified English and those with flapping in General American English, which do not undergo raising.

A common feature in both cases is that the underlying contrast and its related process (here, raising) is 'masked' by some other processes (such as final devoicing and flapping). Such 'masking' effects are divided in two ways: 'counterfeeding masking' for the former case of underapplication, and 'counterbleeding masking' for the latter of overapplication. We clearly see that Turbid OT makes such a masked contrast visible to the constraint that controls the relevant process, and hence the masked process transparent.[5]

3.2. Chain Shift

Next, we will provide a theoretical analysis of chain shifting in the framework of Turbid OT, and demonstrate that Turbid OT can neatly capture a typical case of chain shifting, which Correspondence Theory runs into difficulties in accounting for. A chain shift is a phenomenon where two or more sounds shift stepwise along a certain phonetic scale. The most frequently observed pattern is a chain shift along a vertical vocalic scale, i.e., vowel raising, which is observed synchronically in Western Basque, Basaa, Lena Spanish, and Nzebi.[6] The opaque nature of chain shifting lies in the fact that in the chain shift A → B → C, *only underlying B changes into C, and B derived from A never changes into C*, an underapplication of the process. So what is crucial is whether B is underlying or derived.

---

[5] Turbid OT and Łubowicz's (2003) PC theory might appear somewhat similar in the sense that they have in common the mechanism to make the underlying contrasts visible to some constraints. However, they are different in the nature of output representations. In Turbid OT, the derivational history is evident from, but covert in, its structural representations. There is no step in output representations. But in PC theory, the derivational history is directly represented stepwise as a 'chain,' and the multiple-stepped chains are evaluated by the ranking of PC constraints. In that sense, it is similar to McCarthy's (2007) OT-CC.

[6] For specific examples and analyses, see Kirchner (1996), Moreton and Smolensky (2002), and Łubowicz (2011).

In this section, we will examine a vowel raising chain shift in Western Basque, where in prevocalic position underlying /e/ is mapped onto surface [i] and underlying /i/ is mapped onto surface [i^y], but underlying /e/ is not mapped onto surface [i^y] (de Rijk (1970), Hualde (1991: Ch. 2), Kirchner (1995), and Moreton and Smolensky (2002) among others). This chain shift [e → i → i^y] involves what was called 'counterfeeding on focus' opacity by McCarthy (1999) and Baković (2007). From a rule-based point of view, this fact can be captured by assuming that the raising rule (i → i^y/__V) precedes the other raising rule (e → i/__V). That is, the latter rule creates or feeds an input to the former rule as its 'focus,' but it is too late for the former rule to apply. Because of this counterfeeding order, the former rule underapplies to the derived [i] on the surface even though it is followed by a vowel.

(10) Chain Shift in Western Basque as 'Counterfeeding on Focus'
Input: /seme-V/ 'son' /erri-V/ 'village'
Raising Rule 1 (i → i^y/__V): — erri^y-V
Raising Rule 2 (e → i/__V): semi-V —
Output: [semiV] [erri^{y}V]

In order to analyze this pattern, let us assume, following Kirchner (1995), that the relevant vowels have the following features.

(11) Relevant Vowel Feature in Western Basque

e	i	i^y
−raised	−raised	+raised
−high	+high	+high

Now, we will demonstrate that this pattern of chain shifting poses a serious challenge to Correspondence Theory. More specifically, a 'straight' analysis results in a ranking paradox as in (12).

(12) Straight OT Analysis
　　a. Higher Raising Process: /i-V/ → [iʸV]

/i-V/ [+hi, −rai]	*e[−hi, −rai]/__V	*i[+hi, −rai]/__V	Ident
e V [−hi, −rai]	*!		*
i V [+hi, −rai]		*!	
☞ iʸV/ [+hi, +rai]			*

　　b. Lower Raising Process: /e-V/ → *[iʸV], not [iV]

/e-V/[−hi, −rai]	*e[−hi, −rai]/__V	*i[+hi, −rai]/__V	Ident
e V [−hi, −rai]	*!		
☹ i V [+hi, −rai]		*!	*
☞! iʸV/ [+hi, +rai]			**

To ensure the higher raising process /i-V/ → [iʸV], *i/__V must dominate Ident as shown in (12a); however, the opposite ranking is required to guarantee the lower raising process /e-V/ → [iV]. Otherwise, underlying /e-V/ would be predicted to change into the unwanted *[iʸV] in (12b). In this way, Correspondence Theory falls into a dilemma and cannot capture the whole chain shift [e → i → iʸ] with one and the same ranking.

On the other hand, Turbid OT can capture this raising chain shift without any difficulty, which is shown in (13). The crucial constraints here are *-hi, -rai/__V, an X-Sensitive Con, and *|-hi|, -rai/__V, an |X|-Sensitive Con.

(13) Turbid OT Analysis
　　a. Higher Raising Process: /i-V/ → [iʸV]

/i-V/ +hi, −rai	*−hi, −rai/__V	*|−hi|, −rai/__V	Ident
e V |−hi|, −rai		*!	*
i V +hi, −rai		*!	
☞ iʸV +hi,|+rai|		✓	*

　　b. Lower Raising Process: /e-V/ → [iV]

/e-V/ −hi, −rai	*−hi, −rai/__V	*|−hi|, −rai/__V	Ident
e V −hi, −rai	*!		
☞ i V |+hi|, −rai		✓	*
iʸV |+hi|,|+rai|			**!

*–hi, –rai/__V is equivalent to *e/__V, a ban against [e] from the underlying only, so it excludes the first candidate in (13b) but leaves the first one in (13a) as it is. The constraint *|–hi|, –rai/__V, on the other hand, involves both *i/__V and *|e|/__V, prohibiting [i] unchanged from underlying /i/ as well as [e] derived from underlying /i/, which follows from the entailment relation in (4c). So it excludes both the first and the second candidates in (13a), and the optimal higher raising process /i-V/ → [i^{y}V] is ensured correctly.

This section has demonstrated that Turbid OT can neatly capture the chain shift in question here. In future research, we need to investigate whether this approach can capture various other types of chain shifting than the Western Basque type and compare it empirically with other theoretical approaches such as local conjunction (Kirchner (1995, 1996)) and PC theory (Łubowicz (2003)).

3.3. Fed-Counterfeeding

Another case for Turbid OT over Correspondence Theory, which exhibits a somewhat more complicated pattern than the basic counterfeeding opacity, is 'fed-counterfeeding.' This pattern involves two processes in which the first process feeds the second and the second counterfeeds the first at the same time. The seemingly complex configuration creates an intriguing implication for the logic of OT, and Turbid OT will turn out to reduce it to a very simple reflex of constraint interaction.

For instance, let us examine the following two word-final processes in Lardil, an Australian Tangkic language: apocope, which requires nouns longer than two moras to undergo deletion of the final vowel,[7] and C-deletion, which forces *non-apical* consonants to be deleted in word-final position (Kavitskaya and Staroverov (2010: 256)). Examples are given in (14).

---

[7] This restriction of the deletion target means that even after deletion, the minimal word requirement of this language guarantees a form with the size of a bimoraic/bivocalic foot at least.

(14) Apocope and C-deletion in Lardil
  a. Apocope

stem	non-future accusative	nominative	
/yiliyili/	→ yiliyili-n	yiliyil	'oyster sp'
/mayarra/	→ mayarra-n	mayarr	'rainbow'
/wiwala/	→ wiwala-n	wiwal	'bush mango'

  b. C-deletion

stem	non-future accusative	nominative	
/thurarraŋ/	→ thurarraŋ-in	thurarra	'shark'
/wangalk/	→ wangalk-in	wangal	'boomerang'
/wuŋkunuŋ/	→ wuŋkunuŋ-in	wuŋkunu	'queen fish'

We see that in the nominative case, underlying vowels are deleted word-finally in (14a) and underlying non-apical consonants are deleted word-finally in (14b). Note here that apocope does *not* apply to vowels that are made final by C-deletion, as seen in *thurarra* 'shark' and *wuŋkunu* 'queen fish', which exhibit underapplication of apocope (and thus C-deletion counterfeeds apocope).

But it is evident from (15) that apocope, even in the same order, feeds C-deletion, because C-deletion *does* apply to non-apical consonants that are made final by apocope. This is what 'fed-counterfeeding' opacity in Lardil is like, and the specific derivations discussed so far can be summarized as in (16).

(15) Fed-counterfeeding

stem	non-future accusative	nominative	
/dibirdibi/	→ dibirdibi-n	dibirdi	'rock cod'
/bulumunidami/	→ bulumunidami-n	bulumunida	'dugong'
/muŋkumuŋku/	→ muŋkumuŋku-n	muŋkumu	'wooden axe'

(16) Fed-counterfeeding of Apocope and C-deletion

		Counterfeeding	*Fed-Counterfeeding*
Input:	/yiliyili/	/thurarraŋ/	/dibirdibi/
Apocope:	yiliyil	—	dibirdib
C-deletion:	—	thurarra	dibirdi

Output: yiliyil thurarra dibirdi cf. DYG

What is interesting about the interaction of the two processes is that it looks like the so-called 'Duke of York gambit (DYG)' derivation in the sense that it proceeds as V#→C#→V#. This pattern is difficult to handle in classic OT (Tanaka (2014b, c)). But even more interesting is the 'synergism' or the 'multiplier effect' of mutual feeding in fed-counterfeeding. That is, a counterfeeding order usually blocks the application of the first process that would apply and be fed by the second process if the order were the opposite. But fed-counterfeeding cancels this blockage and activates the original potential for the second process to feed the first, accelerating the mutual feeding power of the two. As a consequence, a form without any apical consonants like *muŋkumuŋku* 'wooden axe' might appear to undergo the two processes spirally until it becomes the minimal word *muŋku* (see footnote 5). But the fact is that the two processes apply only once, and this underapplication for sure makes Correspondence Theory fall into difficulty.

Suppose that there are two markedness constraints involved here: *V/__#, which prohibits vowels in word-final position, and *C-Place/__#, which prohibits codas with a place feature in word-final position under the assumption that apical (coronal, anterior) consonants do not have their own place feature. Then a 'straight' analysis would proceed as shown in (17).

(17) Straight OT Analysis with Fed-counterfeeding
 a. Forms with Apical Consonants: /dibirdibi/ → *[dibird]

/dibirdibi/	*V/__#	*C-Place/__#	Max
di.bir.di.bi	*!		
di.bir.dib		*!	*
☹ di.bir.di	*!		**
☞! di.bird		✓	***

b. Forms without Apical Consonants: /muŋkumuŋku/→*[muŋkumuŋku]

/muŋkumuŋku/	*V/__#	*C-Place/__#	Max
☞! muŋ.ku.muŋ.ku	*		
muŋ.ku.muŋk		*	*!
☹ muŋ.ku.mu	*		*!**
muŋ.kum		*	*!***

The tableaux in (17a,b) mercilessly illustrate that the desired outputs with ☹ are harmonically-bound by the first candidate of each tableau and never come out as optimal.[8]

Now Turbid OT opens a door to solve this problem in a very simple manner, as shown in (18).

(18) Turbid OT Analysis with Fed-counterfeeding
 a. Forms with Apical Consonants: /dibirdibi/ → [dibirdi]

/dibirdibi/	*V/__#	*C-Place/__#	Parse
di.bir.bi#	*!		
di.bir.dib.<i>#		*!	*
☞ di.bir.di.<b><i>#	✓		**
di.bird.<i><b><i>#		✓	***!

---

[8] One possible solution is to use an anti-faithfulness constraint like ¬Max in line with Alderete (1999/2001, 2001) and Horwood (1999), since the stem/nominative relation in (14) and (15) tells a bare fact of subtractive morphology in this language. As exemplified by the following tableaux, this proves to work well if we rank *C-Place/__# over Anchor-R as defined in a way that the rightmost consonant of a stem in the input has a correspondent at the right edge of a word in the output.

/dibirdibi/	*C-Place/__#	Anchor-R	¬Max	Max
di.bir.di.bi		*	*!	
di.bir.dib	*!			*
☞ di.bir.di		*		**
di.bird	✓	*		***!

/muŋkumuŋku/	*C-Place/__#	Anchor-R	¬Max	Max
muŋ.ku.muŋ.ku		*	*!	
muŋ.ku.muŋk	*!			*
☞ muŋ.ku.mu		*		**
muŋ.kum	*!		*	***

However, its effectiveness is specific to morphophonological processes including subtractive morphology, and we are thinking here of a general method to overcome various types of opacity. So we do not adopt a solution with anti-faithfulness here.

b. Forms without Apical Consonants: /muŋkumuŋku/ → [muŋkumu]

/muŋkumuŋku/	*V/_#	*C-Place/_#	Parse
muŋ.ku.muŋ.ku#	*!		
muŋ.ku.muŋk.<u>#		*!	*
☞ muŋ.ku.mu.<ŋ><k><ŋ>#	✓		***
muŋ.kum.<u><ŋ><k><ŋ>#		*!	****

Crucial here are the turbidity-based definitions of the two markedness constraints: *V/_# is a <X>-Sensitive Con such that any of X, X̄, and <X> in its environment is visible and that V in the environment _<X$_n$># is *not* final or banned; conversely, *C-Place/_# is an X-Sensitive Con such that only underlying and surface X in its environment is visible and that *C in the environment _<X$_n$># *is* final and banned. Thus, in (18a, b), the second candidates with invisible <X$_n$> violate *C-Place/_#, while the third candidates with visible <X$_n$> survive *V/_# and become optimal.

Incidentally, postnasal voicing in Japanese (e.g., *sin-ta* → *sin-da* 'died') is known to underapply to cases in which vowels are deleted in colloquial speech, such as *ano-toki* → *an-toki* 'that time' and *oreno-uti* → *oren-ti* 'my house'. This can be simply accounted for if *NC̥, a ban on voiceless obstruents immediately preceded by nasals, is a <X>-Sensitive Con just like *V/_# and the visible deleted vowels actually block the adjacency of nasals and voiceless obstruents in *an<o>toki* and *oren<o><u>ti*.

Finally, Kavitskaya and Staroverov (2010) take up fed-counterfeeding as a challenge to HS and propose a solution within that framework. But we do not adopt it for the reasons mentioned in section 1.

3.4. Input-Sensitive Tone Shift

Let us now turn to the issue of tone, a topic that has played an important role in the development of generative phonology for decades. Kisseberth (2007) points out that H-tone shifting attested in several Bantu languages is problematic for OT because of its opaque nature. The opacity of tone shifting is caused by the fact that *the surface location of an H tone may be computed relative to its underlying location and/or the underlying location of a following tone.* In this section we discuss both types of sensitivity to input tones in Bantu languages, and show how they can be accounted for in Turbid OT.

What we take up here is the pattern of local tone shifting observed in Jita (Downing (1990, 2009)), where H tones surface one syllable to the right of their 'sponsor syllable,' i.e., their underlying location. Examples from Jita adopted from Downing (2009) are presented in (19), where H tones are indicated by acute accent marks, and the underlying sponsors by underlines.

(19) Local Tone Shift in Jita
 oku-bóna   'to get/see'
 oku-bonéra   'to get/see for (applicative)'
 oku-bonérana 'to get/see for each other'

The basic generalization for Jita is that an H tone is realized on the syllable immediately to the right of the underlying sponsor, except if doing so would result in the H tone being realized on the final syllable. As can be seen in the first example of (19), the H tone remains on its sponsor, avoiding a violation of NonFinality(H).

In derivational models, such 'bounded' tone shifts as seen above can be captured in terms of a two-step process in which tone spreading is followed by delinking of the tone from its underlying position (Downing (1990)), as in (20a). But in Turbid OT, such association lines are simply represented in a single output as in (20b).

(20) Spreading and Delinking

Obviously, these are two operations that are ordered in a specific way. In Corresponderce Theory, such ordering of operations is not available, and there is no way but to capture this pattern as tone movement like (20c). However, it is unclear how the locality of movement is ensured and how the underlying location (i.e., the sponsor syllable) can be determined after the movement. This poses a serious problem to Corresponderce Theory.[9]

In Turbid OT, on the other hand, the Jita data can be easily accounted for because all input information is present in the output. This can be shown by the two input-output mappings in (21).

(21) Tone Shift in Jita

	Input	Output	Unattested
a.	oku-bona | H	oku-bóna | H	*oku-boná ◇⃫ H
b.	oku-bonera | H	oku-bonéra ◇⃫ H	*oku-bónéra |⃫ H

As pointed out above, the absence of a tone shift in (21a) can be accounted for by NonFinality(H)-[], which turns out to be a X-Sensitive Con. However, there are two facts that remain to be accounted for. First of all, we need to explain why tone spreading occurs in forms like (21b) in the first place. Second, we need to explain why the original underlying association line is delinked in the output form. As for tone spreading, let us assume that this operation is triggered by the need for an H tone to be binary, i.e., to be associated to more than one tone-bearing unit. Similar Tone-Binarity constraints have been proposed in Cassimjee and Kisseberth's (1998) domain-based approach as well as Zec's (2009) autosegmental approach. In terms of turbid representations, the Tone-Binarity constraint can be assumed to be <X>-sensitive: Binarity(H)-◇. This constraint is satisfied when an H tone is linked to two association lines of *any*

---

[9] In order to deal with tone shift cases like those in Jita, it has been proposed that a gradient alignment constraint that demands a tone to be aligned as far to the right as possible within a word or a phrase (Align-R) interacts with a constraint that restricts the movement of a tone to a directly neighboring tone-bearing unit (Myers (1997) and Yip (2002)). An example of such a constraint is Myers' (1997) anchoring constraint Local, which demands (the syllable hosting) a tone in the output to share at least one edge with (the syllable that hosts) the tone in the input. However, a constraint like Local cannot account for yet another type of phenomenon in which *reference to the location of another input tone* is necessary, as in the Xhosa case discussed below.

type. The reason why the underlying association line | in (21b) appears as bracketed < > in the output can be accounted for by means of another <X>-sensitive Con, Unique-Peak, which is satisfied only when an H tone is linked to a *single non-delinked* association line. This constraint, which reflects the tendency of a syllable with an H tone to stand out as prominent relative to other syllables, is ranked above Binarity(H)-<>, and thereby ensures the unattested form in (21b) does not surface.

The existence of different types of turbidity-sensitive Tone-Binarity predicts that there are also languages in which an H tone must spread twice. Interestingly, such languages do exist. For instance, in Sukuma (Sietsema (1989)), another Bantu language, H tones prefer to be realized *two syllables* to the right of the sponsor syllable, as in (22b). In other words, in Sukuma, tone shifting is non-local.

(22) a. Jita: σ σ́ σ   b. Sukuma: σ σ σ́
          H   H

The local vs. non-local difference between Jita and Sukuma can be neatly accounted for by means of a difference in turbidity sensitivity. As pointed out above, for Jita, the Tone-Binarity constraint can be assumed to be <X>-sensitive, which means it is satisfied when an H tone is linked to two association lines of *any* type. In Sukuma, on the other hand, the relevant constraint can be assumed to be Binarity(H)-|: an H tone is preferably linked to two *inserted* association lines (even if one of these inserted association lines is 'delinked' at the same time due to high-ranked Unique-Peak).

Let us now move on to tone shifting in Xhosa. In this language, whether an underlying H tone can shift to the right depends on whether the target syllable is *not* followed by another H-sponsor syllable, regardless of whether this following sponsor syllable carries an H tone in the output. Kisseberth (2007) points out that this fact is problematic for an output-based autosegmental approach. In order to show this, let us first consider the data from Xhosa verbs with underlyingly toneless stems in (23) and with underlyingly tonal stems (stems in which the initial syllable sponsors an H tone) in (24), which are adapted from Cassimjee and Kisseberth (1998: 81-82). The lengthening of the penultimate syllable is the result of this syllable being stressed.

(23) Toneless Verb Stems in Xhosa
   a. ndi-ya-baala 'I count'
      ba-yá-baala 'they count'
   b. ndi-ya-liima 'I cultivate'
      ba-yá-liima 'to find each other'

(24) Tonal Verb Stems in Xhosa
   a. bá-ya-bóóna 'they see'
   b. bá-ya-boníísa 'they show'
      bá-ya-bonísiisa 'they show clearly'

In the first examples of (23a, b), the first person prefix *ndi-*, the present tense prefix *ya-*, and the stems are all toneless. In the second examples of (23a, b), on the other hand, the H-bearing third person plural prefix *ba-* causes an H tone to surface on the immediately following syllable.[10]

Crucial here are cases of verbs with tonal stems in (24), where the H tone sponsored by a prefix fails to shift at all. The presence of a tone shift in *ba-yá-baala* (23a) and *ba-yá-liima* (23b) and the absence of one in *bá-ya-bóóna* (*ba-yá-bóóna*) (24a) can be explained without making reference to input tones: shifting the H of the prefix *ba-* would result in two adjacent H tones, violating the Obligatory Contour Principle (OCP; Goldsmith (1976/1979)). However, forms like *bá-ya-boníísa* (*ba-yá-boníísa*) and *bá-ya-bonísiisa* (*ba-yá-bonísiisa*) in (24b) can only be explained in terms of the OCP *if there are intermediate forms like bá-yá-bóníísa and bá-yá-bónísiisa, in which spreading has taken place, but delinking has not yet taken place.* As pointed out by Kisseberth (2007),

---

[10] In the case of Xhosa, shifting H tones actually target the antepenultimate syllable, rather than the immediately following syllable. In the examples in (23), these two syllables coincide with each other. Because for the present discussion it is not relevant in what way we can account for a shift to the antepenultimate syllable, we will only focus on cases in which the H tone sponsored by a prefix fails to shift at all.

if constraints only have access to output representations, the blocking of the shift in forms like those in (24b) is unexpected.

Because in turbid representations, all input information is visible in the output, the Xhosa patterns can be easily accounted for. First, the OCP constraint we need is defined from the perspective of turbid representations as in (25). The OCP(H) is a <X>-Sensitive Con that is violated whenever two different instances of H have any association line of |, ⟦⟧, and ◇ linked to adjacent tone-bearing units in the output. The entailment relation of sensitive elements follows from (4d). Given this constraint and turbid output representations, the Xhosa patterns in (24) are accounted for as in (26).

(25) OCP(H)-◇ = <X>-Sensitive Con
Two H tones are not associated to adjacent TBUs, regardless of the nature of the association lines (i.e., |, ⟦⟧, and ◇).

(26) Tone Shift in Xhosa

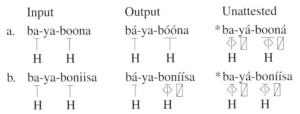

As in the case of Jita, the absence of a shift of the second H in (26a) can be accounted for by the X-Sensitive Con NonFinality(H)-⟦⟧.[11] More importantly, the H tone linked to the prefix fails to shift because this would entail a violation of the OCP(H)-◇. For the same reason, the tone shift from the prefix is avoided in (26b), and only the tone shift within the stem applies here.

In summary, by adopting turbid representations and constraints that re-

---

[11] Note here that a long vowel like *bóó* in (26a) and *níí* in (26b) by penultimate lengthening has a single association line. This may be due to the fact that tone-bearing units in this language are syllables or that penultimate lengthening applies after spreading.

fer to these representations, the need of output H tones to refer to the original input location can be dealt with in terms of a single representation. In a parallel correspondence-based analysis that makes use of autosegmental representations, on the other hand, the opaque behavior of H tones in languages like Jita and Xhosa cannot be accounted for. This is one of the reasons why Cassimjee and Kisseberth (1998) argue in favor of abstract tone domains that are projected by input tones. Turbid OT, using independently motivated representations, makes it possible to account for the OCP-nature and locality of tone shifts without making any reference to such tone-specific domains.

4. Conclusion and Further Issues

We have shown four case studies in which some opaque processes are accounted for by evolving representations and constraints in a new form of containment based on turbidity. This can be done under Turbid OT in thoroughly output-oriented, parallel fashion. Concerning other arguments in favor of Turbid OT, see Tanaka (2014a, b, 2015) for underspecification, Tanaka (2016) for opacity under blocking (underblocking and overblocking), and Tanaka (2014b, c) for the Duke-of-York gambit derivations.

The basic picture of Turbid OT just sketched above will be more clarified by the following supplementary comments. First, containment and correspondence are not incompatible but can stand in tandem by reusing the Parse/Fill constraints in a new conception and renewing the Ident constraint with turbidity. Thus various findings uncovered by Correspondence Theory are still alive in Turbid OT. Second, only markedness constraints are qualified to be turbidity-sensitive, as defined in (3). As for faithfulness constraints, which are not turbidity-sensitive but 'turbidity-prohibitive,' each can be formulated in the following way: Parse as *<X>, Fill as *$\boxed{X}$, and Ident as *$|-\alpha X|$. By 'turbidity-prohibitive,' we mean that turbid representations like *<X>, *$\boxed{X}$, *$|-\alpha X|$ are prohibited. Third, it is not an acquired property whether a certain markedness constraint is an X-Sensitive Con or takes any other form of turbidity. Turbidity is not an acquired property. Rather, a markedness constraint can universally have any form of turbidity in (3), although its exact form relies partially on the constraint's nature: whether it is a constraint on segments, stress, tone, association lines, etc. or a constraint on features. Constraints are universal, and only their ranking can decide whether a certain process exhibits opacity or stays transparent. Finally, we have not shown any empirical advantages or superiority of Turbid OT over other strategies for conquering opacity proposed so far. As stated in section 1, we believe that it has some conceptual advantages over HS in terms of economy and simplicity, but we will leave empirical issues for further research.

In conclusion, correspondence and containment are the two sides of a coin. Correspondence necessarily causes opacity effects, and the effects are sufficiently covered by containment. One needs and entails the other, and one is unseparable from the other. Turbid OT allows the two to stand in tandem and classic OT to revive in parallel.

References

Alderete, John (1999/2001) *Morphologically Governed Accent in Optimality Theory*, Doctoral dissertation, University of Massachusetts, Amherst. [Reproduced by Routledge, New York, in 2001.]

Alderete, John (2001) "Dominance Effects as Transderivational Anti-faithfulness," *Phonology* 18:2, 201-253.

Baković, Eric (2007) "A Revised Typology of Opaque Generalizations," *Phonology* 24, 217-259.

Benua, Laura (1997/2000) *Transderivational Identity: Phonological Relations Between Words*, Doctoral dissertation, University of Massachusetts, Amherst. [Reproduced by Routledge, New York, in 2000.]

Bermúdez-Otero, Ricardo (1999) *Constraint Interaction in Language Change*, Doctoral dissertation, University of Manchester.

Blaho, Sylvia and Curt Rice (2014) "Overgeneration and Falsifiability in Phonological Theory," *La Phonologie du Français: Normes, Périphéries, Modélisation*, ed. by Jacques Durand, Gjert Kristoffersen and Bernard Laks, 101-118, Presses Universitaires de Paris Ouest, Paris.

Cassimjee, Farida and Charles W. Kisseberth (1998) "Optimal Domains Theory and Bantu Tonology," *Theoretical Aspects of Bantu Tone*, ed. by Charles W. Kisseberth and Larry Hyman, 265-314, CSLI Publications, Stanford.

Chomsky, Noam (1964) *Current Issues in Linguistic Theory*, Mouton, The Hague.

de Rijk, Rudolf (1970) "Vowel Interactión in Bizcayan Basque," *Fontes Linguae Vasconum* 2, 149-167.

Downing, Laura J. (1990) *Problems in Jita Tonology*, Doctoral dissertation, University of Illinois, Urbana-Champaign.

Downing, Laura J. (2009) "Optimality Theory and African Language Phonology," *Selected Proceedings of the 38th Annual Conference on African Linguistics*, ed. by Masangu Matondo, Fiona Mc Laughlin and Eric Potsdam, 1-16, Cascadilla Proceedings Project, Somerville, MA.

Goldrick, Matthew (2001) "Turbid Output Representations and the Unity of Opacity," *NELS* 30, 231-245.

Goldsmith, John (1976/1979) *Autosegmental Phonology*, Doctoral dissertation, MIT. [Reproduced by Garland, New York, in 1979.]

Harris, Zellig (1951/1960) *Methods in Structural Linguistics* (4th impression, entitled *Structural Linguistics*), University of Chicago Press, Chicago.

Horwood, Graham (1999) "Anti-faithfulness and Subtractive Morphology," ms., Rutgers University.

Hualde, José (1991) *Basque Phonology*, Routledge, New York.

Kavitskaya, Darya and Peter Staroverov (2010) "When an Interaction is Both Opaque and Trarsparent: The Paradox of Fed Counterfeeding," *Phonology* 27: 2, 255-288.

Kirchner, Robert (1995) "Going the Distance: Synchronic Chain Shifts in Optimality Theory," ms., UCLA. [Available at Rutgers Optimality Archive-66.]

Kirchner, Robert (1996) "Synchronic Chain Shifts in Optimality Theory," *Linguistic Inquiry* 27:2, 341-350.

Kisseberth, Charles W. (2007) "Review of *Tone* by Moira Yip, 2002, Cambridge University Press," *Language* 83:3, 662-664.

Łubowicz, Anna (2003) *Contrast Preservation in Phonological Mappings*, Doctoral dissertation, University of Massachusetts at Amherst.

Łubowicz, Anna (2011) "Chain Shifts," *The Blackwell Companion to Phonology*, ed. by Marc van Oostendorp, Colin Ewen, Elizabeth Hume and Keren Rice, 1717-1735, Blackwell, Oxford.

McCarthy, John J. (1999) "Sympathy and Phonological Opacity," *Phonology* 16:3, 331-399.

McCarthy, John J. (2003) "Comparative Markedness," *Theoretical Linguistics* 29, 1-51.

McCarthy, John J. (2006) "Restraint of Analysis," *Wondering at the Natural Fecundity of Things*, ed. by Eric Bakovic, Junko Ito and John J. McCarthy, 195-219,

Linguistics Research Center, UC Santa Cruz.

McCarthy, John J. (2007) *Hidden Generalizations: Phonological Opacity in Optimality Theory*, Equinox, London.

McCarthy, John J. (2008a) "The Gradual Path to Cluster Simplification," *Phonology* 25:2, 271-319.

McCarthy, John J. (2008b) *Doing Optimality Theory*, Blackwell, Malden, MA and Oxford.

McCarthy, John J. (2009) "Studying Gen," *Journal of the Phonetic Society of Japan* 13:2, 3-12.

McCarthy, John J. (2010) "An Introduction to Harmonic Serialism," *Language and Linguistics Compass* 4:10, 1001-1018.

McCarthy, John J. and Joe Pater, eds. (2016) *Harmonic Grammar and Harmonic Serialism*, Equinox, London.

McCarthy, John J. and Alan Prince (1993) *Prosodic Morphology: Constraint Interaction and Satisfaction*, Technical Report TR-3, Rutgers Center for Cognitive Science, Rutgers University, New Brunswick, NJ.

Moreton, Elliott and Paul Smolensky (2002) "Typological Consequences of Local Constraint Conjunction," *WCCFL* 21, 306-319.

Myers, Scott (1997) "OCP Effects in Optimality Theory," *Natural Language and Linguistic Theory* 15:4, 847-892.

Oostendorp, Marc van (2006) "A Theory of Morphosyntactic Colours," ms., Meertens Institute, Amsterdam.

Prince, Alan and Paul Smolensky (1993/2004) *Optimality Theory: Constraint Interaction in Generative Grammar*, Technical Report TR-2, Rutgers Center for Cognitive Science, Rutgers University, New Brunswick, NJ. [Published by Blackwell, New York, in 2004.]

Sietsema, Brian Mark (1989) *Metrical Dependencies in Tone Assignment*, Doctoral dissertation, MIT, Cambridge, MA.

Tanaka, Shin-ichi (2014a) "Nigori no Hyouzi to Hutoumeisei: Nitieigo no Yuuseion no Sinsou to Hyosou (Turbid Representations for Opacity: The Underlying and Surface Representations for Voiced Obstruents in Japanese and English)," *JELS* 31, 193-199.

Tanaka, Shin-ichi (2014b) "Turbid Optimality Theory: A Containment-Based Solution to Opacity and the DYG Derivations," *Proceedings of the 5th International Conference on Phonology and Morphology*, 177-191, The Phonology-Morphology Circle of Korea.

Tanaka, Shin-ichi (2014c) "Two Phonologies or One?: Some Implications of the DYG for Biolinguistics," *English Linguistics* 31:2, 593-622.

Tanaka, Shin-ichi (2015) "Yuuseisei no Tuyosa kara Mita Nihongo no Hutoumei Gensyou: Nigori no Hyouzi niyoru Toumeika (Opacity from the Viewpoint of Voicing Strength in Japanese: Visualizing with Turbid Representations)," *Nihongo Kennkyuu to Sono Kanousei (Linguistic Studies and their Future Possibilities in Japanese)*, ed. by Takashi Masuoka, 26–51, Kaitakusha, Tokyo.

Tanaka, Shin-ichi (2016) "OCP no Teisikika no Saikentou: Sono Rironteki Itiduke to Seibutu Gengogakuteki Imiai (Rethinking OCP: Its Formulation in OT and Implications for Biolinguistics)," *Hitui Genri no Syatei to Kouryoku ni Kansuru Kenkyuu (A Report in the Grant-in-Aid Research in Basic Science (B) "Studies on the Scope and Effects of the Obligatory Contour Principle)"*, ed. by Masao Okazaki, 37–60, Japan Society for the Promotion of Science, Tokyo.

Trommer, Jochen (2011) *Phonological Aspects of Western-Nilotic Mutation Morphology*, Habilitation thesis, University of Leipzig.

Wilson, Colin (2001) "Consonant Cluster Neutralization and Targeted Constraints," *Phonology* 18:1, 147–197.

Yip, Moira (2002) *Tone*, Cambridge University Press, Cambridge.

Zec, Draga (2009) "Tone and Stress in Prominence-Based Systems," *Formal Approaches to Slavic Linguistics* 17, 269–288.

Zimmermann, Eva (2017) *Morphological Length and Prosodically Defective Morphemes*, Oxford University Press, Oxford.

三重県志摩和具方言における前鼻子音

高山　知明

金沢大学

1. はじめに

　本稿は，三重県志摩地方の濁音の音声実現，とくに前鼻子音の現れ方とそれに関連する事項を取り扱う．

　17世紀初期のロドリゲス『日本文典』『日本小文典』の記事からは，当時の文化的中心地である京において，ダ行とガ行を中心に濁音が前鼻子音で実現されていたことがうかがえるが，その後，この特徴は衰弱・消滅していった．他方，同じ近畿地方の周縁およびその外縁の方言に関しては，前鼻子音の実現が報告されている．具体的には，楳垣（1962）のほか，柴田（1960, 1962）が知られ，近年では岸江・吉廣（2006），中澤（2013）がある．四国や淡路島に関する研究が目立つ一方，それとは反対の，近畿の東側に関する研究は多くない．本稿で取り上げる志摩地方は，近畿南部の東端に位置し，京都を中心とする視点からすれば東側の周縁部ということになる．濁音の変化の進展および地理的分布を知る上で，この地域の状況を把握することは重要である．本稿では，志摩地方のうち，前島半島(さきしま)の和具方言の録音資料にもとづいて，前鼻子音の状態を中心に報告し，関連する問題について論じる．

2. 前島半島の位置

　志摩市（旧志摩郡）にある前島半島は，志摩半島の東南端に位置し，地図に示すように，東側の根元に当たる部分から南下し，大きく向きを西に変えて，西端の御座岬(ござ)に至る．東西に延びた細長い部分はおよそ10kmあまり，幅が南北約1～2kmほどの大きさである．南側に太平洋を臨み，北側の英(あ)

虞湾を包み込むような形状をしており，特に英虞湾側は複雑に入り組んだリアス式海岸が特徴的である．東側から順に 阿児町，大王町，志摩町（旧志摩郡阿児町，大王町，志摩町）に属し，志摩町は半島の東西に延びた部分の大部を占める．志摩町内には，東側の大王町の船越に続き，片田，布施田，和具，越賀，御座の5つの地区がある．

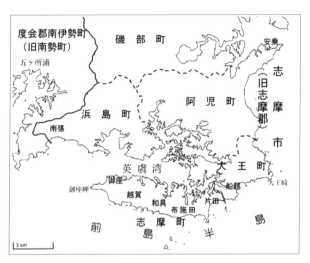

〔地図〕前島半島とその周辺
（「地理院地図・ベースマップ・白地図」国土地理院 http://maps.gsi.go.jp/#9/
38.246809/138.584290/&base=blank&ls=blank&disp=1&lcd=blank&vs=
c1j0l0u0f0&d=vl）をもとに加工作成）

3. 志摩地方の前鼻子音に関する先行研究

楳垣（1962: 112-113）の「三重県方言」の音韻に関する解説によると，「志摩では鼻濁音は語彙的現象として名残りをとどめているものと認められる」とする．ここでいう「鼻濁音」は，ガ行の [ŋ] だけでなく，[ⁿŋ] [ⁿg] [ⁿd] [ᵐb] [ⁿz] のような音声を指している（これらの IPA は楳垣（1962: 112））．「語彙的現象」として具体的に列挙されているのは，「アンゴ（顎）」「フンゴ（ふご）」「クンギ（釘）」「ドング（道具）」「アンブ（虻）」「ジョンブ（丈夫）」「インボ（疣）」「コンバシ（香ばし）」「マンド（窓）」「インド（井戸）」「ニン

ド（二度）」「コナンダ（この間）」「ニンジ（虹）」「サンザイ（さざえ）」「カンジェ（風）」[1] の15語で（順序・表記は楳垣 (1962: 113) に従う），これらのガ，バ，ダ，ザ行音の前の撥音が「鼻濁音」の痕跡であるとする（この点については第9節で再び触れる）．これに従えば，鼻濁音，すなわち前鼻子音は当時すでに過去のものであるということになる．ただ，「志摩」と一口に言っても広域で，そこには多くの地区が存在し，また，地形の複雑さを考慮すると，地区（集落）ごとに方言の特徴が異なることが予想される．

　他方，丹羽 (2000a: 46) の調査によると，志摩町布施田（上述の前島半島内の地区）には次のような特徴が認められるとの指摘がある（ここでいう「鼻濁音」は [ŋ] を指している）．

　　語中のガ行子音は個人差がある．鼻濁音，破裂音，人によってはガ行子音の前に「ン」が入る．今回の調査では，生え抜き4人のうち，鼻濁音が二人，破裂音と「ング」[ⁿg] がそれぞれ一人ずつであった．
　　　例：ワング（地名の「和具」）

布施田は，本稿で報告する和具の東隣りの地区で，いずれも前島半島の中腹部に位置する．生え抜き4人は大正11年から昭和4年生まれとあるが，「『ング』[ⁿg]」の話者がこのうちのいずれであるかは明記されていない．同じく，丹羽 (2000a: 14) の「ガ・ダ・バ行音の前の鼻音」の項目にも次のような説明がある．

　　南三重方言の志摩方言や南牟婁方言地域にガ行の前に「ン」が現れ，[ŋg] となる地域がある．この現象はすべての語に規則的に起こっているので，音声としての特徴である．ただし，現在の若年層では消えている．
　　　例：ケンガ（怪我），ヒンゲ（髭），マンゴ（孫），ワング（地名の和具），アンガル（上がる），エンガ（絵が）

　ダ・バ行の前に「ン」の現れる現象はほとんどの地域で観察されなかった．ただ，熊野市山間部の調査で一部の人に「ン」が聞かれた．これについてはII章で述べることにする．また南牟婁方言では，方言形

---

[1] 当該地域は「セ・ゼ」が [ce], [ze]([dze]) となる．

の中に「ン」の現れる地域もある．これらの「ン」は，かつて一般的な音声の現象であったかもしれないが，現在では語形の地域差となって残っている．

　布施田では，このように，ガ行子音が全般的に前鼻子音で実現されているのに対し，他の行ではそうでないということである．以下に報告する隣りの和具でも，これと同じ状態にある．地理的に連続する地区に共通しており，その点が分布上注目される．

　他方，『日本言語地図』の音声に関する図を見ると，旧志摩郡およびその周辺には前鼻子音の存在を示すデータは見出せない．具体的にいうと，第1図「カガミ（鏡）」，第2図「カゲ（蔭）」，第10図「カゼ（風）」，第15図「カジ（火事）」に該当する標示がない．三重県内に広げて見ても，前鼻子音を示すのはガ行の第1図，第2図の，和歌山県に接する紀和町（旧南牟婁郡）の1か所だけである．実は，和具は前島半島の中で唯一『日本言語地図』の調査地点（調査地点番号6587.42）に選ばれているのだが，当地で調査が実施された1957年の時点ではこれらの調査項目がまだ含まれておらず，該当するデータを欠く．これらの図の志摩（前島半島以外）での調査地点は阿児町安乗（あのり）（前掲地図参照）のみである．そのため，かりに前島半島に前鼻子音が存在していたとしてもデータとして出てこないことになる．

　『日本言語地図』には，これら以外の，語彙に関する項目にもガ行音の音声を細かく記述した図があるので，和具の手掛かりはそれに求めることができるかもしれない．具体的には，(1)に掲げた調査項目の地図で，実際，回答された語にガ行音が含まれる．しかし，その標示には〔g̃〕〔ɣ̃〕に該当するものがなく，いずれも〔g〕になっている．

(1) a. 第86図「においを嗅ぐ」の後部分（「嗅ぐ」）
    b. 第163図「すりこぎ」
    c. 第169図「もちごめ」
    d. 第224図「とかげ」
    e. 第266図「ゆげ」（蒸気—湯の場合）
    f. 第267図「ゆげ」（蒸気—飯の場合）

周辺の調査地点も見てみると，前鼻子音に該当する標示は，(1a)の第86図

の伊勢市横輪(よこわ)（6576.56）の「KAG〔˜g〕U」（嗅ぐ）1例のみで，ほかには見出せない。[2]『日本言語地図』からうかがえる内容は以上のとおりである．そのほか，大阪教育大学方言研究会（1978, 1979）の前島半島を中心とした地域の方言調査報告があるが，前鼻子音に関しては具体的な言及がない．また，前島半島以外の地域になるが，日本放送協会（1966）の志摩郡浜島(はまじまちょう)町南張(なんばり)（現志摩市，前掲地図参照）の談話資料の音声についても前鼻子音は聞かれない。[3]

4. 資料概要

本稿で報告するのは，筆者が1983年1月に当時履修中の授業の課題として出された「方言調査」のレポート作成のために収録した録音資料によるものである。[4]

調査協力者は1900年生まれで，以来，和具を中心に生活を営んできた話者である。[5]

調査方法としては，なぞなぞ形式を基本とした．むろん，学部段階1年次の未熟なものであり，「調査」と呼ぶのは躊躇されるが，なぞなぞ形式による質問と併せて，昔の生活を教えてもらうということで，談話を収録した．結果的にはその談話部分が重要となり，前鼻子音の確認もそれによるところが大きい．当時，すでにご高齢であったにもかかわらず，いろいろな話題についてお話しいただき，120分近くの長さの録音を残すことができた．

---

[2] 横輪は，志摩からは，度会郡南伊勢町（五ヶ所浦）から鍛冶屋(かじや)峠を経て山田（伊勢市中心部）に至る「伊勢路」の途中の山間部にある．

ところで，近畿地方の「KAG〔˜g〕U」（嗅ぐ）の地点は三重県に3か所，奈良県に1か所，和歌山県に2か所，京都府に1か所，兵庫県に3か所（うち，淡路島が2か所）ある．このうち，和歌山・三重・奈良の各1は，和歌山県東牟婁郡本宮町（現田辺市），三重県南牟婁郡紀和町（現熊野市），奈良県吉野郡野迫川村で，紀伊半島の山間部である．

[3] 志摩半島先端部に関しては，上野・相澤・加藤・沢木（1989）の地図によると，ガ行のほか，バ行，ダ行に入りわたり鼻音が標示されている．三重については，その執筆を担当された加藤和夫氏から，当時の記憶として，楳垣（1962）に依るものとのご教示を得た．

[4] 本稿筆者が在籍した筑波大学（第一学群人文学類・言語学主専攻）において必修の音声学概論（城生佰太郎氏担当）の課題として出された．

[5] 調査に協力してくださったのは西岡トシヱ氏（1900年生まれ，志摩町和具字石(いしけ)ケ）で，当地の生活，風習に関する豊かな経験と幅広い知識をお持ちの方であった．

なお，収録の際には，家族の方1名と，調査協力者の紹介者（和具の出身・在住）が同席した．そのため，とくに談話は自然な雰囲気で行うことができた．[6] 以下では，この録音資料に基づいて記述および考察を行う．

5. ガ行の前鼻子音

ガ行子音の音声は (2) のようになっている．語頭では破裂音 [g]，語頭以外（母音間）では前鼻子音 [ᵑg] か，鼻音 [ŋŋ] ～ [ŋ] である．[ᵑg] と [ŋŋ] との違いはしばしば明瞭でない．ガ行音で始まる助詞・接尾辞の類は，語頭以外（母音間）に属する．(3) にはそれぞれの位置別に該当する語を掲げる．問答方式で得た回答と談話中の場合とがあるが，聴取の結果，とくに差が見られないので区別しない．(3b) は多数あるため，品詞等の分類を施す（活用語については終止形で示す）．

音声の同定が困難な例は除いてある．ただし，それは少数にとどまり，収録されているガ行子音を含む語の大半は入っている．

(2) a. 語頭： 破裂音 [g]
　　b. 語頭以外（母音間）： 前鼻子音 [ᵑg]，鼻音 [ŋŋ]（表記上 [ᵑg] と [ⁿg] を区別しない）．全体として，先行する鼻音部分は撥音よりも短く聞こえる．また，同じ語でも，早く発音されると [ŋ] と短くなったり，あるいは，弱まって [ɣ] に近くなる場合がある．助詞・接尾辞の類は短くなって [ŋ] となる傾向が強い．具体的な語は，(3b)【助詞・接尾辞】を参照．
　　c. 語頭以外（撥音の後）： [g] か [ŋ]．
(3) a. 語頭： ガクモン（学問），ガス（「無駄なガス」の中で），ガッコー（学校），ガッコーアガリ（学校上がり〔卒業後〕），ギューニュー（牛乳），ゴー（「ごうが沸く」〔腹が立つ〕で），ゴハン（「白いご飯」の中で），ゴボー（牛蒡），ゴンボ（牛蒡），ゴロネ（ごろ寝），ゴネンセーゴロ（五年生頃）
　　b. 語頭以外（母音間）：【一般名詞】アサガタ（朝方），イソドコギ

---

[6] 調査協力者を紹介し，調査に同席してくださったのは山口源三(げんぞう)氏（当時，三重県立水産高等学校教諭）である．

(磯人漕ぎ)，イチガツ (一月〔一か月〕)，イナサゴチ (〔風名〕)，イマゴロ (今頃)，ウサギ (兎)，オショーガツ (お正月)，ガッコーアガリ (学校上がり〔卒業後〕)，クガツ (九月)，クラガリ (暗がり)，サキガネ (先金〔前金〕)，シゴト (仕事)，ショーガツ (正月)，スリコギ (擂粉木)，タキギ (薪)，タトエゴト (喩え事)，チューガク (中学)，テコギ (手漕ぎ)，ヒガサ (日傘)，ヒグレ (日暮れ)，ヒゴロ (日頃)，ヒョーゲン (表現)，ホーゲン (方言)，モチゴメ (糯米)，ユーガタ (夕方)，ワラシゴト (藁仕事)

【固有名詞】ウガタ (鵜方，地名)，カジヤトーゲ (鍛冶屋峠，地名)，コーゲンドウ (江原道，地名)，シゲ (同僚の人名)，シマグン (志摩郡，地名)，ナガサキ (長崎，地名)，ワグ (和具，地名)

【副詞・形容動詞など】クチグチ (口々)，スグ (直ぐ)，タイガイ (大概)，トギレトギレ (途切れ途切れ)

【動詞】アガル (上がる)，サガス (探す)，チガウ (違う)，ナガメル (眺める)，ナゲル (投げる)，ヒキアゲル (引き上げる)，モグル (潜る)

【助詞・接尾辞】-ガナ (終助詞，とくにヤ〔断定詞〕-ガナの形で)，-ゲ (「おらゲ」「おれゲ」「〜先生＋ゲ」などの形で〔〜の家〕の意)，-ゲナ〜-ゲン (「そげな」「そげん」「こげん」等，指示詞に後接)

c. 語頭以外 (撥音の後): サンガツ (三月)，マンガ (漫画)，クリーニング，ニンゲン (人間)

(2b) 語頭以外 (母音間) は，(3b) に示したように，単純語のみならず，イナサゴチ (←イナサ＋コチ)，サキガネ (←サキ＋カネ)，タキギ (←タキ＋キ)，タトエゴト (←タトエ＋コト)，ヒガサ (←ヒ＋カサ) のように複合語の後部要素が連濁でガ行子音に交替する場合も含まれている．クチグチ (口々) のような繰り返し語の連濁も同様である．この点は，東京方言のいわゆるガ行鼻濁音 [ŋ] の現れ方と一致する．しかし，上野 (2010: 63)，中澤 (2013: 88) で示されたような，形態音韻論的条件，種々の音的条件を考

慮したより詳細な分析は，残念ながら上記で得られたデータだけでは明らかにできない．

　ところで，本資料の聞き取りだけでは，個別の語形について，撥音とガ行子音の連続を，前鼻子音と誤認するおそれがある．すなわち，かりに標準語形に撥音がないところに撥音が来る方言形があったとすると，それを前鼻子音と見誤る危険がないではない．たとえば，「夕方」[juᵑgata] は (3b) の中に分類したが，疑えば，当方言の語形としては実は (3c) に該当するといったことがないとも限らない（とくに1回しか発話されなかった語はその危険が高い）．むろん，このような混入の危険性を完全には払拭できないのだが，全体的に見て前鼻子音の実現がある点は動かない．

6. その他の音韻的特徴

　参考のために，収録された音声資料に基づいて聞き取ることのできる和具方言の音韻的特徴をまとめておく．なお，アクセントについては体系記述に十分なデータが得られないため省く．

(4)　5母音体系であると見られ，(5) を除いて，その音声は伊勢湾岸地域の方言，および近畿中央の方言と大差ない．

(5)　母音音節エは [je] である．語例：エ（柄），エ（絵），エーセーシャ（衛生車），エサ（餌），エンジ（臙脂〔色〕），ウエ（上）．ただ，母音間の場合に，[j] が聞かれないことがある〔コエ（肥），モエル（燃える），タトエゴト（喩え事）〕．

(6)　子音体系および子音の音声実現は，(7) 以下の点を除いて，伊勢湾岸地域の方言，および近畿中央の方言と大差ない．

(7)　セ・ゼは，[ɕe], [ʑe]([dʑe]) で現れる．センコ（線香），イセ（伊勢，地名），ジッセン（十銭），-セン（否定辞．「鳴かせん」「わからせん」など），ゼンブ（全部），ヒゼンカキ（皮癬掻き）など．

(8)　バ行子音は全般的に破裂 [b] がしっかり実現されている印象を受ける．あまり摩擦音化しない．[kabuto]（兜）など．

(9)　ガ行子音は上述の通り．

(10)　語頭のラ行子音は，[dakkaɕeː]（落花生），[dampu]（ランプ），[doː

（樽），[dobjoːɕi]（樽拍子），[doːsoku]（蝋燭），[dzoːɕi]（漁師），[dendzaku]（連尺〔荷袋の1つ〕）のように破裂音もしくは破裂音に傾斜した実現，および破擦音で現れる．ただし，本資料からではダ行と弁別されるか否かは判断できない．

(11) マ行，ナ行子音は，母音間でしばしば長めに聞こえる傾向がある．

上記のうち，(11) についてはさらに客観的な分析を行う必要がある．ガ行が，前鼻子音 [ᵑg] もしくは長めの鼻音 [ŋŋ] で実現されることと平行して，マ行，ナ行の子音が長めに発音される傾向を持つのかもしれない．もし，そうだとすれば，ガ行，ナ行，マ行が同じ鼻音のカテゴリーで共通のふるまいを見せることになり，興味深い．これについては今後の課題である．

7. 主格助詞ナについて

本資料に収録した和具方言では一般に，助詞ガの代わりにナが現れる．そのため，第5節 (3b)【助詞・接尾辞】の中にも助詞ガを挙げていない．具体的に示すと，たとえば，(12) のようにガが期待されるところはナとなる．丹羽（2000a: 49-50）によると，和具の東隣りの布施田でも助詞ナであるとのことである．

(12) a. マムシナ，オル．ドレデモコノヘンノヒトラ，マムシ…（「マムシがおる」．どのような種類でもこの辺の人らは「まむし」という）．
  b. イセナナ，キマルト，コンドァー，マッツァカノホーイイテナ《伊勢がナ，極まると，今度は松阪の方へ行てナ》（秋仕事で，伊勢が終わると今度は松阪のほうへ行って）
  c. マゼモトナワリイヨッテ，アメナフッテクル（南西の方角があやしいから，雨が降ってくる）

助詞ガに対応するナは，『日本言語地図』『方言文法全国地図』を見ても，志摩および紀伊半島南部にプロットがない．同じ n であることから，no 系の一種かと一見思われる．実際，比較的近いところでは，N が静岡県を中心に分布し，愛知県，岐阜県のごく一部にもないわけではない．しかし，母音

a を取る点が容易に説明できないし，また，na そのものがめずらしい（『方言文法全国地図』の「雨が（降ってきた）」に富山県の1例があるのみである）．このようなことから，no 系の1つとして結論するのは躊躇される．ここでは，同じ母音 a を持つ点を考慮して，ガからの変化という線で考える．助詞や接尾辞の類は，(2b)【助詞・接尾辞】に述べたように，全体的な傾向として，機能語の発音弱化のために，前鼻子音というよりも，自然談話中ではそれが弱化した [ŋ] で実現されることが多い．

この傾向を踏まえると，もともと助詞ガがあったとしても，同様に弱化が起こり，通常の発音では [ŋa] となっていたと推定される．ガ行子音の多くが前鼻子音で実現される中で，助詞ガではそのような変異に偏っていたとすると，ガ行子音から遊離して，体系内の [ŋ] の周囲にある他の音素に混同する可能性が出てくる．おそらく，[ŋ] は同じ鼻音の [n] に聞き取られ，その結果，(13) のように，ガからナへと語形の変化が起こったと考えられる．こうして見ると，歴史的経過として比較的無理なく理解することができる．

(13) 主格助詞 *ga [ŋa] > na [na]

もし，このような推定が正しいとすれば，統語上の位置ゆえに生じた音声実現の偏りが語形変化を誘発させる契機を与えたという点で興味深い．ただし，同様の例が全国の分布上にはほとんど見られないという問題が依然残される．なお，和具の周辺地域における助詞ナの地理的分布については大阪教育大学方言研究会 (1979) がある．志摩地方におけるその分布はガ行の前鼻子音を推定する上でも重要な情報であると考える．

本調査協力者よりも新しい世代では，おそらくは周辺地域の方言の影響を受けて，ガに置き換えられつつある（そのことは，調査時に同席された話者の発話からうかがえた）．経過としては，社会言語学的な要因で，ふたたびガに戻ることになる．

8. ガ行四段動詞の撥音便形

当該方言のガ行四段動詞は，コイデ，コイダ（漕）のようなイ音便ではなく，コンデ，コンダ，コンドルのように撥音便を取る．これについても，布施田で同様に撥音便である（丹羽 (2000b)）．(14) に具体例を示す（収録さ

れた形にかかわらず，テ形で示す）．

(14) カグ～カンデ（嗅ぐ），コグ～コンデ（漕ぐ），シノグ～シノンデ（凌ぐ），ナグ～ナンデ（凪ぐ）

撥音便全体の現れ方を把握するためには，丹羽（2000b）のように，マ行，バ行をはじめとして，活用体系の全体像を押さえる必要があるが，収録された資料だけでは網羅的なデータが得られない．

(14) のような撥音便がどのような過程を経て形成されたのかについて考察しようとすれば，結論はどうあれ，少なくとも濁音の前鼻子音との関連性は無視することができない．

(15) コイデ（漕） [koiⁿde] > [konde]

もし，(15) のようなプロセスを想定するとなると，ガ行以外の濁音（とくにダ行）がどのようであったかという点に関わってくる．これに加えて，周辺地域も含めた，動詞の活用体系全般に関する考察も欠かせない．

本稿では，この問題は今後にゆだねざるを得ない．ここでは，前鼻子音に関連する問題として，現象の存在を指摘するにとどめておく．

9. まとめ

歴史的な観点から見ると，本稿の和具方言の状態は，より古く濁音全般に前鼻子音が存在していたとすれば，ガ行子音だけに残った最終段階ということになる．また，地理的には，隣接する布施田と同様の現れ方をしているところから，前島半島の他の場所にも同特徴が分布していたことが考えられる．

この方言のガ行子音は，前鼻子音の他，鼻音 [ŋŋ]～[ŋ] でも実現されていることから，大きな流れとしては，前鼻子音から鼻音 [ŋ] に移行する途上にあるものと見られる（井上 (1971) 参照）．

前島半島は，地理的に近畿の周縁部にあり，京都ですでに失われた濁音の特徴が比較的遅くまで保持されたのであろう．本報告のように20世紀初に生まれた世代において前鼻子音がすでにガ行子音だけに限られていることからすると，他の行のそれは20世紀以前に失われたことになる．これは，現

在でもなおこの特徴が他の行にも見られる（あるいは最近まで見られた），西側の淡路島や四国の状況とは対照的である．

　第3節で言及した楳垣（1962）が指摘するアンブ（虻），カンジェ（風）などの「語彙的現象」に残る「鼻濁音」の痕跡は，本資料からは見出すことができなかった．

　一見するといかにもこれらの語形は前鼻子音の存在を彷彿とさせるが，特定の語に限ってなぜ痕跡が残るのかは不明であり，単純には扱えない．音変化の基本的な見方からすると，もともと撥音であったために，変化の影響を受けず，そのまま残ったと見るのが定石である．以前から存在した撥音であれば，直ちに前鼻子音の痕跡ということにはならない．実際，ニジ（『日本言語地図』によれば和具では NINZI）のように，古くから「3拍」であったことが疑われている語もある（金田一（2003 [1964]: 422-423，〔十二・十・三〕および注3）参照）．

　もし，かりに前鼻子音の痕跡と思われる語が少なからず認められるとしても，なぜそのような形が存在するかについて，より確かな説明を必要とする．その点についても課題が残されている．

参考文献

井上史雄（1971）「ガ行子音の分布と歴史」『国語学』第86集．
上野善道（2010）「鼻濁音考」音声学会2010年度（第24回）全国大会発表要旨・特別講演1，『音声研究』第14巻3号，63．
上野善道・相澤正夫・加藤和夫・沢木幹栄（1989）「音韻総覧」『日本方言大辞典』小学館．
大阪教育大学方言研究会（1978）「志摩　前島方言調査報告」『方言研究年報』続3，12-24．
大阪教育大学方言研究会（1979）『志摩・前島（サキシマ）半島方言事象分布図集』大阪教育大学方言研究会，大阪．
楳垣実編著（1962）「三重県方言」『近畿方言の総合的研究』三省堂，東京．
岸江信介・吉廣綾子（2006）「四国諸方言における入りわたり鼻音について―徳島方言を中心に―」『音声研究』第10巻1号，49-59．
金田一春彦（1964）『四座講式の研究』三省堂，東京．金田一春彦（2003）に所収．
金田一春彦（2003）『金田一春彦著作集　第5巻』玉川大学出版部，町田．
国立国語研究所編（1966-1977）『日本言語地図』大蔵省印刷局．

国立国語研究所編（1989-2006）『方言文法全国地図』財務省印刷局．
柴田武（1960）「高知方言の音声的特徴」『幡多方言』10号（浜田数義），柴田武（1988: 454-458）に所収．
柴田武（1962）「語頭の入りわたり鼻音」『土佐方言』第3集（浜田数義），柴田武（1988: 459-462）に所収．
柴田武（1988）『方言論』平凡社，東京．
中澤光平（2013）「淡路島方言の前鼻音の分布と音韻解釈」音声学会2013年度（第27回）全国大会発表要旨，『音声研究』第17巻3号，88．
日本放送協会編（1966）『全国方言資料 第四巻 近畿編』日本放送協会，東京．
丹羽一彌（2000a）「I 総論」「II 県内各地の方言」『三重県のことば 日本のことばシリーズ24』明治書院，東京．
丹羽一彌（2000b）「三重県志摩町布施田方言の音便形とバ四・マ四動詞」『人文科学論集・文化コミュニケーション学科編』34号，41-49，信州大学人文学部．

〔付記〕
　もう三十年以上も前のことになるが，調査にご協力くださった西岡トシエさん，西岡さんを紹介くださり調査にも同行くださった三重県立水産高校（当時）の山口源三（げんぞ）先生，お世話になった西岡さんのご家族の方，ご近所の電器店の方に対して，改めて厚く感謝申し上げる．
　なお，収録した資料をもとにあらためて成果を公表するにあたり，現在の西岡家の皆様からご承諾をいただいた．また，山口先生のご子息の山口喜博さんにはその仲介の労を取っていただくなど，たいへんお世話になった．
　本稿をまとめるにあたり，金沢大学歴史言語文化学系教授の加藤和夫氏には，三重方言に関してご教示を賜った．
　この場を借りて，お世話になった皆様方に心よりお礼を申し上げる．

Part II

語形成と音韻現象

日本語の名詞形成接尾辞「-さ」と「-み」について*

太田　聡

山口大学

1. はじめに

　形容詞を名詞にする派生接辞の「-さ」と「-み」（例えば，「高い」→「高さ」，「高み」）の振る舞いや用いられ方の異同は，派生形態論（derivational morphology）のメカニズムやメンタル・レキシコン（mental lexicon）——すなわち脳内にある辞書——の構造や役割に興味のある者にとっては，大変面白いテーマを提供してくれる．[1] 本論では，「-さ」と「-み」に関する代表的な論考を振り返った上で，特にそのアクセント付与に関する違いに着目し，そこから，日本語のメンタル・レキシコンの構造に関してどのような提案ができるかを述べることにする．

2. 「-さ」と「-み」が表すものの違い

2.1. Sugioka (1984) の分析

　Sugioka (1984: 127) は，「-さ」は抽象的な状態や特性を表し，「-み」は

---

* 原稿段階で貴重なコメントを与えてくださった山口大学英語学研究会のメンバー諸氏及び本論文集編集委員の先生方に感謝申し上げたい．また，本研究は JSPS 科研費（課題番号 24520545，16K02772）の助成を受けている．

[1] 2003 年の夏にミシガン州立大学で開かれたアメリカ言語学会の言語学講座で，Harald Clahsen 先生（当時 University of Essex）の "The Mental Lexicon" という講義を受講したときのことだが，受講者の中に筆者を含めて日本人が数名いることを知った先生が，「日本人ならば，Hagiwara et al. の *Language* に載った -sa と -mi についての論文はもちろん読んだでしょう．あれは素晴らしかった」と Hagiwara et al. (1999) を絶賛された．このことがきっかけで，私も「-さ」と「-み」の違いについて考えてみるようになった．

その特性を持つより具体的な要素を表すと指摘して，以下の例文を挙げてその違いを説明している（原文は英文であるが，ここでは和文で示した）．

(1) a. 川の深み／*深さにはまった．
b. 川の*深み／深さに驚く．

確かに，(1a) はある川の中の特定的・具体的な場所を指しているが，(1b) はその川を全体的・一般的に捉えており，意味的な違いがある．しかしながら，例えば「彼の話には重みがある」という場合，その話の中の特定的・具体的な箇所を指しているのではなく，全体的な印象を述べていると思われる．よって，抽象的か具体的か，特定的か全体的かといった基準だけでは，「-さ」と「-み」の違いを十分に捉えたことにはならない．[2]

2.2. Hagiwara et al. (1999) の指摘

Hagiwara et al. (1999: 742) では，「-み」がつく名詞形は五感で感じられるという特性を持つ旨が述べられている．なるほど，例えば，「甘み」は味覚，「臭み」は嗅覚，「丸み」は視覚や触覚といった具合に，五感で実際に感じ取られる特徴を「～み」という名詞が表すことは多い．しかし，例えば「○○の有り難みを知る」というような場合には，具体的に見たり触ったりして感じ取る事柄に言及してのではなくて，心・頭の中で思い抱くことを表している．よって，「～み」が五感で感じるものを指すというのも，まだ不十分な面がある．[3]

---

[2] ちなみに，『広辞苑』などの一般的な国語辞典で接辞「み」を引いても，「所・場所を表す」と「程度・状態を表す」といった2種類の働きが挙げられているので，「-み」の意味・働きは複数の観点・基準から論じなくてはなるまい．

[3] 例えば，「有り難み」，「面白み」などの「-み」のつく例は主観的・内面的に感じるものを表すが，「激しさ」，「大きさ」などの「-さ」のつく例は客観的・外面的に捉えられる状態を表す，という違いもありそうである．またそうすれば，味覚や嗅覚で捉える事柄も主観的な面があるので，「甘み」や「臭み」が可能であることと整合する．しかしながら，主観的な表現である「だるい」，「眠い」は「だるさ」，「眠さ」とはなっても「*だるみ」，「*眠み」とはなりそうにないので，意味的・認知的分類基準を定めるのは容易ではない．

なお，「Yahoo! 知恵袋」で，「温かさ」と「温かみ」の違いなどについての質問に対して，以下の回答が挙げられていた (detail.chiebukuro.yahoo.co.jp /qa/question_detail/ q1037795460)．ここでの議論に大いに参考になるので，（用字なども）そのまま引用することにする．

3. 「-み」のつく名詞の一覧とその特徴

　Sugioka (1984) や Hagiwara et al. (1999) は，形容詞に「-み」がついて名詞化した例は約 30 語あると述べているが，具体的にその 30 語が列挙されているわけではない．そこで，『逆引き広辞苑　第五版対応』などを利用して，形容詞に「-み」がついて名詞化したものを拾い上げてみると，以下の (2) のようになる（一応目安としてそれらの分類基準を記したが，区分は難しく，例えば (2c) に挙げたものを (2d) に属させることなども可能である）．

(2) a. 味覚・嗅覚で感じるもの：
　　　苦（にが）み，臭み，渋み，甘み，うまみ，辛（から）み
　b. 視覚・触覚などで感じるもの：
　　　青み，赤み，暖かみ，[4] 温（ぬく）み，痛み，かゆみ，暗み，明るみ，黒み
　c. 物理的・(比喩的に) 知覚的なもの：
　　　高み，深み，柔らかみ，低み，浅み，新しみ，厚み，重み，強み，軽み，[5] 丸み，弱み

　大きく分けるなら…「〜さ」はほぼすべての形容詞に使え「程度の概念」を表します．「〜み」が使える形容詞はきわめて限られていて「主観的特徴」を表します．〈中略〉(「〜さ」は)「状態的なものを，程度概念の名詞に変える」という働きを持っています．つまり，「程度」の幅がある形容詞（したがってほとんどすべての形容詞）・形容動詞に使うことができます．（あたたかさ，柔らかさ，などには，さまざまな程度がありますね．これに対し，例外的に「さ」が使えないのは，程度の幅がない「小高い」というような語です．小高さ，とは通常言いません）〈中略〉「〜さ」がついた名詞については「それは，どのくらい？」という質問が成り立ちます．〈中略〉「〜さ」が使える「大きい，長い，広い，太い，若い」などの，客観的な形容詞に「〜み」が付く例はありません．「丸い」は客観的な語ですが，「丸み」という場合には対象の特徴を【感覚的に】とらえた語になります．（厚さ 3 センチ，とは言うが，厚み 3 センチ，とは言わない．厚みのある人間，とは言うが，厚さのある人間，とは言わない）〈後略〉

[4] 下線を施した「暖かみ，暗み，柔らかみ，新しみ，優しみ」は『逆引き広辞苑』（つまりは『広辞苑　第五版』）には載っていないが，『日本国語大辞典　第二版』や『大辞林　第三版』には載っているので，ここに加えた．

[5] 破線を引いた「軽（かる）み」及び「丸（まる）み」には，「かろみ」，「まろみ」と読む異形もあるが，ここでは省略することにした．

d．心理的なもの：
　　優しみ，有り難み，辛（つら）み，面白み

　これら以外に，古語や俳諧の理念を表す用語なども加えれば，「長み，悪（あ）しみ，うるわしみ，細み，広み」などを挙げることができる．[6] (2b) と (2c) に挙げたもののうち，「明るみ，高み，深み，重み」に対して，「暗み，低み，浅み，軽み」は使用頻度が低いと思われる．例えば，英語の "short, shallow, small" などに対して "long, deep, big" などは肯定的である．よって，"How 〜 ...?" と尋ねるときは，プラスと評価される方を用いる．日本語でも，「背の高さ／部屋の広さはどれくらいですか？」と聞き，（背の低い人や，狭い部屋に住んでいる人に尋ねる場合でも）「背の低さ／部屋の狭さはどれくらいですか？」とは言わない．こうしたことと同様に，「高み」と「低み」などのペアでは，肯定的・プラスと評価される前者の方が用いられやすいと推察できる．[7]

　さて，では (2) に挙げた「-み」のつく名詞に共通する特徴はなんであろうか？ 2.1 節と 2.2 節でも触れたように，1 つの簡明な基準では「-み」のつく例を漏れなくカバーすることはできない．

　多くの健常者と失語症患者から実験によって大量のデータを収集し，その分析を通して「『-さ』のつく名詞は（デフォルト）規則によって作り出されるが，『-み』のつく名詞はレキシコンにリストされている（すなわち，記憶されている）．[8] つまり，不規則動詞と規則動詞の違いを捉えるために，屈折

---

[6] 例えば，「惜しみ，おかしみ，憎しみ，親しみ，悲しみ，楽しみ，寂しみ，苦しみ」などは，動詞（「惜しむ」など）の連用形が名詞化したものと判断できるので（インターネット上で利用できる Weblio 辞書の一種である『日本語活用形辞書』なども参照されたい），ここでの考察対象にはしなかった．また，例えば「嫌（いや）み」を「-み」のついた名詞とする辞書もあるが，本論では「〜い」で終わる形容詞に「-み」のつく例のみを分析対象としており，「いやい」という形容詞があるわけではないので，「嫌み」は除外した．

[7] 年齢を尋ねるときに "How old are you?" と言うからといって，old が肯定的意味で young は否定的意味だというわけではあるまい（その証拠に，「若いですね」や「若く見えますね」などは通例褒めことばになる）．年齢は誰でもより old な方向に進むものなので，"How old ...?" と聞いて失礼ではないのであろう．

[8] 例えば，「あかさ」と「あかみ」を『大辞林 第三版』で引くと，「あかみ」は独立の見出しとして立てられているが，「あかさ」は「あかい」という項目の末尾に派生語形として「『-さ』（名）」と略して示されているだけである．こうしたところに，「-さ」のつく形が規則

形態論 (inflectional morphology) において提案された二重メカニズムモデル (dual-mechanism model) と同じことが，派生形態論においても支持できる」とした Hagiwara et al. (1999) の議論は大変説得力がある．ところで，Hagiwara et al. (1999) では，「連想的記憶に基づく類推的拡張 (analogical extension on associative memory)」という表現（およびそれに類するもの）が幾度も用いられている．例えば，「高い (takai)」の子音を1つ変えた「たさい (tasai)」と，「寒い (samui)」の子音を1つ変えた「さぬい (sanui)」という新造語・無意味語を提示して，それに「-み」をつけて名詞にする場合，どちらの容認可能性が高いかを尋ねるとしよう．そうすれば，（「高み」は存在しても「*寒み」は使われないという元にした語からの類推で，）「たさみ」の方が「さぬみ」よりもよさそうだといった回答が得られるかもしれない．こういった音韻的共通性からの類推は起こりそうである．しかしながら，例えば，(2b) の「温み」や (2c) の「厚み」があるのに，「*寒み・*冷たみ」や「*薄み」は現れないのはなぜであろうか？ 上述のように，否定的な表現は用いられにくいからとするだけでよいのであろうか？ では，(2c) の「高み」や「重み」があるのに，なぜ「*速み・*早み」や「*遠み」などは（否定的な意味合いがあるわけではないのに）使われないのであろうか？

　英語の「～する人［もの］」を表す -er と -or について論じた太田 (2009) では，「-or は -ate や -ct といったつづりで終わる語——ラテン語の知識がある人にはラテン語由来の語と感じられる語——につく」といった分析を行った．つまり，-or のつく語を丸暗記しなくても，-or を用いるべきか否かは基体 (base) の末尾のつづり・発音から予測ができるのである．しかしながら，「-み」がつくか否かが，基体のつづり・発音から決められるということはありそうにない．結局，(2) に列挙した「-み」のつく約 30 語は，そのまま暗記しているとするのが妥当であろう．

的・生産的に作られるので，わざわざ見出し語とする必要はないという編者の判断が働いたことが窺われる．

4. 「-さ」と「-み」は -ness と -ity に対応するのか？

　Sugioka (1984)，Hagiwara et al. (1999)，そして島村 (2002) などは，「-さ」はほとんどすべての形容詞に付加できるが，「-み」は限られた形容詞にしかつかないという生産性 (productivity) の違いが，英語の名詞形成接尾辞の -ness と -ity の違いに似ているとしている．[9] 確かに，-ness のつく語に比べれば，-ity のつく語の数は少ない．例えば，realness と reality は両方可能だが，happiness に対して *happyity は不可である．しかしながら，-ity のつく語は，例えば逆引き辞典の *Walker's Rhyming Dictionary* で確認してみると，1000語以上が掲載されている．30語ほどで，かつ，使用頻度の高いものであれば，(英語の不規則動詞のように) そのまま記憶しているとしても不思議ではない．しかし，1000語以上の -ity のつく語をそのまま暗記しているとは思えない．きっと，「ラテン系の語彙で，-al, -ic(al), -able, -ous などで終わるもの」というように，一定の基準・規則に基づいて判断・生成しているはずである．よって，例の多さ少なさという印象だけから，「-さ」は -ness に，「-み」は -ity に相当するとする単純な議論は納得できないし，重要な相違点を見落としてしまうことになる．

5. レキシコンの構造について

5.1. 語彙音韻論の観点

　Siegel (1974) や Allen (1978) の順序づけられた形態論 (level-ordered morphology) という提案をさらに発展させた Kiparsky (1982) などの語彙音韻論・形態論 (lexical phonology/morphology) では，-ity と -ness などの振る舞いの違いを説明するために，レキシコンが複数のレベル／層 (stratum) に分かれているとした．第I類 (Class I) 接辞と分類される -ity がつ

---

[9]「-さ」は，「-み」と違って，終止形が「～だ」となるいわゆる形容動詞にも付加できる (例：「静かさ」，「さわやかさ」，「*静かみ」，「*さわやかみ」)．この「-さ」の生産性に関連させて補記すると，例えば，「非常識さ」は容認できるが，「*常識さ」とは言えない．これはおそらく，「非常識さ」は「非常識だ」に「-さ」が付加した形として処理されるが，「*常識さ」は名詞の「常識」に「-さ」がついたと捉えられ，「-さ」が形容詞・形容動詞に付加するという範疇上の制限に反することになるからであろう．

く語では，例えば grammátical → grammaticálity といった具合に強勢（stress）の移動が起こるが，第 II 類（Class II）接辞と分類される -ness の場合には，grammátical → grammáticalness のように強勢移動は生じない．こういった違いを生み出す仕掛けとして，語彙音韻論では，次の (3) に示したように，強勢や発音の変化を引き起こす -ity などの接辞付加はレベル 1 と呼ばれる早い段階で起こるが，そうではない -ness などの接辞付加はレベル 2 と呼ばれるそれよりは遅い段階で起こるとし，かつ，強勢付与規則などをレベル 1 に配置した．[10]

(3)　レベル 1：　-ity などの付加　⇄　強勢付与規則など
　　　　　　　　　　　　　　⇓
　　レベル 2：　-ness などの付加

同じレベル 1 で -ity 付加と強勢の計算が行われるのであれば，-ity のつく語では強勢移動が生じうるが，レベル 2 に強勢付与規則がなければ，強勢配置の再計算は起こりようがない．

では，この語彙音論的な発想を，「-み」と「-さ」の違いの説明にそのまま当てはめることができるであろうか？　前節で触れたように，先行研究では，「-み」は -ity に，「-さ」は -ness に相当するとうい主張が，主に生産性の違いに着目して，行われてきた．-ness は，例えば well-formedness, class-consciousness のように，複合語にも付加できる．これは「-さ」にも見られる特徴で，複合語の「塩辛い」，「感慨深い」，「腹黒い」を「塩辛さ」，「感慨深さ」，「腹黒さ」とできる．[11] 一方，「*塩辛み」，「*感慨深み」，「*腹黒み」

---

[10] 例えば，X に -ness がついた語の意味は「X であること」と平明であるのに対して，-ity のついた語の意味はもう少しわかりにくくなることがある．また，-ness と違って -ity は，probity のように語よりも小さな単位に付加できるなどの特殊性もある．よって，-ity などの特殊な性質を備えた接辞の付加を，-ness などの接辞付加よりも先に行うようにするということは，太田（1992）で論じたように，非該当条件（Elsewhere Condition）の考え方—特殊な・特定の（special/specific）規則が一般的な（general）規則よりも先に適用される—とも通じるところがあり，穏当な見解である．

[11] Allen (1978) は，複合語が作られるレベルをレベル 3 とした．そして，例えば non-color-blind, non-homemade のように，non- は複合語にも付加できるので，non- 付加はレベル 3 の過程であるとした．これと並行的に考えれば，複合語にもかなり自由につけられる「-さ」をレベル 3（あるいは第 III 類）接辞としてもよいかもしれない．一方，Kiparsky

とは言えない．では，(3) の図式の -ity のところに「-み」を，-ness のところに「-さ」を当てはめて (4) とすると，どのような予測ができるであろうか？

(4) 　レベル1：「-み」付加　⇄　アクセント付与規則
　　　　　　　　　　　　　⇓
　　　レベル2：「-さ」付加

(4) から予測されることは，もちろん，「-み」のつく語ではアクセントの位置が変わりうるが，「-さ」のつく語ではアクセントが変化することはないということである．ところが，この予測は，事実とはまったく異なるのである．

5.2. 「-さ」と「-み」が生み出すアクセント型

まず，「-さ」がつく元の形容詞と，派生された名詞のアクセント型に注目してみよう．[12] (以下では，例えば「しろい（白い）」のように，いわゆる起伏式アクセント型の語で，ピッチが落ちる箇所のある——アクセント（核）のある——例では，「しろ'い」といった具合にそこにアポストロフィを付した．一方，「まるい（丸い）」のように，いわゆる平板型アクセントになって，ピッチが落ちない例——本論では「無アクセント」の語とも呼ぶ——の場合には，何も付さない．)

(5) 　a.　あかい　→　あかさ
　　　　　かたい　→　かたさ
　　　　　くらい　→　くらさ
　　　　　つめたい　→　つめたさ
　　b.　ふる'い　→　ふ'るさ

(1982) のように，第II類接辞の付加と複合語形成は，どちらもレベル2で起こるとする見解もある．本論の議論にとっては，レベル2とレベル3の区別は重要ではないので，レベル1とレベル2のみを取り上げ，(Kiparsky と同じく，本節では）複合語に付加できる接辞もレベル2に存在することにする．

[12] 以下の (5) および (6) に挙げた語のアクセント型の確認は，『NHK日本語発音アクセント辞典　新版』によって行ったが，このアクセント辞典に載っていない例の場合には，『日本国語大辞典　第二版』を用いて確かめた．

```
       せま'い    →  せ'まさ
       かわい'い  →  かわい'さ, かわ'いさ
       はかな'い  →  はかな'さ, はか'なさ
       あたらし'い →  あたら'しさ, あたらし'さ
       おもしろ'い →  おもし'ろさ, おもしろ'さ
       みぐるし'い →  みぐる'しさ
       うつくし'い →  うつく'しさ
       かがやかし'い → かがやか'しさ
       けばけばし'い → けばけば'しさ
```

まず，(5a) からわかることは，基体が無アクセントならば「-さ」のついた派生形も基本的に無アクセントとなるということである（ただし，「かなしい → かな'しさ，かなし'さ，かなしさ」のように，4モーラ（= 4拍）以上の語になるとアクセントの有無・位置が揺れる場合がある）．一方，(5b) の例のように基体がアクセントを持っているときには，「-さ」がつく派生形のアクセントは，基本的に語末から3番目の音節に置かれる（ただし，下線を付した例のように，「-さ」の直前にアクセントが置かれることもあるが，これは，後半要素が1〜2モーラしかない複合語のアクセントのパターンと同じあることに注目されたい[13]）．

ところで，日本語の名詞のアクセントは，例えば「い'のち，たま'ご，あたま'，さくら」のように，3モーラ語であれば4通りのアクセント型が観察されるので，nモーラ語には (n+1) 通りのアクセント型・配置が存在することになり，かなり複雑であると考えられてきた．そして，どの語がどのアクセント型を取るかは恣意的に社会習慣として決まっているとされた．しかしながら，Kubozono (1996)，窪薗・太田 (1998)，Kubozono (2008)，太田 (2010) などが主張したように，「後ろから2番目の音節が長ければそこに，短ければもう1つ前の音節にアクセントが置かれる」といういわゆるラテン語アクセント規則 (Latin Accent Rule) が，日本語の多くの名詞に適用可能である（例：スト'ーブ，スト'レス）．そして，例えば「ふ'るさ」も，

---

[13] ちなみに，「あ'われ → あわれ'さ，お'ろか → おろか'さ，し'ずか → しずか'さ」のように，形容動詞に「-さ」のついた例では，アクセントが「-さ」の直前に置かれる規則性がある．

後ろから 2 番目の「る」が短いので,もう 1 つ前の「ふ」にアクセントを与えていると分析できる.よって,「-さ」のつく語がアクセントを持つ場合,その位置は,規則で予測可能である.

さて,用言(動詞や形容詞など)のアクセント型は,名詞に比べると単純で,「平板型になるか,後ろから 2 番目のモーラに置かれるかのどちらかである」といったことが,日本語音声の入門書でもよく指摘される(松崎・河野(2010)などを参照).しかしながら,どの形容詞にアクセントがつくかつかないかは,規則等では決められない.例えば,「悪い(waru'i),高い(taka'i),楽しい(tanosi'i)」などと「丸い(marui),硬い(katai),悲しい(kanasii)」などは,音節構造や音素の種類はほぼ同じなので,なぜ前者にだけアクセントがあるのかは説明できない.つまり,アクセントの(位置ではなく)有無は覚えるしかないであろう.

次に,「-み」のつく語のアクセント型を確認してみよう.(2) に挙げた例(およびその基体)のアクセント型を示せば以下のようになる.

(6) にが'い → にがみ'
    くさ'い → くさみ'
    しぶ'い → しぶみ'
    あまい → あまみ
    うま'い → うまみ, うまみ'
    から'い → からみ', からみ
    あお'い → あおみ, あおみ'
    あかい → あかみ
    あたたか'い → あたたかみ, あたたかみ'
    ぬく'い → ぬくみ'
    いた'い → いたみ'
    かゆ'い → かゆみ', かゆみ
    くらい → くらみ
    あかるい → あかるみ
    くろ'い → くろみ'
    たか'い → たかみ, た'かみ
    ふか'い → ふかみ', ふかみ

やわらか'い　→　やわらかみ
ひく'い　→　ひくみ'
あさい　→　あさみ
あたらし'い　→　あたらしみ, あたらしみ'
あつい　→　あつみ
おもい　→　おもみ
つよ'い　→　つよみ'
かるい　→　かるみ
まるい　→　まるみ
よわ'い　→　よわみ'
やさしい　→　やさしみ
ありがた'い　→　ありがたみ, ありがたみ'
つらい　→　つらみ
おもしろ'い　→　おもしろみ

「-み」のつく語では，基体にアクセントがあれば語末にアクセントを配置し，基体にアクセントがなければ，無アクセントになることが優勢なパターンであるとしてよかろう．ところで，語末にアクセントを付与するのは通常の名詞アクセント規則とは異なる．よって，「『-み』アクセント規則」とでも呼ぶべき規則を想定するしかないであろう．[14] ただし，下線を付した例からわかるように，基体にアクセントがあっても，「-み」がつく語は無アクセントになる傾向が徐々に強まっていることが窺える（よって，「『-み』アクセント規則」は不要となりつつあると言えそうである）．

5.3. 提案

結局，(「-さ」と「-み」のアクセントを説明するためには，) 日本語のメンタル・レキシコンは，以下に示したように，「記憶された項目が収められる領域」と「規則等で計算される領域」に分かれた二重構造になっているものと思われる．例えば，「重い」と「強い」を例にとると，これらに「-み」のつく形も記憶された領域に存在し，かつ，それぞれがアクセントを持つか持

---

[14] 二重下線を付した「た'かみ」だけは，ほかの「-み」のついた例と違って，通常の名詞アクセントパターンになっている．

たないかも(アクセント規則が適用されるよりも前の段階で)決まっているものと考えられる([＋acc]は「アクセントを持つ」という素性指定,[－acc]は「アクセントを持たない」という素性指定を意図している).

(7) メンタル・レキシコン

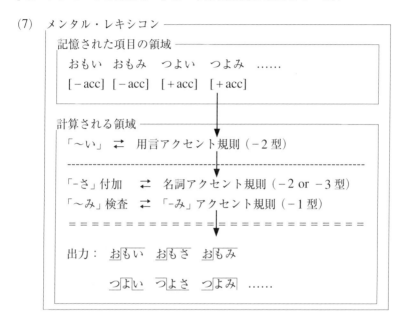

[＋acc]と指定された項目が,(i)「用言アクセント規則」を適用されれば語末から2モーラ目に,(ii)「-さ」を付加された上で「名詞アクセント規則」の適用を受ければ語末から2もしくは3音節目に,(iii)(「-み」の既に付加された状態で)「『-み』アクセント規則」の適用を受ければ語末に,それぞれアクセントを有するようになる.[－acc]と指定された項目にはアクセント規則が適用されず,おしなべて無アクセント語となる.そして,各語は出力欄に示したピッチパターンを持つことになるのである.

6. まとめ

従来の研究では,日本語の「-さ」と「-み」は英語の -ness と -ity に似ているという指摘がよくなされてきた.しかし本論では,「-さ」と「-み」がついた名詞のアクセント型を丹念に検討し,そのユニークなパターンを説明す

るには，英語の接辞の振る舞いの違いを捉えるために提案されてきたメカニズムとは異なるものを仮定しなくてはならないことを論じた．そして，規則的な屈折変化と不規則な屈折変化の分析において唱えられた二重メカニズムモデル（例えば Pinker (1999) などを参照）の考え方が，「-さ」と「-み」が付加される派生過程の説明にも有効であることを示した．

参考文献

Allen, Margaret (1978) *Morphological Investigations*, Doctoral dissertation, University of Connecticut, Storrs.

Hagiwara, Hiroko, Yoko Sugioka, Takane Ito, Mitsuru Kawamura and Jun-ichi Shiota (1999) "Neurolinguistic Evidence for Rule-Based Nominal Suffixation," *Language* 75, 739-763.

Kiparsky, Paul (1982) "From Cyclic Phonology to Lexical Phonology," *The Structure of Phonological Representations (Part I)*, ed. by Harry van der Hulst and Norval Smith, 131-175, Foris, Dordrecht.

Kubozono, Haruo (1996) "Syllable and Accent in Japanese: Evidence from Loanword Accentuation,"『音声学会会報』第 211 号，71-82.

Kubozono, Haruo (2008) "Japanese Accent," *The Oxford Handbook of Japanese Linguistics*, ed. by Shigeru Miyagawa and Mamoru Saito, 165-191, Oxford University Press, Oxford.

窪薗晴夫・太田聡 (1998)『音韻構造とアクセント』研究社，東京．

松崎寛・河野俊之 (2010)『日本語教育能力検定試験に合格するための音声23』アルク，東京．

太田聡 (1992)「可能な派生を制限する 2 つの原理：非該当・最小努力の原理」『英語と英米文学』第 27 号，11-32.

太田聡 (2009)「「〜する人［もの］を表す接尾辞 -or について」『近代英語研究』第 25 号，127-133.

太田聡 (2010)「日本の地名のアクセント型とラテン語アクセント規則との不思議な関係について」『異文化研究』第 4 巻，1-14.

Pinker, Steven (1999) *Words and Rules: The Ingredients of Language*, Basic Books, New York.

島村礼子 (2002)「語を作る仕組み：形態論 2」大津由紀雄ほか編『言語研究入門』89-101, 研究社，東京．

Siegel, Dorothy (1974) *Topics in English Morphology*, Doctoral dissertation, MIT. [Published 1980, Garland, New York.]

Sugioka, Yoko (1984) *Interaction of Derivational Morphology and Syntax in Japanese and English*, Doctoral dissertation, University of Chicago, Chicago. [Published 1986, Garland, New York.]

辞典類

岩波書店辞書編集部編 (1999)『逆引き広辞苑　第五版対応』岩波書店, 東京.

松村明編 (2006)『大辞林　第三版』三省堂, 東京.

NHK 放送文化研究所編 (1998)『NHK 日本語発音アクセント辞典　新版』日本放送出版協会, 東京.

『日本語活用形辞書』(ejj.weblio.jp/cat/dictionary/nhgkt)

日本国語大辞典第二版編集委員会・小学館国語辞典編集部編 (2000-2002)『日本国語大辞典　第二版』小学館, 東京.

新村出編 (1998)『広辞苑　第五版』岩波書店, 東京.

Walker, John (1983) *The Rhyming Dictionary of the English Language*, Revised and Enlarged Edition with Supplement, Routledge & Kegan Paul, London.

Motorola は，混成か接尾辞付加か[*]

本間　猛

首都大学東京

1. 導入

Motorola は，車載の無線機や携帯電話などを作っているアメリカの会社である．この会社の社名である Motorola という語について，窪薗（2008）では，混成語としている．しかしながら，Motorola 社のホームページには，下のような記述がある．

(1) Birth of the Motorola brand
Paul Galvin wanted a brand name for Galvin Manufacturing Corporation's new car radio something memorable. He created the name "Motorola" to suggest sound in motion (from "motor" and the then-popular suffix "ola"). The Motorola brand name became so well-known that Galvin Manufacturing Corporation later changed its name to Motorola, Inc.

つまり，Motorola という語は，motor という語に -ola という接尾辞を付加して作り出したものであるとしているのだ．窪薗（2008）の混成語説と Motorola 社自身が主張する接尾辞付加説とは，どちらが正しいのであろうか．

この論文では，Motorola の由来としては，接尾辞付加説のほうが妥当であることを主張する．さらに，新語創成（neologism）における接尾辞付加の役割について論じる．

---

[*] この論文は，本間（2010）に加筆修正したものである．

2. 混成 (blending) とは何か？

混成語とは，次のような語のことである．

(2) 混成語の例（窪薗 (1998: 58)）
 a. ゴジラ＜ゴリラ＋クジラ
 b. キャベジン＜キャベツ＋ニンジン
 c. バイナラ＜バイバイ＋サヨナラ
 d. バトポン＜バトミントン＋ピンポン

ゴジラは，いわずとしれた怪獣のことで，ゴリラとクジラが元になっているとされる．また，キャベジンは，胃腸薬の名前である．キャベジン[1]は，その成分の1つであるS-メチルメチオニンスルホニウムクロライドが，もともとキャベツの絞り汁のなかから発見されたことにちなんで名付けられている．バイナラは，萩本欽一のテレビ番組「欽ちゃんのどこまでやるの」の中で使われていた言葉で，斉藤清六のギャグである．バトポンは，バトミントンの羽と卓球（ピンポン）のラケットに似た道具を使って行うスポーツの名前である．

これらの例からわかるように，混成とは，似たような意味を持つ2つの単語から新しい語を作り出す過程である．最初の単語の前半部分と2つ目の単語の後半部分を結合することで新しい語が作られる．

窪薗 (2008: 131) によれば，混成という過程には，次のような3つの特性がある．

(3) 混成語の特性
 a. 意味のよく似た2語が混成する．
 b. 1語の前半ともう1つの語の後半が結合する．

---

[1] 「キャベジン」についても，この語が混成語であるか否かについては，議論の余地がある．「キャベジン」の開発元は，興和株式会社であるが，この会社のサイト (http://www.kowa.co.jp/news/2010/cabagin_50th.pdf) では，次のような記述が見られる．「製品名の由来は，キャベツに含まれるという意味の「cabbage in（キャベッジ，イン）」を転じてキャベジンという名称になりました．」（2016年8月現在）「キャベッジ，イン」が元で，「キャベジン」が混成語だとすると，「キャベジン」が全体で4モーラの長さを持つことが，説明できない．

c. 前半を残す語から n モーラ採る場合には，もう 1 つの語の n + 1 モーラ目へと転移する．

　この過程を混成 (blending) と呼ぶのは，(3a) の特性のためだ．コーヒーや紅茶，お酒などでもブレンドという言葉が用いられることがあるが，この場合も，似たものを混ぜ合わせる．2 つの同義語や類義語などを混ぜ合わせて混成語が作られるのである．2 番目の (3b) の特性については，窪薗 (2008) に詳しく論じてあるので，そちらを参照してほしい．

　ここで，特に注目しておきたいのは，3 番目の (3c) の特徴である．これは，単語の長さに関する法則であり，言い換えると，「出来上がった混成語は，元になった単語のうち，2 番目の単語と同じ長さになる」ということだ．(2) の例を見てみよう．(2a) では，ゴリラもクジラもともに 3 モーラなので，どちらの長さにそろえたのか判定不能だが，(2b) では，キャベツが 3 モーラなのに対して，ニンジンは 4 モーラであり，混成語のキャベジンは，後半要素のニンジンと同じ長さで，4 モーラある．バトポンは，後半要素のピンポンの長さ (4 モーラ) である．

　日本語では，単語の長さを測る際にモーラという単位を使う．しかし，英語では，単語の長さを測る際，音節という単位が重要であることがわかっている (窪薗 (1995) や 窪薗 (2002) などを参照)．

　(4)　英語の混成語 (窪薗 (1995: 143))
　　a. smog < smoke + fog
　　b. snark < snake + shark
　　c. spork < spoon + fork
　　d. brunch < breakfast + lunch
　　e. lupper < lunch + supper

1 音節語同士なら，出来上がる混成語も 1 音節語になる (4a-c)．後半要素が，1 音節語の場合は，前半要素が，2 音節語であっても，出来上がる混成語は，1 音節語になる (4d)．後半要素が，2 音節語の場合は，前半要素が 1 音節語でも，出来上がる混成語は，2 音節語になる (4e)．

　日本語の混成語も英語の混成語も，さらには，ほかの言語の混成語も扱うために，(3) を (5) のように言い直すことにする．特に混成語の長さに関

する法則 (3c) が，(5c) のように言い換えられた点に注意してほしい．

(5) 混成語の特性（改訂版）
    a. 意味のよく似た 2 語が混成する．
    b. 1 語の前半ともう 1 つの語の後半が結合する．
    c. 前半要素から n 番目まで採る場合には，後半要素の n + 1 番目へと転移する．ただし，長さを測る単位は，言語によって定められる．（例えば，日本語では，モーラが，英語では，音節が用いられる．窪薗 (1995: 178-189)）結果として出来上がった混成語の長さは，後半要素の元の長さと一致する．[2]

3. Motorola の意味特性

次に (5) の混成語の特性に基づいて，Motorola ついて考察する．窪薗 (2008) は，Motorola は，motorcar と Victrola の混成語だと考えている．

(6) Motorola < motorcar + Victrola（窪薗 (2008: 136)）

この Motorola の謎を解く鍵は，Victrola にある．この節では，まず，Victrola の成り立ちについて，考察してみる．Victrola とは，The Victor Talking Machine Company という会社が開発した蓄音機のことである．Victor という会社の作った製品なのだから，Victrola は，Victor という語に -ola という接尾辞がついてできた語であるといえそうである．もともと Victor は，2 音節であったが，接尾辞 -ola の付加によって，なぜか 2 音節目の母音を失い，1 音節分になってしまったようである．母音が脱落する理由は，今のところあまりはっきりとしたことがいえない．

Motorola 社の社名 Motorola は，もともと社名ではなく，この会社の製品の名前であった．社名の由来となった Motorola という製品は，そもそも，自動車に搭載可能なラジオであった．自動車（motorcar）に搭載可能な Victrola のようなモノという意味合いがこめられていた可能性は，おおいにあ

---

[2] 窪薗 (1995) や窪薗 (2002) などで指摘のある通り，英語の混成語の場合は，音節の途中で切り取られて，混成する場合もあるが，その場合でも，出来上がった混成語の長さは，第 2 要素の単語の音節数と一致する．

る．もしそうであったとすれば，(5a) の混成語の意味特性と照らしてみると，Motorola が混成語であるかどうか微妙である．つまり，Motorcar と Victrola が意味的によく似ていると判断するのが難しいということだ．Motorcar は，自動車であり，Victrola は，オーディオ機器である．機械であるという意味では，類似した意味を持つといえるかもしれないが，これは，十分類似しているといえないのではないだろうか？ 以上の考察から，Motorola が motorcar と Victrola との混成だとすると，意味特性上問題がありそうである．次節では，Motorola という語の長さが問題について考察してみる．

4. 混成語の長さの法則と Motorola

　この混成語の長さの法則 (5c) をふまえて，Motorola の成り立ちを考えてみよう．もし，窪薗 (2008) の主張通り，Motorola が motorcar と Victrola の混成だとすると Motorola は，(5c) の混成語の長さの法則にしたがっていないことになる．後半要素の Victrola は，3 音節なのに，Motorola は，4 音節だからだ．(5c) の混成語の長さの法則によれば，出来上がった混成語は，後半要素の長さと同じになるはずである．したがって，Motorola は，混成語であったとしても，あくまでも，例外的混成語であることになる．

5. 新語創成と接尾辞

　Motorola を motorcar と Victrola の混成によってできた語ではなく，motor + ola のように接尾辞が付いた構造であると考えると，問題になるのは，接尾辞 -ola の地位である．そこで，各種辞書やインターネットを用いて，-ola で終わる単語を集めてみた．下のようなものが見つかった．どの語も 20 世紀初頭に成立したようである．

(7)　-ola で終わる単語[3]
    a. crapola: 名詞．意味 (vulgar slang) Rubbish; nonsense. 語源 crap + -ola (probably modeled on trade names like Shinola, a brand of shoe polish). 出典 AHD.
    b. Crayola: 名詞．意味 a US make of crayons (= coloured pencils or sticks of soft coloured chalk or wax) which have been popular with children for many years and are sold in boxes of different sizes in many countries. Binney & Smith of Easton, Pennsylvania, have produced them since 1903. 出典 OALD.
    c. drugola: 名詞．意味 Bribery with payment or kickbacks made by using illegal drugs as the medium of exchange. 語源 [drug + (pay) ola]. 出典 TFD.
    d. granola: 名詞．意味 a US breakfast food that is a mixture of whole grains, fruits, seeds and nuts (called muesli in British English). It is eaten in a bowl with milk and sometimes sugar. 出典 OALD.
    e. payola: 名詞．意味 the practice of bribing someone to use their influence or position to promote a particular product or interest : if a record company spends enough money on payola, it can make any record a hit. 語源 1930s: from pay + -ola as in Victrola, the name of a make of gramophone. 出典 NOAD.
    f. Pianola: 名詞．意味 (trademark) a piano equipped to be played automatically using a piano roll. 語源 late 19th cent.: apparently a diminutive of piano. 出典 NOAD.
    g. Rock-Ola: 名詞．意味 イギリスの Jukebox のメーカーの名前．出典 TFD.
    h. Shinola: 名詞．意味 (trademark) a brand of boot polish. 語源

---

[3] 出典情報．AHD = American Heritage Dictionary. OALD = Oxford Advanced Learner's Dictionary. NOAD = New Oxford American Dictionary. TFD = The Free Dictionary (http://encyclopedia.thefreedictionary.com/)

early 20th cent.: from shine + -ola. 出典 NOAD.

(7) を眺めてみると，その多くはブランド名や製品名である．ブランド名や製品名でない語（crapola, drugola, payola）は，どちらかというとマイナスな意味合いが含まれているようだ．まず，この点から考察してみる．

payola の語源を見てみよう．payola は，New Oxford American Dictionary（NOAD）によれば，pay に接尾辞の -ola を付けることによって生じたとされる．さらに，この接尾辞の -ola は，Victrola の -ola であるという．Victrola は，上述の通り，Victor 社の開発した蓄音機である．音楽業界の影響力のある人物や放送局などに賄賂を支払うことによって，番組で取り上げてもらい，楽曲を放送してもらう行為を payola と称したのだ．The American Heritage Dictionary of the English Language（AHD）には，payola の成り立ちとして，"Probably pay(off) + -ola, suff.; see crapola." という記述が見られる．

では，次に crapola について，見てみよう．AHD には，その成り立ちとして，crap + -ola (probably modeled on trade names like Shinola, a bland of shoe polish) を示している．その意味が，rubbish や nonsense となるのは，crap のせいである．この語は，AHD には，下のように記述されている．

(8) AHD による crap の記述
Noun (Vulgar Slang.)
1. Excrement.
2. An act of defecating.
3. Foolish, deceitful, or boastful language.
4. Cheap or shoddy material.
5. Miscellaneous or disorganized items; clutter.
6. Insolent talk or behavior.
Intransitive Verb. crapped, crapping, craps
To defecate.
[Middle English crappe, chaff, from Old French crappe, from Medieval Latin crappa, perhaps of Germanic origin.]

つまり，crap だけでも，十分に rubbish や nonsense という意味がある．その crap にさらに，接尾辞の -ola を加えたのは，なぜだろう．これは，AHD の記述がヒントになる．AHD によれば，crapola は Shinola がモデルになったのだ．この Shinola は，靴墨である．この語を用いた次のようなスラングがある．

(9) You don't (or He doesn't) know shit from Shinola.

多少長くなるが，このスラングについて，The Free Dictionary[4] (TFD) から引用しておく．

(10) "You don't know shit from Shinola"
Shinola was immortalized in colloquial English by the phrase "You don't (or He doesn't) know shit from Shinola" which first became widely popular during World War II. Aside from being an amusing bit of alliteration, the phrase implies that the subject is stupid or woefully ignorant. Shit and Shinola, while superficially similar in appearance, are entirely distinct in their function; only one is good for polishing shoes, and anyone who fails to distinguish one from the other must be ignorant or of low. Similar expressions include, doesn't know his ass from his elbow or Sir Henry Wood's doesn't know his brass from his woodwind. (from TFD).

次に，drugola を見てみよう．TFD には，drugola の成り立ちとして，drug + (pay) ola を示している．これは，おそらく，drugola という語が，payola をモデルとして成立したということを表しているのであろう．AHD にも，同様の記述がある．

ここまで，まとめておく．どうやら，-ola には，3つの起源があるようだ．1つは，Shinola を元にしたもので，crapola がこれに続く．もう1つは，Victrola を元にして，payola や drugola を生んだ．最後は，ブランド名などを作る接尾辞だ．

ここまでをまとめて，接尾辞 -ola をその意味にしたがって分類すると，

---

[4] The Free Dictionary (http://encyclopedia.thefreedictionary.com/)

下のようになる.

(11) a. -ola (その1): とるにたらないものを表す接尾辞
例: crapola
b. -ola (その2): 賄賂を表す接尾辞
例: drugola, payola
c. -ola (その3): ブランド名や製品名を作るための接尾辞
例: Crayola, granola, Pianola, Rock-Ola, Shinola, Victrola, Motorola

この節をしめくくるにあたり，(7) の単語に使われている -ola が本当に接尾辞と呼べるかどうか検討してみる．まず，Crayola だが，これは，crayon の一種なので，この語については，-ola が接尾辞であるとは，いえないかもしれない．Shinola がもし，shine に -ola を付加して作られたとすると，Shin の部分の発音が問題になる．どうやら，Shin の部分は shine と同じ発音であったようなので，-ola は，接尾辞であるといえそうだ．そのほかの単語 (crapola, drugola, granola, payola, Pianola, Rock-Ola) については，接尾辞であると考えて，よさそうだ．ただし，granola や Pianola では，多少の調整が行われているとする必要がある．

まず，granola だが，これは，grain + ola なので，綴り字を調整した上で，発音も変えてある．つまり，grain では，強勢のある母音で，rain と韻を踏むが，granola の第一音節は，強勢が失われ，弱母音で発音されている．次に，pianola であるが，ここれは，piano + ola で，語幹の終わりと接尾辞の先頭の母音が重なり，1つの母音として発音されている．このことについては，さらに詳しく考察してみる必要があるので，ここでは，これ以上，踏み込まないこととする．

ここまでをまとめてみる．Motorola や Victrola などに使われている -ola は，20世紀初頭に英語に導入された接尾辞といえる．その意味は，さまざまで，少なくとも (11) に示したように3つある．

6. 接尾辞創成

前節では，-ola が，20世紀初頭に英語に導入された接尾辞であると主張

したが，このように接尾辞が言語の中に新たに導入されること（接尾辞創成）は，ほかにも例があるのだろうか．以下で，接尾辞創成と思われる例を英語から1つと日本語2つ取りあげて考察してみるとにする．

6.1.　-ex と -tex

Thornton (2000) は，英語の商標などに見られる -ex と -tex という形式 (formative) について考察している．その上で，前者は，接尾辞であるが，後者は，textile という語の短縮形であり，短縮複合語 (shortened compound) の後半要素になっていると結論付けている．-tex については，別の機会に考察することにして，以下で，-ex という形式について，考えてみよう．Thornton (2000) では，この形式に関して，その綴り字，音韻論的な側面，語幹の所属する語彙層 (strata) の側面，統語的側面，意味的側面などについて詳細に検討している．

綴り字については，語幹の標準的な綴りから逸脱する場合が多いことが示されている．例えば，Kleenex は，clean に -ex を付加したものだが，語幹の標準的な綴り clean ではなく，Kleen が使われている．これは，多くの商標でよくおこることである．具体例については，Thornton (2000) を参照されたい．

音韻論的な側面として，Thornton (2000) は，語幹が英語の固有語の場合，音韻的最小語 (minimal word, cf. McCarthy and Prince (1986: 60)) になるように切り取りが起こるとしている．英語の場合，音韻的最小語は，重音節である．

(12)　save＞savex
　　　pure＞purex
　　　clean＞Kleenex
　　　correct＞cor＞Korex
　　　blister＞blist＞blistex
　　　wind＞windex

接尾辞 -ex の付加には，語彙層の影響もある．(12) で見たように，英語の固有語彙層 (native stratum) では，語幹が最小語である必要がある．しかし，語幹がラテン語起源の場合は，この最小語制約が当てはまらなくなるよ

うだ.

(13) terminate＞terminex
vagina＞vaginex
femina＞feminex
resin＞resinex

次は，統語的な側面だが，語幹は，名詞でも，形容詞でも，動詞でも良いようで，はっきりした制限がわからない．

(14) 名詞：blister＞blistex
形容詞：pure＞purex
動詞：to correct＞korex

次に，意味的側面を見てみよう．(15) に -ex が使われている具体例をその意味によって分類したものを示す．分類は，Thornton (2000) による．Thornton は，この -ex という接尾辞が実際の綴り字では，-e のかわりに様々な母音の文字が使われる変異があるとしている．

(15) -Vx が付加された語の語幹の意味による分類 (Thornton (2000: 115))
   a. Action performed with the product, or quality resulting from usage of the product:
      e.g., Kleenex, korex, purex (detergent), savex, terminex, tintex
   b. Object or body part of being to which the product must applied:
      e.g., blistex, cutex, feminax, pirlax, sinex Vicks (＜sinus), termex (＜termite), vaginex, windex (＜window)
   c. Quality fo the product:
      e.g., bitrex, purex (salt), primex
   d. Substance present in the product:
      e.g., clorox, resinex
   e. Some element present in the situation in which the product is used:

e.g., pyrex (heat resistant glass, from Greek *pyr* "fire"), wind-ex (wind direction indicators)

以上，英語には，-ex という形式が，さまざまな商標に用いられていることがわかった．この -ex という形式が，現代英語の共時文法の中で接尾辞として働いているかどうかについては，さらに詳しく議論する必要があるが，接尾辞創成の一例になる可能性があると考えてよさそうだ．

6.2. アムラーの「ラー」

次に日本語の「ラー」について考察してみる．インターネットを利用して探してみたところ，下のような語が見つかった．

(16) 接尾辞「ラー」
 アムラー：歌手安室奈美恵のファッションを真似た女性
 アララー：安室奈美恵に真似ているが，なりきれていない女性
 エハラー：スピリチュアルカウンセラー江原啓之を信奉する人
 カミラー：会話の最中に言葉をよく噛む（言葉が詰まる，つっかえる）人
 クチャラー：食べ物を「クチャクチャ」と音を立てて食べる人
 ケチャラー：ケチャップが好きな人
 シノラー：タレント篠原ともえのファッションを取り入れている人
 シャネラー：シャネルのブランド商品を好んで身につける人
 シュノラー：収納好きな人
 セメラー：平安時代の陰陽師である安倍晴明（あべせいめい）のファン
 ネバラー：ネバネバした食べ物が好きな人
 マヨラー：マヨネーズが好きな人

そもそもの起源は「アムラー」にあるようだ．1995 年ころから，使われ始めたようである．アムラーの場合は，amuro の最後の母音を取り除き，子音 /r/ までの「語幹」に英語の -er を付けたと説明ができなくもないが，(16) にあげた例には子音で終わる語幹に -er を付けたと考えられない例も

ある．例えば，カミラーやクチャラー，ケチャラー，シノラー，シュノラー，セメラー，ネバラー，マヨラーがそうだ．これらの例では，語幹（もしくは，短縮された語幹）にラーという接尾辞を付加したと考えた方が，合点が行く．

6.3. オバタリアン

窪薗 (2008) は，オバタリアンを混成の例だとしている．

(17) X- バタリアン
    オバタリアン＜おばさん + バタリアン
    ジベタリアン＜地べた + バタリアン
    ジモタリアン＜地元 + バタリアン

オバタリアンは，漫画家堀田かつひこの同名の4コマ漫画に登場する中年女性のことである．中年女性の中には，無神経で世間に迷惑をかけるものもおり，そのような女性たちを風刺し，漫画に描いた．バタリアンとは1986年に公開されたホラー映画のタイトルであり，日本の映画配給会社東宝東和が英語の battalion（大隊，大群の意）という言葉を元に付けたもの．原題は *Night of the Living Dead* である．

(17) にあげた3つの語は，混成であるとすると，混成語の長さの法則 (5c) に違反していることになる．つまり，混成語であれば，出来上がった語の長さが後半要素の長さと一致するはずであるが，(17) にあげたどの単語も，全体で6モーラあり，後半要素のバタリアンの長さ，5モーラより長い．

(17) の3つの語には接尾辞タリアンが含まれると考えることにすると，上で述べた問題はなくなる．つまり，(18) のように分析するのである．語幹（前半要素）の最初の2モーラと接尾辞のタリアンが接合してできていると考えるのだ．

(18) X- タリアン
    オバタリアン＜おば（さん）+ タリアン
    ジベタリアン＜じべ（た）+ タリアン
    ジモタリアン＜じも（と）+ タリアン

実は，日本語では，語幹から2モーラを取り出し，そこに接尾辞を付加

するプロセスが，複数存在する．Poser（1990）が，Hypocoristic Formation と呼んだ「チャン」を付けるプロセスなどがその例だ．

(19) Hypocoristic Formation (Poser (1990: 81))
　　　akityan＜akira 昭
　　　arityan＜arisa（＜English Alicia）
　　　mayutyan＜mayumi 真弓
　　　osatyan＜osamu 治
　　　makotyan＜ma(＋)koto 真琴
　　　wasatyan＜wa＋sabu＋roo 和三郎

以上，接尾辞創成の例と考えられる現象を英語から1つ，日本語から2つ取り上げて，考察した．

7. まとめ

Motorola は，motorcar と Victrola の混成ではなく，motor に接尾辞 -ola を付加したものであるとすると，この語の成り立ちが端的に捉えられる．さらに，接尾辞創成と考えられる現象を -ola の例の他に，3つ指摘した．今後，接尾辞創成の例をさらに，収集してみる必要がある．

参考文献

本間猛（2010）「Motorola は，混成か接尾辞付加か」『人文学報』第427号，37-46．
窪薗晴夫（1995）『語形成と音韻構造』くろしお出版，東京．
窪薗晴夫（1998）『音声学・音韻論』くろしお出版，東京．
窪薗晴夫（2002）『新語はこうして造られる』岩波書店，東京．
窪薗晴夫（2008）『ネーミングの言語学――ハリー・ポッターからドラゴンボールまで――』開拓社，東京．
McCarthy, John J. and Alan S. Prince (1986) "Prosodic Morphology," ms.
Poser, William (1990) "Evidence for foot structure in Japanese," *Language* 66, 78-105.
Thornton, Anna M. (2000) "On *-ex* and *-tex*," *Extragramatical and Marginal Morphology*, ed. by Doleschal, Ursula and Anna M. Thorton, 107-126, Lincoma Europa, Muenchen.

キラキラネームは音韻的にキラキラしているのか？*
―名前と一般語の頻度分布比較による予備的考察―

北原　真冬

早稲田大学・上智大学

1. はじめに

　本稿は，「キラキラネーム」と呼ばれるものも含む，最近の子どもの名付けについて，その音韻的側面の考察を試みるものである．「光宙（ピカチュウ）」や「希空（ノア）」に代表される，伝統的人名とは異なる一群の名前は，2000年前後から様々なメディア上で盛んに取り上げられるようになり，キラキラネームと呼ばれるようになった．一般的な定義としては伊東（2015）にあるように，「これまでの常識とは異なる漢字の読み方をしたり，これまでの日本語にはなかった音の響きを持っていたりする難読の名前」と言うのが妥当なところであろう．

　耳目を集めるのは，この定義の前半，特に「常識とは異なる」＋「難読」と言う部分であり，本当にその名前を持った人物が実在するかどうか確かめられないまま，珍妙さと奇天烈さにおいて極端な例がよく俎上に上がる．漢字表記からは想像しがたい名前があることは，大学教員として学生の名前に触れていると確かに日々感じられる．しかし，漢字表記が意表を突いている面に気を取られて，名前の持つ音の響き自体が変わってきたかどうかについては，直感ではいささか判断が難しい．

　そこで，定義後半の「音の響き」と言う部分についてどんなアプローチが

---

[*] 本研究のアイデアの萌芽段階から，慶應義塾大学の深澤はるか教授とは様々な議論を重ね，形を整えることができた．深く感謝する次第である．また東京学芸大学の白勢彩子准教授からも貴重なアドバイスをいただいた．もちろん本稿に残る間違いは全て筆者の責任である．なお本研究は，科学研究費補助金（課題番号25370443）の助成を受けている．

可能であるか考えを巡らせることにする．ただ，珍奇なものばかりを集めてもサンプリングとして偏ってしまい，音韻論的に意味のある分析にはなりにくい．本稿では，実在する名前を毎年約 6000 から 1 万名分調査している，明治安田生命（2004-2015）「名前ランキング」の「読み方ベスト 50」を元データとする．そして，名前の持つ音韻的空間が一般語のそれに対して異なるか否か，異なるとすれば，どのように特徴付けられるかについて解析を試みる．なお，一般語に関しては天野・近藤（1999）を参照した．

2. 先行研究

　伊東（2015）は，キラキラネームの「キラキラ感」について，様々な考察を述べているが，「柔らかい音が多い」などの印象論が中心で実証的な議論に乏しい．しかしながら，いわゆる名付け本にある「名付けアンケート」では「名前の音の響き」と「漢字の画数」が最も重視されることを報告している．小林（2009）でも，名付けたい名前を音で思い浮かべ，後から漢字を当てはめる「音から決めるタイプ」が現在最も有力な名付けの方法であると論じている．しかし，何を手がかりとして音を思い浮かべ，何を基準としてその音を選ぶのかについての考察は全くない．佐藤（2007）は，名前における漢字の使用法についての歴史的な考察が中心となっていて，音に関する記述はほとんどなく「今では，快いイメージを喚起するということに命名の力点が置かれているようである」と述べるに留まっている．黒川（2009）は，筆者が探し得た中では唯一，音韻的な考察を中心とした書籍である．しかし，50 音の各行に対する音象徴的なイメージと調音法をゆるやかに結びつけ，例えば「A 音は，口を開ける心地よい開放感がある音．A 音の名前を口にした人は，その持ち主に明るさや開放的な印象をもちます．」というような記述を連ねている．

　ここまで見てきた論考とは大きく異なり，キラキラネームに対して工学的なアプローチを取った山西ほか（2016）という論考も存在する．サポートベクターマシンという機械学習の手法を適用して，人間が直感的に「キラキラネーム」と判定している要因について，言語的特徴として取り出せるものを探っている．しかし，結局のところ言語的特徴として取り出されたのは，(1) 漢字の個数，(2) 読みの発音数，(3) 同一漢字の複数回使用，(4) 異体

漢字の使用，(5) 漢字の音訓読みにない読み方の使用，(6) 漢字の総画数，(7) 漢字と性別の不一致，(8) 読み方がカタカナ単語として存在，の8つであり，純粋に音韻的な特徴と言えるものはない．

　先行研究について筆者の知り得た範囲では，親が名付けという行為に込める思いや，それを規定する社会，世相，流行，意識といったものに関する文化論的な記述は非常に多く，上記の文献でも至る所に顔を出している．松浦・筒井 (2015) では，救命救急室を深夜に訪れるのは「キラキラネーム児」が有意に多い，と批判的にも受け取れる視点を提示している．ネット上の匿名掲示板やブログへの匿名コメントなどの言説を見ると，キラキラネームに対してはかなり辛辣な意見が多い．一方，言語学的には，佐藤 (2007) や小林 (2009) のように，漢字の読み方や「当て字」に関する歴史的な考察が実証的研究の中心となっていて，「キラキラ」の音韻論を展開している論考には残念ながら出会えなかった．従って，本研究の手法はまったくの手探りから始まったものである．次節でその手探りの過程を順次説明する．

3. データの整理と解析方法

　明治安田生命のサイトに公表されている「名前ランキング」には，「名前ベスト100」，「読み方ベスト50」，「人気の漢字ベスト25」という3つの項目について，2004年から2015年までのデータが公開されている．2015年の調査要領によると，「個人保険・個人年金保険の保有契約 約1,134万件を調査．うち2015年生まれの男の子4,278人，女の子4,122人」が2015年分のデータとして集計されている．「名前ベスト100」は実際のところ「名前の表記ベスト100」であって，ある表記がどのような読みに対応しているかは明らかにされていない．「人気の漢字ベスト25」も当然のことながら，単漢字として表記に現れるものを集計しただけであり，音韻にはあまり関係がない．一方，「読み方ベスト50」は漢字とは無関係に，読みの順位を人数，占率（年度ごとの男女それぞれの調査人数における比率）と共に集計している．具体的には以下の表1のようになっている．

順位	読み方	人数	占率
1位	ハルト	119人	2.78%
2位	ソウタ	83人	1.94%
3位	ユウト	77人	1.80%
4位	ハルキ	58人	1.36%
5位	ユイト	50人	1.17%

表1. 2015年男の子の名前，読み方ベスト50のサンプル

このような一覧表が年度ごとに男女それぞれ50位まで公開され，各年度の調査数と共に示されている．本研究では2004年から2015年までの12年分を使用したが，各年度とも同順位となる名前を複数個含むため，年度ごとのサンプル数は50を越えることがある（例えば，同率で49位となる名前が3個あれば，その年度の名前の総数は51個となる）．そのため，12年分の名前の総数は1266であった．なお，表1で第1位の「ハルト」は前年度も1位，「ソウタ」は前年度3位，というように年度をまたいで上位に現れ続ける名前は多数あり，読み方の総異なり語数は204であった．

　これらの名前をカタカナで見渡していると，果たしてこれらは十分「キラキラ」しているのだろうか，という疑念が湧く．実際，あくまで主観的ではあるが，各年度の50位までに現れる名前は，2節で概観した文献が取り上げたものほどには，斬新あるいは常識はずれな響きを持つとは感じられない．しかし，これまでのキラキラネームに関する論考は，漢字の常識的な音訓から乖離した読みが耳目を集めるがために，それにばかり焦点を当てるというバイアスに取り憑かれている．本稿では，音の響きについて「一般語の音韻パターン」と「名前の音韻パターン」の間になんらかの乖離があるのかを，あくまで客観的に検証すべきであると考えた．

　比較すべき音韻パターンとして本稿で取り上げるのは，(i) 音節の軽重，(ii) 子音・母音の連鎖，(iii) 子音セット，の3つである．(i) は音韻論においてはおなじみの基礎的分析単位であり，対象を（子音）+（拗音）+母音からなる軽音節（L）と，軽音節に特殊拍（撥音，促音，長音，二重母音の後部要素）を加えた重音節（H）の2種類の単位の連鎖として分析する．(ii) も，子音（c），母音（v）の連鎖として捉えるという非常にありふれた方法である．本稿では，(i) の単位をさらに細かく切り分けた下位の単位につい

て分析を行う，という点を重視して，撥音，促音，長音を特殊拍甲類（M），二重母音の後部要素を特殊拍乙類（H）として cv 表記とは区別した．これは，日本語の二重母音は真性の二重母音とは言いがたい（御園・平坂(2008)）という意見や，アクセントの配置から見てその後部要素の独立性は低い（田窪ほか(2004)）という意見もあることによる．また，いわゆる拗音（g）を子音とは別の記号として取り入れた．最後に (iii) は母音要素を全て取り除いた残り，ということである．例えば「ハルト」から取り出せるのは /h-r-t/ という子音セットであるが，同じセットを持つものに「ヒロト」や「ヒロタ」がある．また，子音の順序について取り払ってしまうことも可能であったが，順序を入れ替えた子音セットが名前においてはそれほど上位に現れなかったため，今回は考察から外した（順序を取り払うと「テルハ」や「ホタル」も「ハルト」と同じ子音セットということになる）．以上の分析単位の定義をまとめて表2に示す．なお，(iii) 子音セットは，基本的に前川 (2006) にある「日本語話ことばコーパス」の分節音表記に依拠しているが，口蓋化の記号 [j] と鼻濁音の記述を省略した．

(i) 音節の軽重	L(ight): {v, cv, cgv} H(eavy): {vM, vH, cvM, cvH, cgvM, cgvH}
(ii) 子音・母音連鎖	c: {k, g, s, z, S, Z, t, d, C, T, n, h, b, F, v, p, m, r, w} v: {a, i, u, e, o} g: {y} M: {N, Q, V}, V: {aa, ii, uu, ee, oo, ei, ou の後部要素} H: {ai, oi, ui, au の後部要素}
(iii) 子音セット	k, g, s, z, t, d, n, h, b, p, m, r, w: 通常のローマ字通り S:「シ，シャ，シュ，シェ，ショ」の子音部分 Z:「ジ，ジャ，ジュ，ジェ，ジョ」の子音部分 C:「チ，チャ，チュ，チェ，チョ」の子音部分 T:「ツ，ツァ，ツィ，ツェ，ツォ」の子音部分 F:「フ，ファ，フィ，フェ，フォ」の子音部分 v:「ヴァ，ヴィ，ヴ，ヴェ，ヴォ」の子音部分 N:「ン」 Q:「ッ」 y:「ヤ，ユ，ヨ，ャ，ュ，ョ」の子音部分

表2. 分析単位の定義

以上のような道具立てで名前データと一般語データを分析した．名前データは，それぞれのパターンについて表1の「人数」欄にある数値を年度をまたいで全て合計して頻度とした．また，男女の名前データは特に区別せずにすべて結合して用いた．これは，音節やcvパターンなど抽象度が高い分析において大まかな全体像を見ることを第一義としたことによる．一般語は天野・近藤 (1999) にある辞書データから名詞のみを取り出し，朝日新聞における出現頻度データと共に用いた．

4. 結果

まずは，(i) 音節の軽重（HL）パターンについての頻度上位10パターンを表3に示す．名前データについては，この10パターンで尽きており，これ以外の形はない．一方，一般語データでは226パターンが取り出されたが，その中の頻度上位10パターンを示す．

名前データ			一般語データ		
パターン	頻度	例	パターン	頻度	例
LLL	13357	タケル	HH	15429376	向上
HL	10385	ケンタ	LL	8302680	カニ
LL	9477	ソラ	HL	7801049	端子
H	3425	リョウ	LH	7648966	砂糖
LH	1346	リオン	LLL	6798925	こころ
HH	1287	ユウセイ	HLL	5496222	干拓
HLL	591	ユウスケ	H	3441261	本
LLH	173	コタロウ	LLH	2542460	学問
HLH	122	リンタロウ	LLLL	2467369	空梅雨
HLLL	82	リュウノスケ	L	1506258	気

表3. 音節のHLパターンの名前データおよび一般語データにおける上位10

表3から分かるように，名前データと一般語データでは順位が大きく異なる．そこで，まず一般語データのパターンで頻度順位の高いものをx軸に右から並べ，それぞれの頻度をy軸にプロットした上に，名前データの中で該当するパターンの頻度を重ねて表した．

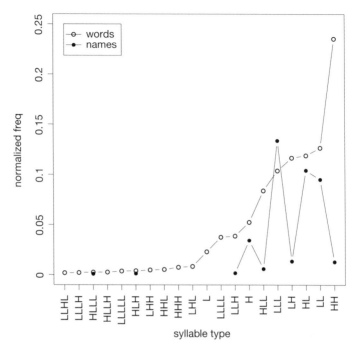

図 1. 頻度順位による一般語音節の HL パターン（x 軸）とその頻度（y 軸），および，名前における HL パターンの頻度

 逆に，名前の HL パターンの頻度順位に沿ってプロットした上に，一般語の中で該当するパターンの頻度を重ねてプロットしたものを図 2 に示す．

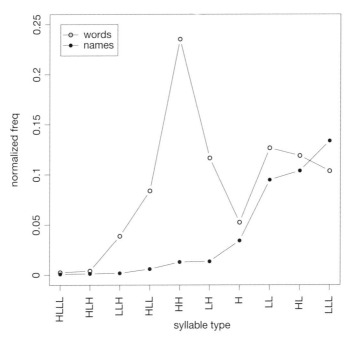

図 2. 頻度順位による名前の HL パターン（x 軸）とその頻度（y 軸），および，その順位において該当する一般語の HL パターンの頻度

なお，表 3 にあるように，頻度データは名前と一般語ではスケールが大きく異なるため，それぞれの延べ語数（名前は 99932 人分，一般語は 65609259 件）で割ったものを図の縦軸に取っている（以下の図も同様）．

(ii) cv パターン，および (iii) 子音セットの分析については，表を省略し，図 1, 2 と同様のグラフを以下に示す．

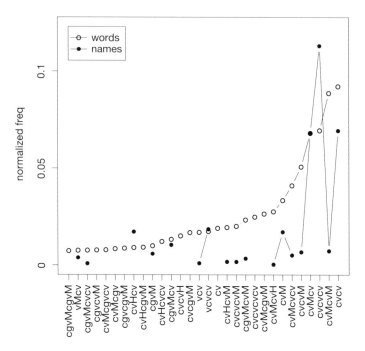

図 3. 頻度順位による一般語の cv パターン（x 軸）とその頻度（y 軸），および，その順位において該当する名前の cv パターンの頻度

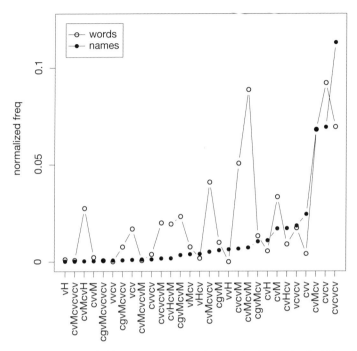

図 4. 頻度順位による名前の cv パターン（x 軸）とその頻度（y 軸），および，その順位において該当する一般語 cv パターンの頻度

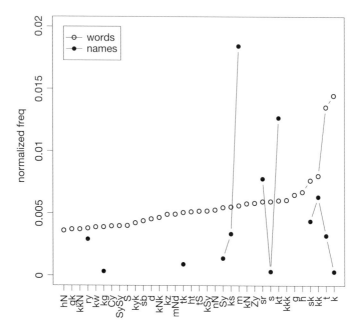

図5. 頻度順位による一般語の子音セットパターン (x 軸) とその頻度 (y 軸), および, その順位において該当する名前の子音セットパターンの頻度

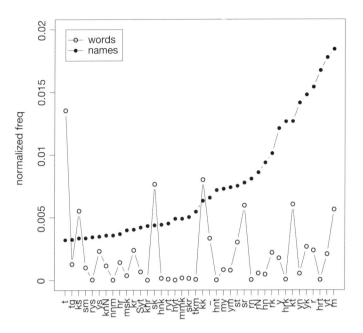

図6. 頻度順位による名前の子音セットパターン（x 軸）とその頻度（y 軸），および，その順位において該当する一般語の子音セットパターンの頻度

5. 考察

　表3および図1, 2に示した HL パターンの対照から観察できるのは，名前と一般語で順位が大きく異なることはもちろんだが，その分布が全く対応していないことである．図1に特によく現れているように，一般語の HL パターンの頻度は第1位の HH が飛び抜けていることを除けば，なだらかに右肩上がりとなっている．その順位に沿って名前データのパターンを並べると頻度は大きく上下に動き，決して一般語の分布に沿わない．名前の頻度分布から読み取れるように，軽音節（L）がおおむね支配的であり，重音節を含むものでは HL（例：ケンタ）だけが高位にある．

　図3, 4に示した cv パターンの対照は，HL パターンよりも現れるパターンの種類が多いため，名前と一般語の乖離がより強く現れている．すなわ

ち，片方を頻度順位に沿って並べると，もう片方が激しくギザギザな分布を取る．図4に現れている細かな差異に注目すると，例えば二重母音を含む cvH とそれ以外の特殊拍を含む cvM の対比は興味深い．cvH は「名前 > 一般語」であるのに対し，cvM では「一般語 > 名前」となっている．もちろんそれぞれの頻度データは母数に対しての比率であって，両者の大小関係は見かけ上のことに過ぎない．しかし，cvM と cvH というきわめて近い音節構造であっても，名前と一般語で分布が大きく異なることは，名前が一般語とは異なった音韻的空間に位置していることを示唆している．

　図5，6に示した子音セットにおいても，名前と一般語は鋭い対照を示している．名前に使われる高位の子音セットを見渡すと，/m/, /y/, /r/, /n/ を含むものが目立ち，伊東 (2015) が指摘したように「やわらかい」音がやや多いことは容易に確かめられる．また，名前において子音が単独で現れるのは，表3の HL パターンと併せて考えると，LL あるいは H に当たることが分かる．例えば最上位の単独の /m/ は「アミ」「モア」「マイ」などとなる．さらに，ここでは図5において名前データが非常にまばらであることを指摘しておきたい．これはすなわち，名前によく使われる子音の組み合わせは，一般語では下位に沈んでいることを示す（なお図5は一般語の上位35までのみを示し，それ以下はグラフに入っていない）．

6. まとめと結論

　いわゆるキラキラネームを含む最近の名前が，音韻的に見て「キラキラ」しているかどうかを検討するため，「名前ランキング」12年分の頻度データと，一般語の頻度データから，(i) HL パターン，(ii) cv パターン，(iii) 子音セット，の3つの観点で名前と一般語の分布傾向を概観した．その結果，名前と一般語の音韻的な空間における分布は大域的に異なっていることが示唆された．本稿で示した考えは，あくまで分析の方向性を探るために手始めに行ったというレベルに留まり，音韻的な洞察に踏み込むまでは至っていないが，今後の見込みとして考えられることをいくつか指摘しておきたい．まず，大域的な頻度の分布が大きく異なることが「キラキラ感」の発生に寄与しているのかどうかを確かめなければならない．ベースラインとしての一般語の特性自体を何らかの形で定式化した上で，そこからの逸脱を定量

的に表現することが望まれる．予想されるのは，全ての「逸脱」が「キラキラ感」を産む訳ではなく，キラキラしない逸脱の道が無数にある中に，名前の音韻的空間を形作る道が何本か隠れているというような図式である．続いて，この「キラキラ感」を要因の一つとして持ちながら，他の多くの要因との相互作用の中で決まる『名付けの音韻文法』とでも言うようなものの探求が必要である．それはおそらく，流行語の発生や新たなブランド名の創出とも共通したメカニズムを根底には持っているに違いない．そしてその先には，音韻論をより生き生きとした動的システムとして捉える文法の見方があるのではないかと想像している．

参考文献

天野成昭・近藤公久 (1999)『NTT データベースシリーズ日本語の語彙特性』三省堂，東京．

伊東ひとみ (2015)『キラキラネームの大研究』新潮社，東京．

小林康正 (2009)『名づけの世相史：「個性的な名前」をフィールドワーク』風響社，東京．

黒川伊保子 (2009)『名前力：名前の語感を科学する』東光社，東京．

前川喜久雄 (2006)『日本語話し言葉コーパスの構築法』第 1 章，国立国語研究所，東京．

松浦ález史・筒井一成 (2015)「臨床研究・症例報告：キラキラネームと ER 受信時間の関係」『小児科臨床』第 68 巻，2113-2117.

明治安田生命 (2004-2015)「名前ランキング」http://www.meijiyasuda.co.jp/enjoy/ranking/index.html

御園和夫・平坂文男 (2008)「二重母音と二母音連続」『関東学院大学文学部紀要』113 号，87-103.

佐藤稔 (2007)『読みにくい名前はなぜ増えたか』吉川弘文館，東京．

田窪行則・前川喜久雄・窪薗晴夫・本多清志・白井克彦・中川聖一 (2004)『音声』(シリーズ言語の科学 2)，岩波書店，東京．

山西良典・大泉順平・西原陽子・福本淳一 (2016)「人名の言語的特徴の分析に基づくキラキラネーム判定」『日本感性工学会論文誌』第 15 巻 1 号，31-37.

英語の形容詞の比較級の語形とフット構造について*

山本　武史

近畿大学

1. 初めに

英語の形容詞の比較を表す形式には，接尾辞を付加して形態的，総合的に表すものと迂言的，分析的に表すものがある．これは，前者の方式で一貫しているドイツ語や後者の方式で一貫しているフランス語と比べると興味深い．

(1) a.　ドイツ語（形態的，総合的）
　　　　jung　　　　jünger　　　　　　jüngst
　　　　interessant　interessanter　　　interessantest
　　b.　フランス語（迂言的，分析的）
　　　　jeune　　　　plus jeune　　　　le plus jeune
　　　　intéressant　plus intéressant　　le plus intéressant
　　c.　英語（混合）
　　　　young　　　younger　　　　　youngest
　　　　interesting　more interesting　　most interesting

比較級については，一般的に 1 音節の形容詞には -er 形，3 音節以上の形容詞には more 形を用いるとされているが，2 音節の形容詞については事情が複雑である．南出（2014）(『ジーニアス英和辞典』第 5 版) "more" の項に次の記述があるが，「以下に述べる基準はあくまで原則であり，詳細は個々の語を参照．」とも書かれている．

---

* 本研究は JSPS 科研費 JP25370567 の補助を受けたものである．

(2) 南出 (2014: "more") より（各グループを表す記号を改変）
   a. 単音節語 通例 -er をつける．
      taller, faster, harder, etc. / ˣmore tall, etc.
      cf. apter, more apt
   b. 2音節語

	-er	more
i. -y, -ble, -tle, -dle	○	×
ii. -ly, -ow, -er, -some	○	○
iii. -ous, -ish, -ful, -ing, -ed, -ct, -nt, -st	×	○
iv. その他	○	○

   例： i. happier, humbler, subtler, idler, etc. / ˣmore happy, etc.
       ii. friendlier, more friendly / mellower, more mellow / cleverer, more clever / handsomer, more handsome, etc.
       iii. more famous, more childish, more useful, more interesting, more pleased, more exact, more urgent, more modest, etc. / ˣfamouser, etc.[1]
       iv. pleasanter, more pleasant / simpler, more simple / quieter, more quiet / stupider, more stupid / commoner, more common / politer, more polite, etc.《◆ii と iv のタイプは6文字の形容詞が多い：s-i-m-p-l-e, p-o-l-i-t-e, etc.》
   c. 3音節以上の語 すべて more をつける．
      more beautiful, more interesting, etc. / ˣbeautifuler, etc.《◆ただし，3音節以上でも un- のつく語は un- を取り除いた語と同じ形になる：(un) happier》

小西・南出（2006）(『ジーニアス英和辞典』第4版)"more"の項の記述は（2）に挙げた第5版のものと少し異なるが，興味深いことに（2b）の2音節語のうち more 形のみ認められるとされている（2b-iii）の例外として次の語が挙げられている．

---

[1] interesting, pleased は2音節ではない．

(3) 小西・南出 (2006: "more") より
例外: more exact, exacter / more honest, 《まれ》honester / more common, 《まれ》commoner / more civil, 《まれ》civiler / more fussy, 《まれ》fussier / more wicked, 《まれ》wickeder / more awful, 《まれ》awfuller.

(2), (3) は各語の辞書項目の記述と異なっている場合もあり，また同じ辞書でも版により記述が異なることから，語によっては用法にかなりの揺れがあることが予想される．

2. Google 検索の結果

(2), (3) に挙げられている形容詞の比較級両形の使用比率を明らかにするため，検索サイト Google (www.google.com) のフレーズ検索[2]によりアメリカ合衆国内の英語のウェブページを検索してヒット数を比べた．フレーズ検索で例えば "more fast" を検索すると比較級以外の例もヒットし，また副詞の用法も除外することができないが，おおまかには各形容詞の比較級の両形の使用比率を知ることができると思われる．以下の (a), (b-i)～(b-iv), (c) はそれぞれ (2) の分類に対応し，(b-iv)' は (3) に例外として挙げられている語のうち (2) に含まれていないものである．また，各カテゴリー内では -er 率の高いものから低いものへと並べてある．

(4)

a. 1 音節　-er: ○／more: ×

原級	-er	more	-er + more	-er 率
fast	452,000,000	641,000	452,641,000	99.9%
hard	210,000,000	498,000	210,498,000	99.8%
tall	40,200,000	122,000	40,322,000	99.7%
apt	574,000	628,000	1,202,000	47.8%

---

[2] "faster", "more fast" のように検索語句を引用符で囲む．

b-i. 2音節 -er: ○／more: ×

原級	-er	more	-er + more	-er 率
happy	69,900,000	531,000	70,431,000	99.2%
idle	513,000	66,700	579,700	88.5%
humble	468,000	519,000	987,000	47.4%
subtle	651,000	8,730,000	9,381,000	6.94%

b-ii. 2音節 -er: ○／more: ○

原級	-er	more	-er + more	-er 率
friendly	5,940,000	554,000	6,494,000	91.5%
mellow	357,000	491,000	848,000	42.1%
clever	435,000	650,000	1,085,000	40.1%
handsome	317,000	633,000	950,000	33.4%

b-iii. 2音節 -er: ×／more: ○

原級	-er (-ller)	more	-er + more	-er 率
useful	1,474 (771)	23,400	24,874	5.93%
exact	18,800	510,000	528,800	3.56%
famous	14,000	516,000	530,000	2.64%
childish	1,350	140,000	141,350	0.955%
modest	28,700	4,290,000	4,318,700	0.665%
urgent	2,020	486,000	488,020	0.414%
(pleased)	535	701,000	701,535	0.0763%

b-iv. 2音節 -er: ○／more: ○

原級	-er	more	-er + more	-er 率
quiet	21,500,000	685,000	22,185,000	96.9%
simple	68,300,000	3,210,000	71,510,000	95.5%
stupid	604,000	989,000	1,593,000	37.9%
polite	74,100	521,000	595,100	12.5%
pleasant	245,000	6,320,000	6,565,000	3.73%
common	480,000	36,000,000	36,480,000	1.32%

b-iv′. 2 音節　-er: △／more: ○

原級	-er (-ller)	more	-er + more	-er 率
fussy	101,000	62,700	163,700	61.7%
wicked	38,800	237,000	275,800	14.1%
honest	22,200	491,000	513,200	4.33%
awful	7,520 (6,000)	194,000	201,520	3.73%
civil	5,550 (1,060)	523,000	528,550	1.05%

c.　3 音節以上　-er: ×／more: ○

原級	-er (-ller)	more	-er + more	-er 率
beautiful	45,800 (25,000)	17,900,000	17,945,800	0.255%
interesting	3,590	49,100,000	49,103,590	0.00731%

　検索結果を見ると，(2), (3) で同じ範疇に分類されているものでも -er 率に大きな幅があることが分かる．[3] 特に，-er 率に囲みを付したものは南出 (2014: "more") の記述と大きく異なるものである．

　(2) では -ble, -tle, -dle は (b-i) に，-ple で終わる simple は (b-iv) に分類されているが，上のデータを見る限りは -ple だけを別扱いする理由は見当たらない．[4] また，(4) で happy は (b-i) に，fussy は例外として (b-iv′) に分類しているが，-er 形のみ許されるとされている -y も実際には語により -er 率に大きな幅があるので，まとめて (b-ii) とするのが適当であろう．[5] したがって，以下では次の (5) の分類によって論を進めることにする．なお，(iii′) は (iii) の語尾を持ちながら -er 形も可能であるとされているものであり，(iv) は -er 率により (iv-1), (iv-2) に分けた．なお，表内の囲みは形容詞化接尾辞である可能性があるものであるが，これについては次節で触れる．

---

　[3] (2a) の apt についてはこの語の項目で用法によって使い分けがあることが示されている．

　[4] 小西・南出 (2006: "more") では -ple は -ble, -tle, -dle とともに (b-i) に分類されている．

　[5] 例えば rainy, cloudy, worthy の -er 率はそれぞれ 99.7%，71.4%，21.8% である．

(5) 2音節語
　　○：使用率 10% 以上
　　△：使用率 10% 未満だが，使用の記述がある
　　×：使用率 10% 未満で，不使用の記述がある

	-er 率 (%)	-er	more
i.　-ple, -ble, -tle, -dle	95.5 ～ 6.94	○～△	○～×
ii.　-y, -ly, -ow, -er, -some	99.2 ～ 33.4	○	○～△
iii.　-ous, -ish, -ful, -ing, -ed, -ct, -nt, -st	5.93 ～ 0.0763	×	○
iii'.　honest, awful, pleasant, exact		△	○
iv-1.　quiet	4.33 ～ 3.56	○	△
iv-2.　stupid, polite, wicked, common, civil	96.9 37.9 ～ 1.05	○～△	○

3. 分析

Hilpert (2008) は，形容詞の比較級の両形の選択に (6) のような要因が関与していることを統計的に示している．[6]

(6) a. -er 型になる傾向がある要因
　　　語末の /i/(/li/ を除く．), 原級の使用頻度の高さ，原級の使用頻度に対する比較級の使用頻度の高さ
　　b. more 型になる傾向がある要因
　　　音節数の多さ，語末の /l (子音連続を除く．), r, li/, 語末の子音連続（成節子音を含む．），語末の強勢，形態素数の多さ

これらの要因は先行研究で言及されているもので，Hilpert はそのそれぞれを統計的に検証しているが，その手法に問題がないわけではない．例えば語末に /l, r/ があると more 型になりやすいという結果は，すべての子音を調べた上での結果ではない．また，子音連続の場合，simple のように成節子音を含むものと honest のようにそうでないものを同列に論じることにも無理がある．また，なぜある要因がある型の選択につながるのかについては十分に明らかにされていない．本論では (6) のすべての要因を論じること

---

[6] このほかにも統語的な要因が指摘されている．

はできないが，(5) の 2 音節語についての記述の検討を中心に両形の選択に関する音韻的な理由を探る．

3.1. 形態構造

(6b) に示されている通り，形態上複合的な形容詞は more 型になりやすい．Simpson and Weiner (1989) (*OED*[2]) "*-er*[3], *suffix*" の項には次の記述がある．

(7) "In mod.Eng. the comparatives in *-er* are almost restricted to adjs. of one or two syllables; longer adjs., and also disyllables containing any suffix other than *-y* or *-ly*, having the periphrastic comparison by means of the adv. *more*."

(2c) にあるように 3 音節以上の形容詞は more 型になるが，これは 3 音節以上で接尾辞を含まない形容詞は difficult, parallel 等，ごく少数しか見られないことも一因であろう．前節の (5) では，形容詞化接尾辞もしくはその可能性があるものに囲みを付けたが，(5iii) の -ous, -ish, -ful, -ing, -ed を持つものが more 型になるとされているのはこれらが接尾辞であるからであろう．

-y, -ly で終わる形容詞には cloudy, creamy, friendly, lovely のように明確に形容詞化接尾辞を含むもののほか，busy, early, holy, silly のようにそうではないものもある．(7) に記されているように -y, -ly は接尾辞であっても -er 形を許すので，この点は音韻的な観点から議論しなければならない．

-y, -ly とは対照的に，(5) では -ct, -nt, -st はそれ自体接尾辞ではないにもかかわらず，これらの語尾で終わるものは more 型になるとされている．Leech et al. (2001) による 1,035 語の形容詞のリストから各語尾で終わるものを抜き出してみると次のようになる．

(8) a. -ct

direct, correct, perfect, distinct, exact, abstract, compact, intact, select

b. -nt

recent, present, current, ancient, constant, silent, brilliant, distant, violent, pleasant, frequent, pregnant, urgent, decent, giant, content, absent, patient, instant

c. -st

honest, modest, Marxist, eldest

上記の語のうち，(8c) の Marxist は明確な接尾辞を持つので more 型が予想される．また，eldest も明確な接尾辞を持つが，それ自体最上級であるので比較変化をしない．よって (8c) で考慮すべきは honest, modest となる．Leech et al. (2001) には含まれていないが，earnest もここに入る．

次に (8b) であるが，present, content, absent 以外は形容詞化接尾辞である -ant, -ent を含むことから more 形が好まれると考えてよさそうである．この中で pleasant, urgent は自由形態素 please, urge と関連づけられ，前者は (2b-iv) に入っている．また，present, absent は比較変化をしない．

以上のことから，(8) の中で音韻的な理由から比較級の形を説明すべきものは (a) のすべて，(b) の content, (c) の honest, modest ということになる．

次に (5ii) の -some を考える．この接尾辞を持つ2音節の形容詞は少なく，上記 Leech et al. (2001) の形容詞のリストに入っているのは handsome のみである．また，収録語句数約 40,000 の Landau (2000) には handsome 以外に3つの形容詞が含まれているが，Google 検索の結果によると -er 率はいずれもそれほど高くない．

(9) -some, 2音節

原級	-er	more	-er + more	-er 率	語基
handsome	317,000	633,000	950,000	33.4%	hand??
lonesome	2,920	16,000	18,920	15.4%	lone
awesome	564,000	7,690,000	8,254,000	6.83%	awe
gruesome	2,850	194,000	196,850	1.45%	grue?

handsome は歴史的には hand から派生したものであるが，現在の話者にとっては語源的なつながりが感じられないであろう．したがって，-some は (5iii) に，handsome はその例外として (5iii') に分類してもよいかもしれない．同様に，(5iii') の awful (-er 率 3.73%) は日常的に最もよく使用

されると思われる「ひどい」という意味では awe との意味的なつながりが希薄であると考えられる．また，同じく (5iii′) の pleasant (-er 率 3.73%) は please との意味的つながりはあるものの，母音短縮を受けている．このような意味的・音韻的変化は形態的複合性を曖昧にする．(5iv-2) の stupid, wicked, civil についても，これらが接尾辞を持つという話者の意識は薄いであろう．

3.2. 音韻構造

前節での議論を踏まえ，本節では音韻的な観点から以下の点を考察する．

(10) a. -ple, -ble, -tle, -dle (5i) で終わるものはなぜ -er 型になるのか？
     b. -y, -ly, -ow, -er (5ii) で終わるものはなぜ -er 型を許容するのか？
     c. -ct, -nt, -st (5ii) で終わるものはなぜ more 型になるのか？

3.2.1. 音節数—-ple, -ble, -tle, -dle; -y, -ly

-er 型か more 型かの選択に音節数が深く関わっているのは事実であるが，これが入力である原級の音節数の制限か出力である -er 形の音節数の制限かという問題がある．例えば commoner の -er 率 (1.32%) が低いのは，2 音節語に -er が付加されにくいのか，それとも -er で終わる 3 音節語が認められにくいのかどちらであろうか．n 音節の原級に -er が付加されると必ず (n + 1) 音節になるのならどちらでも同じようなものであるかもしれないが，実はそうではない．1 音節の原級に -er が付加されると 2 音節になるが，2 音節語に -er が付加されると必ず 3 音節になるわけではなく，第 2 音節が成節子音を含む場合，2 音節になる場合もある．[7]

(11)   -er 率
     a. tall   ['tɒːl]   1 音節
        taller   ['tɒː.lɚ]   2 音節   99.7%
     b. common ['kɑː.mən] 2 音節

---

[7] 音節数の判断については Wells (2008) に従った．ただし，音節境界の位置および音声表記は変更してある．以下の例も同じである．

	commoner	[ˈkɑː.mə.nɚ]	3音節	1.32%
c.	simple	[ˈsɪm.pl̩]	2音節	
	simpler	[ˈsɪm.plɚ]	2音節	95.5%
d.	idle	[ˈaɪ.dl̩]	2音節	
	idler	[ˈaɪd.lɚ]	2音節	88.5%
e.	subtle	[ˈsʌ.tl̩]	2音節	
	subtler	[ˈsʌ.tl̩.ɚ]	3音節	6.94%

この結果を見ると，-er 形が2音節になるということがこの形が認められる条件であることが分かる．すなわち，多くの話者は simpler, idler は2音節，subtler は3音節で発音していることが見てとれる．したがって，多くの話者にとって simple, idle, subtle は次のような音韻表示を持つと考えられる．

(12) a.　simple /ˈsɪmpl/, idle /ˈaɪdl/　　b.　subtle /ˈsʌtəl/

また，これとは別に，語内に母音接続がある場合には音節縮約により音節数が減少する場合がある．quiet のように原級自体に母音接続がある場合のほか，[8] 原級が弱母音 /i/ で終わる場合には -er が付加されると母音接続が生じ，どちらの場合も本来3音節の -er 形が2音節になりうる．-y, -ly で終わる形容詞が -er 形を許容するのはこのためであると思われる．[9]

(13)　　　　　　　　　　　　　　　　　　　　　　-er 率
	quiet	[ˈkwaɪ.ət → ˈkwaɪ̯ət]	2→1音節	
a.	quieter	[ˈkwaɪ.ə.tɚ → ˈkwaɪ̯ə.tɚ]	3→2音節	96.9%
b.	happy	[ˈhæ.pi]	2音節	
	happier	[ˈhæ.pi.ɚ → ˈhæ.pi̯ɚ]	3→2音節	99.2%

---

[8] 動詞化接尾辞 -en は通常1音節の形容詞および名詞にしか付かないが，quiet には付く．
[9] Wells (2008) は (11e) の subtler が [l̩] の非成節化により2音節になる ([ˈsʌ.tl̩.ɚ → ˈsʌt.lɚ]) 可能性を示しているが，-er 率は 6.94% と低い．これについてはこの種の音節縮約と (13) の母音連続由来の音節縮約との間に起こりやすさの違いがあることが考えられる．

3.2.2. フット構造

そもそも，なぜ -er 形の音節数に制限があるのであろうか．強勢に中立な接尾辞の中には，特定の強勢位置を持った語基にしか付加されないものがある．例えば Burzio (1994: 293) によると，形容詞化接尾辞 -ish は後ろから1番目か2番目の音節に強勢がある基体にしか付かない．これはフット構造に起因する制限であると考えられる．

-er 形に音節数の制限があるのも，同様にフット構造の問題であると考えられる．-er 形が2音節フットに収まる場合はこの形が好まれ，そうでない場合は -er 率が低くなる．

(15)　　　　　　　　　　　　　　　　　-er 率
　　a.　(tállϕ)$_F$　　　1音節
　　　　(táller)$_F$　　　　2音節　　　99.7%
　　b.　(cómmon)$_F$　　　2音節
　　　　(cómmo)$_F$ner　　3音節　　　1.32%
　　c.　(símple)$_F$　　　2音節
　　　　(símpler)$_F$　　　2音節　　　95.5%

unhappy のように否定の接頭辞 un- が付いた3音節形容詞の比較級は (2c) にもあるように un- の付いていない形容詞に準ずるが，これは un- が付いた形容詞と元の形容詞とで比較級の形を揃えようという心理が働くという理由以外に，un- 自体がフットを形成することから語幹のフット構造に影響を与えないという理由もあると思われる．Hilpert (2008: 398) が挙げている untrustworthy が4音節にもかかわらず -er 形を許すこともフット構造から説明できる．

(16)　a.　(háppier)$_F$ / (ùn)$_F$ (háppier)$_F$
　　　b.　(ùn)$_F$ (trúst)$_F$ (wòrthier)$_F$

3.2.3. 弱強格形容詞—exact, polite

-er 形の好まれる条件が2音節フットに収まることであるとすると，弱強格 (iamb) の形容詞も1音節語と同じように振る舞うことが予想される．しかし，弱強格形容詞の -er 率は1音節語のものと比べて明らかに低い．3節

で音韻的な説明が必要であると述べた more 型になる形容詞のうち, (8a) の -ct で終わるものは perfect 以外すべて弱強格であり, (8b) の content もそうである.

(17)   -er 率
  a. e(xáctϕ)$_F$ 2 音節
    e(xácter)$_F$ 3 音節   3.56%
  b. po(líteϕ)$_F$ 2 音節
    po(líter)$_F$ 3 音節   12.5%

窪薗 (1998: 139-141) は英語の形容詞・副詞の比較級・最上級の形式が -er/-est 型から more/most 型に移行していることを指摘しつつ,「英語が強勢拍リズムを持ち, 強勢の衝突を避けようとする限り, 限定用法として用いられる 1 音節の形容詞が more, most の形式に移行する可能性は低いものと思われる.」と述べている.

(18) 窪薗 (1998: 141) より
  a. *a more big bag
  b. a bigger bag

ここで弱強格の 2 音節形容詞の場合にどうなるか考えてみよう.

(19) a. a more polite man
  b. a politer man

後続する名詞との強勢衝突という点では (19a) は (18a) と同様に避けられるはずであるが, そうではない. また, (19b) は (18b) と同様に好まれるはずであるが, polite の -er 率は 12.5% しかない. この事実はどのように解釈すればいいのであろうか.

弱音節である -er と異なり more は強音節であるので, more 形の場合は more と形容詞との強勢衝突も考慮に入れなければならない. (18a) の big は bag だけでなく more とも強勢衝突を起こしている. これに対し, (19a) では弱強格の polite は man と強勢衝突を起こしているだけである. つまり, 後続の名詞の影響がなくても more big は more polite よりもリズム的に悪いということになる.

以上を強弱格（trochee）の 2 音節形容詞も含めて整理してみよう．下線は強勢衝突を起こしている箇所を示している．

(20)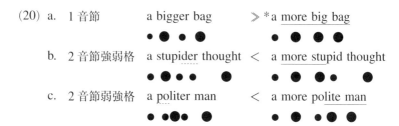

形態的な変化による比較級・最上級から迂言的な形式への移行というおそらく音韻に関わらない流れがある一方，それ自体強音節である more は強勢衝突の原因にもなる．stupid のような 2 音節強弱格形容詞の場合は more 形は強勢衝突を引き起こしはするが元の -er 形では問題であった 2 音節フットに後続する弱音節を回避する効果がある．polite のような 2 音節弱強格の形容詞は原級と同様，初頭音節に強勢を持つ後続の名詞と強勢衝突を起こすが，元の -er 形では問題であった 2 音節フット前の弱音節が先行する強音節 more と後続の強音節に挟まれるため安定する．一方，big のような 1 音節形容詞の場合は，-er 形は原級で問題になる後続の初頭音節に強勢を持つ名詞との強勢衝突は生じず，more 形は後続名詞との強勢衝突が回避できないばかりか more と形容詞の間にも新たな衝突が生じてしまう．したがって窪薗（1998: 139-41）が指摘するように迂言形へ移行する可能性は低いと思われる．

3.2.4. 強弱格形容詞の末尾音

(5ii) に挙げられている語尾の中で -ow, -er は -y, -ly と違い音節縮約を引き起こさないが，なぜ -er 形が認められるのであろうか？ これはこれらの語尾が共鳴音で終わっているからであると思われる．接尾辞を持ちながら -er 形が認められる同じく (5ii) に属する handsome と (5iii′) の awful, (5iv-2) の common, civil も共鳴音で終わっている．[10] また，音節縮約とし

---

[10] Adams (2012: §3.5.5) は happy, yellow, little, common などのよく使われる形容詞の末尾の母音や成節子音を stray segment/syllable とし，これらを 1 音節としている．

て分析した happy, friendly などの例も共鳴音で終わっている.

　一方, (5iv) の quiet (96.9%), stupid (37.9%), wicked (14.1%) はかなり高い -er 率を示すが, これらは /t, d/ で終わっている. つまり, -er 形が認められる 2 音節形容詞は共鳴音か /t, d/ で終わるということができる.

　Hammond (1999: 197, 250) は 1 形態素の強弱格形容詞の語末子音はほぼ舌頂音 (coronal) [t, d, n, l, ɹ] に限られるとしている.[11] これはそのような制限を持たない名詞の形 (Hammond (1999: 196, 249)) と対照的である.

　(5ii) の handsome は舌頂音ではない [m] で終わっているが, 1 形態素の強弱格形容詞の語末子音として非舌頂音でも共鳴音である [m] は適格であると考えられる. 先述の Leech et al. (2001) の形容詞のリストには random, bottom が含まれており, また, このリストには含まれていないが solemn も [m] で終わる. bottom は名詞からの転換であるとしても, random は明らかに形容詞である. 参考のため, Google 検索による random, solemn の -er 率を次に掲げる.[12]

(21)

原級	-er	more	-er + more	-er 率
random	145,000	527,000	672,000	21.6%
solemn	3,750	139,000	142,750	2.63%

　このように考えると, (5) で -er 形が可能であるとされている (i, ii, iv) は強弱格形容詞の語末子音 [t, d, m, n, l, ɹ] すべてを含んでいることになり, 語末子音が 1 つである形容詞は多かれ少なかれ -er 形が見られるということになる.

---

[11] Dixon (2005: 11) は唇音, 軟口蓋音, /s/ で終わる 2 音節形容詞は -er 形が許されないとして superb, elastic, famous を例に挙げているが, 強勢型は考慮に入れていない. この例はそれぞれ弱強格, 接尾辞 -ic, -ous の存在が more 形が選択される理由であろう. しかし, Hammond の指摘と同じく /s/ が含まれていないことは興味深い.

[12] solemner は -er 率が低いが, これは longer, stronger, younger が原級にはない [g] を加えて発音されるのと同様に, [n] が発音されることによって第 2 音節が重音節になっている可能性がある. 重音節の影響については次に論じる.

3.2.5. 強弱格形容詞末尾の子音連続—perfect, honest, pleasant

(5iii) の語尾のうち -ct, -nt, -st は子音連続であるので，強弱格の場合は -er 形になると後ろから 2 番目の音節が重くなる（数字は -er 率）．

(22) (pérfec)_Fter (3.30%), (pléasan)_Fter (4.33%), (hónes)_Fter (3.73%)

一般に強弱弱格（dactyl）で第 2 音節が重い (óH)_Fσ 型（H は重音節）のフットは自由に生じることができず，Hammond (1999: 257–258) によると，1 形態素の名詞の場合，cárpenter, cávalry, cháracter のように最後の音節が [i] か成節子音で終わっていなければならないという．1 形態素の形容詞でこのような形を持つものには sínister があるが，この語は sinístér という型も許す．また，これにさらに形容詞化接尾辞が付加された sinistral の存在を考えると，sinister は基本的には名詞と認識されているとも考えられる．(óH)_Fσ 型のフットは形容詞においては名詞よりもさらに嫌われると考えてよいだろう．

上記の事実は次のように解釈できる．前述の Hammond (1999) による指摘の通り，強弱格の名詞の語末子音は形容詞に比べて重いものが許される．これは名詞の方が形容詞よりも語頭に強勢を置こうとする傾向が強いことを意味する．接尾辞を持つ 3 音節語においてもこの傾向は同じである．例えば，母音で始まり強勢を持たない接尾辞を見た場合，名詞化接尾辞は強勢に対して中立なものが多いのに対し，形容詞化接尾辞は強勢の移動を許すものが多く，(óH)_F 型の語基にこれらの接尾辞が付加された場合，名詞は強勢が移動せず (óH)_Fσ 型になるが，形容詞は σ(Hσ)_F 型に移行する．

(23) a. 名詞化接尾辞：-age, -er, -ist, -or, -y
(cólum)_Fnist[13], (góver)_Fnor, (hárves)_Fter, (hónes)_Fty, (mónar)_Fchist, (mónar)_Fchy, (páren)_Ftage
b. 形容詞化接尾辞：-al, -ant, -ar, -ic, -ive, -ous
co(lúmnar)_F, mo(llúscous)_F, mo(méntal)_F, mo(méntous)_F, mo(nárchal)_F, mo(nárchic)_F, pa(réntal)_F, pro(dúctive)_F,

---

[13] [n] のない形もあり，この場合は第 2 音節に重音節は生じない．

su(ffíxal)_F, tri(úmphal)_F, tri(úmphant)_F

比較級を作る -er は屈折接尾辞であるので，(23b) に見られる派生接尾辞と異なり強勢位置を変えることができない．したがって，(22) のような形は stupider 等と同じく最終音節が舌頂破裂音で始まってはいるが (óH)_Fσ 型のフットが嫌われて -er 率が低くなるものと思われる．

4. 終わりに

本論では -er 形と more 形の選択に関わる音韻的な条件がフット構造によるものであることを明らかにした．比較級の語形選択の問題は，派生接辞の選択と異なり意味的には全く同一の 2 形の選択で，音韻的条件が浮き彫りになるという点で興味深い．本論では形容詞の比較級のみ扱ったが，Google 検索の結果によると，最上級は少し違った様相を示す．また，副詞も扱っていない．今後の研究が待たれる．

参考文献

Adams, Matthew E. (2012) *The Comparative Grammaticality of the English Comparative,* Doctoral dissertation, Department of Linguistics, Stanford University.

Burzio, Luigi (1994) *Principles of English Stress,* Cambridge University Press, Cambridge.

Dixon, Robert M. W. (2005) "Comparative Constructions in English," *Studia Anglica Posnaniensia* 41, 5-27.

Hammond, Michael (1999) *The Phonology of English: A Prosodic Optimality-Theoretic Approach*, Oxford University Press, Oxford.

Hilpert, Martin (2008) "The English Comparative—Language Structure and Language Use," *English Language and Linguistics* 12(3), 395-417.

小西友七・南出康世（編集主幹）(2006)『ジーニアス英和辞典』第 4 版，大修館書店，東京．

窪薗晴夫 (1998)『音声学・音韻論』（日英語対照による　英語学演習シリーズ 1），くろしお出版，東京．

Landau, Sydney I., ed. in chief (2000) *Cambridge Dictionary of American English*, Cambridge University Press, Cambridge.

Leech, Geoffrey, Paul Rayson and Andrew Wilson (2001) *Word Frequencies in*

Written and Spoken English: Based on the British National Corpus, Longman, London.

南出康世（編集主幹）(2014)『ジーニアス英和辞典』第 5 版，大修館書店，東京.

Simpson, J. A. and E. S. C. Weiner, eds. (1989) *The Oxford English Dictionary*, 2nd ed., Oxford University Press, Oxford.

Wells, J. C. (2008) *Longman Pronunciation Dictionary,* 3rd ed., Pearson Education, Harlow.

Part III

日本語アクセントと形態論

ピッチ・アクセント言語に於ける無アクセントとは*

吉田　優子

同志社大学

1. 本稿の目標

日本語では，ピッチ・アクセントの語彙指定，もしくは付与された分節音には高ピッチが知覚され，また，近隣の分節音に波及するとされている．ここではいわゆるアクセントがない，無アクセント語になぜ高ピッチが知覚されるのか，関西方言，特に大阪方言に焦点を当て，その仕組みを考察したい．

2. アクセントとは？

ピッチ・アクセント言語に於けるアクセントの定義としてはアクセント核の直後にピッチの下がり目があるものとする．

2.1. 無アクセントとは？

3拍から構成される和語の例を挙げると，共通語においては無アクセント語，すなわち，高ピッチの後に下がり目の来ないもの，としては1タイプ，大阪，京都等の関西方言では2タイプある．まず，共通語の例を挙げると：

(1)　共通語　　L H H　　　L H H -H
　　　　　　　さくら　　　さくら -が

---

* 本研究はJSPS科研費基盤研究C（課題番号：JP16K02648）の助成を受けたものである．

これは語彙指定により語末アクセントのある語，例えば助詞を付けると助詞の部分からピッチが下がるあたま'と対照すると，無アクセント語では後続する助詞などに高ピッチが認められることによって初めてアクセントが無いことがわかる．聞き分けが困難なのみならず，音響的にも区別は難しい(Pierrehumbert and Beckman (1988))．高ピッチは語頭の第一拍を除いてアクセント位置から左側の文節音に波及すると考えられている．

　大阪方言では3拍和語には特殊な語彙（マッチ等，促音を含むもの）を除き，語末アクセントはないので，語末の拍が高ピッチを持っていればそれはアクセントの語彙指定の無い語であることがわかる．共通語と同様，大阪方言でもアクセントによる高ピッチなのか，無アクセント語に現れる高ピッチなのか，聞き分けは困難であり音響的にも有意差は見受けられない．無アクセント語はピッチが左方向に波及するもの（2a）としないもの（2b）の二通りに分かれる．共通語とは異なり，第一拍にまで高ピッチが波及する．

(2) 大阪方言　a.　H H H　-H
　　　　　　　　　さくら　-が
　　　　　　　b.　i) L L H　　ii) L L L　-H
　　　　　　　　　うさぎ　　　　うさぎ　-が

どちらの場合（2a, b）にも右端に高ピッチが認められ，特に（2b）のピッチ型では判りやすいのは，音韻領域の末尾に高ピッチが現れている．
このデータを踏まえて音韻領域の末尾のステータスについて考察を進める．

3. 語末のアクセント

　共通語において，3拍語では語末の語彙アクセントは少なく，減少傾向にある（Yoshida (1999a)）ことを報告したが，大阪方言に於いては語末のアクセントは先述の特殊な場合以外にはなく，2拍語に於いても語末アクセントのものは：

(3) a.　L H　-L　　　b.　L D　　-L　（D は下降ピッチ）
　　　かき　-が　　　　　かきい　-が
　　'oyster - nom.'

の 2 通りのピッチ型があった．(3b) の牡蠣では，下降ピッチは「き」の上にアクセントがあり，母音が伸びるかたちでピッチが下降するものであり，1990 年代生まれの話者のデータ[1] からは完全に消滅しているが，以前は使われていたこのピッチ型については，語末のアクセントを回避するかたちと考えられ，語末のアクセントを避ける傾向があったと言えよう．

　語彙アクセントのない場合，領域末尾の拍に高ピッチが知覚される．語彙指定アクセントではないことが判るのは，後続の同一音韻領域に入る格助詞部分に高ピッチが知覚され，語が単独の場合に認められた語末の高ピッチは知覚されなくなるからである．

　共通語では句を並列すると時間軸上先に現れたアクセントが融合した句のアクセントとなり，そのアクセントから右はピッチが下がる (4a)．語彙アクセントのない名詞句と動詞を組み合わせると，後続の動詞と同一の音韻領域を構成し，その動詞に語彙アクセントがあれば，そのアクセントを主要部とするピッチ型となる (4b, c)．関西方言に於いては，アクセントのない名詞句に動詞を後続させた場合，名詞句部分の領域の末尾にアクセントがあるようなピッチ型となる (5b, c)．

(4)　共通語　　　　　　　　　**slow speech**　/　**connected speech**
　　a.　たま'ご-を　た'べた　　LHL-L　HLL　/　LHL-L　LLL
　　b.　うなぎ-を　た'べた　　LHH-H　HLL　/　LHH-H　HLL
　　c.　さかな-を　た'べた　　LHH-H　HLL　/　LHH-H　HLL
(5)　関西方言　　　　　　　　**slow speech**　/　**connected speech**
　　a.　たま'ご-を　たべ'た　　LHL-L　LHL　/　LHL-L　LLL
　　b.　うなぎ-を　たべ'た　　LLL-H　LHL　/　LLL-H　LLL
　　c.　さかな-を　たべ'た　　HHH-H　LHL　/　HHH-H　LLL

関西方言において名詞句単独では判別できなかったが，その高ピッチが，動詞が後続することによって実はアクセントとして機能していることが判る．これは句の最右端の，すなわち，句の音韻領域の末の拍（正確には Nucleus（核点））は語彙指定アクセントのない名詞句の主部の位置として「確保」さ

---

[1] 1990 年代生まれに関しては著者の採取した 2 人の住吉出身・在住の女性話者のデータである．

れていることを示す.

　(6)　　φ [xx...xx]　　（φ は句領域（phrasal domain）を示す）

ではこの二つの変種においてどうして節，文におけるピッチの使われ方が違うのか検討してみよう．共通語，大阪方言のどちらにおいても，例えば名詞句では phrasal domain（句領域）の中に lexical domain（語彙領域）がある analytic（分析的）な結合をする．

　(7)　　φ[_L [名詞]-助詞]　　（_L は語彙領域（lexical domain）を示す）

すなわち音韻領域はその統語的範疇によって振る舞いを変えると考える．名詞句においては語彙領域が分析的に句領域に位置する構造をとるために，このタイプの領域では語彙のアクセントがその主部として句領域の主部に投射される．アクセントのない語は語彙領域を持たず，語が単独で発話されて音韻領域となるか，助詞などの clitic が後続することによって名詞句となり，句としての領域を構成する．アクセントのない領域は主部のない領域であるかというとそうではなく，どの音韻領域にも主部がなくてはならない（Kaye (1990)）．この句領域の右端部分はその領域の主部として確保されているために，高ピッチが知覚され，これが「拡張」することになる．

　次に，句同士の結びつきを検討する．

4.　句の並列と主部の選択

　共通語と関西方言の句同士の「統語的な結びつき」の違いによりピッチ型が変わると考える．発話の中で形態素，そして句が連結されるにあたってANALYTIC（分析的）な配列となるか，もしくは NON-ANALYTIC（非分析的）に結合されるかという統語的な結びつきによって現れる違いである．Kaye (1995) では英語の不規則動詞，例えば keep の過去形，kept のように不規則な型を持つものは，音韻的に算出されるのではなく，例えば規則的な活用をする grieved のように [[gri:vφ]-dφ]（Kaye の枠組みでは領域末には核点があることを前提としていて，英語のこのような場合には空の核点，φ）と分析的な結合をするものとは異なり，本質的に語彙的であると提唱されている．この英語のケースの場合に決め手となるのは母音長である．

kept においては keep の長母音 [iː] は原形をとどめず，短母音の [ɛ] となっている．分析的な音韻領域内にある動詞の母音長は過去形においても，すなわち過去の要素 -(e)d が後続する場合にも長さを保っているのは原型 *grieve* が分析的な音韻領域として認識され，結合のアウトプットに反映されるからである．

　共通語の名詞句と動詞の組み合わせでは，名詞のピッチ型は語彙アクセントのない名詞の場合，単語，もしくは句として単独で現れない限り，領域が構成されない（Yoshida (1999a)）．関西方言の場合はどうだろう．

　語彙アクセントのある名詞句は名詞句と動詞の連鎖に於いてそのアクセントをアウトプットに投射する．語彙アクセントのない名詞を含む名詞句と動詞の組み合わせでは共通語の場合とは大きく異なり，名詞句の末尾にアクセントがあるかのようにピッチの下がり目が現れる．これを Yoshida and Zamma (2001) では京都方言の例を挙げ，pseudo accent（疑似アクセント）と呼んでいたが，ここでは逆に句アクセントとして音韻領域の最終核点が確保されるため，語彙アクセントはこの位置を避けて付いていることを提唱する．

　Yoshida (1999a, b) では共通語においては語彙指定がされなかった場合に音韻領域の右端に当該の音韻領域の主要部として高ピッチが認識されるという考えを示している．これも昨今の語彙アクセント指定の無い語が増加の一途（Yoshida (1999a)）であることや，関西方言の状況を鑑みると，こちらが優先条件と言えるかもしれない．この後，語彙領域にとっての領域末のステータスを検討したのち，句領域の結合について，さらに吟味することにする．

5. 語彙領域 (Lexical Domain) における主部の選択

5.1. 語彙アクセントの分布と特徴

　関西方言の和語の語彙指定によるアクセント位置の考察に入る．そもそも語彙指定がどのような過程でなされているのか，その分布を一緒に考慮に入れて考えてゆく．その上で，この語彙指定と音韻領域末のアクセントとの関連を検討する．ここで分布の観察をするのは，大阪といえども北のほうでは京都の変種とかなり近くなり，南のほうに行くと奈良，和歌山の変種と近づ

いてくるので，杉藤（1995）のデータベースで集められている大阪市内の変種に絞る．

このデータベースにおいて二世代に亘ってのピッチ型のデータの記録があり，高年層と区別されている 1910 年から 1930 年代生まれと，若年層とされている 1960 年代生まれの記録である．現在，ちょうど 1990 年代生まれのデータを実際にとりながら検討してゆく．サンプルの取り方として平安時代から使われている語彙に絞る検索機能を使い，この方法でいわゆる和語，もしくは和語に近いものに絞ってゆく．

次の表に大阪方言のピッチ型をまとめる．ピッチの高い部分を H，高くないところを便宜上 L，D は降下を，A は上昇ピッチを示す．1 拍語の上昇ピッチに関しては 1990 年代生まれにおいても使う話者はいるが，降下に関しては使わなくなっている．

(8)

モーラ数	1	2	3	4
	H エ（エガ）	HH ハシ（ハシガ）	HHH カタチ（カタチガ）	HHHH クレナイ（クレナイガ）
	\ D \ ナガ（ナガ）	HL クサ（クサガ）	HLL アブラ（アブラガ）	HLLL ウグイス（ウグイスガ）
			HHL カガミ（カガミ ガ）	HHLL クダモノ（クダモノガ）
				HHHL サカズキ（サカズキガ）
	／ A キ（キ/ガ）	LH フネ（フネガ）	LLH ウサギ（ウサギガ）	LLLH モトドリ（モトドリガ）
		\ LD アメ（アメ\ガ）	LHL ミドリ（ミドリ ガ）	LHLL ナデシコ（ナデシコガ）
				LLHL クチナシ（クチナシガ）

もう一つ，カガミのような HHL 型の単語は 1990 年代生まれのデータでは半数が LHL の中高型になり，無アクセントとなったものも見受けられる（吉田（2016））．総じてこの表と付記から大阪方言のアクセントについて言えることは：

(9) 1. アクセント核は語末には稀である．
    2. アクセント核とその左側の近隣の分節音が高ピッチを共有する

型は 1990 年代生まれのデータでは消滅している．
3. 無アクセントの場合は高ピッチを単語内全般に共有するものと最終拍のみに高ピッチのつくものがある．
4. 無アクセント語の高ピッチの共有は Initial Lowering の見られる共通語とは異なり，語（音韻領域）全体に渡る．

ここで語末のアクセントが特殊な場合を除いて無いこと，ピッチの波及は全体に行き渡ること，そしてアクセント位置の分布から語彙アクセントの付与の過程について考察する．

大阪・東京アクセント辞典（杉藤（1995））には 65,928 語の大阪，および東京のアクセント記録があり，大阪方言に関しては大阪市内在住の 1916 年〜 1932 年生まれの高年層三人と若年層からは 1960 年代前半生まれの三人のデータが記録されている．また，平安時代から記録のある語彙を絞ることができる．和語の定義は難しいが，1,300 年前から使われている語彙に絞ることによって有意義な程度に漢語，漢語の複合語，借用語は排除することができる．そうして検索をかけてみると 3 拍和語に関しては 424 語見つかる．これ以上長い語，すなわち 4 拍の語を探してみても，おお・かぜ，もみじ・ば，ふえ・ふき，など，ほぼ例外なく複合語や派生語であることがわかるので，アクセントの語彙的性質は見えにくいと考え，そうすると形態素境界を持たない語としては 3 拍の和語が最も長いものといえるので，3 拍和語の観察をする．

割合としては圧倒的に無アクセント語が多く，HHH のものが高年層で 44.58％，若年層で 44.65％，LLH のものは高年層 12.42％で若年層が 19.02％と増加傾向にある．1990 年代生まれにおいては LLH のものが増え，23.46％を占め，HHH に関しては 38.39％となっているが，やはり最も多いのがこの無アクセントである．

2 拍和語の総数 538 語の分布に関しては以下の通り，HL が圧倒的に多く，さらに増加傾向である．LD に関しては減少しているうえ，1990 年代生まれにおいてはもう使われていない．また，各話者によって数のばらつきの他に，語彙のばらつき，すなわち，このピッチ型を持つ語彙が話者ごとに異なることも特筆すべきであろう．各アクセント型の語数は高年，若年それぞれ 3 人の平均語数である．

(10)

	高年	若年	差
HH	153.67 (28.56%)	154.33 (28.69%)	0.66 (0.13%)↑
HL	259.33 (48.20%)	288 (53.53%)	28.67 (5.33%)↑
LH	78.33 (14.56%)	86 (15.99%)	7.67 (1.43%)↑
LD	46.67 (8.67%)	9.67 (1.79%)	37 (6.88%)↓

3拍和語ではどうか．こちらは著者の採取した1990年代生まれのデータも見ることができる．

(11)

	高年層の語数(平均)	若年層の語数(平均)		1990年代生	
HLL	87.3 (20.58%)	85.66 (20.20%)	↓	67 (15.88%)	↓
LHL	57 (13.44%)	47 (11.08%)	↓	94 (22.27%)	↑↑
HHL	38 (8.96%)	21 (4.95%)	↓	0 (0%)	↓↓
LLH	52.66 (12.42%)	80.66 (19.02%)	↑	99 (23.46%)	↑
HHH	189 (44.58%)	189.33 (44.65%)	↑	162 (38.39%)	↓

杉藤（1995）の高年層と比べて若年層に減少傾向にあった中高型が，1990年代生まれには著しく増えている（吉田 (2016)）．この年代の意識として大阪方言においては中高のピッチ・パターンが多いという認識があり，これは外来語やグリ'コのような新出語，[2] 外来語の省略（省略複合）語のピッチがユニ'バ（ユニバーサル・スタジオ），マク'ド（マクドナルド），ファミ'マ（ファミリー・マート），スタ'バ（スター・バックス）などのように中高になることからも伺え，中高型の和語の増加と新出語の中高化と同時に増加傾向となっている．

　この度の1990年代生まれの調査から判ったことは，この年代の話者にお

---

[2] 中井（2002）においてカン'ペ（カンニングペーパー）の例を挙げ，「ごく最近発生した「若者ことば」では，発生時からもともとL2（L2＝中高）かもしれない．」とあるが，まさにその通りであろう．

いて中高であった94語，もう一人の話者においては80語観察されたのだが，前者が中高（LHL）で発話したもののうち，古いデータでのアクセント型に一貫性のないものを取り除いた92語において（うち，二人の話者に共通して中高になっていたものは45語），パターンの変化は以下のようであった．

(12)   92語中   45語中
   a. LHL → LHL   25   19   維持型
   b. HHL → LHL   19   12   ピッチ共有のなくなったもの
   c. HLL → LHL   18   4   語頭アクセントから中高へ
   d. HHH → LHL   24   8   無アクセントから中高へ
   e. LLH → LHL   6   2   無アクセントからLHLへ

高年のデータでは他のアクセント型だったものが1960年代生まれではHLLに変わっていたものもみられたが，このような語においても1990年代生まれではLHLに変わっていたものもある．また，概して現代っ子には馴染みの薄い古い語彙（例えばカブラなど話者が使わないと答えた語など）において中高にする傾向も見られたことからも，新出語と同様，アクセントを第二拍に付ける傾向が見られた．

5.2. 語彙アクセントの付与過程

どのように語彙アクセント位置が決まるかを簡単に説明しておく．まず，2拍語を観察すると，圧倒的にHLが多かった．これは英語の二音節語において，語彙的に指定されていない限り，第一音節にストレス・アクセントが付与されるのと同様で，trochaic foot（強弱脚）が構築されていると考える（吉田（2013））．これと考え併せて，音韻領域の末尾は領域の主部のために確保されているので，どちらからの条件を考えても第一拍目にアクセントを付与することとなる．

(13)

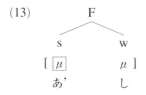

3拍語においては右端から強弱脚の構築があり，第一拍は degenerate foot となり認可主がなく，主部を投射できないので右側の foot の主部が語全体を認可することとなる．このため中高型が増加していると考えられる．

(14)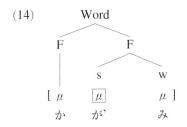

6. 句領域の結合からわかること

6.1. 共通語と大阪方言を含む関西方言と，句におけるピッチ型

ではどうして高ピッチは近隣の拍に「波及」したりしなかったりするのであろうか，これは句領域の結合からその「波及」の性質が見えてくる．

(15) 共通語　　　　　　　　　　**slow speech**　/　**connected speech**
　　 a. たま'ご-を　たべる　　　LHL-L　LHL　/　LHL-L　LLL
　　 b. さかな-を　たべ'る　　　LHH-H　LHL　/　LHH-H　HHL

2つのアクセントのある句が並列する場合，左側の句の主部が統合された句の主部として投射され (15a)，左側の句にアクセントがない場合 (15b) は左からスキャンしてまず見つかるアクセント，すなわち右側の句のアクセントが統合された句，XY の主部として投射され，あたかも最初から同一の領域内にあったかのように Y のアクセントから左側に最初の拍を除き高ピッチが観察される．関西方言では同じようにアクセントのある句の配列で共通語とは全く異なった主部の選択が見られる．

(16) 関西方言　　　　　　　　　**slow speech**　/　**connected speech**
　　 a. たま'ご-を　たべ'た　　　LHL-L　LHL　/　LHL-L　LLL
　　 b. うなぎ-を　たべ'た　　　LLL-H　LHL　/　LLL-H　LLL
　　 c. さかな-を　たべ'た　　　HHH-H　LHL　/　HHH-H　LLL

[φ[X]φ[Y]] において関西方言では XY 両方にアクセントがある場合には共通語と同じように左側の句の主部が統合された句の主部として投射される．代わって左側の句，X にアクセントのない場合が二通り，高ピッチが領域の右端のみにあるもの (13b) と領域全体に高ピッチがあるもの (13c) とあるが，どちらの場合にも，語彙アクセントではないにもかかわらず，句 X の末尾にあたかもアクセントがあるかのように，その直後にピッチの下がり目がある．ここからわかることは，関西方言においては句の領域の結合が必ず分析的 [φ[X]φ[Y]] であり，共通語ではアクセントのある句は同様な分析的結合をするのに対し，アクセントのない句 X は [X [Y]] のように結合していることがわかる．

　句の切れ目の「主張」として共通語では左端の拍は低くあらわれ，また大阪方言においてはかが'みなどが HHL のピッチ型から LHL に変わってしまって，すなわち最初の拍を「高くしない」ことによって領域の切れ目を示そうとする方向に向かっていると考えられる．1990 年代のアクセントなし型 2 種類 LLH と HHH において表 (11) にみられるように最後の拍のみ高いものが増加傾向にあるのもこの証拠であろう．

　高ピッチは波及するというよりは，領域の構成により，当該の音韻領域内での主部の音声解釈として，共通語では領域の第一拍を避けて主部から左に高ピッチが付く，大阪方言は主部のみ，もしくは主部から左へ領域内の左端まで高ピッチを付けるということである．

7. おわりに

　ピッチ・アクセント言語において音韻領域主部の音声解釈という理解により，ピッチ型が決まるという一考察をした．関西方言に焦点を当て，語彙アクセントとしての主部も，音韻領域の末尾に確保された主部も，音声解釈としては同じであることを論じた．

参考文献

Kaye, Jonathan (1990) "'Coda' Licensing," *Phonology* 7, 301–330.
Kaye, Jonathan (1995) "Derivations and Interfaces," *Frontiers of Phonology*, ed. by

Jacques Derand and Francis Katamba, 289-332, Longman, London/New York.

中井幸比古（2002）『京阪系アクセント辞典』勉誠出版，東京．

Pierrehumbert, Janet B. and Mary E. Beckman (1988) *Japanese Tone Structure*, MIT Press, Cambridge, MA.

杉藤美代子（1995）『大阪・東京アクセント音声辞典』CD-ROM，丸善，東京．

Yoshida, Yuko (1999a) *On Pitch Accent Phenomena in Standard Japanese*, School of Oriental and African Studies (1995), Dissertations in Linguistics 1, Holland Academic Graphics, The Hague. pp. 234.

Yoshida, Yuko (1999b) "Phonological Domains and Binary Inter-nuclear Licensing for Pitch Accent," *Phonologica 1996: Syllables—Proceedings of the 8th International Phonology Meeting*, ed. by J. Rennison and K. Kühnhammer, 355-371, Holland Academic Graphics, The Hague.

吉田優子（2013）「2モーラ和語のアクセントと無声化母音」『コミュニカーレ』第2号，21-41，グローバル・コミュニケーション学会，同志社大学．

吉田優子（2014）「大阪方言の韻律における世代間変容に見る韻脚構造」東京音韻論研究会，招待講演．於：東京大学．

吉田優子（2016）「大阪方言らしさとは？ 3モーラ和語における中高型」『現代音韻論の動向：日本音韻論学会20周年記念論文集』，日本音韻論学会（編），104-105，開拓社，東京．

Yoshida, Yuko Z. and Hideki Zamma (2001) "The Accent System of the Kyoto Dialect of Japanese—A Study on Phrasal Patterns and Paradigms," *Issues in Japanese Phonology and Morphology*, ed. by J. van de Weijer and T. Nishihara, 223-249, Mouton de Gruyter, Berlin/New York.

日本語複合動詞のアクセント特性について*

田端　敏幸

千葉大学

1. はじめに

　印欧語では，一般に，動詞の不定詞をそのまま名詞として使用することができる．西洋古典語は言うに及ばず，現代のヨーロッパ諸語にもその性質は受け継がれている．実は，日本語の動詞体系にも「転成名詞」と呼ばれる形式に類似の現象が観察されるのである．この「転成名詞」が英語やラテン語の不定詞と平行的な機能をもつことは次のような例で確認することができるであろう．[1]（1）において下線でマークした部分が具体例である．

（1）a. Errāre est hūmānum.
　　 b. To err is human.
　　 c. yo'mu ～ yomi'-ga　　読む～読みが（甘い）
　　 d. noboru ～ nobori-ga　　登る～登りが（きつい）

　日本語のデータ（1c-d）に注目すれば，日本語の転成名詞にはアクセントをもつもの（例：「読み」yomi'-ga）とそうでないもの（例：「登り」nobori-ga）が存在することがわかる．この区別は動詞のアクセント情報に由来するものであると考えるのが自然であろう．というのは，アクセント動詞に対応する転成名詞は尾高に，無アクセント動詞に対応する転成名詞は平板式にな

---

　* 本研究は日本学術振興会科学研究補助金基盤研究（C）（課題番号 245204194）の助成を受けている．
　[1] 転成名詞という用語は秋永（1998）に従う．ここではラテン語と英語の実例を示すにとどめる．

るという相関関係が見られるからである。[2] 日本語の動詞はアクセントの有無が語彙情報として定まっており，この情報を転成名詞が引き継ぐと考えられる．動詞アクセントと転成名詞間におけるアクセントの引き継ぎを (2) に示す．

(2)

動詞		転成名詞		
アクセント有り	読む yo'mu	読み（が）	yomi'(ga)	尾高
アクセント無し	登る noboru	登り（が）	nobori(ga)	平板

動詞のアクセント情報が引き継がれる現象は「〜方（かた）」といった語形成にも観察される．無アクセント動詞とアクセント動詞を比較すれば次のようになる．(3a-c) は無アクセント動詞，(3d-f) はアクセント動詞に基づく語形成である．無アクセント動詞に基づくものは平板式であるが，アクセント動詞に基づくものはその情報（起伏式）が「〜方（かた）」にも引き継がれていることがわかるであろう．

(3) アクセント情報の引き継ぎ現象「〜方（かた）」
    a. 忘れる 〜 忘れ方 wasure + kata
    b. 登る 〜 登り方 nobori + kata
    c. 行く 〜 行き方 iki + kata
    d. 読む 〜 読み方 yomi + ka'ta/yomi + kata'(ga)
    e. 食べる 〜 食べ方 tabe + ka'ta/tabe + kata'(ga)
    f. 生きる 〜 生き方 iki + ka'ta/iki + kata'(ga)

以上，動詞のアクセント情報が転成名詞などに引き継がれる現象を確認したが，日本語には V + V 型の複合動詞（構成要素が動詞）が存在する．[3] それは次のようなものである．ここで注目すべきは，複合動詞のアクセントは

---

[2] 動詞のアクセント情報（アクセントの有無）が転成名詞に引き継がれ，そして，アクセント動詞の転成名詞は動詞とは異なる位置にアクセントがある．Łubowicz (2012) の「対立関係の保持」という考え方を想起させる現象であるとも言える（英語でも to impo'rt 〜 an i'mport のように，動詞と名詞がアクセント対立を示すことがある）．

[3] 英語にも，一見したところ V + V のような形式，例えば "make-believe" のようなものは存在する．しかし，"a make-believe sleep"（たぬき寝入り）という形式が示すように，これは動詞ではない．

その終止形が示すように,現代日本語ではすべて起伏式として実現することである.構成要素が両方とも無アクセント動詞であっても,複合動詞はアクセントをもつわけである.(4)にV+V型複合動詞の実例を示す.[4] (4)からわかるように,複合動詞は構成要素のアクセント情報(アクセント動詞と無アクセント動詞の区別)の如何にかかわらず,例外なしにアクセント動詞として実現するのである.

(4)

	V + V	終止形	
a.	ki(−accent)+kazaru(−accent)	ki+kaza'ru	着飾る
b.	naki(−accent)+dasu(+accent)	naki+da'su	泣き出す
c.	tabe(+accent)+owaru(−accent)	tabe+owa'ru	食べ終わる
d.	huri(+accent)+dasu(+accent)	huri+da'su	降り出す

複合動詞からも転成名詞を規則的に作り出すことができるが,複合動詞の転成名詞はことごとく平板式になることが知られている.(5)でそれを確認しておこう.

(5)

	複合動詞	転成名詞
a.	着飾る	着飾り
b.	泣き出す	泣き出し
c.	食べ終わる	食べ終わり
d.	降り出す	降り出し

動詞と転成名詞の間にはアクセント情報の引き継ぎがあるにもかかわらず,複合動詞のアクセントは転成名詞に引き継がれていないのである.複合動詞のアクセントはなぜ転成名詞に引き継がれないのであろうか.以下,本稿ではこの現象を説明するために二つの分析案を検討し,結論として,複合動詞のアクセントは語彙情報ではない(したがって,引き継ぐべきアクセントが存在しない)という分析を提案する.

---

[4] Kawahara (2015), McCawley (1968), Labrune (2012) などでも,現代日本語では複合動詞が原則的にアクセントをもつという報告がなされている.

2. 2つの分析案を検討する

これまで，単純動詞のアクセントは転成名詞に引き継がれるが，複合動詞のアクセントは転成名詞に引き継がれず，転成名詞が必ず平板式（無核）になるということを確認した．この現象を説明するために，以下で，二つの分析を検討してみよう．

2.1. 音韻制約 Nonfinality に基づく分析

この分析では，動詞の転成名詞がアクセント情報を引き継ぐのを原則とし，複合動詞でも当然，アクセントが引き継がれるはずであると考えることになる．しかし，複合動詞のアクセントを転成名詞が引き継ぐと不都合が発生するわけで，その不都合を，音韻制約 Nonfinality に求める分析である．この制約は複合語が語末音節にアクセントをとることを禁止するもので，その有効性が示されてきた．[5] この制約が機能していると考えれば，(6) に示すように，複合動詞のアクセントを引き継いだ形式 (6a) はただちに排除することができる．

(6)

/tabe + aru'ku ～ tabe + aruki/	Nonfinality
a. tabe + aruki'	*!
b. tabe + a'ruki	
c. tabe + aruki	

この方法の問題点は，(6b) と (6c) の候補のうちなぜ平板式の (6c) が最適候補として選ばれるのかということであろう．(6c) を最適候補とするためには別の制約を用いて (6b) を排除しなければならないからである．他方，(7) に示すような O+V 型の複合名詞では Nonfinality を満たすのに平板式（無核）ではなく典型的な複合名詞のアクセント型が用いられる．[6]

---

[5] Kubozono (1995), Prince and Smolensky (1993) など参照．また，理論的な枠組みは異なるが Poser (1990) は末尾フットを韻律外要素とすることによって，複合名詞アクセントが末尾近くに置かれないことを説明しようとした．

[6] 「山歩き」のような形式は /yama' + aruki'/ のような入力に基づいて候補選択が行われていると考えておく．「山歩き」は */yama-aruku/ という動詞の転成名詞ではないのである．

(7) a. yama + a'ruki
    b. mono + ho'si
    c. mimoto + si'rabe

(7) に示したような O+V 型の複合名詞も，Nonfinality を利用すれば，たしかに語末アクセントをもつ形式は排除できる．しかし，(8) に示すように，(8b) と (8c) のうち (8b) を最適候補とするためには Nonfinality に加えて何らかの制約が必要になるのである．

(8)

/yama'/ + /aruki'/	Nonfinality
a. yama + aruki'	*!
b. yama + a'ruki	
c. yama + aruki	

　複合動詞の転成名詞「食べ歩き」が平板式であるのに対し，動詞句「山を歩く」を名詞化した「山歩き」は平板式ではなく典型的な複合名詞アクセントをとる．「山歩き」に代表される OV 型の複合名詞は内心構造をもち，右端要素が主要部として機能している．このような場合の複合名詞は，通常の複合名詞と同じ仕組みでアクセントが与えられると考えることができる．これに対して，複合動詞の転成名詞は OV タイプの複合名詞とはまったく異なるアクセント型を示すのである．この違いは両者の形態構造に起因すると考えられる．「食べ歩く」のような複合動詞は構成要素間に主従関係はなく，右側要素が主要部として機能しているわけではない．例えば，「乗り回す」〜「乗り回し」はある種の「回す行為」として定義するわけにはいかない．なぜなら，「乗り回し」は「回し」の一種ではないからである．このことから，V+V の複合動詞は右端要素が主要部ではないことがわかるであろう．他方，「山を歩く」〜「山歩き」のペアは右端要素の「歩く」および「歩き」が主要部として機能し，ある種の「歩く」行為が中心的な意味であると考えても不都合はない．このような語構造の違いが異なるアクセント型に反映されていると考えられる．

2.2. 不完全指定理論再訪
　複合動詞が表面上はアクセントをもちながら（有核），その転成名詞が必

ず平板式（無核）として実現することはすでに繰り返し述べてきた．ここで，その特性を説明するもうひとつの方法を検討したい．この分析は，単純動詞とは異なり，複合動詞のアクセントは「語彙情報ではない」という考えに基づく．

単純動詞の場合は，もしアクセント動詞なら，その転成名詞は必ずその語彙情報（アクセント）を引き継ぐ．他方，無アクセント動詞の場合には引き継ぐべきアクセント情報が存在しないので，その転成名詞はデフォルトの音調つまり平板式（無核）になるのである．

日本語の動詞はアクセント情報に関しては「アクセント」と「無アクセント」に二分されるが，アクセント位置は，その動詞がもつアクセントに関する語彙情報と，接辞がもつ文法情報とが併合して，一定の位置に定まると考えることができる．アクセント動詞 /tabe/(Accent) に終止形語尾 /ru/(Present) を付加するか，過去を示す /ta/(Past) を付加するかでアクセント位置は異なるのである．例えば，(9) に示すように，終止形（現在）接尾辞はアクセント動詞がもつアクセント情報を語尾の直前に実現させる．これは動詞の持つ語彙情報 [Accent] と接尾辞の文法情報 [Present] が併合した結果であると考えることができる．[7]

(9) [tabe' + ru] (Accent, Present)

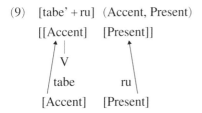

語尾が過去を示す /ta/ の場合には，アクセントの置かれる位置が現在終止形とは異なり，末尾から3モーラ目になる．この場合も動詞のアクセント情報と語尾がもつ文法情報が併合し，一定の位置にアクセントが実現するわけである．[8]

---

[7] Lieber (1980, 1989) の feature percolation 方式で素性の併合過程を示す．以降，アクセントの存在は [Accent] のような素性で示す．
[8] 現在形と過去形のアクセントが異なる位置に実現することに関しては Yamaguchi (2010) を参照されたい．

(10) [ta'be + ta]（Accent, Past）

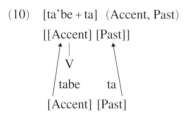

　単純動詞のアクセントは動詞の語彙情報 [Accent] が接尾辞のもつ文法情報と併合してしかるべき位置に実現することを確認したわけであるが，複合動詞のアクセントはこのようなモデルでは説明できない．というのも，複合動詞はその終止形が必ず「有核」として実現するからである．例えば「着飾る」のような複合動詞は，その構成要素（「着る」「飾る」）がともに無アクセント動詞であるにもかかわらず，複合動詞としてはあたかもアクセント動詞のようなふるまいを示す．ここで，複合動詞のアクセントは構成要素がもっている語彙情報ではなく，複合動詞形成という形態操作に付随して登場するデフォルト的な音韻特性であると考えてみよう．このような立場に立てば，複合動詞にはアクセント情報が存在しないという結論になるのである．アクセント情報が存在しないのであるから，その転成名詞にはアクセントが引き継がれず，平板式（無核）になることが保証される．では，複合動詞がアクセントをもつのはなぜであろうか．ここに登場する音韻制約は「複合語はアクセントをもたなければならない」というものである．[9] あらゆる複合動詞がアクセント動詞のようなふるまいを示すのはこの制約を満足するためだという見通しがつけられるであろう．複合動詞はデフォルトアクセント付与を受けているが，語彙情報としてはアクセントが存在しないのである．例えば「着飾る」といった複合動詞には次に示すような併合が発生する．複合動詞自体にはアクセント情報が存在しないため，この併合では [ØAccent, Present] がもたらされる．複合動詞は語彙情報としてのアクセントをもたないが，音韻制約 Compound Accent が作用するために，それを満足するための手段として導入されるのが基本音調 HL である．

---

[9] Nishimura (2013) 参照．

(11)   [present] (ØAccent, Present)

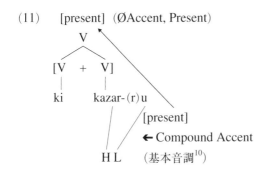

複合動詞はアクセント情報をもたないため,その転成名詞は当然ながら平板式にならざるを得ないのである.複合動詞のアクセントは複合語形成に付随する現象だからである.

さて,複合動詞形成のアクセントは語彙的なものではなく,デフォルト値としてもたらされたものであるというのが本稿の立場であるが,語形成に伴って一定の現象がデフォルト的にもたらされるのは音韻部門に限るわけではなく,統語部門でも観察することができる.ここではよく知られている現象として,ドイツ語の不定詞が名詞に転用される場合を考えてみよう.

ドイツ語も英語と同様に,不定詞はそのまま名詞として機能し,例えば,動詞"schreiben (to write)"はおよそ次のような語形成プロセスを経て名詞に転用されると考えることができる.ここで問題になるのは,不定詞を名詞化する場合,何らかのジェンダーが指定されなければならないということである.ドイツ語の名詞は必ず何らかのジェンダー(男性,女性,中性のいずれか)指定を受けなければならない.具体的には,ドイツ語では不定詞が名詞として機能する場合には中性の指定を受けることになる.それを(12)に示す.

(12)

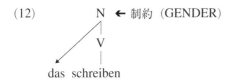

---

[10] Haraguchi (1977) に従って HL を基本音調とする.

(12) における矢印のプロセスは，不定詞を名詞に転用する場合，その名詞形が中性になるという事実である（中性の定冠詞 "das" でそれを示す）．ドイツ語には「N（名詞）には必ずジェンダーの情報がなければならない」という制約（GENDER）が存在すると考えることができる．一般に，名詞のジェンダーは語彙情報であるが，不定詞を名詞に転用する場合，個々の動詞が語彙情報としてジェンダー情報をもつというのは言語システムとしては非常に不経済であり，そのような仕組みが存在するとは考えにくい．[11] 不定詞を名詞として用いる場合は「中性」にするという「規則性」で捉える方がより簡潔な記述になるのである．

不定詞の名詞用法とは異なり，派生接尾辞を用いて動詞から名詞を作り出す場合には，その接尾辞が語彙情報として名詞のジェンダーを決定する．[12] 例えば，名詞形成接尾辞 "-ung [feminine]" による派生語のジェンダー指定がその一例である．それを (13) に示す．

(13)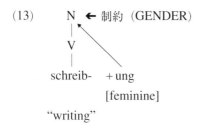

"writing"

これに対して，(12) に示したような不定詞の名詞化は接尾辞がジェンダーを決定するのではない．語形成の操作そのものが中性のジェンダーをもたらすと考えるべきである．これは語形成に伴うデフォルト値の導入と考えられる現象である．[13]

内心構造をもつドイツ語の名詞は一般にその主要部（右端要素）がもつジェンダー情報を引き継ぐわけであるが，例えば "Hamburg" のような地名

---

[11] Archangeli (1988) などの不完全指定理論を想起されたい．

[12] 右端要素が主要部となるわけである．Williams (1981) 参照．

[13] デフォルト値のジェンダー付与という考えは Pinker (1999) でも紹介されているが，デフォルト値の導入はジェンダー付与にとどまらず，Batman → *Batmen/Batmans のような複数形式にも観察される．"Batman" は内心構造をもたないため，語彙情報に基づいた man → men のような複数形成は用いられないのである．

に関しては，そのジェンダーは「中性」である．ここで想起すべきは "Burg" という名詞は定冠詞がつけば "die Burg" となり明らかに「女性」である．しかし "Hamburg" はもはや内心構造としては理解されず，たとえ "Burg" が女性であっても，地名としてはデフォルトの「中性」となるのである．(14) に示すように "Hamburg" は内心構造をもたないので，制約 GENDER によりデフォルトの「中性」が与えられるが，"Burg" は語彙情報として「女性」のジェンダーをもつ．[14]

(14) ジェンダー（ドイツ語）

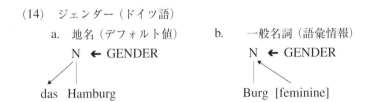

また，類似の現象として，ラテン語における不定詞の名詞用法がもたらすジェンダーのデフォルト値を挙げることができる．ラテン語の不定詞も名詞に転用できるが，ラテン語にはドイツ語のように性を示す冠詞が不定詞につくわけではない．しかし，不定詞が名詞に転用されたときに「中性」のジェンダーが導入されるのは次のような場合である．(15) のような文において，述語形容詞は必ず何らかのジェンダーを取らなければならないが，不定詞の転用名詞は必ず中性にするという決まりがある．このような場合も，形容詞のジェンダーは構文がもたらしたものであって，動詞の不定詞が個別にジェンダー素性を語彙情報としてもっているわけではないのである．

---

[14] 千葉大学の清野智昭氏によれば，ドイツ語の地名はごく一部の例外を除けば中性名詞として実現する．例外とは "Rheingau, Neumark" といった語で，これらは "der Gau" および "die Mark" が語全体のジェンダーを決定し，それぞれ男性名詞，女性名詞になるわけである．このようなものは内心構造が意識されている可能性がある．

(15) ラテン語

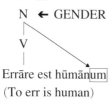

Errāre est hūmānum
(To err is human)

　日本語の複合動詞は [V+V]ᵥ のような構造をもつが，すでに述べたように，どちらかの構成要素が主要部として機能しているわけではない．つまり，複合動詞には語彙情報としてのアクセントは存在しないのである．[15] したがって，表面上はアクセント動詞であるかのようにふるまう複合動詞のアクセントは「複合語はアクセントをもつ」という音韻制約によってもたらされたものであると考えるのが妥当である．以上が本稿の主張である．

(16)

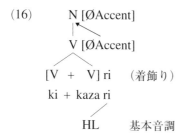

　転成名詞は動詞のアクセント情報を引き継ぐが，アクセントが存在しない複合動詞の転成名詞は (16) に示すように，動詞からは [ØAccent] を引き継ぐことになる．したがって無核の「平板式」になるのが当然なのである．複合動詞で観察される表面上の「アクセント」は音韻制約 Compound Accent がもたらす現象で，基本音調 HL が実現したものであると考えるのが妥当であると思われる．平板式のピッチ型は，基本音調 HL の H を右端に対応させることによって得られる．ただし，語頭が低ピッチで開始することと，不要になった L の削除という操作が必要になる．この結果 /kikazari/

---

[15] Nishimura (2013) は複合動詞が主要部をもたない "dvandva compound" であるという主張を展開しているが，本稿もその立場を取る．

はLH型の音調として実現することになる.[16]

(17)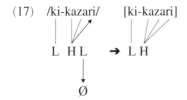

3. おわりに

　日本語には他言語と同様，動詞を名詞に転用する操作が存在する．転成名詞と呼ばれるものがそれである．この転成名詞形成に関して，単純動詞と複合動詞はアクセント型が大きく異なることを見てきた．単純動詞のアクセント情報は転成名詞に必ず引き継がれるが，複合動詞には一見したところアクセントがあるにもかかわらず，転成名詞は必ず平板式（無核）として実現する．本稿は転成名詞が引き継ぐのは語彙情報としてのアクセントであるという見通しをたてて，複合動詞にはアクセント情報が存在しないという主張をおこなった．複合動詞がアクセント動詞であるかのようにふるまうのは音韻制約 Compound Accent の効果であり，複合動詞には転成名詞が引き継ぐべきアクセントは存在しないというのが結論である．それゆえ，複合動詞の転成名詞は必ず平板式（無核）になるのである．

参考文献

秋永一枝 (1998)「共通語のアクセント」『NHK 日本語発音アクセント辞典』, NHK 放送文化研究所（編）, 174-221, NHK 出版, 東京.

Archangeli, Diana (1988) "Aspects of Underspecification Theory," *Phonology* 5, 183-208.

Haraguchi, Shosuke (1977) *The Tone Pattern of Japanese: An Autosegmental Theory of Tonology*, Kaitakusha, Tokyo.

---

[16] 平板式の音調は単に語頭の L（境界音調）と H だけで記述することも可能であるが，ここでは複合動詞のデフォルトアクセントをもたらすのに用いた HL を転成名詞にも使用するという方法で表示しておく．代案については Kawahara (2015) を参照されたい．

Ito, Junko and Armin Mester (2003) *Japanese Morphophonemics*, MIT Press, Cambridge, MA.
Kawahara, Shigeto (2015) "The Phonology of Japanese Accent," Online: http://www.researchgate.net/publication/280136131
Kiparsky, Paul (1973) "'Elsewhere' in Phonology," *A Festschrift for Morris Halle*, ed. by Stephen R. Anderson and Paul Kiparsky, 93-106, Holt Rinehart and Winston, New York.
Kubozono, Haruo (1995) "Constraint Interaction in Japanese Phonology: Evidence from Compound Accent," *Phonology at Santa Cruz* 4, 21-38.
Labrune, Laurence (2012) *The Phonology of Japanese*, Oxford University Press, Oxford.
Lieber, Rochelle (1980) *On the Organization of the Lexicon*, Doctoral dissertation, MIT. [Reproduced by IULC, 1981.]
Lieber, Rochelle (1989) "On Percolation," *Yearbook of Morphology* 2, 95-138.
Łubowicz, Anna (2012) *The Phonology of Contrast*, Equinox, Sheffield.
McCawley, James D. (1968) *The Phonological Component of a Grammar of Japanese*, Mouton, The Hague.
McCawley, James D. (1977) "Accent in Japanese," *Studies in Stress and Accent, Southern California Occasional Papers in Linguistics* 4, ed. by Larry M. Hyman, 261-302, Department of Linguistics, University of Southern California.
Nishimura, Kohei (2013) *Morphophonology of Japanese Compounding*, Doctoral dissertation, University of Tokyo.
Pinker, Steven (1999) *Words and Rules*, Harper Collins, New York.
Poser, William (1990) "Evidence for Foot Structure in Japanese," *Language* 66, 78-105.
Prince, Alan and Paul Smolensky (1993) "Optimality Theory: Constraint Interaction in Generative Grammar," ms., Rutgers University and University of Colorado. [Published in 2004, Blackwell, Malden.]
Williams, Edwin (1981) "On the Notions 'Lexically Related' and 'Head of a Word'," *Linguistic Inquiry* 12, 245-274.
Yamaguchi, Kyoko (2010) "The Differences in Accentuation between the Present and the Past Tenses of Verbs in Japanese," *Journal of the Phonetic Society of Japan* 14:3, 1-10.

ナガラ節における音調の形成と変異

那須　昭夫

筑波大学

1. はじめに

　本稿では，「動詞連用形＋ナガラ」からなる従属節（ナガラ節）において生じつつある音調変異の実態と性格を記述するとともに，変異を支える機序について最適性理論に基づく考察を試みる．まず第2節でナガラ節の音調の特性と近年見られる変異の実態について述べ，続く第3節で現象の性格に関する記述的考察を行い，ナガラ節での音調変異が対立の中和・規則の単純化・後部主導性を指向した現象であることを論じる．その考察を踏まえて，第4節では音調変異のしくみについて理論的見地から考察し，ナガラ節での音調変異が制約の階層関係の変動を通じて捉えられることを明らかにする．

2. 現象

2.1. ナガラ節の音調

　動詞の連用形に接続する付属語の中には，先行する動詞の式表示の違いに応じて異なる音調を作るものがある．並行動作を表す助詞「ナガラ」はそのひとつで，これを含む従属節の音調には（1）に示す二通りの型がある．（以下，＝は平板型であることを，］は声の下がり目を示す．）

(1) a.　泣く＝　　ナキ-ナガラ＝　　b.　成］る　　ナリ-ナ］ガラ
　　　 洗う＝　　アライ-ナガラ＝　　　　 習］う　　ナライ-ナ］ガラ
　　　 比べる＝　クラベ-ナガラ＝　　　　 調べ］る　シラベ-ナ］ガラ

平板動詞にナガラが続く（1a）では節全体も平板式となり，起伏動詞にナガラが続く（1b）では節全体も起伏式となる．この振る舞いから，和田（1969）はナガラ節の音調に「いわゆる式保存の法則に従っ」た性質があるとする．近畿方言の複合語音調などと同じく，前部要素（前接動詞）の式表示が節全体の式表示を代表することを踏まえた観察である．木部（1983a）も，ナガラ節の音調形成過程では前接動詞が決定力を持つことから，ナガラを「前部主導型」の付属語に分類している．また田中宣廣（2005: 96）は，ナガラのような「前接自立語の声調が及ぶ」タイプの付属語アクセントを「声調式」と呼んでいる．[1] この呼称は簡明なので，本稿でも以下適宜これを用いる．

2.2. 「平板動詞＋ナガラ」節での起伏化

ナガラ節の音調形成は（1）に見るとおり極めて規則的で，前接動詞の式表示（平板／起伏）さえ指定されれば節全体の音調も自動的に予測できる．木部（1983b）の言を借りると「無核の用言につく時と有核の用言につく時とで，『句』のアクセントが異なっている」のが特徴で，そこには動詞のアクセント体系に準じた二型の対立が成り立っている．

ところが，近年，ナガラ節の音調にはこの規則性に従わない型が観察されるようになってきた．「泣く，洗う，比べる」などの平板動詞にナガラが続くときに，節全体が本来期待される平板式にはならず，起伏式の音調が現れる（2）のような事例（起伏化）である．

(2)　ナキ-ナ] ガラ，アライ-ナ] ガラ，クラベ-ナ] ガラ

栗木（2015）および那須・栗木（2015）は，都内の中学校に通う生徒を対象とした調査を通じて，「平板動詞＋ナガラ」からなる 2048 項目の節のうち 65% において起伏化が認められたことを明らかにしている．この結果から，ナガラ節での起伏化は今日の共通語において進行しつつある萌芽的なアクセント変異の1つと見ることができる．65% という数値は，この現象が単なる偶発的な言い誤りの類ではないこと，および，変異の背景に体系的な要因と合理的な機序が働いていることを示唆している．

---

[1] この場合の「声調」とは語に備わっている「音の高低関係の調子」（田中宣廣（2005: 45））のことであり，共通語では平板式／起伏式の別が該当する．

3. 起伏化の音韻論的性格

3.1. 対立の中和

「平板動詞＋ナガラ」節での起伏化 (2) の性格としてまず注目すべき点は，それが対立の中和に向かう変異だということである．(1) に見たように，ナガラ節の音調は前接動詞での二型の音調対立をそのまま引き継ぐ形で決まるが，平板動詞含みの節で起伏化が生じると，この対立が解消されてしまう．

(3) a. 泣く＝　　ナキ-ナ］ガラ　　　b. 成］る　　ナリ-ナ］ガラ
　　　洗う＝　　アライ-ナ］ガラ　　　　習］う　　ナライ-ナ］ガラ
　　　比べる＝　クラベ-ナ］ガラ　　　　調べ］る　シラベ-ナ］ガラ

これに類する中和現象としては，ほかにも形容詞や複合動詞でのアクセント変化がある．まず形容詞では，終止形で「一，二類の一型化」（清水 (1970)）が進みつつあるほか，活用形においても型の中和が進んでいる（稲垣 (1984)，日比谷 (1993)，小林 (2003)，田中ゆかり (2003)，三樹 (2007, 2008)）．過去形のアクセントを例に示す．

(4) a. 従来型　　　　　　　　　　　b. 新型
　　　アカ］-カッタ（第 1 類）　　　　アカ］-カッタ（第 1 類）
　　　シ］ロ-カッタ（第 2 類）　　　　シロ］-カッタ（第 2 類）

複合動詞でも，かつては前部動詞の式表示に応じて全体の型が決まるという規則性（いわゆる「山田法則」）があったものが (5a)，近年では前部動詞の式表示がいかなるものであれ常に中高型で実現される傾向 (5b) が著しい（相澤 (1992)，塩田 (2013)）．

(5) a. 従来型　　　　　　　　　　　b. 新型
　　　踏む＝　フミ-ダ］ス　　　　　　踏む＝　フミ-ダ］ス
　　　取］る　トリ-ダス＝　　　　　　取］る　トリ-ダ］ス

本稿で検討の対象としているナガラ節での音調変異 (3) も，従前あった二型の対立が失われる方向へと進みつつある点で，上述の諸現象と同様，対立の中和を指向した変異と見ることができる．

3.2. 規則の単純化

　対立の中和は，アクセント規則の単純化という一面も持ち合わせている．上に言及した形容詞（4）および複合動詞（5）のいずれにおいても，従前の型では当該形式の前部を占める要素の式表示の別がアクセント形成上重要な手がかりとして働いていたものが，新型では前部要素の式表示に全く依存しない形でアクセントが作られている．

　同様のことはナガラ節での音調変異においても起きている．従来のパターン（6a）では節の音調決定に際して前接動詞の語彙音韻情報（式表示）が参照されるのに対して，新たなパターン（6b）ではもっぱら一定の位置に声の下がり目を作るという，より単純化した規則に基づいて音調が作られている．

(6) a.　従来型　　　　　　　　　　　b.　新型
　　　　泣く＝　ナキ-ナガラ＝　　　　　　泣く＝　ナキ-ナ］ガラ
　　　　成］る　ナリ-ナ］ガラ　　　　　　成］る　ナリ-ナ］ガラ

　注目すべきは，(4b)(5b)(6b) にそれぞれ示した新型アクセントが，すべて無標の型としての性格を備えていることである．形容詞 (4b) については小林（2003）の言う「N−1」の型（語幹末尾拍が核となる型）に統合しており，複合動詞 (5b) に関しては起伏動詞の無標型である「次末核型」（川上（2003））に落ち着いている．ナガラ節の新型音調 (6b) についても，常に形態素境界の直後に声の下がり目が起こる点などは，3拍語を後部要素に持つ複合名詞の無標アクセント (7) と軌を一にする振る舞いである．

(7)　ス］ガタ　　ウシロ-ス］ガタ　　（後ろ姿）
　　　ココ］ロ　　オンナ-ゴ］コロ　　（女心）
　　　アタマ］　　イシ-ア］タマ　　　（石頭）
　　　クスリ＝　　ネムリ-グ］スリ　　（眠り薬）

こうした振る舞いから，ナガラ節に生じつつある新たな音調変異は，語彙依存的規則から無標型生成規則へと向かうアクセント規則の変容を反映した現象として捉えることができる．

3.3. 後部主導性

加えて，ナガラ節での音調変異は，助詞ナガラの音調特性の変質という観点からもその性格を論じることができる．

田中宣廣 (2005) は，動詞連用形に接続する付属語の音調には「声調式」のほかに「支配式」と呼ばれるタイプもあることを指摘している．[2] 支配式は「前接語のアクセントに関わりなく，自身の型に引きつけてしまう」（田中宣廣 (2005: 96)）のが特徴で，たとえば助動詞「マス」などはこの種の音調を備えた付属語の一例である．

(8) a. 泣く＝　　ナキ-マ]ス
　　b. 成]る　　ナリ-マ]ス

マスは，前接動詞が平板式 (8a) であれ起伏式 (8b) であれ，常に付属語の初頭拍で声の下がる型を作るが，この振る舞いはナガラ節の新たな音調 (6b) においても同様に見られる．助詞ナガラはいわば，従前の「声調式」からマスと同様の「支配式」へとその性格を変えつつあると言える．

「声調式」から「支配式」への変化とは，木部 (1983a) の術語を借りると，ナガラの音調特性が本来の「前部主導型」から「後部主導型」へと変わりつつあることに等しい．すなわち，かつては節全体の音調を決定する力が前部要素（前接動詞）にあったものが，近年では後部要素（ナガラ）へと移りつつある．この後部主導型の性格は，複合名詞アクセントの特徴として夙に知られている．周知のとおり，複合名詞ではアクセント形成に際して後部要素の音韻特性が決定力を発揮し，前部要素がいかなるアクセントを持っていようとも，後部要素が共通していれば常に一定の型が作られる．

(9) a. ハ]ル＋ヤスミ]　　ハルヤ]スミ　　（春休み）
　　b. ナツ]＋ヤスミ]　　ナツヤ]スミ　　（夏休み）

これと同様の振る舞いがナガラ節の新たな音調 (6b) にも見られることから，ナガラ節の音調形成のあり方は，複合名詞と同様の「後部主導型」へと傾きつつあると見てよい．

---

[2] このほか「独立式」「下接式」と呼ばれる類型もあるが，本論には直接関わらないので説明を省く．詳しくは田中宣廣 (2005) 参照．

4. 音調変異の機序

前節までの検討を踏まえ，この節ではナガラ節の音調形成ならびにその変異を支える機序について最適性理論（OT）に基づく分析を試みる．なお，従来の音調（6a）と新たな音調（6b）とを区別するために，以下ではそれぞれの音調の現れる節を「声調式ナガラ節」・「支配式ナガラ節」と呼ぶ．

4.1. 音韻制約

周知のとおり，共通語アクセントの体系では，①ある語がアクセント核を持つか否か（式表示）と②アクセント核がどの位置に生じるか（核位置）の二点が，型の弁別に寄与する情報として重要である．この二段階の弁別情報は，ナガラ節の音調形成においても機能している．(1) に見たように，声調式ナガラ節では①前接動詞の式表示が節全体に継承され，かつ，②節が起伏式になる場合には声の下がり目が助詞ナガラの初頭拍に置かれる（動詞の核は消失する）．この二点を自律分節理論における多元表示の枠組みに沿って述べると，①音調平面での計算では前接動詞の音調に忠実な出力が求められ，②強勢平面での計算においてはナガラに備わる核指定に忠実な出力が求められていることになる．[3]

ここで，前接動詞および助詞ナガラをそれぞれ「語根」「接尾辞」と位置づけると，[4] 上述の特徴に関わる音韻制約として次の3つを挙げることができる．

---

[3] 強勢平面はその本義としては強勢アクセント言語での頂点位置計算に関わる理論的装置なので，高低アクセント言語である日本語とは一見無関係であるように思われるかもしれない．しかし，強勢のシステムを持たない日本語であっても，アクセントの頂点の「位置」が弁別的音韻情報として働く点は強勢言語と特徴を等しくする．本稿では，「高低アクセントは，高低のメロディーが結びつけられる抽象的なレベルでは，いわゆる『強勢』と同様，強勢平面（Stress Plane）において処理されるべきものである」との原口（1994: 2）の見解を承け，日本語においても核位置の計算のデバイスとして強勢平面が役割を果たしていると考える．

[4] ナガラが接尾辞と解されることについては木部（1983a）に指摘がある．木部は「独立しない形に続いて語形変化のないもの」を「接尾辞式」の付属語としたうえで，この種の形態素は「付属語と言うよりは接尾辞と考えた方がよい」と述べている．

(10) a. FAITH-TONE-Root
語根の音調指定は節全体の音調指定と一致する．
b. FAITH-ACCENT-Affix
接尾辞に備わる核は節全体でも同一位置に保たれる．[5]
c. FAITH-ACCENT-Root
語根に備わる核は節全体でも同一位置に保たれる．

(10a) は音調平面における計算（式表示の継承）に関わる忠実性制約であり，(10b, c) は強勢平面での計算（核位置の継承）に関わる忠実性制約である．以下，各制約の詳細について見る．

4.1.1. 音調指定の一致：(10a)

共通語アクセントにおける下げ核は，理論上，「HL」からなる音調素が分節に連結した構造として捉えられる（Haraguchi (1977), Pierrehumbert and Beckman (1988)）．ここで，ある出力形が下げ核を具有している（HLが連結している）状態を素性 [+T] で表し，無核の（HL が連結していない）状態を素性 [-T] 表すと，声調式ナガラ節での式表示のあり方は次の対応関係を以て記述できる．

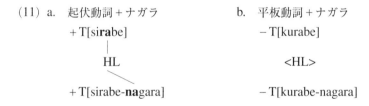

起伏動詞を含む形式（11a）では，動詞単独の形と節の形との間で HL 音調素を具有するという特徴（+T）が一致している．他方，平板動詞を含む形式（11b）では，動詞も節も HL 音調素を持たないという点（-T）において特徴が一致している．このような動詞と節での音調指定の一致を求めるのが FAITH-TONE-Root 制約（10a）である．端的に述べると，この制約は動詞の音調指定（+T または -T）がナガラ節全体にも忠実に継承されることを要

---

[5] (10b, c) の制約の内実は核の保持（MAX）および核位置の同一性（NO-FLOP）からなるが，本論では簡略のため FAITH とまとめて示す．

4.1.2. 核位置の継承：(10b, c)

ナガラ節が起伏式で実現される場合，すなわち「起伏動詞＋ナガラ」からなる節では，ナガラの初頭拍に声の下がり目が起こる．これはナガラに指定されたアクセント核が節全体に継承されることによる．一方，起伏動詞に指定されたアクセント核は消えてしまう．たとえば起伏動詞「調べ（る）」を含むナガラ節のアクセントは「シラベ-ナ] ガラ」ではあっても「*シラ] ベ-ナガラ」ではない．この事実から，(10b) と (10c) の間には次の階層関係があることが分かる．

(12)　Faith-Accent-Affix (10b) > Faith-Accent-Root (10c)

一方，同じ声調式ナガラ節でも平板動詞を含む「比べながら」などの形式では，節全体が平板式になるのでナガラのアクセント核は継承されない．その代わり平板動詞「比べ（る）」の音調指定が節全体に継承される．このあり方を保障するには，さらに次の制約階層が必要である．

(13)　Faith-Tone-Root (10a) > Faith-Accent-Affix (10b)

声調式ナガラ節では，動詞の音調（式表示）を節全体に継承すること (10a) のほうが，ナガラの核を継承すること (10b) よりも優位な要求として働いている．(13) の階層関係はこの要求を反映している．

4.1.3. OCP 効果

ところで，(13) の制約階層には一点だけ不備が残されている．起伏動詞を含むナガラ節の音調「シラベ-ナ] ガラ」は (13) の 2 つの制約をともに満たすが，実はもう 1 つ，(13) を十全に満たす候補がある．起伏動詞および助詞ナガラに指定されたアクセント核を両方とも継承した次のようなパターンである．

(14) *シラ] ベ-ナ] ガラ

むろんこうした重起伏型は実際には現れないのだが，(13) の制約階層だけではこのパターンを排除できないところに問題がある．

重起伏型の音調（14）では単一の音調形成領域（節）に声の下がり目が二つ含まれているが，その構造を Pierrehumbert and Beckman (1988: 124) の提案に倣って図示すると次のようになる．

(15)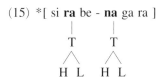

(15) では同じ属性（HL）を含む音調 T が隣接関係にあるが，こうした構造は OCP 制約に抵触する．つまり重起伏型の音調（14）が適格でないのは，それが OCP 違反を伴う構造であるからにほかならない．

Ito and Mester (1998, 2003: 29–32) は，OT における OCP 制約の扱いについて考察する中で，ある有標性制約への違反を 2 回伴う構造を不適格とみなす自己連接制約 (self-conjoined constraint) の有効性を主張している．その論によると，日本語の音調現象における OCP 効果は次の 2 つの制約を通じて捉えられるという．

(16) a. *HL　　下降型の複合音調は有標である．
　　 b. *HL$^2_\delta$　HL 音調は単一の領域$_\delta$で共起してはならない．[6]

(16a) は下げ核を含む構造を有標とする制約で，(16b) はその自己連接制約である．(16b) への違反は，何らかの領域$_\delta$で (16a) への違反が二度生じている場合に発生する．[7] (14) に示した重起伏型の音調を排除するには，これらを含む次の制約階層が最低限必要である．

(17) *HL$^2_\delta$ > Faith-Accent-Affix (10b) > *HL

この制約階層では，ナガラのアクセント核が出力に保持される傍ら，それ以外の要素（前接動詞）の核を同時に保持することは *HL$^2_\delta$ 制約の働きによって許されない．つまり重起伏型音調は排除される．

---

[6] ここでは Ito and Mester (1998) による制約形式を用いる．
[7] 本稿で検討中の現象ではナガラ従属節が「領域$_\delta$」に該当する．

4.2. 制約階層

以上の議論を踏まえて，以下ではナガラ節の音調形成を司る制約階層の性質について考察する．

4.2.1. 声調式ナガラ節

(1) に見たように，声調式ナガラ節では前接動詞の式表示に応じて節の音調に区別が起こるのが特徴である．換言すると，声調式ナガラ節では前接動詞と節全体とで音調指定の忠実な一致が求められる．

まず起伏動詞を含む声調式ナガラ節では，ナガラに指定されたアクセント核が表出することで節全体が起伏式となり，動詞と節とで音調指定（+T）が一致する．他方，平板動詞を含む声調式ナガラ節では，ナガラの核が消えて節全体が平板式で実現されることで，動詞と節の音調指定（−T）が一致する．以上の振る舞いは，次の (18) に示す制約階層により保障される．（紙幅の都合上，以下，制約の名称は略称で示すほか，一部の制約については記述を割愛する．[8]）

(18) 声調式ナガラ節

この階層の有効性について，まずは起伏動詞「成る」を含むナガラ節「成りながら」での音調形成を一例として見る．

---

[8] 割愛するのは (10c) FAITH-ACCENT-ROOT 制約である．(12) に示したとおり，この制約は FAITH-ACCENT-Affix 制約の下位にあるが，声調式ナガラ節／支配式ナガラ節のいずれにおいても最適形の選出に際して決定的な役割を果たす機会がない．そこで記述の簡略と理解の便宜を優先し，考察上不可欠の制約のみを示すこととした．ただし，言うまでもなく，これは FAITH-ACCENT-Root 制約が階層中に存在しないことを意味するものではない．この制約は FAITH-ACCENT-Affix 制約に常に支配される位置にあり，かつ，*HL 制約と同等階層にある (FAITH-ACC (Af)>...> FAITH-ACC (Rt), *HL)．

(19)　ナリ-ナ］ガラ

/$_{(+T)}$**na'ri** + **na'gara**/	*HL$^2_\delta$	F-Tone (Rt)	F-Acc (Af)	*HL
a.　$_{+T}$[**na'ri**-**na'gara**]	*!			**
b.　$_{-T}$[nari-nagara=]		*!	*	
c.　$_{+T}$[**na'ri**-nagara]			*!	*
→ d.　$_{+T}$[nari-**na'gara**]				*

重起伏を含む(19a)「*ナ］リ-ナ］ガラ」は，最上位の自己連接制約への違反により排除される．平板型の(19b)「*ナリ-ナガラ=」は動詞に指定された起伏式の特徴(+T)を失っているため，Faith-T(Rt)制約への違反を伴う．また(19c)の「*ナ］リ-ナガラ」は，起伏式の音調を維持してはいるものの，ナガラのアクセント核が継承されていないためにFaith-Acc(Af)制約への違反を生じてしまう．この競合の結果，ナガラの核を継承することで起伏式の音調を維持した(19d)「ナリ-ナ］ガラ」が最適形として出力される．

(18)の制約階層は，平板動詞を含むナガラ節の音調についても適切な予測を示すことができる．平板動詞「泣く」を含む節「泣きながら」を例に，最適形選出の様子を(20)に示す．(平板動詞含みのナガラ節については，動詞部分に核を含む「*ナ］キ-ナガラ」のような候補は考察の本質には関わらないので省略する．当面の議論に直接関わる候補だけを示す．)

(20)　ナキ-ナガラ=

/$_{(-T)}$naki= + **na'gara**/	*HL$^2_\delta$	F-Tone (Rt)	F-Acc (Af)	*HL
→ a.　$_{-T}$[naki-nagara=]			*	
b.　$_{+T}$[naki-**na'gara**]		*!		*

上の競合において決定的な役割を果たすのはFaith-T(Rt)制約である．動詞に指定された平板式の特徴(-T)を継承した(20a)「ナキ-ナガラ=」はこれを満たすが，起伏型の(20b)「*ナキ-ナ］ガラ」では動詞と節とで音調指定が一致しないため，Faith-T(Rt)制約が破られる．

4.2.2. 支配式ナガラ節

続いて，今度は支配式ナガラ節の音調をもたらす制約階層について見る．支配式ナガラ節では，(3) に見たように，前接動詞の式表示の如何を問わず常に起伏型の音調が現れる．すなわち平板動詞の音調指定（－T）が節全体に継承されない点が顕著な特徴である．

この点を理論的文脈を以て換言すると，支配式ナガラ節では音調形成に際して FAITH-T(Rt) 制約の働きが不活性化していると言える．その一方で，支配式ナガラ節ではナガラのアクセント核が節全体の音調にも継承されることから，FAITH-ACC(Af) 制約が最適形選出に際して決定力を発揮する．この文法状態は次の制約階層によって表現できる．

(21) 支配式ナガラ節

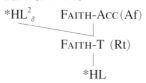

この階層が支配式の音調を適切に予測できることを，平板動詞「泣く」を含むナガラ節「泣きながら」を例に見る．((20) と同様，当面の議論に直接関わる候補だけを示す．)

(22) ナキ-ナ] ガラ

$/_{(-T)}$naki = +**na'gara**/	$*HL^2_\delta$	F-ACC (Af)	F-TONE (Rt)	*HL
a. $_{-T}$[naki-nagara =]		*!		*
→ b. $_{+T}$[naki-**na'**gara]			*	

これまで再三指摘してきたとおり，ナガラ節における近年の音調変異を特徴づける振る舞いとは，「平板動詞＋ナガラ」節に起伏式の音調（ナキ-ナ] ガラ）が現れることにほかならない．上表に見るように，この振る舞いはFAITH-ACC(Af) 制約が FAITH-T(Rt) 制約に対して支配的な地位を占めることで生じる．

ちなみに (21) の制約階層は，「起伏動詞＋ナガラ」からなる節の音調に関しても問題なくその事実を捉えることができる．

(23)　ナリ-ナ] ガラ

/$_{(+T)}$**na'ri** + **na'gara**/	*HL$^2_\delta$	F-Acc (Af)	F-Tone (Rt)	*HL
a.　$_{+T}$[**na'ri-na'gara**]	*!			**
b.　$_{-T}$[nari-nagara =]		*!	*	
c.　$_{+T}$[**na'ri**-nagara]		*!		*
→ d.　$_{+T}$[nari-**na'gara**]				*

4.3. 制約階層の変動と音調変異

以上検討したように，近年生じつつあるナガラ節での音調変異は，制約階層に生じる限局的なリランキングを反映した現象として分析できる．(24)にまとめるように，隣接する2つの忠実性制約（Faith-T(Rt), Faith-Acc(Af)）の上下関係が入れ替わることにより，声調式から支配式への変異がもたらされる．

(24)　a.　… Faith-T(Rt) > Faith-Acc(Af) > …（声調式:(18)）
　　　b.　… Faith-Acc(Af) > Faith-T(Rt) > …（支配式:(21)）

Faith-T(Rt) 制約の下降は，前接自立語の式表示の別が節全体に及ぶという声調式音調の特徴が，ナガラ節から失われることを意味する．反対に Faith-Acc(Af) の上昇は，「前接語のアクセントに関わりなく，自身の型に引きつけてしまう」（田中宣廣 (2005: 96)）という支配式の特性が，助詞ナガラに新たに備わったことを意味する．先に3.3節において，ナガラ節での音調変異の背景には助詞ナガラの音調特性の変質があることを指摘したが，この変質は，上に示した制約のリランキングを通じて捉えることができる．

本稿の分析のもう1つの利点は，ナガラ節での音調変異が本質的には「平板動詞＋ナガラ」からなる形式での起伏化を契機とした現象であることを捉えられる点にある．(24) に示したリランキングを通じて音調に直接の影響が現れるのは，(20) と (22) の対比からうかがえるように，平板動詞を含むナガラ節だけである．一方，起伏動詞を含むナガラ節では，支配式音調を保障する制約階層 (21) の下でも相変わらず起伏式の音調が得られる．ナガラ節における音調対立の中和（3.1節）は，「平板動詞＋ナガラ」からなる節

での音調形成が「起伏動詞＋ナガラ」節に生じるパターンと同一化することで起こるものであり，本稿の分析ではこうした記述的事実も過つことなく捉えることができる．

5. おわりに

　本稿では，ナガラ節の音調に近年生じつつある変異を取り上げ，この変異の性格について記述的考察を与えるとともに，音韻制約の相対的な上下関係の交替という観点を通じて変異の機序が捉えられることを示した．

　ただし，この変異は現在なお進行中の段階にある．ナガラに前接する平板動詞の拍数などにより起伏化の割合にばらつきが見られるなど（那須・栗木 (2015)），変異の帰趨は必ずしも定まっているわけではない．本稿では制約のリランキングという機序を通じて変異前後の文法状態の相違を捉えたが，ナガラ節の音調形成を司る制約階層の状態はいまだ流動的で，むしろ同一の話者の中でも（18）と（21）との間で随時ゆれていると見るのが実態に近いところであろう．

参考文献

相澤正夫（1992）「進行中のアクセント変化―東京語の複合動詞の場合―」『研究報告集』第 13 集（国立国語研究所報告 104），195-265．

Haraguchi, Shosuke (1977) *The Tone Pattern of Japanese: An Autosegmental Theory of Tonology*, Kaitakusha, Tokyo.

原口庄輔（1994）『音韻論』（現代の英語学シリーズ 3），開拓社，東京．

日比谷潤子（1993）「形容詞アクセントの変化と変異―実時間における変化と現時点における変異―」『慶應義塾大学言語文化研究所紀要』第 25 号，207-218．

稲垣滋子（1984）「アクセントのゆれに関わる要素について」『現代方言学の課題 2 記述的研究篇』，平山輝男博士古稀記念会（編），281-307，明治書院，東京．

Ito, Junko and Armin Mester (1998) "Markedness and Word Structure: OCP Effects in Japanese," ms., University of California, Santa Cruz. [Available on Rutgers Optimality Archive, http://roa.rutgers.edu, ROA-255-0498.]

Ito, Junko and Armin Mester (2003) *Japanese Morphophonemics: Markedness and Word Structure*, MIT Press, Cambridge, MA.

川上蓁（2003）「東京アクセント末核型の行方」『国語研究』第 66 号，1-11．

木部暢子（1983a）「付属語のアクセントについて」『国語学』第 134 号，23-42.

木部暢子（1983b）「用言の活用形とアクセント」『文献探究』第 12 巻，1-10，文献探究の会，福岡.

小林めぐみ（2003）「東京語における形容詞アクセントの変化とその要因」『音声研究』第 7 巻 2 号，101-113.

栗木風香（2015）「首都圏地域における動詞接続付属語アクセントの変容」平成 26 年度筑波大学大学院教育研究科修士論文.

三樹陽介（2007）「首都圏方言形容詞アクセントの多様性」『国学院大学大学院紀要 文学研究科』第 39 巻，171-182.

三樹陽介（2008）「首都圏方言の形容詞アクセントの複雑さ──「-クナイ」「-クナル」の形を例に──」『國學院雑誌』第 109 巻 7 号，1-15.

那須昭夫・栗木風香（2015）「若年話者に生じつつある付属語アクセントの変化──ナガラ節での起伏化傾向──」『第 29 回日本音声学会全国大会予稿集』128-133.

Pierrehumbert, Janet B. and Mary E. Beckman (1988) *Japanese Tone Structure*, MIT Press, Cambridge, MA.

清水郁子（1970）「東京方言のアクセント」『方言研究の問題点』，平山輝男博士還暦記念会（編），134-172，明治書院，東京.

塩田雄大（2013）「NHK アナウンサーのアクセントの現在──複合動詞を中心に──」『現代日本語の動態研究』，相澤正夫（編），236-258，おうふう，東京.

田中宣廣（2005）『付属語アクセントからみた日本語アクセントの構造』おうふう，東京.

田中ゆかり（2003）「首都圏方言における形容詞活用形アクセントの複雑さが意味するもの──「気づき」と「変わりやすさ」の観点から──」『語文』第 116 巻，119-195.

和田實（1969）「辞のアクセント」『国語研究』第 29 号，1-20.

擬似形態素境界が複数挿入される可能性について[*]

小川晋史　　儀利古幹雄
熊本県立大学　　大阪大学

1. はじめに

本稿においては擬似形態素境界[1]が1語中[2]に複数（回），循環的なプロセスで挿入される可能性について示す．主張の根拠としては，9モーラ無意味薬品名を用いた標準語のアクセント聞き取り判断テストの結果を用いる．

1.1. 研究の背景と将来的に明らかにしたいこと

本稿の内容は，将来的に（1）のような違いの説明に資することを目指した研究である．

(1) 南メキシコ vs. 南カレドニア
　　([^{0}]: 平板型アクセント，[⁻]: アクセント核，[#]: 形態素境界)
　a. みなみ^0　めきしこ^0 → みなみ#め⁻きしこ（南メキシコ）
　b. みなみ^0　かれどにあ^0 → みなみ#かれどにあ^0（南カレドニア）

上記（1）の複合語の後部要素である「メキシコ」と「カレドニア」は単独だと平板型で発音されるが，それらを後部要素にした複合語では，前部要素が

---

[*] 本稿は関西音韻論研究会（PAIK）において2012年3月16日に口頭発表した内容に加筆修正したものである．また，本稿は第2著者に対する科学研究費補助金・若手研究（B）「日本語アクセントの平板化に関する実証的研究」（課題番号：23720238）の助成を受けた研究成果の一部である．実験に協力して下さった皆さんに感謝申し上げる．

[1] 擬似形態素境界は形態論的な概念ではなく音韻論的な概念であることに注意されたい．

[2] 本稿において特に説明なく「単語」あるいは「語」という語を用いる場合，音韻論的な語ではなく形態論的な語を意味する．

同じ「南（みなみ）」であるにもかかわらずアクセント型に違いが出る．(1a)は後部要素の初頭モーラにアクセント核が置かれるパターンを示すが，(1b)は平板型になるのである．記述的な傾向として後部要素が比較的長い平板型の語だと複合語全体が平板型になることは指摘されているが（秋永 (1985)，など），その原理を明らかにしようとした研究は管見の限り存在しないようである．

1.2. 本稿で明らかにしたいこと

　実在の薬品名であって，かつモーラ数も同じである語であっても，アクセントの異なるものが存在している．例えば本稿が行った予備実験の結果では以下の (2) と (3) では平板型アクセントをとる率が大きく異なっている．

(2)　平板になりにくい9モーラの実在薬品名
　　　メルカプミダゾリン（平板率50%（5/10 人））
(3)　平板になりやすい9モーラの実在薬品名
　　　ジプレキサントニン（平板率80%（8/10 人））

これらの語のアクセントが平板型になるのを予測すること，あるいは平板型になる理由や平板率の違いを説明することは，先行研究から得られている知見だけでは不可能だと考えられる．本稿はこの背景として擬似形態素境界が1語中に複数回挿入される可能性があるということを考えており，その可能性を示す実験結果を提示する．

2. 仮説の前提となる概念

　本稿における仮説を次節で述べるが，その前に仮説の前提となる概念（用語）について述べておく．まずは「擬（似）複合構造」・「擬似複合語構造」・「擬似複合語」（および「擬似形態素境界」・「擬似語境界」）といった一連のものが挙がる．そもそもは佐藤 (2002) における「擬複合構造」が最初であるが，その後，窪薗 (2004) や窪薗・小川 (2005) などでも用いられている．本稿にとって重要なのは，一連の用語に共通する比較的長い語については，形態的に単純語であっても，音韻的には，一般的な（形態的な）複合語と類似の擬似複合語として扱われるという考え方である．窪薗 (2004) や窪薗・

小川（2005）では，複合語と同様のプロセスにおいて語アクセントの決定や短縮語形成がなされるという主張がなされており．この主張に基づくと以下の (4a) と (4b) が平行的なプロセスであるということになる．

(4) アクセント決定と短縮語形成の例（［＋］：擬似形態素境界）
    a. コンペティション＝コンペ＋ティション

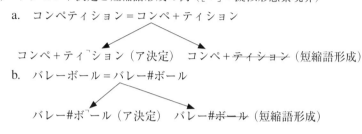

    コンペ＋ティ⌐ション（ア決定）   コンペ＋ティション（短縮語形成）
    b. バレーボール＝バレー#ボール

    バレー#ボ⌐ール（ア決定）   バレー#ボール（短縮語形成）

次に，上と関連した重要な概念（用語）として「擬似平板化形態素」（儀利古（2009））がある．これは擬似複合語を前提とした概念で，一般的な（形態的な）複合語の場合の平板化形態素（McCawley（1968））と同様のもの，すなわち擬似複合語の場合の平板化形態素が存在すると考えるものである．儀利古（2009）に基づけば，平板化形態素の1つである「-党」が付いた複合語が平板型アクセントになる例 (5b) が，擬似平板化形態素の1つである「-リン」を"含む"語が平板型アクセントになる例 (5a) と平行的なプロセスであるということになる．

(5) 擬似平板化形態素と平板化形態素（儀利古（2009））
    a. インスリン＝インス＋リン^0（実在語）
       プリリリン＝プリリ＋リン^0（非実在語）
    b. 社会党＝しゃかい#とう^0（実在語）
       ビビデバビデ党＝ビビデバビデ#とう^0（非実在語）

3. 本稿の仮説

先行研究で主張されていることをまとめると (6)(7) のようになる．(6) については，(6a, b) の例外は考えにくく，(6c, d) については傾向であって例外もあり得るようである．

(6) 擬似形態素境界の挿入位置（窪薗・小川（2005））
   a. 語の長さが5モーラ以上のときに擬似形態素境界が挿入される．
   b. 擬似形態素境界を挿入するときに，音節を分断しない．
   c. 語を半分の長さに分ける位置に挿入される傾向がある．
   d. 前部要素≧後部要素になるように挿入される傾向がある．
(7) 擬似平板化形態素（医学・化学用語における語末の /Cin/[3]）

(儀利古（2009））

これらを前提に，本稿による新たな主張（8）を付け加えて仮説とする．

(8) **上記の（6）にしたがって擬似形態素境界が挿入された後，5モーラ以上の要素が残っていれば，その要素に対して擬似形態素境界の挿入がもう一度なされる．**

ここで示した主張（8）が正しければ，(6)(7)(8) を組み合わせることによって（2）(3) で挙げた語の平板型アクセントが出現する理由（および平板率）は以下のように説明される可能性がある．

(9) 9モーラの実在薬品名が平板型になる仕組み
   a. メルカプミダゾリン→メルカプ＋ミダゾリン
      →メルカプ＋ミダゾ＋**リン**^{0}
   b. ジプレキサントニン→ジプレキ＋サントニン
      →ジプレキ＋サント＋**ニン**^{0}

なお，(9a) の「メルカプ＋ミダゾリン」(i.e.「4＋5」の挿入方法）は (6c, d) から「OK だが少数派」の擬似形態素境界挿入方法と考えられる．(6c) には当てはまるが，(6d) には当てはまらないからである．(6a-d) の全てに当てはまる「5＋4」の「メルカプミ＋ダゾリン」の方が多数派で，「4＋5」の「メルカプ＋ミダゾリン」は（例外的に）一部出現する可能性があるという程度であろう．一方で，(9b) の「ジプレキ＋サントニン」は6モーラ目が特殊モーラであるため，「5＋4」の「ジプレキサ＋ントニン」にすると (6b) に反してしまう．そのため「4＋5」の「ジプレキ＋サントニン」の可能性が非常

---

[3] C は任意の子音を表し，「-リン /-rin/」「-ミン /-min/」などが含まれる．

に高くなる．このように考えると，(9a) と (9b) では平板型がともに許容され得るのだが，平板型が許される割合としては (9b) の方が高いと予測されるのである．

4. 実験

前節で述べた主張 (8) を検証すべく実験を行った．

4.1. 内容

語末に /Cin/ を含む 9 モーラ無意味語のアクセントを聞いての許容度判定実験を行った．同じ 9 モーラの語であるが，被験者が聞く音声には語中の特殊モーラの位置が異なる語が含まれている．それぞれの語が最大で 4 通りのアクセントで発音される．4 通りの内訳は，無核（「0」）が 1 通り，有核（「−3」「−4」「−5」）が 3 通りである．[4] 特殊モーラにアクセント核が置かれる発音は実験に用いなかった．それぞれのアクセントについて，「化学薬品名のアクセントとして『OK』あるいは『NG』」で被験者に判断してもらった．語に含まれる母音の種類は /a/ のみ（語末を除く）に限定した．語中の特殊モーラは撥音と引き音を用いた．被験者が聞いた音声の録音者は東京出身の 30 代女性である．実際の聞き取り判断実験においては，本稿で結果を分析する「実験語」だけでなく実在の薬品名を「ダミー語」として提示した．語順についてはランダマイズされており，すべての被験者について異なる順番で音声の提示がなされている．[5] 被験者は 10 名で，[6] 東京・埼玉・神奈川出身の 20 代である．被験者には 1000 円分の図書カードを進呈した．実験に使った語の例を音節構造別に 1 つずつ示しておく．実験に使った全ての語については付録を参照されたい．

---

[4] 「0」が平板型，「−3」「−4」「−5」はそれぞれ語末から何モーラ目にアクセント核が置かれる型かを示す．

[5] 当然ながら，音素配列が同じ語について異なるアクセントで発音されている音声は，それぞれを別の音声ファイルにして取り扱った．

[6] (10c) についてのみ，10 名中の 8 名のデータしか録れなかったため 8 名分を使用する．

(10) 実験語の例（μ: モーラ，N: 撥音，S: 撥音または引き音）
    a. ガタラナカタチャミン（$\mu\mu\mu\mu\mu\mu\mu$N）
    b. ラガハンタファラリン（$\mu\mu\mu$S$\mu\mu\mu\mu$N）
    c. マハダナンサファリン（$\mu\mu\mu\mu$S$\mu\mu\mu$N）
    d. パカヤファマンナミン（$\mu\mu\mu\mu\mu$S$\mu\mu$N）[7]

(11) 各被験者が実験中に聞いた音声数
    (10a)の音節構造を持つ語 15 語×アクセント 4 通り = 60
    (10b)の音節構造を持つ語 15 語×アクセント 4 通り = 60
    (10c)の音節構造を持つ語 15 語アクセント 3 通り[8] = 45
    (10d)の音節構造を持つ語 9 語×アクセント 3 通り = 27
    ダミー語 12 語×アクセント 2 通り[9] = 24
<u>　　　　　　　　　　　　　　　　　　　　　　合計 216 音声</u>

4.2. 結果の予測

擬似形態素境界の挿入位置には（6b）の条件があるために，語中の特殊モーラの位置によって擬似形態素境界の挿入位置が限定されると考えられる．したがって，以下の（12）から（15）に図示したようなアクセント許容が予測される．（6d）が傾向であるため，（6a-c）から擬似形態素境界の挿入位置が 2 通り予想される場合は，両方とも許容され得るとした．ただし，許容度が高いと予測される方（＝前部要素が後部要素より長くなる方）を太い矢印で示している．

---

[7] (10d) については，今回実験を行った語の語中特殊モーラは撥音 (N) のみである．
[8] 特殊モーラにアクセント核が置かれる発音は実験に使用しなかったため，(10c) と (10d) の音節構造を持つ語では，アクセントは 4 通りでなく 3 通りである．
[9] 「ダミー語」については無核と有核がそれぞれ 1 通りずつの 2 通りを提示した．

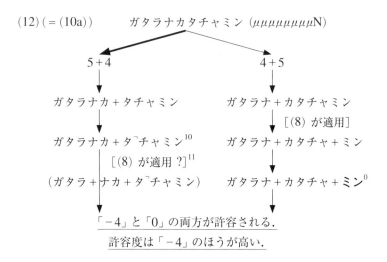

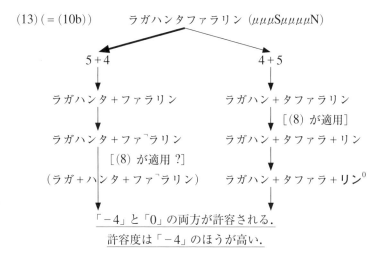

---

[10] 後部要素が4モーラ以下なので，一般的な複合語アクセント規則と同様の原理によって後部要素の初頭にアクセント核が置かれると考える．(13) (14) の「5+4」の例も同じ．

[11] 本稿では前部要素に対して (8) が適用されているかどうかの判断ができない．前部要素に (8) が適用されているかどうかが実験結果の予測に影響しないからである．

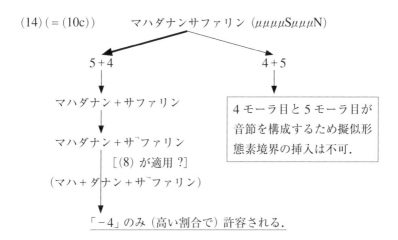

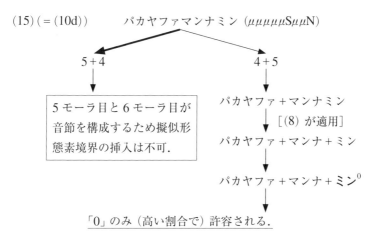

4.3. 結果

許容度判定実験の結果を以下の表1で示す．表1の内容を棒グラフで表したものが図1である．

		アクセント型許容度			
		0	−5	−4	−3
a.	$\mu\mu\mu\mu\mu\mu\mu$N	43.3%	60.0%	88.0%	60.0%
	cf. (10a)	(65/150)	(90/150)	(132/150)	(90/150)
b.	$\mu\mu\mu$S$\mu\mu\mu\mu$N	41.3%	44.7%	71.3%	60.0%
	cf. (10b)	(62/150)	(67/150)	(107/150)	(90/150)
c.	$\mu\mu\mu\mu$S$\mu\mu\mu$N	12.5%	N/A	91.7%	42.5%
	cf. (10c)	(15/120)		(110/120)	(51/120)
d.	$\mu\mu\mu\mu\mu$S$\mu\mu$N	67.8%	68.9%	N/A	57.8%
	cf. (10d)	(61/90)	(62/90)		(52/90)

表1. 構造別のアクセント型許容度[12]

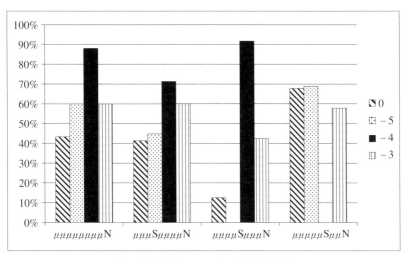

図1. 構造別のアクセント型許容度

4.4. 議論

本稿で実施した実験は複数のアクセント型のなかから1つを強制選択さ

---

[12] $\mu\mu\mu$S$\mu\mu\mu\mu$N および $\mu\mu\mu\mu$S$\mu\mu$N 構造の語の語末撥音を引き音に変えた語で実験すると，平板型アクセントが一切許容されなかった．すなわち，語末が /Cin/ でない場合には平板型アクセントは許容されない．この事実は儀利古（2009）の主張を裏付けるものである．

せる実験ではないので，本稿の主な分析対象ではない「−5」や「−3」のアクセントについても「OK」と判断されているものがある．これら「−5」や「−3」が比較的高い率で許容される理由については，先行研究で得られている知見では説明が難しいと同時に，本稿でも現時点では明確な説明ができないことを認めなければならない．「−5」については「4+5」の位置に擬似形態素境界の挿入がなされたものの，(8) あるいは擬似平板化形態素が働かなかったために複合語アクセント規則が適用された例と言えそうであるが，本稿の実験では完全な証明はできない．もっとも，「−5」の構造別の許容度を見ると，「5+4」で擬似形態素境界が挿入できない，すなわち「4+5」にしか擬似形態素境界が挿入できない構造（$\mu\mu\mu\mu S\mu\mu N$）において最も許容度が高い．これは「−5」が出現するのは擬似形態素境界の挿入が「4+5」のときであるという傍証となるだろう．以下では，「−4」と「0」について考える．

「−4」については「5+4」の位置に擬似形態素境界が挿入できる語，すなわち 6 モーラ目が特殊モーラではない語における最も典型的なアクセントパターンであるという予測が (12)-(14) からなされていたが，表 1(a)-(c) のいずれの構造においても最も許容度が高いのは「−4」であるという結果が出た．これは予測通りといえるだろう．

「0」については (12)-(15) で次のような 3 段階の許容度の予測がなされていた．

(16) 「0」の許容度予測
  $\mu\mu\mu\mu\mu\mu\mu N$ および $\mu\mu\mu S\mu\mu\mu N$：　許容される
  $\mu\mu\mu\mu S\mu\mu N$　　　　　　　　　：　許容されない
  $\mu\mu\mu\mu\mu S\mu\mu N$　　　　　　　：　高い割合で許容される

図 1 から「0」に関する部分だけを取り出すと図 2 のようになり，許容度によって 3 つのグループに分かれることが確認される．「0」についても予測通りといえるだろう．

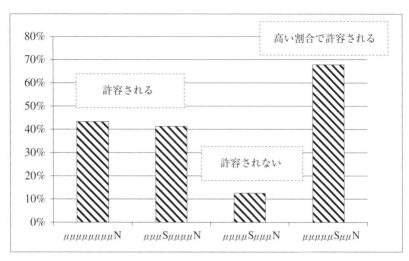

図 2. 構造別の平板型アクセント許容度

　以上の「-4」および「0」についての実験結果から，(12)-(15) の予測は正しいといえる．(12)-(15) の予測は擬似形態素境界が複数回挿入されるという本稿の主張 (8) を前提としなければ導けないものであるから，本稿の主張が正しいことを示しているといえるだろう．

5. 平板化形態素と擬似平板化形態素

　本稿で述べたい内容の中心は前節で述べたが，言及しておくべきことがある．それは平板化形態素と擬似平板化形態素の性質についてである．平板化形態素については平板化形態素が単独で右側要素として関わる場合にのみ語のアクセントを平板化するという性質が知られている（窪薗 (1993)）．この窪薗 (1993) に基づくと，例えば「地方線（ちほうせん^0）」と「新幹線（しんか￥んせん）」のアクセントの違いは以下のように説明される．(17) の下線部は平板化形態素（ここでは「-線」）の作用域である．

(17)　「地方線（ちほうせん^0）」と「新幹線（しんか￥んせん）」
　　　a.　ち#ほ￥う　せ￥ん　→　ちほう#せん^0
　　　b.　し￥ん　かん#せん^0　→　しん#か￥んせん

(17a) では平板化形態素「線」が「地方線」全体における単独右側要素なので,「地方線」という複合語全体が平板化される.しかし,(17b) で「線」が単独右側要素になるのは「幹線」という語が形成される段階であり,「新幹線」という語が形成される段階での右側要素は「線」単独でなく「幹線」である.「新幹線」全体における単独右側要素でない「線」は平板化形態素としての力を発揮することがなく,「新幹線」は平板型アクセントにならない.その結果,一般的な複合語アクセント規則によって有核アクセントとなるのである.つまり,「{新}{{幹}{線}}」のような右枝分かれ構造の語においては,平板化形態素が複合語の最も右端の位置にあったとしても,単独の要素でない限り平板化形態素の働きが複合語全体に及ぶことがないのである.そして,右枝別れ構造の複合語については「{えー}#{{ほんこん}#{がた}^{0}}」(A 香港型)や「{ぱんしん}#{{だい}#{し゚んさい}}」(阪神大震災)のようにアクセントが1つにまとまらない例があることも知られている(窪薗(1999)).

一方で,擬似複合語構造が関係する場合に,「{えー}#{{ほんこん}#{がた}^{0}}」(A 香港型)のような,音韻的に1つにまとまらないアクセントが出現することは無いようである.すなわち,「ラガハンタファラリン」という語で「{ラ゚ガハン}+{タファラ+リン^0}」のようなアクセントは観察されない.この理由としては2つの可能性があるように思われる.1つ目の可能性は平板化形態素と擬似平板化形態素でそもそも性質が異なるというものである.すなわち,「平板化形態素は自身が単独の右側要素である場合でなければアクセントを平板化する力を発揮しないため,語内部の枝分かれの仕方によっては平板化形態素を右端に含みながらも『新幹線(しんか゚んせん)』のように有核アクセントになる語が存在するが,擬似平板化形態素にはそのような制限がなく,擬似平板化形態素が語の最も右端にあれば,その語全体が平板型アクセントになる.」という可能性である.もう1つの可能性は,平板化形態素と擬似平板化形態素の性質に差はないが,擬似複合語構造における枝分れの仕方に制限があるというものである.すなわち,「平板化形態素も擬似平板化形態素も単独の右側要素である場合でなければ力を発揮しないという点で共通しているが,擬似複合語構造がそもそも右枝分かれ構造になりにくい.」という可能性である.例えば,「ラガハンタファラリン」が「5+4」か「4+5」になるとすれば,(i)「{ラガハンタ}+{ファラリン}」→

「{{ラガ}+{ハンタ}}+{ファラリン}}」，あるいは，(ii)「{ラガハン}+{タファラリン}}」→「{ラガハン}+{{タファラ}+{リン}}」のように擬似形態素境界が入ると考えられる．しかしながら，後者 (ii) のような「{ラガハン}+{{タファラ}+{リン}}」という右枝分かれ構造においてアクセント付与がなされる前に「{{ラガハン}+{タファラ}}+{リン}}」という左分かれ構造に再構成しているのではないだろうか．この再構成については，擬似複合語には意味の"支えがなく，"擬似複合語の要素を成す（擬似）形態素の意味から枝分かれ方向を決めることができない点に根拠を求めることができるかもしれない．擬似複合語は一般的な複合語と違い，意味に"とらわれることなく"枝分かれ方向を決めることができるというわけである．[13]

　以上，平板化形態素と擬似平板化形態素の性質に関連して2つの可能性を述べたが，本稿の内容からどちらか一方の可能性に確定されるものではない．ただし，背景にある原理は今後の課題としても，擬似複合語の最も右端の位置に擬似平板化形態素がある（＝擬似平板化形態素が語の最も右の位置に表れるような位置に擬似形態素境界が入る）状況において，擬似複合語全体が平板型アクセントになるという前提で行った本稿の実験には一定の妥当性があるといえるだろう．

6. 結論

　本稿では擬似形態素境界が1語中に複数入る可能性を示した．「擬似形態素境界は形態素境界と同様に1語中に複数入り得る」と表現すると，擬似形態素境界がより形態素境界に近い性質を持っていることを示したように感じるかもしれないが，実はこれは言葉遊びであって，そうではない．なぜなら，擬似形態素境界は音韻的概念であり，形態素境界に近い／遠いと言うことにあまり意味はないからである．むしろ，本稿の内容によって擬似形態素境界（および擬似複合語）という概念から一般的な複合語アクセント規則を

---

[13] ちなみに，上記 (ii) の「4＋5」の場合に枝分かれの再構成をしているのではなく，一括処理で「ラガハンタファラリン」→「ラガハン＋タファラ＋リン」と擬似形態素境界を挿入して，より無標な（擬似）左枝分かれ構造「{{ラガハン}+{タファラ}}+{リン}}」を作っている可能性も否定はできない．この場合，(8) の主張に若干の修正が迫られることになる．(8) では擬似形態素境界が循環的なプロセスで挿入されるとしているからである．

見ることができる基盤が整ったといえるのではないだろうか．すなわち，擬似形態素境界（=『音韻的な切れ目』）が挿入される位置を予測する際（(6)）に「形態素境界の位置に挿入される」を書き加えることで，これまで擬似複合語と呼んでいたものと一般的な複合語と呼んでいたもののアクセントの違いが音韻的観点からは無いに等しくなる．(6) は改新されて，擬似なのか否かは問題にならず，一般に5モーラ以上の語のアクセントを決めるルールの一部となる．これまでの複合語アクセント規則（秋永（1985），など）と，擬似複合語のアクセント規則を統合したルールは以下のようになると思われる．

(18) 5モーラ以上の語のアクセントが決定される基本ルール
　a. 語の長さが5モーラ以上のときに『音韻的な切れ目』が挿入される．
　b. 『音韻的な切れ目』は形態素境界の位置に挿入される．
　c. 形態素境界が無い場合は，語を半分に分ける位置に挿入される．
　d. 『音韻的な切れ目』を (b)(c) に従って挿入しても，5モーラ以上の要素が残る場合は，その要素にも『音韻的な切れ目』が (c) に準じて挿入される．
　e. 最も右端の『音韻的な切れ目』の周辺にアクセント核が置かれる．但し，最も右端の要素が擬似平板化形態素の場合は語全体が平板型になる．最も右端の要素が平板型形態素の場合は1つ左の要素までを平板型にする．

これによって，(1) で示した一般的な複合語におけるアクセントの違いも説明できるようになる．

(19) 南メ˥キシコ *vs.* 南カレドニア^0
　a. みなみ^0＃めきしこ^0 → みなみ＃＋めきしこ
　　　　　　　　　　　　　 → みなみ＋めきしこ
　　　　　　　　　　　　　　　（後部要素が5モーラ未満）
　　　　　　　　　　　　　 → みなみ＋め˥きしこ
　b. みなみ^0＃かれどにあ^0 → みなみ＃＋かれどにあ
　　　　　　　　　　　　　　 → みなみ＋かれど＋にあ

(後部要素が5モーラ以上)
→ みなみ＋かれど＋にあ^0
(※地名の /-Cia/ は平板化形態素)

以上が本稿で述べたかったことである．

　もっとも，本稿の中で述べたような問題点も残っている．本稿の実験でも許容された「-5」や「-3」の説明ができない点が先行研究から一貫した問題点である．また，5節で述べた平板化形態素と擬似平板化形態素の性質の違いについてはより詳細な議論を必要とするだろう．それから，{電子}#{{顕微}#{鏡}}^{0}のような，3要素から成る右枝分かれ構造の語が平板型になる理由については先行研究と同様に例外的な扱いをして，「顕微鏡^0」のアクセントが複合語全体に引き継がれるといった規則を考えざるを得ない．

参考文献

秋永一枝 (1985)「共通語のアクセント」『NHK 日本語発音アクセント辞典』(「──解説・付録──」)，NHK 放送文化研究所(編)，70-116, 日本放送協会，東京．

儀利古幹雄 (2009)『日本語における語認識と平板型アクセント』博士論文 (神戸大学文化学研究科)．

窪薗晴夫 (1993)「日本語複合語における平板化形態素の作用域について」『日本語・日本文化研究』第3号，9-18, 大阪外国語大学日本語学科．

窪薗晴夫 (1999)『日本語の音声』岩波書店，東京．

窪薗晴夫 (2004)「音韻構造から見た単純語と派生語の境界」『文法と音声 IV』，音声文法研究会(編)，123-143, くろしお出版，東京．

窪薗晴夫・小川晋史 (2005)「「ストライキ」はなぜ「スト」か？──短縮と単語分節のメカニズム──」『現代形態論の潮流』，大石強・豊島庸二・西原哲雄(編)，155-174, くろしお出版，東京．

McCawley, James D. (1968) *The Phonological Component of a Grammar of Japanese*, Mouton, The Hague.

佐藤大和 (2002)「外来語における音節複合への区分化とアクセント」『音声研究』第6巻1号，67-78．

付録

	実験語	語中特殊拍
(10a)	**ガタラナカタチャミン**	なし
	パハガラマファカリン	なし
	サワガダザラパジン	なし
	キャタラカガタラチン	なし
	ダバサラカラパニン	なし
	ヤナジャカマナカリン	なし
	バザサタパファラミン	なし
	カパナジャサラファジン	なし
	シャマナラファタラチン	なし
	ガカハナサナタニン	なし
	ハタナマサナファリン	なし
	ガラハカマナラニン	なし
	ラカファダガラザミン	なし
	パラタカパナマリン	なし
	ナパマジャサカラミン	なし

	実験語	語中特殊拍
(10c)	マハダナンサファリン	撥音
	カファザランパタミン	撥音
	ナバガナンサナジン	撥音
	ワパナマンラカチン	撥音
	サパラカンラマニン	撥音
	ハガラカンダファリン	撥音
	ガファタカンマラニン	撥音
	バファカナンサナミン	撥音
	ハファカナーパタリン	引き音
	チャザダカーナパミン	引き音
	パカマナハータラジン	引き音
	ラファカダザーカラチン	引き音
	ジャナパサタータラニン	引き音
	カパラターファマリン	引き音
	ガワマガーカダニン	引き音

	実験語	語中特殊拍
(10b)	**ラガハンタファラリン**	撥音
	マバヤンガパナミン	撥音
	ザチャカンファラパジン	撥音
	タヤバンパガラチン	撥音
	ダラサンサハバニン	撥音
	ファガパンパカララリン	撥音
	ナガカンタラマニン	撥音
	ガラタンナパラミン	撥音
	ナハラーマバサリン	引き音
	ガダザータガラミン	引き音
	バヤラーラカラジン	引き音
	タザガーマガラチン	引き音
	ハファザーサラマニン	引き音
	ハバマーザマファリン	引き音
	サラファーマカラニン	引き音

	実験語	語中特殊拍
(10d)	パカヤファマンナミン	撥音
	ファサマザバンガリン	撥音
	バマサタサンパシン	撥音
	マガラカランダリン	撥音
	ザマシャラカンサミン	撥音
	ヤザワダファンサリン	撥音
	ジャナワカダンナリン	撥音
	カダファヤナンガミン	撥音
	ラカパナパンカジン	撥音

	ダミー語	
	インスリン	
	オロナイン	
	アスピリン	
	ラニチジン	
	グリセリン	
	ドーパミン	
	アセチレン	
	プロカイン	
	クルクミン	
	ブテナフィン	
	コラーゲン	
	システイン	

Part IV

音声知覚・生成とL1獲得

"Good Infant-directed Words" Do Not Sound
like "Good Japanese Words."*

Reiko Mazuka[1,2], Akiko Hayashi[3] and Tadahisa Kondo[4]

Riken Brain Science Institute[1], *Duke University*[2],
Tokyo Gakugei University[3] *and Kogakuin University*[4]

1. **Introduction**

When adults talk to infants and young children, they modify their speech. This type of speech is called "motherese" or "infant-directed speech (IDS)." IDS is known to differ from adult-directed speech (ADS) in various ways, for example, an overall higher pitch, exaggerated intonation, and shorter utterances than ADS. Importantly, IDS is considered to facilitate infants' acquisition of language (Soderstrom (2007), for review). For example, an exaggerated intonation in IDS would facilitate infants' task of parsing speech stream, since prosodic boundaries roughly correspond to syntactic phrases as well. It has also been proposed that segments in IDS tend to be hyperarticulated, which facilitates infants' acquisition of segmental categories. Nonetheless, the link between a specific characteristic of IDS and how it may help infants' language acquisition is correlational, and critical evaluation of these proposals is difficult.

In the present paper, we try to investigate the link between a specific property of IDS, and how it may or may not be related to infants' language acquisition by focusing on one of unique properties of Japanese IDS. In the Japanese language, it has been noted that the use of special-

---

* We thank Haruo Kubozono for his assistance in testing college aged adults. The research reported in this chapter was supported in part by Grant-in-Aid for Scientific Research S (16H06319) to the first author, and by the NINJAL collaborative research project 'Cross-linguistic Studies of Japanese Prosody and Grammar'.

ized vocabulary is particularly prevalent (Murata (1960, 1968), Murase, Ogura and Yamashita (1992), Ogura (2006), Tsuji, Nishikawa and Mazuka (2014)). In this paper, we will call them Infant-directed vocabulary (IDV). Relevantly, individual items of Japanese IDV often bear little resemblance to corresponding adult words phonologically. It is because many of them are derived from onomatopoeia or mimetics, and they often involve repetition of single syllables or bi-syllabic units. For example, "maNma" for 'gohan' (food), and "waNwaN" for 'inu' (dog).

To quantify what kinds of words are used as IDV, Mazuka, Kondo, and Hayashi (2008) surveyed Japanese mothers, asking them to list IDV items they would use themselves. They found that the majority of IDV items were indeed phonologically unrelated to the adult forms of the words. Instead, they tend to take specific prosodic forms; namely 3-mora, 2-syllable, Heavy-Light (HL) form (e.g., maN.ma), or 4-mora, 2-syllable Heavy-Heavy (HH) form (e.g., waN.waN). To examine whether these forms actually occur frequently in Japanese IDS, they analyzed a corpus of Japanese IDS (RIKEN-Japanese mother-infant conversation corpus, R-JMICC, Mazuka, Igarashi and Nishikawa (2006)), and compared it to the ADS spoken by the same mothers. In addition, following sources were also examined; a different corpus of spoken Japanese (Corpus of Spoken Japanese, CSJ, Maekawa (2006)), written texts from newspaper articles (from the 'Asahi Newspaper'; Amano and Kondo (2000)), and all content words listed in the Japanese dictionary (Shinmeikai Kokugo Jiten 'Shinmeikai Japanese Dictionary,' Amano and Kondo (1999)). They found that one of the IDV word types, HL-type words, occurred more frequently than any other types of words in IDS. Interestingly, this form (HL-type) did not occur frequently in any of the adult Japanese data they analyzed.

As discussed above, the fact that the prominent form of IDV is not a property of adult Japanese has significant implications for our understanding of IDS, since IDS properties have been assumed to facilitate language acquisition by highlighting and/or enhancing specific aspects of adult language. Learning an IDV item "waNwaN" for dog is not likely to make it easier for infants to learn the adult word 'inu,' nor would it offer a benefit of learning a prominent pattern of the target language, in the same manner that a trochaic word form in English IDV, such as "doggy" or "mommy," would. Then, what roles, if any, would Japanese IDV serve for Japanese infants?

In order to address this question, it is important to examine where the specific properties of Japanese IDV came from? In the literature, it has been noted that IDV forms are similar to the word form young children produce in their early production (Murata (1960, 1968)). On the basis of this, it has been argued that the properties of IDVs are derived from children's early production, i.e., mothers are trying to produce words in a similar form infants would produce themselves. It is also possible that Japanese adults learned IDVs from hearing specific lexical items of IDV, e.g., "aNyo" and "neNne," either when they were growing up or from other adults using them. Alternatively, it is possible that native speakers of Japanese have an intuitive sense of good IDV forms, reflecting their underlying phonological knowledge for a good word for young children, although they may not occur frequently in day-to-day adult Japanese. In this case, native speakers' sense of good IDV forms are likely to be independent of actual lexical knowledge for specific word.

To examine whether either of these predictions is valid, we conducted a series of rating studies with Japanese adults. We report parts of the results from two of the rating experiments in which adult native speakers of Japanese were asked to rate nonsense words in terms of how good they sound as IDV's or Japanese words. We will combine the results of these experiments with those from other rating experiments (Mazuka and Hayashi (2003), Mazuka, Hayashi, Takahashi and Kondo (2004)).

If IDV forms are derived from infants' early production, and mothers are producing these forms because they are trying to imitate children's production, a mother who has an extensive experience interacting with her own infant should have a better sense of what good IDV forms should sound like compared to college-age adults whose experience interacting with young children are limited. If, alternatively, native speakers of Japanese have the intuitive sense of what a good IDV should sound like, reflecting their underlying phonological knowledge, even college-age adults should have a good sense of IDV-ness, and that their IDV-ness ratings should be similar to that of mothers. Additionally, if the IDV properties reflect an underlying linguistic knowledge of Japanese word form, items that receive high ratings as IDV may also be rated as good Japanese words.

2. Rating Experiments

2.1. Material

A total of 711 nonsense words were selected from two previous rating studies with Japanese adults (Mazuka and Hayashi (2003), Mazuka, Hayashi, Takahashi and Kondo (2004)). In the first rating study, 107 college-aged adults were asked to rate how good a nonsense word sounds like when compared to an IDV. A total of 755 words were created, such that they varied in terms of the length of words (1, 2, 3, or 4 mora), types of segments (vowels and consonants), whether they contained one of the special morae (long vowel, H; geminate obstruent, Q; moraic nasal, N), and where they occurred. Each word was rated on a 7 point scale, from "This word sounds like a very good IDV, 7" to "This word does not sound like an IDV at all, 1". Stimuli were divided into 4 sets, and each participant rated approximately 300 of the stimuli which were visually presented in kana-characters on a computer screen. In the second study, a separate group of 57 college-aged adults were asked to rate a different set of nonsense words. A total of 1,452 nonsense words (961 4-mora words, 323 3-mora words, and 168 1- and 2-mora words) were included. In addition, 84 filler items were also included.

From these studies, 98 items from the first rating study and 613 items (including 84 filler items) from the second study, a total of 711 items were selected for the present study. There were 35 1-mora, 91 2-mora, 214 3-mora, and 371 4-mora words. Among other factors, 3- and 4-mora words were systematically varied in terms of their repetition patterns as shown in Table 1. Among 4-mora words, 19 patterns were created without heavy syllables so that either consonants alone, vowels alone, or both consonants and vowels varied. Additionally, 16 patterns were also tested in which the positions of heavy syllables were varied. Similarly, 12 patterns were created with 3-mora words.

Table 1.
Patterns of 4- and 3-mora words examined in the present study. Either consonants, vowels, or both consonants and vowels were varied systematically to test how these patterns contribute to Japanese native speakers' ratings on IDV-ness and Japanese-ness. Actual test items also varied in the types of consonants and vowels. But not all combinations of vowels and consonants were tested in all of the patterns. Thus, not all examples listed below were actually used in the survey. Figures 1 and 2 do not show the results from all patterns. L = light syllables, H = heavy syllables, S = special mora.

Pattern	Consonant	Vowel	Mora	Syllable	Examples	*kana*-characters
4-mora words without heavy syllables						
1	AAAA	AAAA	AAAA	LLLL	papapapa	ぱぱぱぱ
2	ABAB	AAAA	ABAB	LLLL	pakapaka	ぱかぱか
3	AABB	AAAA	AABB	LLLL	papakaka	ぱぱかか
4	ABBA	AAAA	ABBA	LLLL	pakakapa	ぱかかぱ
5	ABAC	AAAA	ABAC	LLLL	pakapata	ぱかぱた
6	ABCB	AAAA	ABCB	LLLL	pakataka	ぱかたか
7	ABCD	AAAA	ABCD	LLLL	pakatama	ぱかたま
8	AAAA	ABAB	ABAB	LLLL	papupapu	ぱぷぱぷ
9	AAAA	AABB	AABB	LLLL	papapupu	ぱぱぷぷ
10	AAAA	ABBA	ABBA	LLLL	papupupa	ぱぷぷぱ
11	AAAA	ABAC	ABAC	LLLL	papupape	ぱぷぱぺ
12	AAAA	ABCB	ABCB	LLLL	papupepu	ぱぷぺぷ
13	AAAA	ABCD	ABCD	LLLL	papupepo	ぱぷぺぽ
14	ABAB	ABAB	ABAB	LLLL	pakupaku	ぱくぱく
15	AABB	AABB	AABB	LLLL	papakuku	ぱぱくく
16	ABBA	ABBA	ABBA	LLLL	pakukupa	ぱくくぱ
17	ABAC	ABAC	ABAC	LLLL	pakupate	ぱくぱて
18	ABCB	ABCB	ABCB	LLLL	pakuteku	ぱくてく
19	ABCD	ABCD	ABCD	LLLL	pakuteme	ぱくてめ
With heavy syllables						
20	ASAA	ASAA	ASAA	HLL	paNpapa	ぱんぱぱ
21	AASA	AASA	AASA	LHL	papaNpa	ぱぱんぱ
22	AAAS	AAAS	AAAS	LLH	papapaN	ぱぱぱん
23	ASAS	ASAS	ASAS	HH	paNpaN	ぱんぱん
24	ASBB	ASAA	ASBB	HLL	paNkaka	ぱんかか

25	ASBS	ASAS	ASBS	HH	paNkaN	ぱんかん
26	ASBC	ASAA	ASBC	HLL	paNkata	ぱんかた
27	ASAA	ASBB	ASBB	HLL	paNpupu	ぱんぷぷ
28	ASAS	ASBS	ASBS	HH	paNpuN	ぱんぷん
29	ASAA	ASBC	ASBC	HLL	paNpupe	ぱんぷぺ
30	ASBB	ASBB	ASBB	HLL	paNkuku	ぱんくく
31	ASBS	ASBS	ASBS	HH	daNkuN	ぱんくん
32	ASBC	ASBC	ASBC	HLL	paNkute	ぱんくて
Different special morae						
33	AS1AS2	AS1AS2	ASAS	HH	paHpaN	ぱーたん
34	AS1BS2	AS1AsS2	ASBS	HH	paQkaH	ぱっかー
35	AS1BS2	AS1BS2	ASBS	HH	paNkuH	ぱんくー
3-mora words with no heavy syllables						
1	AAA	AAA	AAA	LLL	papapa	ぱぱぱ
2	ABA	AAA	ABA	LLL	pakapa	ぱかぱ
3	AAB	AAA	AAB	LLL	papaka	ぱぱか
4	ABB	AAA	ABB	LLL	pakaka	ぱかか
5	ABC	AAA	ABC	LLL	pakata	ぱかた
6	AAA	ABA	ABA	LLL	papupa	ぱぷぱ
7	AAA	AAB	AAB	LLL	papapu	ぱぱぷ
8	AAA	ABB	ABB	LLL	papupu	ぱぷぷ
9	AAA	ABC	ABC	LLL	papupe	ぱぷぺ
With special morae						
10	ASA	ASA	ASA	HL	paNpa	ぱんぱ
11	AAS	AAS	AAS	LH	papaN	ぱぱん
12	ASB	ASB	ASB	HL	paNpu	ぱんぷ

Among 3-mora words, patterns 10 and 12 were Heavy-Light (HL) bi-syllabic forms that were found prominently in IDV survey. Also among 4-mora words, patterns 23, 25, 28, 31 and 33–35 were Heavy-Heavy (HH) bi-syllabic forms that were also found frequently in IDV. In addition, the study was designed to test the possibility that a bimoraic units, that are not a heavy syllable, may also contribute to the impression of IDV. They are often found in onomatopoeia and mimetic words, such as "nadenade" or "gatagoto," and may make a word sound like a good IDV word. It has been proposed that a bimoraic unit may serve a foot-like function in Japanese phonology (Porser (1990)). If true, a word containing bimoraic units may be judged as a good Japanese word or an IDV as well.

The 711 items were divided into 5 sets, so that one participant rated 142 or 143 items. The order of the items were randomized and printed into a paper-and-pencil survey.

2.2. Participants

In the IDV-ness survey, 152 Japanese parents with infants and/or young children (150 mothers and 2 fathers, 27–42 years of age, $M = 33.03$) answered the survey, which they received by mail. They were asked to rate the nonsense words listed in the survey in terms of how good each item sounds like as an IDV on 7 a point scale, from "sounds like a very good IDV word (7)" to "does not sound like an IDV word at all (1)". In the Japanese-ness survey, 147 college-aged adults (81 female, 18–27 years of age, $M = 18.98$) answered the survey in a linguistics class. The items in the survey were identical to the IDV-ness survey. But the participants in the Japanese-ness survey were asked to rate how good each item sounds like as a Japanese word on a 7 point scale from "it sounds like a very good Japanese word (7)" to "does not at all sound like a good Japanese word (1)".

2.3. Results

IDV ratings collected in the previous ratings study were extracted for the items that were also used in the present study. The combined results consisted of three sets of ratings for the same nonsense words; IDV-ness ratings by mothers (and fathers), IDV-ness ratings by college-age adults, and Japanese-ness ratings by a separate group of college-aged adults.

In order to analyze what kind of word forms are judged as good IDV or good Japanese word, 3-mora and 4-mora words with and without heavy syllables were analyzed separately. For the sake of clarity, results of some of the word types are not included in Figures 1 and 2. Figure 1a shows a subset of results for 3 mora-words without heavy syllables. The top panel shows the mothers' ratings of IDV-ness, middle panel shows the IDV-ness ratings of college-age adults, and the bottom panel shows the Japanese-ness ratings of college-age adults. Comparison of three graphs shows that the IDV-ness ratings of mothers and college-age adults are much more similar to each other than to the Japanese-ness ratings, although college-aged adults gave lower IDV-ness ratings in general than mothers. For example, when vowels are changed keeping consonants unchanged (i.e., vowel-change condition), IDV-ness ratings were generally higher than when consonants were changed. However, this pattern was reversed in Japanese-ness ratings. When vowels and consonants are repeated, i.e., AAA pattern, they are rated higher in IDV-ness, while ABC patterns were rated lower than other patterns. In the Japanese-ness ratings, in contrast, neither AAA was rated higher than others, nor were ABC patterns rated lower than others.

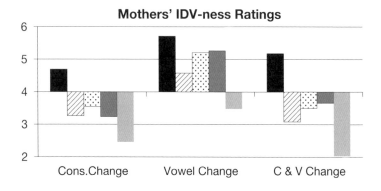

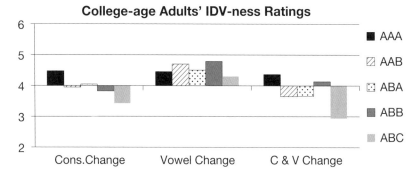

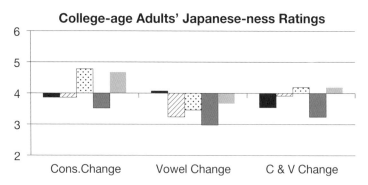

Figure 1a. Mothers and college-age adults' IDV-ness and Japanese-ness rating for 3-mora words without heavy syllables.

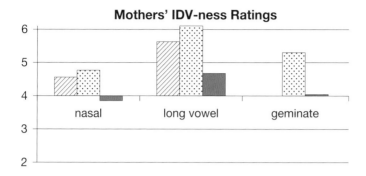
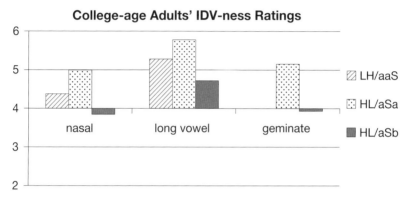
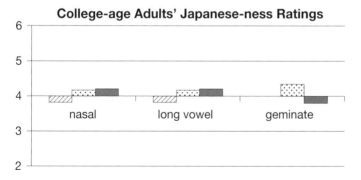

Figure 1b. Mothers' and college-age adults' IDV-ness and Japanese-ness ratings for 3-mora words with heavy syllables.

Figure 1b shows the 3-mora words with a heavy syllable. Again, mothers and college-aged adults showed very similar pattern of IDV-ness ratings, as opposed to the Japanese-ness ratings. As mentioned above, 3-mora, 2-syllable, Heavy-Light (HL) form was the most prominent IDV form among actual IDV items Japanese mothers reported to use. Both mothers and college-age adults gave the highest IDV-ness ratings for the HL/aSa (i.e., paNpa) pattern, showing their intuitive judgment that this is a good IDV form, and it is consistent with the actual lexical items used in infant-directed speech. Interestingly, although it was also an HL form, aSb pattern was not rated as a good IDV form. Among actual IDV items, many HL/aSb forms were reported, for example, "aNyo" for *ashi* (foot), "taQchi" for *tatsu* (stand up). Further studies are needed to examine what may contribute to this discrepancy.

Figure 2a shows a subset of 4-mora words without a heavy syllable. Consistent with 3-mora words, mothers and college-age adults' IDV-ness ratings of 4-mora words showed a similar pattern, while the Japanese-ness ratings showed a different pattern. The tendency that vowel changes being rated higher than consonant changes was also consistent with 3-mora words. The tendency that AAAA pattern was rated higher than ABCD pattern was also consistent with 3-mora words. The fact that AAAA pattern did not receive high Japanese-ness ratings or that ABCD pattern did not receive low ratings was consistent with 3-mora word results also.

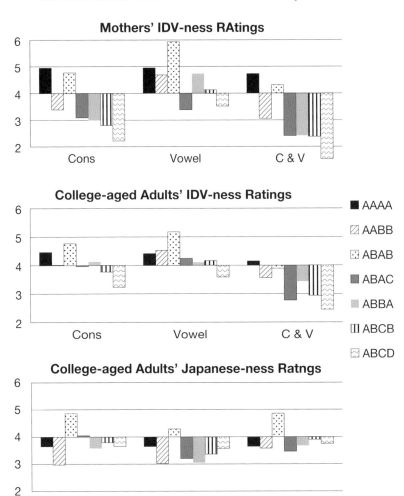

Figure 2a. IDV-ness and Japanese-ness ratings for 4-mora words without heavy syllables.

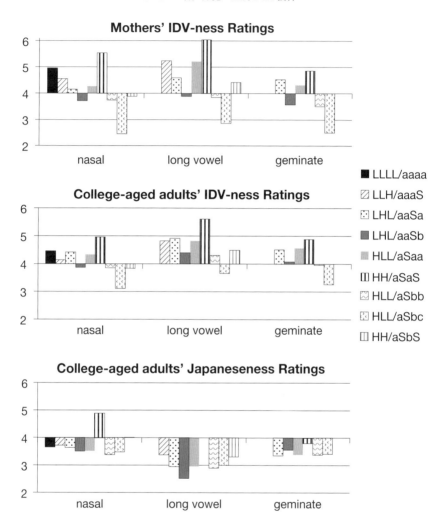

Figure 2b. IDV-ness and Japanese-ness ratings for 4-mora words with heavy syllables. LLLL/aaaa forms were included for comparison.

In addition, 4-mora word stimuli were designed to examine a potential role that 2-mora unit may play. For the present study, we examined 4 types of 2-mora unit; 1) Two moras were repeated as in AABB, or in the middle position, as in ABBA, 2) Two mora unit repeated in ABAB pattern, 3) ABAC pattern in which the second and forth mora changed, and 4) ABCB pattern in which the first and third mora changed. The results showed that ABAB pattern, especially when vowels changed, received highest IDV-ness ratings. Interestingly, ABAB forms also received high Japanese-ness ratings. In contrast, none of the other 2-mora units received high ratings either as IDV or Japanese words.

Figure 2b shows the results for the 4-mora words with heavy syllables. Once again, mothers and college-age adults gave similar patterns of IDV-ness ratings compared to Japanese-ness. Similar to 3-mora words results, HH/aSaS pattern but not HH/aSbS pattern, received high IDV-ness ratings. Recall that among 3-mora, 2-syllable words, HL were rated high in the IDV-ness only when the first and the last mora were the same, i.e., aSa pattern, but not in aSb form. In the actual IDV items collected from the mothers (Mazuka et al. (2008)), both aSa and aSb occurred frequently among HL forms. In contrast, the pattern among 4-mora 2-syllable, HH words, aSaS form (i.e., waNwaN, buHbuH) occurred much more frequently than aSbS forms (baQchiH, goQkuN). Thus, the IDV-ness ratings were consistent with the actual IDV items mothers reported to use.

The pattern of results indicate that mothers and college-age adults were very similar in their IDV-ness ratings, while the same stimuli were rated very differently in terms of their Japanese-ness. To quantify how close the IDV-ness ratings were between mothers and college-age adults, the correlations among mothers' ratings of IDV-ness, college-age adults' ratings of IDV-ness, and college-age adults' Japanese-ness ratings were calculated. For this calculation, 529 items were used from the second one of the two previous rating studies (excluding 84 filler items from a total of 613 items). Recall that separate groups of participants were tested in the two previous rating studies. This ensured that all of the college-age adults' IDV-ness rating came from a single group of participants. For each item, an average of mothers' and college-age adults' ratings of IDV-ness and an average of Japanese-ness ratings by college-age adults were calculated. Using these data, Pearson's correlation coefficients were computed for the 529 items. The results are shown in Table 2. Consistent with the patterns we found in Figures 1 and 2, the correlation between mothers and college-age adults on their IDV-ness ratings was .867, which was exceedingly high in a rating study of this type. In contrast, mothers' IDV-ness ratings had zero correlation with college-age adults' ratings of Japanese-ness. College-age adults' IDV-ness ratings showed a statistically significant negative correlation with the Japanese-ness ratings from another group of college-age adults. This means that for college-aged adults, the more IDV-like an item was, the less Japanese-like it was.

Table 2.
Correlations among Mothers' ratings of IDV-ness, college age adults' IDV-ness, and college age adults' Japanese-ness ratings. N = 529 items. Correlation coefficients are Pearson's Correlation coefficients.

	Mothers' IDV-ness	College-age adults' IDV-ness	College-age adults' Japanesenes
Mothers' IDV-ness	1.00	0.867 P<.001	−0.02 n.s.
College-age adults' IDV-ness		1.00	−0.23 p<.001
College-age adults' Japanese-ness			1.00

3. Discussion

An important characteristic of Japanese IDS is that they use a specialized vocabulary in high frequency. But IDV bare little phonological resemblance to the corresponding adult word. The present paper examined what kinds of words are judged as good IDV forms by native speakers of Japanese; both mothers and non-mothers. A large number of nonsense words were created such that they varied in their word length both in morae, and syllables, and the pattern of repetition in vowels and consonants

(Table 1). The results revealed that the two forms that were found frequently in actual IDV lexical items, 3-mora 2-syllable HL form and 4-mora 2-syllable HH form, received high IDV-ness ratings both by Japanese mothers and college-age adults, revealing that both groups of Japanese native speakers had an intuitive sense of what a good IDV word should sound like, independent of actual lexical knowledge for specific word. The correlation between mothers and college-age adults in their IDV-ness ratings were exceedingly high, nearing almost .9, suggesting that this intuitive sense of what a good IDV sound like, is not something one needs to learn through their interaction with young children.

As mentioned in the introduction, the predominant view in the field is that the Japanese IDV forms come from infants' early production. If true, it is predicted that mothers who have extensive experience interacting with young children should have a stronger sense of what good IDV should sound like. But the results from the current study showed that college-age adults who had little opportunity to learn what young children's production sound like were almost as good as mothers in rating a large set of nonsense words in terms of IDV-ness. This is consistent with the alternative view, namely, the IDV forms must reflect an underlying linguistic knowledge of Japanese native speakers. At the same time, the IDV-ness is distinct from Japanese-ness, as the zero and minus correlation between IDV-ness and Japanese-ness ratings demonstrate.

The results of the present study showed that the specific forms that occur prominently in IDV are not learned through one's interaction with children. We are still left with a question of whether the IDV forms play some useful roles for infants and children trying to learn the Japanese language. Since learning an IDV item, such as "waNwaN" for dog is not likely to make it easier to learn the adult word "inu," some experts have advised against using IDV, arguing that IDV forces children to learn the name of things twice (Kubota, 2009). Much more research is needed to answer this question with Japanese infants and children. Nonetheless, eliminating one of the predominant views regarding the origin of IDV in Japanese is an important step forward towards understanding how specific features of IDS may contribute to children's language acquisition.

References

Amano, Shigeaki and Tadahisa Kondo (1999) *Nihongo no Goitokusei* (*Lexical Properties of Japanese*)*: Vol. 1, Tango Shinmitsudo* (*Word Familiarity*), Sanseido, Tokyo.

Amano, Shigeaki and Tadahisa Kondo (2000) *Nihongo no Goitokusei* (*Lexical Properties of Japanese*)*: Vol. 7, Shutsugenhindo* (*Frequency*), Sanseido, Tokyo.

Kubota, Kisou (2009) *Tensai-no Wo Tsukuru Zero-saiji Kyoiku* (*How to Educate Infants for a Genius-brain*), Daiwa Shobo, Tokyo.

Mazuka, Reiko, Yosuke Igarashi and Ken'ya Nishikawa (2006) *Input for Learning Japanese: RIKEN Japanese Mother-Infant Conversation Corpus*, The Institute of Electronics, Information and Communication Engineers, Tokyo.

Mazuka, Reiko and Akiko Hayashi (2003) "What Does a Good Akachan-Kotoba Sound like?: Japanese Adults' Intuitive Judgments about a Good Child-Directed Vocabulary," paper presented at the International Workshop on Origin of Language, Kyoto, Japan.

Mazuka, Reiko, Akiko Hayashi, Maki Takahashi and Tadahisa Kondo (2004) "What Does a Good Baby-word Sound like?: Japanese Adults' Intuitive Judgments about a Good Child Directed Vocabulary," poster presented at 14th Biennial International Conference on Infant Studies, 2004, Chicago.

Mazuka, Reiko, Tadahisa Kondo and Akiko Hayashi (2008) "Japanese Mothers' Use of Specialized Vocabulary in Infant-directed Speech: Infant-directed Vocabulary in Japanese," *Origin of Language reconsidered*, ed. by N. Masataka, Springer Verlag, Tokyo.

Murata, Kōji (1960) "Ikugijo no Kenkyu (A Study of Child-rearing Vocabulary)," *Shinrigaku Kenkyu* 31(6), 33–38.

Murata, Kōji (1968) *Youji no Gengo Hattatsu* (*Children's Language Development*), Baifukan, Tokyo.

Murase, Toshiki, Tamiko Ogura and Yukie Yamashita (1992) "Ikujigo no Kenkyu (1). Doobutsu Meishoo ni Kansuru Hahaoya no Shiyoogo: Ko no Getsurei ni yoru Chigai (A Study of Child-rearing Vocabulary (1). Mothers' Use of Animal Terms: Effects of Children'S Age)," *Annual Bulletin of Shimane University Faculty of Education* 17, 37-54.

Ogura, Tamiko (2006) "How the Use of 'Non-adult Words' Varies as a Function of Context and Chidren'S Linguistic Development," *Society for Language Science* 103-120.

Poser, William J. (1990) "Evidence for Foot Structure in Japanese," *Langauge* 66 (1), 78-105.

Tsuji, Sho, Ken'ya Nishikawa and Reiko Mazuka (2014) "Segmental Distributions and Consonant-vowel Association Patterns in Japanese Infant- and Adult-directed Speech," *Journal of Child Language* 41(6), 1276–1304.

Soderstrom, Melanie (2007) "Beyond Babytalk: Re-evaluating the Nature and Content of Speech Input to Preverbal Infants," *Developmental Review* 27, 501–532.

言語共通の音韻発達遅滞評価をめぐって[*]

上田　功

大阪大学

1. はじめに

　幼児の音韻体系獲得の遅れは，すべての言語に観られ，研究者の関心を引いてきた．しかしながらこの領域は，複数の学問分野が交差する領域であり，各分野の研究手法や基本的な考え方の違いなどから，学際的な研究は進まなかった．研究史を紐解くと，最初は発達心理学，そして言語病理学で研究が進んだため，言語学からのアプローチは遅れた．またこの領域は，当初から，言語聴覚士等，主として臨床に携わる者の実践報告的研究が盛んであったが，音韻論のような理論的な研究をおこなう者との連携がうまくとれてこなかった．さらに研究対象の言語の問題もある．長い間，研究対象といえば英語であり，他の言語における研究は質量ともにまったく英語には及ばなかった．

　さて，近年このような状況は，徐々に改善されてきている．発達障害の諸問題は，医学，社会科学，人文学の各分野が協働しなければ解決できないという認識が広がり，また現実的な臨床と抽象的な音韻理論のどちらも音韻発達の諸問題を研究する上で欠かせないという理解も，徐々に共有されるようになってきた．さらに研究が英語以外の言語でも盛んになってくるにつけ，音韻発達の遅れには，言語間の普遍性と言語ごとの個別性が存在することが

---

[*] 本稿のプロジェクトの紹介部分は，プロジェクト責任者の May Barnhardt, Joseph Stemberger 両先生のカナダ政府への申請書と内容が重なるところが多い．ご助言いただいた両先生に謝意を表したい．

わかってきた.

このような研究の発達を念頭に置いて，本稿では，音韻獲得の遅れについて，そのメカニズムを11言語間で比較対照することで，上記の普遍性と個別性を解明しようとする，現在進行中の国際的なプロジェクトを概観し，11言語に共通の原則から作成された調音能力アセスメントテストの日本語版を紹介し，現在までの全体的な研究経過と日本語における研究の進捗状況を説明する．

2. プロジェクトの概略

2.1. 目的

これまで言語学研究者が言語発達に観られる普遍性と個別性を研究する目的は，それが自然言語の理解に資するからであり，また，言語聴覚士等の臨床従事者は，実際に調音獲得が遅れている幼児の診断と訓練に利用するために，そのような研究結果が必要であった．ところが近年，アメリカ合衆国やカナダ等では，様々な言語を話す幼児に対応する必要性が高まっており，他の言語における知見が不可欠になってきている (Davis et al. (2005))．しかしながら，これまで蓄積されてきた研究成果は，すべて英語におけるものと言っても過言ではなく，また英語以外を対象にした研究も，1言語のみを対象にした研究であり，複数の言語間で比較対照したものはほとんどなく，あったとしても，手法としては，年齢や性別，遅れの程度などの条件を度外視して，英語においてなされた先行研究と比較するものがほとんどであった．このような状況に鑑みて，本稿で紹介するプロジェクトの目的は，11言語間で音韻獲得の遅れを比較し，発達に係わる言語普遍性と個別性を特徴づけることにある．

2.2. 研究の背景

これまで獲得に関する普遍と個別が議論されてこなかったわけではない．Jakobson (1941) の有名な「有標性」に始まり，いわゆる「普遍性論者」は，言語間で共通する獲得過程を認めてきた (Davis and MacNeilage (1995), Vihman (1992))．その一方で，同じ言語内，あるいは異なった言語間でも顕著な個人差が認められている (Ferguson and Farewell (1975), Beckman et al. (2003)). また言語内での出現頻度が, 獲得の順序を左右するという報告もなされている (Pye et al. (1987), Slocum et al. (2005), Zamuner (2003)). さらに音素的対立に関係する微細な音声的差異が, 言語間の獲得時期に影響を与えるとの研究もある (Li and Edwards (2006)).

　これらいずれの立場を取るにせよ, 複数の言語間の比較研究は, 著しく数が限られており (Bortolini and Leonard (1991), Fox and Dodd (2001), Goldstein (2005)), ほとんどの研究が, 臨床現場で使用される, 子音と母音のリストと簡易なプロセス分析への言及にとどまっており, 結果として, 音節や語の発達や分節音間の相互作用, 弁別素性や語構造等への言及がきわめて不十分になっている.

2.3. 言語の選択

　対象となる11の言語は次のような基準で選択された. 1) 研究経費や時間, 被験者を見つけられるか否か (研究の実行可能性). 2) 研究従事者が当該言語の母語話者, もしくはそれに準ずる能力をもっているかどうか (研究者の運用能力). 3) 音韻獲得に対する視野を広げるために, できるだけ多くの語族からタイプの異なる言語を選んでいるか (多様性). 以上の基準で選ばれた言語とそのデータが収集される地域は, 以下の通りである. アラビア語 (クウェート), ブルガリア語 (ソフィア), ドイツ語 (ケルン), ハンガリー語 (ブダペスト), アイスランド語 (レイキャビク), 日本語 (東京, 大阪), 朝鮮語 (現在のところ在米韓国人のもの), 中国語 (上海), スロベニア語 (リュブリアナ), スペイン語 (アンダルシア, メキシコシティー). これらの言語に関しては, 程度の差はあるものの, 調音の遅れに関する相当数の研究が存在することも重要な点である.

2.4. 検証すべき仮説

　さて, このプロジェクトでは, 検証を試みようとする仮説がいくつかあり, それを基盤として, データが収集されている. まず言語の普遍性に関係する有標性は, 調音に係る生理的な制約と, 認知プロセスに係る制約に内在すると考えられる. そこで, 普遍性に関する仮説としては, 次のような事項が挙げられる (Davis and MacNeilage (1995), Locke (1983)).

(1) 幼児は次の事項に関して，より高い正確さを示すことが予測できる：a. 開音節の単純な語形 b. 母音 c. 破裂音，鼻音，わたり音に関する調音 d. 声帯振動開始の早い破裂音と摩擦音

(2) (1) からの帰結として，次のような逸脱が予測できる：a. 特に語中，語末での弱音節化と子音脱落 b. 摩擦音の破裂音への置換 c. 文脈依存の有声化 d. 同化，挿入，語位転換

(3) 次の項目は欠けているか周辺的であると予測できる：a. 複雑な語形（2音節以上で尾子音や子音連続等と含むもの）b. 摩擦音と流音 c. 上記 (1d) 以外の形態の声帯振動 d. 前舌円唇母音，二次調音子音等，複雑な調音

(4) (3) からの帰結として，以下の項目は相対的に見られにくいと予想できる：a. 子音挿入や子音連結の生成による語形の複雑化 b. 調音方法において，摩擦音や流音による他の音の置換 c. 語頭の無声化 d. 声門音による置換 e. 促音化歯擦音

これに対して，言語個別の仮説も検証の対象になる．上述した音韻単位に関する有標性は，その出現頻度と影響しあって，言語ごとに異なってくる（Archangeli and Pulleyblank (1994)）．この出現頻度に係わる仮説は次の通りである．

(5) 普遍的な有標性に関係なく，分節音や語構造の目録において，少数しか種類をもたない言語は逸脱が少ない．語形一般に関しては，基本的にCVの言語，強勢に関しては，固定強勢の言語，子音や母音に関しては，数の少ない言語等がこれにあてはまる．

(6) さらに音韻的対立が多くの語の弁別に係わってくるほど，早い段階で獲得される．さらに出現頻度と複雑さ両方が作用して，個別言語において，獲得についての予測を可能ならしめる場合がある．

(7) もし複雑な構造の単位が当該言語において，低い出現頻度を示す場合は，もっとも獲得困難なケースであると予想できる．以上，大きく7つの仮説の検証を目的としている．

2.5. 分析の枠組

本プロジェクトでデータ分析の枠組として使われるのは，非線状音韻論を

折衷的に取り入れた，制約に基づく音韻理論である（Bernhardt and Stemberger (1998))．「折衷」の理由は，臨床にたずさわる言語聴覚士にとって，複雑な形式化による負担を最小限にとどめるという点にある．具体的には，分節音は弁別素性で分析され，音節，フット等のプロソディーは構造を重視し，素性と構造の相互関係も調べる．

2.6. プロジェクトの重要性

本プロジェクトの意義は，何よりもすべての言語に共通した被験者の選定，そしてデータ収集法と分析方法を採用することで，音韻獲得と逸脱をいわば同じ土俵に上げて比較対照するところにある．これによって，言語普遍的，言語個別的，そして被験者に個別的な音韻獲得の諸相が明らかになり，研究結果は言語学と言語障害学双方に裨益することになる．

3. 日本語のデータ収集と分析について

3.1. これまでの調音検査と評価

プロジェクトの主たる作業は，被験者の調音を評価することとその結果を音韻理論によって分析することの二点に大別される．本節では，音韻発達の評価方法について概観する．評価テストは，目標音が含まれた語の絵を見せて発音させる検査が主たるもので，音節検査や，自由発話を引き出す絵等が付属する．日本では，初期には田口・笹沼（1964）が使用されていたが，近年は日本音声言語医学会（編）（1981）が使用されることが多い．このスクリーニングテストは，編著者が言語学の専門家ではないので，音韻論の立場から見ると，不十分な点が散見される．まず検査語に関しては，検査目標音をすべての位置で網羅的に発音させておらず，また後続する母音が1種類だけというように，音韻環境に配慮が足りない．音節の検査は，子音と母音の組み合わせに配慮が見られるものの，検査者が音節を発音し，被験者がこれを復唱する形式になっている．要するに意味と切り離されて，聞いた刺激に対する反応を見るものが主となっている．また語構造に対する配慮が欠けており，語のモーラ数も限られており，また語を形成する音節の組み合わせの量的側面（軽＋重，重＋軽等）は，まったく考慮されていない．さらにアクセントやイントネーションは検査対象にもなっていないように思える．さ

らに評価においても，皮相的な音素レベルのものであり，弁別素性は使われない．

3.2. 構音検査

　上記のような問題を可能な限り改善して，音韻理論に立脚した構音検査を製作した．原案は University of British Columbia の School of Speech Pathology and Audiology 関係者で，日本人の研究員を主体としたチームである．それに筆者が目を通し，改訂を加えたものである．検査語は約110あり，付録に載せているが，それぞれの語の写真を見せて，発音させるのは，従来の方法と変わりはない．また部分的にストーリー性をもたせて，発展的な自由発話を誘導できる部分もある．発音は微妙なものを音響分析できるように，可能な限り性能の良いデジタルレコーダーとマイクロフォンを使用して記録される．但し，仰々しい録音機材に威圧感を感じる被験者には，やむを得ず簡便な機器を使用することもある．検査シートはエクセルにIPAで正しいターゲットが書かれており，被験者の発音をその横にやはりIPAで記述する．上述した検査対象語の音韻環境であるが，語頭と語中の両方を検査し，後続する母音との組み合わせも，できるだけ母音の種類を考えたものにした．ただ検査語が多くなれば，被験者には負担が増えることになるので，限界もある．またピッチアクセントの標記方法は，当初 H と L を各音節に結びつける方がわかりやすいとも考えたが，結局スペース等の問題から，IPA の高低の平板ピッチ記号を，母音の上に記すことにした．

3.3. 研究の現状

　プロジェクトが発足してから約10年が経とうとしているが，11の言語が同じようにスタートしたわけではない．それまで研究責任者である，Bernhardt, Stemberger 両教授と共同研究をおこなってきた言語の研究者にとって，このプロジェクトはその延長線上にあるので，研究の進度はそれだけ進んでいる．プロジェクトメンバーは, The International Association of Clinical Phonetics and Linguistics, International Child Phonology Conference 等の国際会議で，個別の研究報告のみならず，随時パネルを立ち上げて，成果を発表している．日本語に関しては，プロジェクトの発足後に参加を依頼され，「日本語班」を立ち上げたが，残念ながら研究の進行は他の言

語に比べて遅く，これまで5名の構音の遅れを示す幼児（いわゆる機能性構音障害児）のデータを収集して，分析したにとどまっている．これは，ことばの問題で医療機関にかかる幼児は，純然たる構音の遅れが原因であることはほとんどなく，多くの場合，口蓋裂や難聴等の器質的問題であったり，運動性の構音障害であったり，また自閉症スペクトラムによるコミュニケーションの問題であったりするからである．また昨今の個人情報の保護が叫ばれているが，これに関して，研究に係わってもらうにあたっては，保護者の許可をいただく承諾書にサインしてもらう必要があるが，この日本語版をブリティッシュコロンビア大学の倫理委員会に諮り，許可を得るまでに，2年近くを要していることも原因となっている．

3.4. 分析例

上述した事例の音韻分析は，Ueda, Tabata and Yamane（2013）で報告しているが，本稿ではこの発表には含まれなかった事例（Case 1 とする）について紹介する．紙幅の関係で，逸脱した発音を示した語のみを下記の（6）に挙げる．ここで Target forms は目標検査語の発音（即ち大人の発音）であり，Phonetic forms は当該の幼児が実際発音した形を示す．また自由発話で得られた目標音を含む語も，（9）のように，追加的に記述しておく必要がある．

(8) Case 1 (A)

Target forms	Phonetic forms	Gloss
àtsúi	àteúi	hot
òbá:sàɴ	òbá:ɕàɴ	grandmother
òdʑí:sàɴ	òdʑí:ɕàɴ	grandfather
mìzú	mìzú	water
tɕì:sái	tɕì:ɕái	small
dʑó:	dʑó:	elephant
dzúbòɴ	dzúbòɴ	trousers
dó:nàtsù	dó:nàtɕɯ˞	donut
dzàrú	dzàrɯ˞	strainer
kàzé	kàzé	wind

gjòːzá	gjòːdʑa´	dumpling
ɸùːsén	ɸùːɕéN	balloon
sáN	ɕáN	three
sémpùːkì	ɕémpùːkì	electric fan
sènséː	ɕèɲɕéː	teacher
sóːdʑìkì	ɕóːdʑìkì	vacuum cleaner
kùtsú	kùtɕú	shoes
ɕíŋkàNsèN	ɕíŋkàɲɕèN	bullet train
çìzá	çìdzá	knee
ɾéːzòːkò	ɾéːdzòːkò	refrigerator
ɾísù	ɾíɕù	squirrel

(9) Case 1 (B)

Target forms	Phonetic forms	Gloss
nàŋásódé	nàŋáɕóde	long sleeve
ɸúdʑìsàN	ɸúdʑìɕàN	Mt. Fuji

(8) と (9) から観察できることは，目標音 /s/, /z/, /ts/, /dz/ が，それぞれ [ɕ], [z], [tɕ], [dʑ] に置換されていることである．調音位置という点では，歯音が歯茎硬口蓋音に置換されているが，同じ歯茎音の /d/ は目標音と同じに発音されているので，これは歯擦音に限られた置換であると考えられる．

分析としては，次のように音韻制約に言及して，形式化する．

(10) *歯茎歯擦音：歯茎の歯擦音は許されない．（口蓋化）

本プロジェクトでは，形式化そのものが目的ではないので，逸脱音の原因となっている音韻制約の性格がわかれば十分である．この子どもの音置換は，正常な音韻発達でも観察される場合が多く（本間 (2000)），報告されている臨床例と比較することで，日本語内での普遍性と個別性を考えることができる．[1] さらに，他の言語と比較することによって，言語普遍的な性格付けをおこなうことも可能である．例えば英語の歯擦音は，歯茎音の口蓋化より

---

[1] 歯茎歯擦音はこの置換以外にも，破擦音化するタイプ，閉鎖音化（いわゆる stopping）するもの，口蓋化と破擦音化をあわせもつタイプなどがある．置換のパターンに関しては，かなりの程度まで類型化が可能である．

も，むしろ後部歯茎音の歯茎音化（いわゆる脱口蓋化）の方が一般的である (Hodson (1980), Ingram (1989))．このように他言語との比較により，言語普遍的な有標性に関して議論することができる．

4. 今後の課題と計画

本稿では，複数の言語に共通の基準を基にして音韻発達遅滞の評価や分析おこなうプロジェクトのアウトラインを紹介し，これが臨床のみならず音韻理論や言語獲得理論に対して貢献することを，日本語の事例を考えながら論じてきた．本プロジェクトはあくまでの現在進行中のものであり，まだまだ不十分な点が多い．今後の課題としては，上述した理論的指標に沿って，ケーススタディーを数多くおこない，多言語間の比較研究ができるようにデータを蓄積し，また各事例の分析を積み重ねることが一番の課題である．

本プロジェクトは Yvan Rose 教授を中心とする，CHILDES プロジェクトのデータベースである PhonBank とも協働している (Rose and MacWhinney (2014))．[2] プロジェクトメンバーは，収集したデータ（音声データを含む）と分析結果を提供する．PhonBank は多様なプログラムを備えており，例えば，(8) の Case 1 の事例は，(10) のように「口蓋化」というキーワードのもとにデータベース化されるので，検索者が palatalization, Japanese と打ち込めば，たちどころにこの事例にアクセスすることができる．さらに palatalization, crosslinguistic とすれば，各言語の口蓋化の事例がすべて選択され，検索者はそのデータを検討することができるのである．もちろんこれらの事例は音声ファイルが付属しているので，音響的分析も可能である．

これまで音韻獲得に係わる研究は，データを集めることが第一の，そしてある意味で最大の関門であった．PhonBank の理念に賛同し，協力している本プロジェクトのメンバーは，この最初にして最大の問題で，これからの研究者が躓かないように願い，貴重な自分のデータと分析結果を提供しているのである．今後，本プロジェクトから多くの音韻獲得研究が生まれることを期待して本稿を終える．

---

[2] PhonBank については，http://childes.psy.cmu.edu/phon/ を参照のこと．

付録（検査語）

àtsɯ́i, àɕí, àçírɯ, àrí, èbí, èhóɴ, ìnɯ́, ìteíɲó, òmándzɯ́ː, òɲí, òɲíɲìrì, òbáːsàɴ, òkáɕi, òdʑíːsàɴ, òːkíː, ɯ̀dón, ɯ̀sáɲí, ɯ̀é, mádò, mámè, míkàɴ, mìmí, mìzɯ́, mé, mòmó, móːɸɯ̀, nàŋáŋɯ́tsɯ́, nékò, nàmí, nòrí, ɲí, ɲìndzíɴ, páɴ, pánda, píːmàɴ, pòpːɯ́kóːɴ, básɯ̀, bíɴ, bòːɕí, bótàɴ/bòtáɴ, bɯ̀tá, tákò, tàmáŋò, tánɯ̀kì, té, tèbɯ́kɯ̀rò, tòːɸɯ́/tóːɸɯ̀, tòkéí, tòmbó, tsɯ̀kí, tɕàíró, tɕìːsái, dénɕà, dóːnàtsɯ̀, dzàrɯ́/zàrɯ́, dzóː/zóː, dzɯ́bòɴ/dzɯ̀bóɴ/zɯ̀bóɴ/zɯ́bòɴ/, dzámɯ̀, dzìténɕà, kásà, kàzé, kàwá, kéːkì, kí, kíŋgjò, kòínóbòrì, kɯ̀tsɯ́, kɯ̀teí, kjɯ́ːkjɯ̀ːɕà, kjɯ́ːrì, gámɯ̀, gítàː, górìrà, gòmíbákó, gjòːzá, gjɯ̀ːɲɯ́ː, ɸɯ̀tón, ɸɯ̀ːséɴ, sáɴ, sémpɯ̀ːkì, sènséí/sènséː, sóːdzìkì, sɯ̀íká, sɯ̀ɕí, ɕàɕíɴ, ɕìŋkánsèɴ, ɕìpːó, ɕóːbòːɕà, çìkóːkì, çí, çìzá, hàná, hàpːá, hóɴ, ráːmèɴ, réːzòːkò, rìŋŋó, rísɯ̀, róbòtːò/ ròbótːò, rɯ́mìtɕàɴ, jáɲì, jàkjɯ́ː, jàmá, jórɯ̀, jɯ̀bí, jɯ̀kí, jɯ̀kídárɯ̀mà, ɰáɲì, ɰàríbáɕí

参考文献

Archangeli, Diana and Douglas Pulleyblank (1994) *Grounded Phonology*, MIT Press, Cambridge, MA.

Beckman, Mary E., Kiyoko Yoneyama and Jan Edwards (2003) "Language-specific and Language-universal Aspects of Lingual Obstruent Productions in Japanese-acquiring Children," *Journal of the Phonetic Society of Japan* 7, 18-28.

Bortolini, Umberta and Laurence Leonard (1991) "The Speech of Phonologically Disordered Children Acquiring Italian," *Clinical Linguistics & Phonetics* 5, 1-12.

Davis, Barbara, Sophie Kern, Peter MacNeilage, Dilana Koçbas and Inge Zink (2005) "Vocalization Patterns in Canonical Babbling: A Cross-linguistic Perspective," paper presented at the Xth International Association of Child Language Congress, Berlin, Germany.

Davis, Barbara L. and Peter MacNeilage F. (1995) "The Articulatory Basis of Babbling," *Journal of Speech and Hearing Research* 38, 1199-1211.

Ferguson, Charles and Carol Farwell (1975) "Words and Sounds in Early Language Acquisition," *Language* 51, 419-439.

Fox, Annette and Barbara Dodd (2001) "Phonologically Disordered German-speaking Children," *American Journal of Speech-language Pathology* 10, 291-307.

Goldstein, Brian (2005) "Substitution Patterns in the Phonology of Spanish-speaking Children," *Journal of Multilingual Communication Disorders* 3, 153-168.
Hodson, Barbara (1980) *The Assessment of Phonological Processes*, The Interstate, Danville, IL.
本間慎治 (2000)『機能性構音障害』建帛社，東京．
Ingram, Davis (1989) *Phonological Disability in Children*, 2nd ed., Cole & Whurr, London.
Jakobson, Roman (1968) *Child Language, Aphasia, and Phonological Universals*, Mouton, The Hague ((1941) *Kindersprache, Aphasie, und Allgemeine Lautgesetze*, Uppsala Universitets Arsskrift Uppsala.)
Li, Fangfeng and Jan Edwards (2006) "Contrast and Covert Contrast Covert Contrast in the Acquisition of /s/ and /ʃ/ in English and Japanese," poster presented at the Xth Conference on Laboratory Phonology, Paris.
Locke, John L. (1983) *Phonological Acquisition and Change*, Academic Press, New York.
日本音声言語医学会構音障害小委員会（編）(1981)『構音検査法』千葉テストセンター，千葉．
Pye, Clifton, David Ingram and Helen List (1987) "A Comparison of Initial Consonant Acquisition in English and Quiché," *Children's Language* 6, ed. by Katherine Nelson and Anne van Kleeck, 175-190, Erlbaum, Hillsdale, NJ.
Rose, Yvan and MacWhinney Brian (2014) "The PhonBank Project: Data and Software-assisted Methods for the Study of Phonology and Phonological Development," *The Oxford Handbook of Corpus Phonology*, ed. by Jacques Durand, Ulrike Gut and Gjert Kristoffersen, Oxford University Press, Oxford.
Slocum, Laura, Jan Edwards and Mary Beckman (2005) "Cross-linguistic Acquisition of Voiceless Lingual Fricatives," poster presented at the American Speech & Hearing Association Annual Conference, San Diego.
田口恒夫・笹沼澄子 (1964)『ことばのテストえほん』日本文化科学社，東京．
Ueda Isao, Yusuke Tabata and Noriko Yamane (2013) "Some Functional Misarticulation Systems in Japanese," paper presented at *Knowledge Mobilization for an International Cross-linguistic Study of Children's Speech Development*, University of British Columbia, Vancouver, Canada.
Vihman, Marilyn (1992) "Early Syllables and the Construction of Phonology," *Phonological Development: Models, Research, Implications*, ed. by Charles Ferguson, Lisa Menn and Carol Stoel-Gammon, 393-422, York Press, Monkton, MD.
Zamuner, Tania (2003) *Input-based Phonological Acquisition*, Taylor & Francis, New York/London.

日本語分節音の音韻要素表現とその内部構造

松井　理直
大阪保健医療大学

1. 序論

1.1. 離散的カテゴリーとプロトタイプカテゴリー

　言語カテゴリーの表象については，よく知られているように，大きく分けて2種類のアプローチが議論されてきた．1つはある属性を持つか持たないかという二項対立に基づく離散的カテゴリーの考え方，もう一方は属性の連続的な変化を認めるプロトタイプカテゴリーの考え方である（Tayler (2004))．

　このうち，離散的カテゴリーは古典的カテゴリーとも呼ばれており，二項対立を成す素性の連言によって定義されるという特徴を持つ．これは，離散的カテゴリーが矛盾律と排中律に従うことを意味している．これに対し，プロトタイプカテゴリーの性質は，典型的な成員（メンバー）に関する情報を中心として，家族的類似性そして連続的な分布性を示す．その結果，カテゴリー間には重複が許され，明確なカテゴリー境界が保証されない．また，質的なカテゴリーだけでなく，量的なカテゴリーを含む．

1.2. 研究の目的

　こうした言語的カテゴリーの中で，音韻カテゴリーは定性的な形態音韻現象を適切に説明できる情報であると共に，実時間上に展開される定量的な音声情報の必要十分な入力でもある．音韻素性から音声情報を導出する過程については様々な議論があるが，もし直接解釈されるものであるなら，音韻素性は離散的カテゴリーとプロトタイプカテゴリーの性質を止揚したような性質を持っていなければならない．こうした音韻素性の表現方法の1つに，

要素理論（Harris (1994), Nasukawa and Backley (2016)）で扱われる音韻要素（phonological element, particle）を挙げることができる．本稿は，日本語の分節音を扱う上で適切と思われる音韻要素の体系について議論を行ったものである．

2. 音韻カテゴリーと要素理論

2.1. 音韻情報に関する離散的カテゴリー

音韻論でしばしば用いられる二値的弁別素性（binary distinctive feature）は離散的カテゴリーの一種であり，ソシュールの言う「差異の体系」という記号の性質を明示できるシステムである．二値的弁別素性では，各素性はプラスかマイナスのいずれかの値を取るため，2種類の弁別素性があると最大で $2^2 = 4$ 種類のカテゴリーを区別でき，3種類の弁別素性では最大で $2^3 = 8$ 種類のカテゴリーが区別されていく．したがって，日本語の5母音体系を弁別素性で表すなら，(1)に示すように最低でも3種類の弁別素性が必要となる．

(1) 二値的弁別素性による日本語5母音の完全指定

	i	e	a	o	ɯ
high	+	−	−	−	+
low	−	−	+	−	−
back	−	−	+	+	+

しかし，(1)のような弁別素性では，5つのカテゴリーはうまく区別できるが，3種類の素性を用いているにも関わらず，8つのカテゴリーを区別することはできない．これは [high] 素性と [low] 素性が独立していないこと，すなわち [+high, +low] という素性束が許されないことに起因している．その結果，(1) のシステムでは，スイスドイツ方言のように母音の高さについて [i], [e], [ɛ], [a] といった4段階の対立を持つ言語体系を適切に表示することができない．こうした言語の母音体系を表示するためには，母音の高さに関して (1, 2, 3, 4) といった多値の素性表現を用いるか，あるいは [high], [low] という素性の代わりに [high], [mid] という素性を導入する必要がある．この素性束を用いると，狭母音は [+high, −mid]，半狭母音は

[＋high, ＋mid]，半広母音は [－high, ＋mid]，そして広母音は [－high, －mid] として表現でき，素性間の依存関係が生じない．

2.2. 弁別素性の不完全指定

弁別素性が従属関係にある場合，ある弁別素性の値（あるいは複数の弁別素性値）から別の弁別素性を導出することが可能になる．例えば (1) では，[＋high] から [－low] であることが予測でき，[＋low] であれば [－high] であることが必然的に決まっていく．こうした余剰的情報を除くことで弱不完全指定 (weak underspecification) された情報が得られる．さらに徹底不完全指定理論 (radical underspecification) では，予測情報のみならず，既定値 (default value) となる弁別素性値も全て表示から省く．例として，(1) を不完全指定表示にすると (2) のような情報になる．

(2) 日本語5母音に関する (a) 弱不完全指定と (b) 徹底不完全指定

(a)

	i	e	ɑ	o	ɯ
high	＋	－		－	＋
low	－		＋	－	
back	－	－	＋	＋	＋

(b)

	i	e	ɑ	o	ɯ
high		－			
low			＋		
back	－	－			

徹底不完全指定を受けた (2b) に従うと，日本語の母音体系では /u/ 音が一切の素性値を持たない無標の母音であると言ってよい．こうした性質は (3) に示す日本語の基本的挿入母音が /u/ 音であり，/u/ 以外の挿入母音は (4) のような特殊な環境でしか生起しないといった現象をうまく説明する．逆に，最も有標な母音は /e/ 音であり，実際，母音 /e/ は日本語5母音の中で最も出現頻度が少ない（染田 (1966)）．この性質は，オノマトペにおける /e/ 音の否定的な音象徴（例えば，ゲーゲー，ベロベロなど）にも反映されていると思われる．

(3) "splash" : [sɯpɯrɑeːɯ], "club": [kɯrabɯ], "Fleagle": [ɸɯriːgɯrɯ] etc.

(4) "tread": [toriːdo], "why": [howai], "march": [mɑːtɕi], "large": [rɑːzi]

2.3. 窪薗 (1999) による日本語の母音融合現象

しかし，不完全指定理論が形態音韻現象において常に妥当な予測を行うとは限らない．その例として，窪薗 (1999) で取り上げられている日本語の母音融合現象を取り上げてみよう．代償延長を伴う母音融合の主な例を (5) に示す．

(5) a. /oi/ → [eː] : 酷い→ひでー，凄い→すげー
　　b. /oe/ → [eː] : 例えれば→たてーれば，萎える→ねーる
　　c. /ou/ → [oː] : 王子→おーじ，公園→こーえん
　　d. /ui/ → [iː] : 熱い→あちー，寒い→さみー
　　e. /ae/ → [eː] : 帰る→けーる，お前→おめー
　　f. /au/ → [oː] : 問うた→とーた，淡海→あうみ→おーみ (近江)
　　g. /ei/ → [eː] : 映画→えーが，先生→せんせー
　　h. /eu/ → [(j)oː] : てふてふ (蝶々) →ちょーちょー，ねう (尿) →にょー
　　i. /iu/ → [(j)ɯː] : いう (言う) →ゆー，りう (龍) →りゅー
　　j. /ea/ → [(j)ɑː] : これは→こりゃー，〜しては→〜しちゃー
　　k. /oa/ → [ɑː] : 〜ことは→こたー

窪薗 (1999) は，これらの現象について，融合後の母音音価が先行母音の [high] に関する素性値と後続母音の [low] および [back] に関する特性を組み合わせることで決定されると分析している．例えば (5a) であれば，/o/ 音の [−high] 素性と /i/ 音の [−low, −back] 素性を組み合わせると，[e] 音：[−high, −low, −back] に融合されるという予測がつく．小野 (2015) が指摘する「消える→けーる」のような sonority が高くなる母音連続の融合を除くと，窪薗 (1999) の分析がほぼ通用する．逆にいえば，母音融合の計算を行うためには [high, back. low] の値が適切に分かっている必要があり，不完全指定情報に基づくと，こうした母音融合の音価をうまく予測できるとは限らない．

まずうまくいく例として，やはり (5a) を見てみよう．弱不完全理論 (2a) に従うと，先行母音 /o/ からは [−high] の情報が，後続母音 /i/ からは [−back] の情報が分かるが，[low] の素性値は取り出せない．したがって，これらの情報を合わせると [−high, −back] のみとなり，さらに [−high]

という情報からは [low] の素性値を予測できないため，融合した結果の母音素性は [−high, +low, −back] か [−high, −low, −back] のいずれかとなる．このうち前者の組み合わせは，日本語の母音素性 (1) で認められていない．したがって，後者の [−high, −low, −back] が生き残り，母音融合の音価を [eː] として決定できる．

しかし，(5f) の母音連鎖 /au/ になるとこうしたプロセスがうまく機能しない．(2a) に基づくと，先行母音の /a/ は [high] の情報を持っておらず，後続母音 /u/ も [+back] の情報は存在するものの [low] の情報は持っていないため，これらの情報を統合すると [+back] のみが指定されていることになる．弱不完全指定理論では [back] 素性に関する含意関係を持たないので，母音融合の結果が [ɯ], [o], [ɑ] のいずれの音価になるのかを決定することができない．徹底不完全指定理論のように既定値を使うにしても，[+high], [−low] が補完されるため，融合後の母音は [ɯ] 音になることを誤って予測してしまう．最初から徹底不完全指定理論に従ったとしても同様で，母音連鎖 /au/ に対し，(2b) の表からは先行母音の /a/ の [high] 素性値を取り出せず，後続母音 /u/ からも [low], [back] の素性値を取り出すことができない．したがって，これらの情報を統合するとやはり一切の素性値を持たない default 母音，すなわち [ɯ] 音を誤って予測する．結局の所，不完全指定を用いた場合，融合母音の計算を行う前に全ての素性値の補完が行われていなければならない．

上田 (1996)，太田・氏平 (2014)，小野 (2015) の分析は，こうした問題を解決できており興味深い．ただし，これら分析は融合後の母音にのみ注目しており，(5h-j) に見られる先行子音の口蓋化現象は取り扱われていない．本稿では上田 (1996) の分析を踏襲しながら，音韻要素の内部構造について議論を行う．結果として，音韻要素には言語のカテゴリー論を統合する機能があり，また母音融合に限らず，多くの音韻変化を統一的に扱う力があることを述べる．

3. 音韻原子要素とその内部構造

3.1. 那須川による阻害音の要素理論分析

日本語の分節音を構成する原子要素の構造については，那須川よる一連の

研究が最も詳しい (Nasukawa and Backley (2016) など). 彼の研究では, 単独の原子要素 N, H, ʔ, U は各々 [N], [h], [ʔ], [u] という実体を持つ. この性質を核にして, 要素 N はプロトタイプとして有声性や鼻音性 (periodicity) の性質を, 要素 H は無声音源の摩擦性 (aperiodicity) を, 要素 ʔ は閉鎖性を, 要素 U は唇音の性質を担う. これにより, 例えば両唇子音は (6) のような複合要素を成す. Nasukawa and Backley (2016) はこの表示に従って, 日本語の唇音退化 [p] → [ɸ] → [h]/[w] を, {H, ʔ, U} → {H, U} → [h] : {H}／[w] : {U} という音韻要素の削除として捉えている.

(6)　[p] : {H, ʔ, U}　　[b] : {N, H, ʔ, U}　　[m] : {N, U}
　　 [ɸ] : {H, U}　　　 [β] : {N, H, U}　　　 [w] : {U}

しかし, 日本語の音韻体系の中では (6) の表示は 1 つの問題を持つ. 有声破裂音 [b] であっても無声性と関わる摩擦要素 H を持つということは, 要素 ʔ は閉鎖にのみ関わり, 破裂音の開放は要素 H によってもたらされることを示す. つまり, [p] 音や [b] 音は「破裂音」であって, 「閉鎖音」ではないことを意味する. 確かに, 英語の破裂音は音節末子音になった場合であっても開放を持ち得ることからも, 「破裂」であると言ってよいだろう. 一方, 日本語の [p], [t], [k] 音は, 母音の後続しない促音部 (音節末子音) では開放がない. つまり, [pɑ], [tɑ] の p 音や t 音が開放されるのは後続する母音 [ɑ] の影響であり, 服部 (1951) が指摘するように日本語の破裂音は正確には閉鎖音である. したがって, 日本語の p, b, t, d, k, g 音は摩擦要素 H を持たないと考えた方がよい.

しかし, ここで日本語の p 音が閉鎖音で要素 H を持っていないとすると, p 音は {ʔ, U} という構造を持つことになり, p 音が [ɸ] : {H, U} 音に唇音退化を起こす過程を自然に説明することができなくなる. また, 要素理論では, 無声破裂音の無声性は無声の口腔内音源 (摩擦音限) というプロトタイプ的性質から, 要素 H が担う. ここで p 音が閉鎖音 {ʔ, U} という構造を持っているとすると, 無声性を実現する口腔内音源の性質が存在しないことになってしまう.

3.2.　中線的接触要素 C の導入

この問題を解決するために, 破裂音と類似した発音を持つ日本語のラ行子

音の調音動態を見てみよう．図1は「あら」「いり」「うる」のエレクトロパラトグラフィ（EPG）パターンで，最前列の2列が歯茎，次の2列が後部歯茎，その後の3列が硬口蓋，最後の1列が軟口蓋における舌の接触パターンを表す．図1(a) の「あら」における子音部の EPG パターンでは側面狭窄が全く見られず，側面接近音 [ɑlɑ] で発音されている．これに対し，図1(b) の「いり」は硬口蓋の狭窄が増加する [irʲi]，図1(c) は後部歯茎に接触する [ɯɾɯ] に近い．

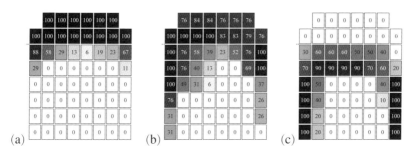

図1. 日本語のラ行子音における異音の EPG 例（a：あら　b：いり　c：おろ）

　日本語のラ行子音は弾き音とされるが，図1から，日本語ラ行子音の本質的な調音動作が中線的接触をもたらす舌尖の挙上動作にあり，弾き音の持つ側面狭窄は必須でないことが分かる．図1(b), (c) の側面狭窄は，狭母音の状態から舌尖を挙上させることによって引き起こされる付随的な現象に過ぎない．これは日本語母語話者の /l/–/r/ 弁別性を考える上でも示唆を与えるであろう．

　このことから，本稿では図1の EPG パターン全てに観察される「中線的接触（contact）」をもたらす要素 C を導入する．単独の原子要素 C は [l] 音に近いプロトタイプカテゴリーであるが，破裂音・鼻子音・側面接近音といった中線的接触を持つ調音は全て内部構造にこの音韻要素 C を持つ．

3.3. 要素 H の定義変更

　中線的接触要素 C を導入した場合，破裂音の完全閉鎖は中線的接触と共に「側面狭窄」によって実現されることになる．この側面狭窄は，摩擦音とも関わりが深い．このことから，本稿では摩擦要素 H を「側面狭窄要素」

と捉え直すことを提案する．この定義変更は，摩擦音としての要素 H には影響を与えないが，破裂音／閉鎖音の表示に違いをもたらす．すなわち，従来の要素理論では破裂音は要素 H と要素 ? を持ち，閉鎖音は要素 ? のみを持つが，本稿のアプローチでは破裂音も閉鎖音も中線的接触要素 C と側面狭窄要素 H を持ち，破裂音と閉鎖音に違いが生じない（要素間の支配関係は異なる）．

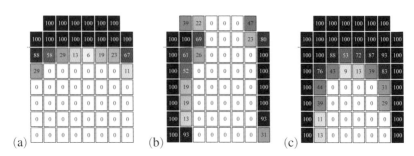

図 2. 歯茎における要素 C（[l]），要素 H（[s]），要素 C・H（[t]）の接触パターン

3.4. 周辺要素 U：日本語の母音ウにおける非硬口蓋性

要素理論では，母音のプロトタイプとして単独ではア音・イ音・ウ音になる原子要素 A, I, U を認める．これらの要素は，複合要素になった時には一般的に各々開口性，硬口蓋性，円唇性をもたらす．日本語でも，開口性は母音の狭広の対立に，硬口蓋性は直音と開拗音の対立に関わるので，要素 A, I の性質に問題はない．しかし要素 U については平唇 [ɯ] の存在から言っても問題を残す．

ここで，日本語のウ音における調音点の変異を観察してみよう．図 3(a) はイ音の EPG パターンで，硬口蓋に広い側面狭窄を持つ前舌母音であることが分かる．一方，図 3(b) は標準的なウ音の EPG パターンで，軟口蓋に調音点を持つ後舌母音であり，硬口蓋より前方には側面狭窄が観察されていない．

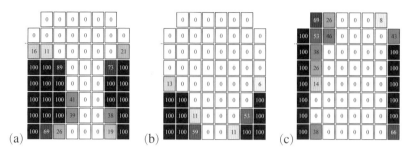

図3. (a) イ音 (b) ウ音 (c) 特殊な環境下におけるウ音の EPG パターン

　これに対し，図3(c) は「涼む」のズ音における母音ウの EPG パターンで，図2(b) の s 音に類似したパターンを持つ．つまり，日本語のウ音の調音位置は軟口蓋だけでなく，「歯茎」であってもよい．そして図3(b)，(c) は，図3(a) のような硬口蓋での強い狭窄を持たないという点で共通する．これは，日本語のイ音—ウ音の対立が [∓back] ではなく，[±palatal] ([±front]) に基づくことを示す．なお，[+back] と [−palatal] が同義ではない点に注意されたい．すなわち，[+back] は歯茎を含まないが，[−palatal] は歯茎をも指示し得る．

　以上の議論から，日本語の要素 I は [+palatal] の性質を含有し，要素 U は [−palatal] の性質を内包すると考えてよい．換言すると，日本語における調音位置の中心は硬口蓋であり，要素 I がこの中心点を意味するのに対し，要素 U はこの中心点を除く周辺位置（唇・歯茎・軟口蓋など）を指定する機能を担う．

3.5. 各原子要素の内部構造

　要素理論では，分節音の構成単位は音韻要素であり，それより小さな弁別素性は音韻操作を受ける対象ではない．しかし，それは弁別素性が存在しないということではなく，各原子要素は 3.2 節〜 3.4 節で議論した特徴を反映する弁別素性を持つ．これは，音韻要素が離散的カテゴリーとプロトタイプカテゴリーを統合する単位であることを意味する．

　この音韻要素に内在する弁別素性は，強素性と弱素性という区別を持つ (Charette (1991))．強素性はプロトタイプとしてその要素を特徴づける中心的な性質であり，弱素性は付随的な性質を表す．これにより，音韻要素は

弁別素性の完全指定／不完全指定という問題も吸収できる．表1に，日本語音韻体系に関わる原子要素の内部構造を示す（最小限の素性のみを示し，他は省略する）．四角枠で囲まれている素性が強素性であり，他の素性が弱素性となる．

表1．日本語における音韻要素の内部構造

	開口性	硬口蓋性	周辺性	鼻音性	狭窄性	接触性
	A	I	U	N	H	C
consonantal					+	+
sonorant	+	+	+	+	ボックス−	+
voiced	+	+	+	ボックス+	−	+
nasal				+	ボックス−	−
contact	ボックス−	−	−	+	−	ボックス+
lat. constriction	−			+	ボックス+	
strident	−	−	−		+	−
high	ボックス−	+	+		ボックスϕ	ボックスϕ
low	+	−	−			
palatal	−	ボックス+	−	−	−	−
grave	+	−	+(++)			−
labial			+			

4. 日本語分節音の音韻要素表示

4.1. 複合要素の支配関係

要素理論では，分節音が複合要素から構成される場合，要素間に支配関係を許す．本稿では，支配要素 X と依存要素 Y の関係を X>Y と表記する．X＝Y なら等位関係を，X≧Y は相互支配関係を表す．X≧Y の場合は，X が Y を支配するか等位関係であるかは任意だが，Y が X を支配することはない．この支配関係の元で，各音韻要素が持つ弁別素性は (7) の強さで分節音に引き継がれる．

(7) a． 強素性は弱素性より常に強い．
　　b． 支配要素の素性は依存要素の素性より優先される．

この結果，分節音に引き継がれる弁別素性は，支配要素の持つ強素性が最も

優先され，次に依存要素の強素性，次いで支配要素の弱素性，そして最も引き継がれにくいのが依存要素の弱素性の順になる．ただし，X＝Y という等位関係においては支配関係が対等なので，強素性同士あるいは弱素性同士の弁別素性値が＋／－で対立する場合，素性値は打ち消し合う．また，X≧Y という相互依存関係では，X の素性が実現された後，Y の素性が実現される．

4.2. 日本語分節音の音韻要素表示

表 1 の音韻要素を用いると，日本語分節音は (8)-(12) の構造を持つ．一般的に両唇音は要素 U が最も支配的であるのに対し，軟口蓋音の要素 U は他の要素と対等関係を取る（歯茎音は次節参照）．また，閉鎖音は要素 C が要素 H を支配するか対等関係を持つのに対し，歯擦音は要素 H が要素 C を支配し，ハ行摩擦音は「後続母音の要素」が要素 H を支配する．なお有声阻害音は，無声阻害音の構造に要素 N を要素 H の対等関係あるいは支配関係として組み込む．Appendix に，これらの構造から (7) に従って導出される弁別素性値を示す．

(8)　母音および接近音
　　　[ɑ] : A　　[i] : I　　[u]/[ɯ] : U　　[e] : I＞A　　[o] : U＞A　　[j] : I
　　　[w]/[ɰ] : U　　[ã] : A＞N　　[ĩ] : I＞N　　[ũ]/[ɯ̃] : U＞N

(9)　両唇音およびハ行子音
　　　[p] : U＞C＞H　　[b] : U＞C＞N≧H　　[m] : U＞N＞C
　　　[ɸ] : U＞H　　[β] : U＞N≧H　　[ç] : I＞H　　[h] : A＞H

(10)　歯茎音および歯茎硬口蓋音
　　　[t] : C＞H　　[d] : C＞H＝N　　[n] : N＞C　　[ɾ] : C
　　　[s] : H＞C　　[z] : H＝N＞C　　[ɕ] : H＞C≧I　　[ʑ] : H＝N＞C≧I
　　　[t͡s] : C≧H　　[d͡z] : C≧H＝N　　[t͡ɕ] : C≧H≧I　　[d͡ʑ] : C≧H＝N≧I

(11)　軟口蓋音および口蓋垂音
　　　[k] : H＝U＝C＞C　　[g] : N≧H＝U＝C＞C　　[ŋ] : N＞U＝C＞C
　　　[ɣ] : N≧H＝U

(12)　開拗音：直音の構造に，要素 I を最も弱い依存要素として組み込む．

4.3. 要素 U の特殊性

前項の (8)-(12) に示した音韻要素は，日本語の音韻体系における最も単純な構造であるが，内部構造として Appendix に示すような弁別素性の対立関係が保たれる限り，より複雑な要素構造を持っていてもよい．その1つの要因として，要素 U の振る舞いを見てみよう．表1に示した通り，現代日本語における要素 U は強素性を持たない唯一の音韻要素である（元々は [+labial] を強素性として持っていた）．したがって，要素 U が他の音韻要素に支配されている時，特に要素 C に支配される依存要素となっている時には，(7) の性質から，要素 U の持つ弁別素性は分節音の特性に反映されない．言い換えるなら，依存要素となる要素 U は構造の中に存在していても存在していなくても，分節音の性質としては同一である．したがって，(10) の歯茎音などは (13) に示す少し複雑な構造を持っていてもよい．要素 U が強素性を持たないという性質は，この要素が日本語において最も無標な原子要素であることを意味している．

(13) 歯茎音および歯茎硬口蓋音
    [t] : C>H>U   [d] : C>H=N>U   [n] : N>C>U   [ɾ] : C>U
    [s] : H>C>U   [z] : H=N>C>U   [t͡s] : C≧H>U
    [d͡ʑ] : C≧H=N>U

4.4. 音韻要素から見た母音融合 (5) の分析

こうした音韻要素表現から，窪薗 (1999) で議論されている母音融合 (5) を捉え直すと，(14) のようになる．全てに共通する性質として，後続母音の原子要素が融合した母音（以後，融合母音）の支配要素となっている点に注目されたい．以下，この現象をもたらす最上位の制約を「ε2>ε1」と呼ぶ．

(14) a. /oi/ → [eː] : {U>A} + {I} → {I>A}　（除外：要素 U）
　　 b. /oe/ → [eː] : {U>A} + {I>A} → {I>A}　（除外：要素 U）
　　 c. /ou/ → [oː] : {U>A} + {U} → {U>A}
　　 d. /ui/ → [iː] : {U} + {I} → {I}　（除外：要素 U）
　　 e. /ae/ → [eː] : {A} + {I>A} → {I>A}
　　 f. /au/ → [oː] : {A} + {U} → {U>A}

g. /ei/ → [eː] : {I>A} + {I} → {I>A}
h. /eu/ → [(j)oː] : {I>A} + {U} → {U>A}　（要素 I は先行子音の拗音）
i. /iu/ → [(j)ɯː] : {I} + {U} → {U}　（要素 I は先行子音の拗音）
j. /ea/ → [(j)ɑː] : {I>A} + {A} → {A}　（要素 I は先行子音の拗音）
k. /oa/ → [ɑː] : {U>A} + {A} → {A}　（除外：要素 U）

　また，多くの場合，先行母音・後続母音の音韻要素が融合母音を含む「音節」に何らかの形で引き継がれている．この性質を引き起こす制約を「Parse(Ɛσ)」と呼んでおく．(14c, e, f, g) は融合母音自体に要素が引き継がれている例である．一方，(14h, i, j) は硬口蓋要素 I が融合母音に引き継がれていないが，先行子音に取り込まれているため，制約 Parse(Ɛσ) に違反しない．なお，硬口蓋要素 I を依存要素として取り込むことで，先行子音は直音から開拗音に変異する．

　問題となるのは，(14a, b, d, k) の例で，一見すると要素 U が融合母音にも先行子音にも引き継がれていない．すなわち，Parse(Ɛσ) に違反するように見える．ここで 4.3 節の議論に基づいて，(14a) の「酷い→ひでー」の融合過程を考えてみよう．「(ひ)どい」の入力 {{C>H=N, U>A}, {I}} に対するいくつかの出力候補は表 2 のような制約違反を犯す．なお，制約 SimpleStr は，要素表現は (8)–(12) に示す単純な構造でなければならず，余剰的な構造 (13) を持ってはいけないことを意味する．この制約が Parse(Ɛσ) より低いランキングにある場合，要素 U が先行子音に組み込まれた余剰的構造を持つ候補が他の候補に勝つ．これは，母音融合前の音節内の原子要素は融合後の音節に全て取り込まれている点で，(14h, i) の原子要素 I が先行子音に取り込まれていることと並行的である．ただし，要素 I は強素性 [+palatal] によって先行子音を開拗音に変化させるが，要素 U は強素性を持たないため先行子音の音価に影響を与えない．

表2. 全ての原子要素が音節に組み込まれる解が最適になる場合

{{C>H=N, U>A}, {I}}		ε2>ε1	Parse(εσ)	SimpleStr
a.	(ひ) ずー： {C≧H=N, U}	*!	**	
b.	(ひ) だー： {C>H=N, A}	*!	**	
c.	(ひ) じー： {C≧H=N, I}		**	
d.	(ひ) じょー：{C≧H=N>I, U>A}	*!		
e.	(ひ) でー： {C>H=N, I>A}		*!	
f. ☞	(ひ) でー： {C>H=N>U, I>A}			*

なお，制約 SimpleStr が制約 Parse(εσ) より高い位置にランクされている場合でも，表3のように結果的には正しい解が選ばれる．ただし，表3の最適解に要素 U が取り込まれていないことから分かる通り，この制約ランキングでは (14h, i) のような要素 I が先行子音に取り込まれるという現象を適切に説明することができない．したがって，日本語の母音融合に関わる制約としては，表2に示したランキングのほうが妥当であると考えられる．

表3. 最も単純な音韻要素構造が選ばれる場合

{{C>H=N, U>A}, {I}}		ε2>ε1	SimpleStr	Parse(εσ)
a.	(ひ) ずー：{C≧H=N, U}	*!		**
b.	(ひ) だー：{C>H=N, A}	*!		**
c.	(ひ) じー：{C≧H=N, I}			**
d.	(ひ) じょー：{C≧H=N>I, U>A}	*!		
e. ☞	(ひ) でー：{C>H=N, I>A}			*
f.	(ひ) でー：{C>H=N>U, I>A}		*!	

5. 総合論議

以上，離散的カテゴリーである弁別素性を内部構造として持つプロトタイプ的性質を持った音韻原子要素によって，窪薗 (1999) で取り上げられている母音融合の現象を先行子音の変異も含めて適切に説明できることを見た．主要な論点は，原子要素が離散的カテゴリーとプロトタイプカテゴリーを止

揚する性質を持っていること，また弁別素性の対立関係が保持されている限り，分節音を構成する原子要素の組み合わせに一定の自由度が認められることである．

　原子要素はプロトタイプとしての性質を持つため，内部構造として離散的な弁別素性のみならず，その性質に関する定量的分布をも持つ．この性質によって，定性的な音韻情報と定量的な音韻情報との自然な接続も可能になる．松井（2015）の議論に基づき，原子要素を C/D モデル（藤村（2007））の入力情報になっているとして，日本語閉鎖音の弱化現象（通時的現象としては唇音退化，共時的現象としては有声閉鎖音 [b], [g] の摩擦化など）を考えてみよう．C/D モデルは音節を最小単位とし（表 2 や表 3 の入力情報が音節を単位とする集合になっているのはこのためである），基底状態を成す母音の上に，インパルス応答関数（IRF）の性質を持つ子音が局所的な影響を与える形で調音動態の定量的計算を行う．図 1 に示したラ行子音の変異は，母音が基底状態を成すという性質を反映した典型例といってよい．ここで今，要素 C が依存要素である場合に，この要素に内在する IRF のパルス強度が減少するとしよう．図 3 から分かる通り，パルスが弱くなると子音の持続時間が短くなり，基底状態（母音の舌位）からの距離（1 を超えると摩擦，2 を超えると完全閉鎖）も減少する．この結果，入力情報としては要素 C を持つ破裂音であっても，音声実現としては摩擦音になってしまう．これが，母音間の有声閉鎖音 [b], [g] などが [β], [ɣ] に摩擦化する共時的現象のプロセスである．しかし，これが音韻現象として定着してくると，図 3 の弱い IRF は要素 C のパルス弱化ではなく，通常のパルス強度を持った要素 H の IRF であると再解釈されていく．すなわち，パルスの弱化という定量的な音声変異が，要素 C>H から要素 C の欠落した要素 H への変化という，定性的な音韻情報の変化に置き換わる．これが，[p]: {U>C>H} → [ɸ]: {U>H} → ハ行子音：{＿>H} ／ [w]: {U} という通時的な唇音退化を引き起こす．

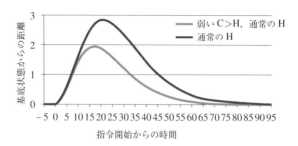

図 3. 母音間における有声破裂音の摩擦化と IRF 強度

　また音韻要素は，変異音の分布を単純な計算で予測し得る．例えば日本語の音素 /g/ は，破裂音 [g] と共に鼻音 [ŋ] と摩擦音 [ɣ] を異音として持つ．これは [g] 音が N≧H＝U＝C>C という構造を持つためで，要素 H や要素 C が依存要素であることから，定量的にこれらのパルス強度が弱化しやすい．要素 H か要素 C のパルス強度の弱化は，定性的には要素 H か要素 C の欠落に相当するため，[ŋ]: N>U＝C>C という鼻音化と [ɣ]: N≧H＝U という摩擦化のいずれもが可能であることが分かる．これに対し，音素 /b/ は摩擦音 [β] には変異し得るものの，鼻音 [m] を変異音として持たない．なぜなら，[b]: U>C>N≧H から要素 C が欠落した場合には摩擦音 [β]: U>N≧H に変わりうるが，[b] 音から要素 H が欠落した場合には U>C>N という構造になり，これは鼻音 [m]: U>N>C の構造にはなり得ないからである．さらに音素 /d/ に関しては，鼻音 [n] のみならず（破擦音が関与しない限り）摩擦音 [z] も異音として現れない．これも，[d]: C>H＝N から要素 H が欠落しても支配関係の違いから [n]: N>C には変異せず，同じく C>H＝N から要素 C が欠落しても [z]: H＝N>C にならないことから理解できよう（そもそも [d] 音における要素 C は支配要素であって依存要素ではないので，パルス強度の弱化自体が起こらない）．

　以上，離散的カテゴリーとプロトタイプカテゴリーの性質を併せ持つ要素表現が，分節音の変異を定量的・定性的に説明できることを見た．しかし，支配構造（Nasukawa (2014)）や言語における内在的弁別素性の違いなど，残された課題も多い．これらの問題点について，また稿を改めて議論を行う予定である．

参考文献

Charette, Monica (1991) *Conditions on Phonological Government*, Cambridge University Press, Cambridge.

藤村靖 (2007)『音声科学原論——言語の本質を考える』岩波書店, 東京.

Harris, John (1994) *English Sound Structure*, Blackwell, Oxford.

窪薗晴夫 (1999)『日本語の音声』岩波書店, 東京.

松井理直 (2015)「日本語の母音無声化に関する C/D モデルの入力情報について」『音声研究』第 19 巻第 2 号, 55-69.

Nasukawa, Kuniya (2014) "Features and Recursive Structure in Phonology," *Nordlyd* 41.1, 1-19.

Nasukawa, Kuniya and Phillip Backley (2016) "The Role of Elements in the Development of Japanese *h*,"『音韻研究』第 19 号, 51-58.

小野浩司 (2015)「同化としての母音融合」*Journal of the Faculty of Culture and Education*, 19(2), 187-196, Saga University.

太田貴久・氏平明 (2014)「最適性理論による日本語の母音連続の分析と制約の統計的検討」*The Lark Hill* 36, 13-34.

染田利信 (1966)「出現頻度から見た子音および母音の特性」『天理大学学報』第 17 巻 3 号, 24-45.

Tayler, John R. (2004) *Linguistic Categorization*, Oxford University Press, Oxford.

上田功 (1996)「連母音融合に関わる音韻変化とその変異形をめぐって」『言語研究の領域: 小泉保博士古稀記念論文集』, 上田功・高見健一・蓮沼昭子・砂川有里子 (編), 79-92, 大学書林, 東京.

Appendix 要素表現 (8) ～ (12) に基づく日本語分節音の内部構造

	[a]	[i]/[j]	[u]/[w]	[e]	[o]	[p]	[b]	[m]	[ɸ]	[β]	[ç]	[h]	[t]	[d]	[n]	[s]	[z]	[ɕ]	[ʑ]	[r]	[k]	[g]	[ŋ]	[ɣ]	[N]
consonantal	−	−	−	−	−	+	+	+	+	+	+	+	+	+	+	+	+	+	+	+	+	+	+	+	+
sonorant	+	+	+	+	+	−	−	+	−	−	−	−	−	−	+	−	−	−	−	+	−	−	+	−	+
voiced	+	+	+	+	+	−	+	+	−	+	−	−	−	+	+	−	+	−	+	+	−	+	+	+	+
nasal	−	−	−	−	−	−	−	+	−	−	−	−	−	−	+	−	−	−	−	−	−	−	+	−	+
contact	−	−	−	−	−	+	+	+	−	−	−	−	+	+	+	−	−	−	−	+	+	+	+	−	+
constriction	−	−	−	−	−	−	−	−	+	+	+	+	−	−	−	+	+	+	+	−	−	−	−	+	−
strident	−	−	−	−	−	−	−	−	−	−	−	−	−	−	−	+	+	+	+	−	−	−	−	−	−
high	−	+	+	−	−	−	−	−	−	−	+	+	−	−	−	−	−	+	+	+	+	+	+	+	+
low	+	−	−	−	−	−	−	−	−	−	−	+	−	−	−	−	−	−	−	−	−	−	−	−	−
palatal	−	+	−	+	−	−	−	−	−	−	+	−	−	−	−	−	−	+	+	−	−	−	−	−	−
grave	+	−	+	−	+	+	+	+	+	+	−	−	−	−	−	−	−	−	−	−	+	+	+	+	+
labial	−	−	+	−	+	+	+	+	+	+	−	−	−	−	−	−	−	−	−	−	−	−	−	−	−

語末 F0 上昇が母音の長短判断に及ぼす影響：
Takiguchi et al.（2010）の再検証*

竹安　大

福岡大学

1. はじめに

音の長さの知覚は，その音の物理的な持続時間だけでなく，基本周波数（F0）によっても影響を受けることが知られている．例えば，母音の F0 に変動がある場合には，F0 の変動がない場合と比べて，その母音が音声的または音韻的に長いと判断されやすいことが，英語をはじめとする様々な言語において報告されている（Lehiste (1976), Cumming (2008), Inoue (2009), Yu (2010)）．日本語においても，こうした母音長の判断に対する F0 変動の影響が存在することが指摘されているが（Kinoshita et al. (2002)），影響の現れ方は語内の位置や F0 変動の方向性（上昇／下降）によって異なることも指摘されており（Takiguchi et al. (2010)），日本語における F0 変動と母音長の判断の関係にはまだ明らかにされていない点が残されている．

本研究では，日本語の語末母音における F0 の上昇が母音の長短判断に与える影響について，知覚実験の結果をもとに議論する．まず，日本語の母音の音韻長の知覚と F0 変動の関係に関する先行研究で明らかにされていることをまとめ，主に Takiguchi et al. (2010) で未解決のまま残されていた問題点を中心に，本研究で扱う論点を整理する．そのうえで，未解明の問題点

---

* 本研究は，筆者が三重大学に所属していた時期に収集したデータを近年の研究によって得られた知見をもとに再分析したもので，2010 年 7 月 10 日の PAIK（関西音韻論研究会）における発表内容に大幅な修正を加えたものである．本研究のデータ収集および分析は，JPSP 科研費（課題番号「25871012」「26284059」）の助成を受けて実施したものである．

を明らかにすべく実施した知覚実験の結果を報告する．

2. 日本語の母音の音韻長に対する F0 変動の影響

　日本語における母音の音韻長の判断には，その母音の持続時間が主要な手がかりとなるが（藤崎・杉藤（1977）），母音の長短の判断にはこれ以外にも発話速度（Hirata and Lambacher (2004)），隣接する音節の母音持続時間（竹安・儀利古（2010）），F0 パターン（Kinoshita et al. (2002)）など，様々な要因が関与することが知られている．

　F0 の変動が母音の音韻的長短の判断に与える影響（以下，F0 変動の影響とする）の有無は，母音の持続時間と F0 を操作して作成した刺激を用いた知覚実験によって検証されてきた．Kinoshita et al. (2002) は，男性の日本語話者によって読まれた /zAza/（A = a, i, u）という 2 音節語の F0 を操作して平板から下降に至る 10 段階の刺激を作成して 2 択の同定実験を行い，F0 は持続時間ほど強い手がかりではないが，持続時間が曖昧な場合には F0 が下降するほど長母音だと判断される率が上がることを明らかにした．Inoue (2009) は，日本語話者が発音した /mama:ma/ の持続時間と F0 を操作して平板および中高に聞こえる [mamama]–[mama:ma] の連続体を作成し，同定実験を行ったところ，音節内でのアクセント下降を伴う中高の方がそうではない平板型よりも判断境界値が低かったことを報告している．Lehnert-LeHouillier (2010) は，エストニア語の話者が発音した単音節語（[tV]–[tV:]; V = a, e, i）から作成した母音連続体を用いて知覚実験を行ったところ，F0 が平坦である場合と比べ，F0 が下降する場合の方が母音が長いと判断されやすかったことを報告している．同様の手法による実験を行った Lehnert-LeHouillier (2007) でも，同様の結論が得られている．

　さらに，F0 変動の方向性（上昇／下降）と語内の位置によって，F0 変動の影響の現れ方が異なることも指摘されている．Takiguchi et al. (2010) は，日本語話者が発音した 3 音節の無意味語 /mamama/ の語頭および語末の母音持続時間と F0 を操作して平坦・下降・上昇の 3 タイプの刺激系列を作成し，長母音か短母音かの同定実験を行ったところ，ほかの先行研究で指摘されている通り，語頭・語末のどちらにおいても，日本語話者は下降する F0 を持つ刺激の判断境界値が平坦な F0 を持つ刺激の判断境界値よりも低

かった（つまり，日本語話者は F0 下降を持つ母音を長母音だと判断しやすかった）ことを報告している．一方，F0 上昇の影響は，語末では F0 下降と同様の傾向が観察されたが，語頭では影響の現れ方が正反対となり，F0 上昇を伴う刺激の方が F0 変動のない刺激よりも長母音だと判断されにくかったことを報告している．F0 変動の方向性および語内の位置の影響については，竹安 (2012a, b) にも同様の報告がある．

F0 上昇の影響の現れ方が語頭と語末で異なることに対し，Takiguchi et al. (2010) は F0 変動が弁別的であるかどうかが原因である可能性を指摘している．Takiguchi et al. (2010) の解釈では，語末の F0 上昇は平叙文・疑問文の区別に弁別的に働くため，F0 の変動が長母音の知覚を促進する方向に働くが，語頭の F0 上昇は日本語（東京方言）においては余剰的な要素であるため，長母音の知覚を促進することはないと説明される．しかしながら，この説明では F0 が弁別的に働くことと長母音の知覚がなぜ関係するのかはわからないままである．従来，F0 変動の影響が生じるメカニズムに関しては，F0 に変動がある場合には母音の知覚上の持続時間が増すというような人間の聴覚特性に基づく説明や，音節内ピッチ下降が長母音と共起するという日本語の音韻体系に基づく説明がなされてきており，語末における F0 上昇に関して疑問文／平叙文の区別と母音の長短の判断が関係するという Takiguchi et al. (2010) の説明はこの点において大きく異なっている．よって，疑問文／平叙文の区別と母音の長短の判断の間に関係性があるのかどうか，実験により確認してみることは重要なことであると考える．

また，Takiguchi et al. (2010) で報告されている「語内の位置の影響」についても，慎重に解釈すべきである．Takiguchi et al. (2010) で用いられた刺激を見ると，語頭における F0 上昇は 150 Hz から 200 Hz への上昇であるのに対し，語末における F0 上昇は 200 Hz から 300 Hz への上昇となっており，上昇の開始時点の F0 と上昇幅がともに異なっている．したがって，もし語末における F0 上昇の起点を低く設定し，上昇幅も小さくした場合，母音の長短の判断に関して語頭で見られたものと同じ方向性の影響が生じる可能性も否定できない．F0 上昇の開始点における F0 の値が結果に影響するかどうかを調べることにより，Takiguchi et al. (2010) における語内の位置によって F0 上昇の影響の現れ方が異なるという指摘が妥当であるのかどうか検討してみる必要がある．

以上のように，F0 変動が母音の長短判断に影響することは疑いようのない事実であるが，F0 変動（特に F0 上昇）の影響の現れ方や F0 変動が母音の長短判断に影響を及ぼすメカニズムは必ずしも明らかにされているとは言えない状況にある．そこで，本研究では，先行研究で提示されている F0 上昇に関する解釈の妥当性を検証する実験を行う．具体的には，3 音節語の語末母音の長短判断について，以下の 2 点を検討する．

(1) F0 上昇開始時点の F0 の違いによって，母音の長短判断に対する F0 上昇の影響の現れ方が異なるかどうか
(2) 疑問文／平叙文の区別（知覚）と，母音の長短判断に対する F0 上昇の影響の現れ方に関係があるかどうか

(1) により，Takiguchi et al. (2010) で報告されている語内の位置による F0 上昇の影響の現れ方の違いが F0 上昇開始点の違いによるものである可能性を検討する．また，(2) により，語末の F0 上昇と平叙文・疑問文の区別とを結び付けた Takiguchi et al. (2010) の説明の妥当性を検討する．以上の 2 点を検討するため，本研究では語末の F0 上昇について，上昇開始時点の F0 が異なる刺激と F0 に上昇のない刺激を用意し，それらについて母音の長短の判断してもらい，F0 上昇の起点の F0 が母音の長短の判断に影響するかどうかを調べる．加えて，母音の長短の判断と，疑問文／平叙文の判断の間に何らかの関係性があるかどうかを調べることで，F0 上昇の影響が平叙文／疑問文の判断と関連して生じたものであるかどうかも調べる．

3. 知覚実験 1

3.1. 刺激

本実験における音声刺激は，日本語話者（女性，静岡方言）が単独で発音した平板型の無意味語「ママ マ」から作成された．なお，この音声は，Takiguchi et al. (2010) で刺激作成に用いられたものと同一のものである．無意味語は話者にとっての自然な速さで読まれた．刺激作成に用いられたトークンのセグメント持続時間は以下の通りであった．

	C1	V1	C2	V2	C3	V3
/mamama/	23	88	57	121	66	167

表 1. 刺激作成元の音声の子音・母音持続時間 (ms)

本実験における変数は第 3 音節目の母音持続時間（127 ms ～ 267 ms まで，20 ms 刻みで 8 段階），第 3 音節目の F0 上昇開始直前の F0(200 Hz, 130 Hz の 2 段階），ピッチ変動の度合い（±0 st，+2.5 st，+5.0 st の 3 段階）の 3 つとし，これらを掛け合わせることで 48 通りの刺激を作成した．刺激作成の手順は以下の通りであった．

まず，語末の母音の持続時間を 127 ms から 267 ms まで 20 ms 刻みで 8 段階に変化させ，聴覚上「ママ マ」から「ママ マー」に聞こえる音声連続体を作成した．持続時間の操作には praat (Boersma and Weenink (2009)) を用い，語末の母音の中央部付近の声帯振動周期を除去または複製して行った．すべての操作はゼロ交点において行われた．

次に，刺激が低高高（以下，LHH とする）または低高低（以下，LHL とする）に聞こえるよう，F0 を以下のように操作した．LHH の系列については，無意味語の始点の F0 を 150 Hz とし，その後 180 ms かけて 200Hz まで線形に上昇し，そのまま語末まで 200Hz を水平に維持した．LHL の系列の F0 は，150 Hz から始まり 180 ms かけて 200 Hz まで上昇する点は LHH の系列と同じであるが，第 3 音節の開始点（語頭から起算して 290 ms 地点）から 110 ms かけて 200 Hz から 130 Hz まで線形的に下降し，その後水平なまま保たれるという点が異なっている．すなわち，LHH と LHL の系列の違いは第 3 音節の F0 のみにあり，第 2 音節の終点までは両系列は音響的に同一のものが用いられている．

最後に，LHH，LHL の両系列について，第 3 母音開始から 40ms 経過した時点（語頭から起算して 400 ms，LHL の F0 が 130 Hz に到達する時点）から語の終点までの間に F0 が 2.5 st または 5.0 st 線形上昇する音声も作成し，語の終点まで水平に保たれるものを含めて 3 パターンの F0 下降を設定した．以上のように，第 3 音節目の母音持続時間（8 段階），第 3 音節目の母音のベースの F0（2 段階），語末にかけての F0 下降の度合い（3 段階）の掛け合わせにより，48 種類の刺激を作成した．

3.2. 被験者

112名の日本語話者が実験に参加した．112名はすべて三重大学に通う学生である．以下の表は被験者の出身地の内訳を示したものである．被験者の出身地は様々であり，表から明らかなように，被験者は愛知県と三重県出身者が大半であったが，それ以外の地域出身者も含まれていた．なお，被験者の出身地が実験結果に大きな影響をおよぼすことはなかったため，以下では被験者の出身地を議論の対象とはしないこととする．

三重	48	岡山	2	富山	1
愛知	34	岐阜	2	長崎	1
奈良	6	静岡	2	兵庫	1
大阪	3	京都	1	福岡	1
滋賀	3	島根	1	宮崎	1
和歌山	3	千葉	1	山口	1
				計	112

表2. 知覚実験1の被験者の人数（出身県別）

3.3. 手順

実験は，実験参加に同意した学生30〜40名を1つのグループとして，合計で3グループに対して実施した．実験の実施に当たっては，三重大学共通教育センターの教室および設備を使用させていただいた．刺激の提示回数は1回ずつとし，ランダムな順序に並び変えたものを3通り作成しておき，各グループに1つを割り当てた．すなわち，グループによって刺激の提示順序は異なっていた．被験者にはラウドスピーカーから流れてくる音声を聞き，それが「ママ」・「ママー」のどちらであったかを回答するように依頼した．被験者はあらかじめ配布された回答用紙に記載されている選択肢の片方に丸をつけることで回答した．回答用紙は「ママ」が左側の列に配置されているものと，「ママー」が左側の列に配置されているものの2種類を用意し，被験者に無作為に割り当てた．

3.4. 予測

Takiguchi et al. (2010) は，母音の長短の判断に対してF0上昇が与える影響の出方が語内の位置によって異なると指摘したが，Takiguchiらの刺激

では語頭に比べ語末のF0上昇の起点のF0の値が高く，上昇幅も大きかった．もし，Takiguchiらが指摘している「語内の位置の影響」が実際にはF0操作の違いに起因するものであるならば，本研究の実験におけるLHHとLHLの系列で母音の長短の判断に与える影響が異なり，LHH系列ではF0上昇が長音の判断を促進するのに対し，LHL系列ではF0上昇が長音の判断を抑制するはずである．

3.5. 結果

以下の図は各条件における長音判断率を，表はProbit分析に基づく長音判断境界値（50％判断地点となる第3音節の母音持続時間）示したものである．F0上昇の影響の有無について調べるために，長音判断率を依存変数とし，第3音節目の母音持続時間（連続変数），第3音節目のベースのHz（名義変数：200 Hz, 130 Hz），F0の変動（名義変数：±0 st, +2.5 st, +5.0 st）を独立変数とするロジスティック回帰分析を行った．その結果，LHH, LHLの両系列において，F0上昇が長音判断境界値に影響を与えており，上昇の度合いが大きいほど判断境界値が下がることが明らかとなった（$B = 0.207$, $W^2 = 75.5$, $df = 1$, $p < 0.001$）．また，系列ごとの判断境界値を比較す

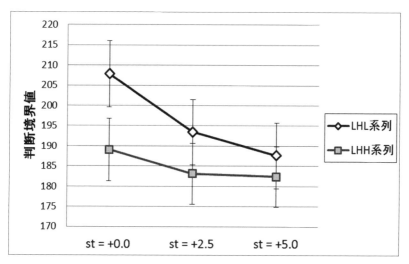

図1. 知覚実験1の各系列の長音判断境界値（probit分析による）

ると，LHH 系列の方が LHL 系列よりも小さな判断境界値を取る，すなわち，LHH 系列の方が長音だと判断されやすいことも明らかとなった（$B = 0.83$, $W^2 = 73.5$, $df = 1$, $p < 0.001$）．

系列とベースの F0	F0 の変動	長音判断境界値 (ms)	長音判断境界値の 95% 信頼区間 (ms)	
			下限	上限
LHL 系列 130Hz	±0.0 st	207.9	199.6	216.1
	+2.5 st	193.5	185.4	201.5
	+5.0 st	187.7	179.5	195.7
LHH 系列 200Hz	±0.0 st	189.1	181.4	196.8
	+2.5 st	183.2	175.6	190.7
	+5.0 st	182.4	174.9	189.9

表 3. 知覚実験 1 の各系列の長音判断境界値（probit 分析による）

3.6. 考察

F0 上昇開始時点の F0 の値が高い LHH 系列の方が，F0 の値が低い LHL 系列より長音だと判断されやすかったことから，母音の長短判断はベースとなる母音の F0 に影響を受けるといえる．中国語母語話者にも同様の傾向が観察されることが Yu (2010) によって指摘されていることから，F0 が高いほうが低い場合よりも音が長いと判断されやすいという傾向は日本語に限ったことではないようである．

また，F0 上昇と判断境界値の関係を見ると，これら 2 つの系列は判断境界値自体に差があるものの，語末の F0 上昇が長音の判断を促進するという点ではどちらも同じ傾向を示しており，Takiguchi et al. (2010) の実験における語末の F0 上昇の影響の現れ方とも共通している．つまり，Takiguchi らの F0 上昇の現れ方が語内の位置によって異なるという実験結果は，語内の位置ごとに刺激の F0 設定が異なっていたために生じたわけではないと判断できる．

先行研究と本研究における実験の結果から，語末における F0 上昇が長音の判断を促進することが明らかとなった．Takiguchi et al. (2010) は，語末の F0 上昇が長音の判断を促進することについて，語末では F0 上昇が疑問

文と平叙文の区別に弁別的に働くために生じたとする仮説を提示している．この点については，知覚実験 2 で議論する．

4. 知覚実験 2

F0 上昇の影響が平叙文／疑問文の判断と関連して生じたものであるかを調べるために，知覚実験 1 の LHH 系列と LHL 系列において，それぞれどの程度の F0 上昇があれば疑問文だと感じられるのかを調べる実験を行う．用いる刺激は，知覚実験 1 と同様に LHH 系列と LHL 系列の 2 系列からなり，第 3 音節目の母音持続時間とピッチ変動の度合いの設定が異なる点を除けば同一のものである．

4.1. 刺激

知覚実験 2 における音声刺激は，知覚実験 1 で刺激作成元となったものと同じ音声をもとに作成された．

知覚実験 2 における変数は第 3 音節目の母音持続時間（127 ms と 267 ms の 2 段階，それぞれ「ママ マ」と「ママ マー」に対応），第 3 音節目の F0 上昇開始直前の F0（200 Hz，130 Hz の 2 段階），ピッチ変動の度合い（-1 st～$+7$ st まで，1 st 刻みで 9 段階）の 3 つとし，これらを掛け合わせることで 36 通りの刺激を作成した．刺激作成における操作の方法は知覚実験 1 と同様である．

4.2. 被験者

99 名の日本語話者が実験に参加した．99 名はすべて三重大学に通う学生である．以下の表は被験者の出身地の内訳を示したものである．被験者の出身地は様々であり，表から明らかなように，被験者は愛知県と三重県出身者が大半であったが，それ以外の地域出身者も含まれていた．なお，被験者の出身地が実験結果に大きな影響をおよぼすことはなかったため，以下では被験者の出身地を議論の対象とはしないこととする．

三重	43	和歌山	3	滋賀	1
愛知	27	鳥取	2	東京	1
奈良	4	兵庫	2	福岡	1
大阪	4	秋田	1	山口	1
静岡	4	大分	1		
岐阜	3	京都	1		
				計	99

表 4. 知覚実験 2 の被験者の人数（出身県別）

4.3. 手順

　実験は，実験参加に同意した学生 30～40 名を 1 つのグループとして，合計で 3 グループに対して実施した．実験の実施に当たっては，三重大学共通教育センターの教室および設備を使用させていただいた．刺激の提示回数は 1 回ずつとし，ランダムな順序に並び変えたものを 3 通り作成しておき，各グループに一つを割り当てた．すなわち，グループによって刺激の提示順序は異なっていた．被験者にはラウドスピーカーから流れてくる音声を聞き，それが尋ねられているように聞こえるかどうかを判断するよう依頼した．被験者はあらかじめ配布された回答用紙に記載されている選択肢（疑問・平叙の 2 種類）の片方に丸をつけることで回答した．回答用紙は選択肢「疑問」が左側の列に配置されているものと，「平叙」が左側の列に配置されているものの 2 種類を用意し，被験者に無作為に割り当てた．

4.4. 予測

　先の知覚実験 1 では，LHH 系列でも LHL 系列でも，F0 上昇が長母音の知覚を促進する働きを示すことが明らかとなった．Takiguchi et al. (2010) の解釈によれば，日本語（東京方言）では語末の F0 上昇が平叙文と疑問文の区別に弁別的に働くことから，F0 上昇が長母音の知覚を促進する方向に働く．知覚実験 1 では，LHH 系列でも LHL 系列でも F0 の上昇度合いが増すほどに判断境界値が低くなっていた．知覚実験 2 では，LHH 系列，LHL 系列ともに F0 上昇の度合いが増すほど疑問文であるという判断が増えていくものと予測されるが，Takiguchi らの説明が正しければ，F0 上昇と疑問文の判断の相関の程度は LHH 系列と LHL 系列とで近いものとなる

ことが期待される．

4.5. 結果

以下の図は各条件における長音判断率を示したものである．長音判断率を依存変数とし，第3音節目の母音持続時間（名義変数：127 ms, 267 ms の2段階），第3音節目のベースのHz（名義変数：200 Hz, 130 Hz），F0の変動（連続変数）を独立変数とするロジスティック回帰分析の結果，F0(st)の上昇度合いが大きくなるほど疑問文の知覚率が高くなることが明らかとなった（$B = 0.600$, $W^2 = 637.5$, $df = 1$, $p < 0.001$）．さらに，LHH の系列に比べ，LHL の系列は疑問文だと判断されにくいことがわかった（$B = 3.189$, $W^2 = 782.6$, $df = 1$, $p < 0.001$）．また，V3 持続時間が長いほうが短い場合よりも疑問文だと判断されやすいことも明らかとなったが（$B = 0.004$, $W^2 = 39.6$, $df = 1$, $p < 0.001$），図からも明らかなように，V3 持続時間の影響は系列の違いによる影響よりも小さなものであった．

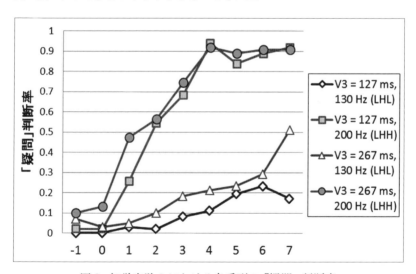

図 2. 知覚実験 2 における各系列の「疑問」判断率

4.6. 考察

疑問文だと判断されるかどうかは，LHH 系列であるか LHL 系列であるか，すなわちベースとなる母音の F0 が高いか低いかによって大きく異なっ

ていた.F0 上昇と疑問文の判断の相関の程度は LHH 系列と LHL 系列で近いものとなることが予測されたが,実験結果は予測に反するものであった.知覚実験 1 の F0 操作(±0 st,+2.5 st,+5.0 st)と対応させてみると,知覚実験 1 の LHH 系列の刺激は,+2.5 st 程度の上昇であっても,半分以上の被験者に疑問文であると聞こえるような音声であったのに対し,LHL 系列の刺激は+5.0 st の上昇がある場合でさえ 4 人に 1 人程度の被験者にとってしか疑問文に聞こえないようなものであったと推測できる.語末の F0 上昇が長母音の知覚を促進するという傾向は LHH 系列にも LHL 系列にも共通して観察されることから,疑問文だと判断されるかどうかという問題と,語末で F0 上昇が長母音の判断を促進するという問題は別の次元の事柄であると解釈できる.

5. 総合的考察

　本研究では,語末での F0 上昇が母音の長短判断に与える影響について,主に Takiguchi et al. (2010) の主張を再検証する形で知覚実験を行った.結果として,語末における F0 上昇が長音の知覚を促進するという Takiguchi et al. (2010) の実験結果は本研究でも再現され,また,この F0 上昇の影響は語のアクセント型(平板・中高)によらず観察されることも新たに明らかになった.一方で,語末での F0 上昇が母音の長短判断に影響を及ぼすのは語末の F0 上昇が疑問文と平叙文の区別に弁別的に働くためであるとする Takiguchi らの説明は,妥当性に欠けることがわかった.では,それに代わるものとしてどのような説明が可能なのかを以下で考察したい.

　そもそも,Takiguchi et al. (2010) が疑問文と平叙文という説明を持ち出したのは,Takiguchi らの実験結果における F0 変動の方向性(上昇・下降)と語内の位置の影響をすべて統一的に説明しようとしたためであった.もう一度 Takiguchi らの実験結果と本研究の実験結果を整理すると,以下のようになる.

		F0 上昇	F0 下降
Takiguchi et al. (2010)	語頭	長音の判断を抑制	長音の判断を促進
	語末	長音の判断を促進	長音の判断を促進
本研究	語末	長音の判断を促進	

表 5. Takiguchi et al. (2010) と本研究の実験結果のまとめ

ここから明らかなように，語頭の F0 上昇のみがほかとは異なる振る舞いを示しており，それ以外の条件では F0 変動があると長音の判断が促進されている．ところで，本研究の知覚実験では，F0 上昇の開始点を複数設定することにより，平板型と中高型に聞こえる刺激の系列を要して実験を行った結果，F0 上昇の度合いのみならず，F0 上昇の開始点も母音の長短の判断に少なからず影響することが明らかとなっている．そこで，この F0 変動の開始点の F0 という観点を加えて Takiguchi らの実験結果を再解釈すると，以下のようになる．

		F0 上昇		F0 下降	
		F0 変動の開始点	比較対象となるF0変動のない系列のF0開始点	F0 変動の開始点	比較対象となるF0変動のない系列のF0開始点
Takiguchi et al. (2010)	語頭	低 (150 Hz)	高 (200 Hz)	高 (300 Hz)	高 (200 Hz)
	語末	高 (200 Hz)	高 (200 Hz)	高 (200 Hz)	高 (200 Hz)
本研究	語末	低 (130 Hz)	低 (130 Hz)		
	語末	高 (200 Hz)	高 (200 Hz)		

表 6. Takiguchi et al. (2010) と本研究の実験結果の再解釈

このように見ると，長音の判断が抑制されていた語頭での F0 上昇のみ，F0 変動開始点（150 Hz）よりも，比較対象となる F0 変動なしの系列の F0 開始点（200 Hz）よりも低くなっており，それ以外の部分，つまり長音の判断が促進された部分では，F0 変動開始点と比較対象となる F0 変動なしの系列の F0 開始点が等しいか，もしくは F0 変動開始点のほうが高くなっている．本研究の知覚実験 1 で示されていたように，F0 変動開始点が低い場合には，高い場合と比べて判断境界値が高くなる（長音の判断が抑制される）．よって，Takiguchi らの実験における語頭の F0 上昇系列が F0 変動なしの系列よりも判断境界値が高くなったのは，F0 上昇の有無の問題という

よりも，F0 変動開始点が低かったためである可能性がある．[1] これが正しければ，例えば語頭において比較する F0 変動なしの系列の開始点を 150 Hz にして比較すれば，語頭の F0 上昇も長音の判断を促進するという結果になることが予測されるため，今後新たに知覚実験を実施するなどしてこの点を検証することができよう．仮にこの通りになるとすれば，F0 変動（上昇・下降とも）は語内の位置によらず，長音の知覚を促進するという説明で実験結果全体を統一的に捉えられるであろう．

　ここまでの議論は，母音の長短判断に対する F0 上昇と F0 下降の影響が同じメカニズムによって生じたものだという前提で進めてきたが，この前提が正しいかどうかは別途検討してみる必要がある．同様に，語内の位置によって全く異なる知覚のメカニズムが働いている可能性も否定できない．F0 が低い場合よりも高い場合のほうが長く感じる，F0 に変動がない場合よりも変動がある場合のほうが長く感じると言った人間の聴覚特性に基づく説明だけでなく，個別言語の音韻体系に基づいて語頭・語末における F0 変動の影響をそれぞれ説明することも可能かもしれない．[2] これらの点は今後の検討課題としたい．

6. 結論

　本研究では，日本語の語末母音における F0 の上昇が母音の長短判断に与える影響について，主に Takiguchi et al. (2010) の主張を再検証する形で知覚実験を行った．その結果，語末の F0 上昇が長音の知覚を促進するという Takiguchi らの主張は妥当であることを明らかとなった．さらに，F0 上

---

[1] 実際に，本研究の知覚実験 1 において，LHL (L) 系列の F0 上昇が +2.5 st, +5.0 st の時の判断境界値（それぞれ 193.5 ms, 187.7 ms）を，LHH(H) 系列の F0 上昇が ±0.0 st (200 Hz で平坦) の時の判断境界値 (189.1 ms) と比較すると，F0 上昇がある場合に長音の判断が促進されるとは必ずしも言えなくなる．これは F0 上昇の影響と F0 開始点の影響が独立に存在しているためであるが，これらの 2 つの要因が Takiguchi et al. (2010) の実験結果における語頭 F0 上昇の特異な振る舞いを生み出した可能性があるということである．

[2] 例えば，Lehnert-LeHouillier (2007/2010) は，F0 下降の影響が生じる理由について，日本語の音韻体系において音節内ピッチ下降が生じうるのは長母音を含む音節のみであるという共起関係に基づく説明を提示している．

昇の影響と F0 変動の開始時点での F0 の影響が独立して存在することを示し，これらの影響を分離することにより，解釈が困難だった Takiguchi らの実験結果を全体としてうまくとらえることができる可能性を指摘した．

参考文献

Cumming, Ruth (2008) "Should Rhythm Metrics Take Account of Fundamental Frequency?" *Cambridge Ocassional Papers in Linguistics* 4, 1-16.

Inoue, Miyoko (2009) "Perception of Japanese Quantity by Swedish Speaking Learners: A Preliminary Analysis," *Proceedings of the XXIIth Swedish Phonetics Conference (FONETIK 2009)*, 112-115.

Kinoshita, Keisuke, Dawn M. Behne and Takayuki Arai (2002) "Duration and F0 as Perceptual Cues to Japanese Vowel Quantity," *Proceedings of the 7th International Conference on Spoken Language Processing*, 757-760.

Lehiste, Ilse (1976) "Influence of Fundamental Frequency Pattern on the Perception of Duration," *Journal of Phonetics* 4, 113-117.

Lehnert-LeHouillier, Heike (2007) "The Influence of Dynamic F0 on the Perception of Vowel Duration: Cross-linguistic Evidence," *Proceedings of the 16th International Congress of Phonetic Sciences*, 757-760.

Lehnert-LeHouillier, Heike (2010) "A Cross-linguistic Investigation of Cues to Vowel Length Perception," *Journal of Phonetics* 38, 472-482.

竹安大 (2012a)「語頭における F0 変動と母音の長短の知覚」『名古屋芸術大学研究紀要』第 33 号，133-139.

竹安大 (2012b)「F0 変動と母音の長短判断について―愛知および三重方言話者の場合―」『*Philologia*』第 43 号，81-93，三重大学英語研究会.

Takiguchi, Izumi, Hajime Takeyasu and Mikio Giriko (2010) "Effects of a Dynamic F0 on the Perceived Vowel Duration in Japanese," *Proceedings of Speech Prosody 2010* [CD-ROM], 100944: 1-4.

Yu, Alan C. L. (2010) "Tonal Effects on Perceived Vowel Duration," *Laboratory Phonology* 10, ed. by C. Fougeron et al., 151-168, Mouton de Gruyter, Berlin.

アクセント型と位置の視点から見る長母音の知覚*

薛　晋陽

山西大学

1. 研究目的

　本研究の目的は，日本語母語話者の長母音の知覚は長母音の位置によって差があるかどうか，またアクセント型の違い（平板型と頭高型）や，falling pitch を伴うかどうかによって，日本語話者の長母音の知覚にどのような影響を与えるかを解明することである．そして，中国語を母語話者とする日本語上級学習者（以下は「日本語上級学習者」と略称する）と日本語母語話者とを比較し，日本語上級学習者に日本語母語話者と同じ傾向があるかどうかを調べる．

2. 先行研究

　助川・前川・上原（1998）は，日本語母語話者は，語末位置における長母音の短母音化に気付くのが鈍感であるということを知覚実験によって明らかにした．彼らは「どれが高校付きの大学？」というキャリア文にある「高校」の語中，語末位置にある長母音の長さを 10msec ずつ短くし，「高校」に聞こえるか聞こえないかを 4 人の日本語話者に判断してもらった．その結果，4 人中 3 人が語末位置にある長母音の長さの変化に鈍感であることが分かった．しかし，刺激音の情報（原音の語中母音・語末母音の持続時間など）については記載されておらず，被験者の数も少ないため，追加実験を行う必要がある．更に，Nagano-Madsen（1990），Kinoshita et al.（2002）などの研

---

*　本研究は筆者の博士論文に基づき，修正を加えたものである．

究によると，falling pitch を伴う場合，日本語母語話者が母音を長母音であると知覚しやすいということが明らかになっている．そこで本稿で知覚実験を行った結果，falling pitch が母音長をより長母音に知覚させやすいという特徴は母音の長さが曖昧な場合のみに観察され，先行研究と一致した．

3. 実験

3.1. 刺激語の選択

知覚実験の刺激音としては，語中位置にも語末位置にも長母音を含み，平板型と頭高型の違いで意味を弁別する語が望まれる．そして，子音の違いによる影響をさけるため，「高校」（平板型）と「孝行」（頭高型）を刺激語に選んだ．1名の日本語標準語話者（女性，静岡県出身）に，「彼は … と言った」というキャリア文に「高校」「孝行」をそれぞれ入れて10回ずつ発音してもらい，語中と語末の母音持続時間を測定し，それが語全体の長さに占める割合を出した．その結果，母音の持続時間には語中・語末の位置による有意な差も，平板型・頭高型による有意な差も見られなかった（図1）．言い換えると，語のどの位置にあるか，また，アクセント型の違いを問わず，長母音の持続時間は同じであることが確認された．

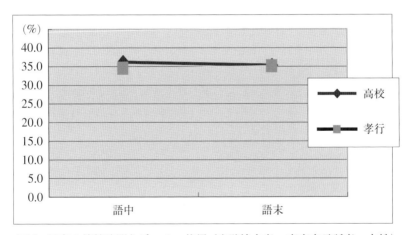

図1. 母音の持続時間とピッチ，位置（実験協力者，東京方言話者，女性）

したがって，もし知覚実験で母音の長さの知覚に，位置や，アクセント型

の影響が見られるのであれば，それは長母音の持続時間が異なるために生まれた差ではなく，日本語話者の知覚上の差であるといえる．

3.2. 刺激音の作り方
3.2.1. 「高校」の場合

1名の日本語標準語話者（女性，静岡県出身）に「彼は高校と言った」というキャリア文を10回発音してもらい，SUGI で録音した．この10回のうち，語中長母音の持続時間と語末長母音の持続時間が最も近いものを抽出した（語中：146msec，語末：144msec）．次に，語末の「校」を切り取り，語頭の「高」をコピーし，「校」のあった場所に入れ替え，語中母音の持続時間と語末母音の持続時間が等しくなるように刺激音を作った．

そして，語中母音の長さを固定し，語末の母音を4周期，16msec（1周期は4msec）ずつ短縮し，146msecから66msecまで6段階の刺激音を作った．また，同様に，語末母音の長さを固定し，語中の長母音も146msecから66msecまで6段階に分けて短縮した．語末と語中あわせて，計12個の刺激が得られた．

3.2.2. 「孝行」の場合

1名の日本語標準語話者（女性，静岡県出身）に「彼は孝行と言った」というキャリア文を10回ずつ発音してもらい，SUGI で録音した．そして，10回の中で，語中長母音の持続時間と語末長母音の持続時間が最も近似しており，「高校」の持続時間とも最も差が少なものを刺激音に選んだ．

次に，語中の母音長を固定し，語末の母音長を3周期，15msec（1周期は5msec）ずつ短縮し，145msecから70msecまで6段階の刺激音を作った．同様に，語末の母音長を固定し，語中の母音長を146msecから71msecまで6段階に分けて短縮した．アクセント核が残るように「孝行」の音節境界から逆向きに母音の長さを短くした．語中と語末あわせて，計12個の刺激音が得られた．

表1に「高校」と「孝行」の各段階の母音の持続時間を提示する．

	0		1		2		3		4		5	
	語中	語末	語中	語末	語中	語末	語中	語末	語中	語末	語中	語末
高校	146	146	130	130	114	114	98	98	82	82	66	66
孝行	146	145	131	130	116	115	101	100	86	85	71	70

表1. 各段階の刺激音の持続時間（msec）

　得られた音声の1周期の持続時間は平板型の「高校」の場合は4msecであり，頭高型の「孝行」の場合は5msecであるため，各段階の母音長を厳密に等しくするのは困難であったが，表3が示すように，6段階までは「高校」と「孝行」刺激音の母音長の長さに見られた差が語中は0〜5msec，語末は0〜4msecであり，それほど大きな差ではなく，比較することが可能であると考えられる．

3.3. 刺激音の提示と実験の手順

　「高校」を例に実験の手順を説明する．「孝行」の場合も同様である．作成した12個の「彼は高校と言った」を音声プログラムで，パソコンの画面でランダムに被験者に提示した．各刺激音は8回提示し，1名の被験者から計96個の答案が得られた．刺激と刺激の間には3秒置き，流れた音声が「彼は高校と言った」に聞こえた場合はキーボードの「Y」を，聞こえない場合はキーボードの「N」を押すように指示した．3秒以内に反応がない場合は，次の刺激音が自動的に流れるようにした．

3.4. 被験者

　日本語母語話者12名（近畿方言話者9名，東京方言話者3名）に実験に協力してもらった．表2に被験者情報を載せる．

日本語話者	出身地	性別	年齢
被験者1	神戸	男性	52歳
被験者2	大阪	男性	23歳
被験者3	大阪	男性	20歳
被験者4	神戸	女性	20歳
被験者5	横浜	女性	22歳
被験者6	名古屋	男性	25歳
被験者7	大阪	男性	26歳
被験者8	大阪	男性	29歳
被験者9	静岡	女性	33歳
被験者10	神戸	女性	21歳
被験者11	神戸	女性	26歳
被験者12	大阪	女性	28歳
平均年齢			27.08歳

表2. 日本語母語話者の被験者情報

同様の実験を日本語上級学習者3名にも協力してもらった．表3はそれらの被験者情報である．

	出身地	性別	年齢	日本語学習暦
被験者1	中国湖北省	女性	32歳	2.5年
被験者2	中国湖南省	女性	28歳	8年
被験者3	台湾	男性	29歳	6年
平均年齢			29.7歳	5.5年

表3. 日本語上級学習者の被験者情報

4. 結果

4.1. 日本語母語話者

まずは，日本語母語話者の結果について述べる．図2に刺激音が「高校」である場合に得られた結果を示す．

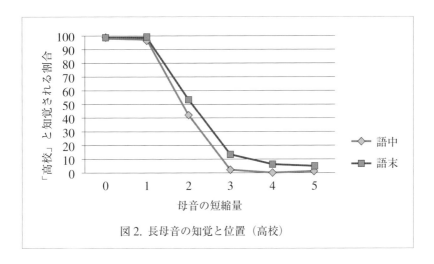

図2. 長母音の知覚と位置（高校）

縦軸は「高校」と判断された割合を表し，横軸は母音の短縮量を表す．右に行けば行くほど，母音の持続時間が短い．当然，語中，語末，いずれの場合においても，母音の持続時間が短くなるにしたがって，「高校」と判断される割合が下がっていく．また，語末の線が語中の線より右側にあり，語中より語末の方が，母音長の短縮に鈍感になるように見えるが，カイ2乗検定をかけてみた結果，有意差が認められなかった（$\chi^2 = 1.238$, df = 5, p = 0.266 n.s）．ここでは助川・前川・上原（1998）と同様の結果が得られなかった．つまり，平板型の「高校」に対して，語中・語末という位置の違いは日本語母語話者の母音長の知覚に影響を与えないといえる．

次に，「孝行」の結果を見る（図3）．

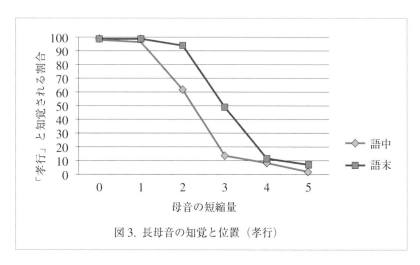

図3. 長母音の知覚と位置（孝行）

　縦軸は刺激音が「孝行」と判断された割合を表し，横軸は母音の短縮量を表す．右に行けば行くほど，母音の持続時間が短い．図3が示すように，語中の場合においても，語末の場合においても，母音の持続時間が短くなるにしたがって「孝行」と判断される割合は下がっていく．また，語末の線が語中の線より右側にあり，語中より語末において，母音長の時間変動に鈍感になるという結果が得られた．カイ2乗検定をかけた結果，有意差が認められた（$\chi^2 = 21.085$, df = 5, p = 0.001）．刺激2と刺激3の間に語中・語末の最も大きな差が見られた．刺激2のときは，「孝行」と判断される割合は語末において93.8%で，100%に近い一方，語中では61.6%であり，半数ぐらいしかない．刺激3の場合は，「孝行」と判断された割合は語末において49.0%であるのに対し，語中の場合は13.5%である．それらをまとめると，頭高型の「孝行」において，当該母音が語中位置にあるか語末位置にあるかの違いによって，母音長を知覚する際に差が見られた．語中位置にある母音と比べて，語末位置にある母音のほうが母音の持続時間が短くてもそれを長母音と知覚しやすいといえる．これは頭高型を有するHHの音節構造を持つ2字漢語は短母音化が起こりやすいという言語事実にも一致している．

　最後に，「高校」と「孝行」と比較しながら議論を行う．まず，語中位置に絞って見ると，「孝行」も「高校」も，刺激0〜1では長母音と判断された割

合はほぼ100%で，刺激3で急に0%近くに下がった．しかしながら，刺激2では，それぞれ61.5%，41.7%に減り，「孝行」と「高校」の長母音の知覚に対する率に19.8%の差が見られた．カイ2乗検定をかけた結果，有意差が認められた（$\chi^2 = 16.154$, df = 5, p = 0.006）．つまり，語中位置の場合，「高校」の「高」と「孝行」の「孝」との間に，刺激2の場合のみ差が見られ（19.8%），「孝行」の「孝」は「高校」の「高」よりも長母音と知覚されやすいということが明らかである．「高」と「孝」の違いは，「高」は falling pitch を伴わないが，「孝」は伴うというところにある．先行研究 Kinoshita et al.（2002），Nagano-Madsen（1990）と一致した結果が得られた．

　次に，長母音と知覚される割合を語末位置に絞って見る．語末位置では「孝行」と「高校」の間に更に大きな差が見られ，特に刺激2，刺激3の場合が顕著である．刺激0から刺激2にかけて，「孝行」の「行」を長母音と判断される割合はほぼ100%であるが，「高校」の「校」が母音と判断される割合は53.1%だけである．刺激3の場合においても，語末の母音を長母音と判断する割合が，「孝行」は49%で，「高校」は僅か13.5%である．

　この結果から，日本語母語話者の母音長の知覚は，語末位置においては，その前の音節にアクセント核があるかどうかによって，かなり影響を受けることがわかる．具体的には，前の音節にアクセント核を有する場合，後ろ（語末）に来る音節の母音の長さが物理的に短くても，それが長音と判断される傾向がある．本研究ではこの現象を「アクセント核効果」と呼ぶ．

　上述した実験結果をまとめると，日本語母語話者は語中位置においても，語末位置においても，平板型を有する刺激と頭高型を有する刺激との間に大きな差を見せた．詳しく言えば，母音長が同じである場合，頭高型を有する語の方が長母音と感じやすいという結論になる．

4.2. 日本語上級学習者

　次は，日本語上級学習者の結果について述べる．図4は刺激音が「高校」である場合に得られた結果である．

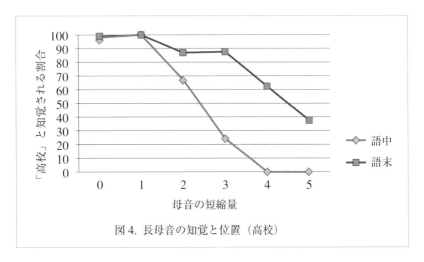

図 4. 長母音の知覚と位置（高校）

　縦軸は刺激音が「高校」に聞こえた割合を表し，横軸は母音の短縮量を表す．右に行けば行くほど，母音の持続時間が短い．日本語上級学習者は図 4 のように，母音の持続時間が短くなるにしたがって，「高校」と判断する率が下がっていく．語末の線が語中の線より極端に右側にあるが，これは日本語母語話者と異なり，語中より語末の母音長の短縮に鈍感になる傾向を示している．

　語末位置に絞ってみると，長母音の判断基準が日本語母語話者と比べ，かなり緩くなり，刺激 5 の場合でも「高校」の「校」を 40％ぐらいは長母音と判断していることがわかる．

　次に，「孝行」の結果について分析する．図 5 は刺激音が孝行である場合に得られた結果である．

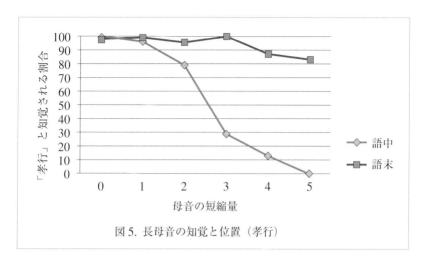

図 5. 長母音の知覚と位置（孝行）

「孝行」の場合は，日本語母語話者と同様に，語中より語末の方が，母音長の時間変動に鈍感になる結果が得られた．

最後に，長母音の判断率と位置，アクセント型の影響についてみる．「孝行」の「行」は母音の短縮量にかかわらず，100％から80％の割合で長母音と判断されるところ（「孝行」の語末）に注目されたい．これは「高校」の「校」を長母音と判断される割合が，刺激3から刺激5にかけて，87.5％から37.5％に下がるところ（「高校」の語末）と対照的である．日本語上級学習者の場合も，日本語母語話者と同じような「アクセント核効果」が見られるという結論になる．また，語中位置にある「高校」の「高」と「孝行」の「孝」とを比べると，刺激2において「孝」を長母音と知覚する割合は79.2％である一方，「高」を長母音と知覚する割合は66.7％と，12.5％低い．これは，「孝行」の「孝」には falling pitch があることに原因があると考えられる．これも日本語母語話者と似たような傾向を示している．

5. 結論

本研究の結果をまとめると，以下の3点が挙げられる．

まずは，母音長を知覚する際に平板型の「高校」は，語中・語末という位置の違いに大きな差は見られなかったが，頭高型の「孝行」は，語中より語

末において日本語話者が母音長の短縮に鈍感になるという事実が知覚実験で明らかとなった.

次に，falling pitch を伴う場合には，日本語母語話者は母音の長さが短くても，それを長母音と知覚しやすいということが本研究の実験で明らかとなった．日本語上級学習者の場合においても，類似の傾向が見られた．

最後に，日本語母語話者の長母音知覚に「アクセント核効果」が働いていることを発見した．具体的には，母音の長さを知覚する際に，その母音に先行するセグメントがアクセントを有する場合は正の影響を受け，母音の持続時間が物理的に短くても，知覚的には長母音と感じやすい．この現象の理由は日本語の長母音の短母音化現象にあると思われる．薛 (2014) によると，平板型の語と比べ，頭高型を有する語のほうが語末長母音の短母音化を起こしやすいということがわかった．日本語母語話者に見られる知覚上の特徴がこの言語事実と一致している．そして，この「アクセント核効果」は日本語上級学習者の場合でも見られた．

6. まとめ

本稿は，知覚実験を行い，日本語母語話者が母音の長さを知覚する際の特徴を調べた．平板型の「高校」は，語中位置においても，語末位置においても，母音の持続時間が短くなるにしたがって，長母音と知覚された割合が下がっていくが，位置による違いは認められなかった．頭高型の「孝行」においては，語中位置と比べて，語末位置において母音長の時間変動に鈍感であるということがわかった．つまり，語末位置にある母音の長さが物理的に短くても，語中位置よりも長母音として知覚されやすいということがいえる．また，falling pitch を伴う場合と伴わない場合とを比較して，falling pitch を伴う場合は母音がより長母音として知覚されやすいという，先行研究に支持した結果が得られた．

以上のような日本語母語話者に見られた母音長の知覚の特徴については，日本語上級学習者においても類似の傾向を示している．また falling pitch の影響は中国語母語話者にも観察された．しかし，中国語は母音の長さに弁別性を持たないため，この影響が中国語母語話者の生得的な能力なのか，それとも学習レベルの向上にしたがい，知覚的にも日本語母語話者と類似の傾

向を示したのかについては，これから学習レベルを分けて研究する必要がある．

参考文献

Kinoshita, Keisuke, Dawn M. Behne and Takayuki Arai (2002) "Duration and F0 as Perceptual Cues to Japanese Vowel Quantity," *Proceeding of 7th International Conference on Spoken Language Proceeding,* 757–760.

Nagano-Madsen, Yasuko (1990) "Influence of Fundamental Frequency Pattern on the Perception of the Vowel Mora in Japanese," *PHONUM* 1, 31–35, *Report from the Department of Phonetics.*

薛晋陽 (2014)「日本語における長母音の短母音化」博士論文，神戸大学．

助川泰彦・前川喜久雄・上原聡 (1998)「日本語長母音の短母音化現象をめぐる諸要因の実験音声学的研究と音声教育への示唆」『言語学と日本語教育』，アラム佐々木幸子(編)，81–94, くろしお出版，東京．

Part V

借用語音韻論とL2習得・知覚

What Neural Measures Reveal about Foreign Language Learning of Japanese Vowel Length Contrasts with Hand Gestures*

Spencer D. Kelly and Yukari Hirata
Colgate University

1. Introduction

It has been well documented that people gesture with their hands as they speak and that the two modalities together form a tightly integrated system of meaning (Kendon (2004), McNeill (1992, 2005)). These theories on gesture-speech integration originated in the realm of language production, but researchers have shown that this integrated relationship extends to the comprehension domain as well (Hostetter (2011), Kelly et al. (2010)). The majority of research on gesture comprehension has focused on semantic and pragmatic functions of gesture, but relatively little research has studied the impact of gesture on phonetic processes (Kelly (in press)). The present study explores this question in the domain of phonetics and phonology of a foreign language (FL).

Many FL words require learners to accurately perceive novel phonemes not contained in their first language (L1). While previous studies have examined this phonological dimension in speech science (Strange (1995), Hirata et al. (2007)), the relationship between this phonological/perceptual ability and the ability to learn the meaning of new words has received

---

* This study was supported by National Science Foundation Grant No. 1052765 given to the authors. We thank Timothy Collett and Joe Alfonso for programming the training and testing part of our experiment. Finally, we thank the excellent undergraduate researchers as part of the Center for Language and Brain who helped create the stimuli and collect that data: April Bailey, Jessica Huang, Carmen Lin, Michael Manansala, Kristen Weiner, and Zach Zhao.

much less attention (but see Wong and Perrachione (2007)). Baddeley and colleagues propose a model that combines the phonological and semantic challenges of learning a new language: "When the phonological loop—which is involved in auditory working memory—processes novel speech sounds, it makes it hard to transfer those novel sounds into stable long-term memories for new words (Baddeley et al. (1998)). For example, when adults are asked to remember words in a language containing phonologically familiar sounds (e.g., from one's native tongue), they rely minimally on the phonological loop when encoding the words into long-term memory and performance is good. However, when asked to remember words that have novel speech sounds, the phonological loop is heavily burdened and performance suffers (Papagno et al. (1991), Papagno and Vallar (1992)).

Given this research, gestures might then be useful in highlighting novel speech sounds when learners are exposed to FL phoneme contrasts that are difficult to perceive. There have been only a handful of studies investigating the role that gestures play in learning to perceive novel FL phonemes (Hirata and Kelly (2010), Hirata et al. (2014), Kelly et al. (2014)). For example, Hirata and Kelly (2010) exposed native English-speakers to videos of speakers producing Japanese long and short vowels with and without long sweeping gestures (shown in the Syllable condition in Fig. 1). Unexpectedly, participants did not learn to perceive the long/short vowel contrasts in the speech-gesture condition any better than a speech alone condition.

To follow up on this surprising finding, Hirata et al. (2014) introduced varying levels of complexity to the gestural instruction in an attempt to push learners even harder. One level of complexity was using hand movements that were not intuitive to English learners (see the Mora gestures[1]

---

[1] Unlike English, where words are broken up into syllables, the Japanese language is one in which words are broken up into "moras" (Vance (1987)). Briefly, words that contain short vowels like [seki] are broken up into two moras, just as it is broken up into two syllables. On the other hand, the word [se:ki], while a native English speaker differentiates into two syllables, would actually be broken up into three moras because the long vowel [se:] is considered to contain two moras.

in Figure 1) to encourage them to perceive the phonemes in a different way. Because the linguistic concept of "moras" is very foreign to English speakers, the prediction was that Mora gestures may provide a unique window into the timing of Japanese phonemes (similar to the idea of how "mismatching" gestures can spur learning, Goldin-Meadow (2005)). A second level of complexity involved asking learners to mimic the gestures they observed during the instruction, with the rationale that actively imitating gestures may promote deeper embodied learning than passively observing them (Cook et al. (2008), Iacoboni (2009), Montgomery et al. (2007)). Given the amount of evidence highlighting the positive role of gestures in higher-order and lower-order language comprehension in L1, the results of the study by Hirata et al. (2014) were also surprising: The outcomes, in terms of auditory/phonological learning, were the same regardless of whether learners observed Mora or Syllable gestures, and it did not matter whether they imitated or just observed them. The same pattern was evident in vocabulary learning as well (Kelly et al. (2014)).

The present study builds on this previous research by employing a more sensitive measure of learning: Event-related potentials. ERPs have been a useful tool in studying the role of gesture in L1 processing by illuminating neural mechanisms that are not possible using traditional behavioral measures (e.g., Biau and Soto-Faraco (2013), Kelly et al. (2004), Özyürek et al. (2007)). This sensitivity would be impossible with traditional behavioral measures such as reaction time. For example, Biau and Soto-Faraco (2013) showed that gestures modulate phonemic processing of speech within 100 ms, suggesting that gestures influence very low-level and early sensory aspects of speech. This provides important additional information to behavioral studies (e.g., using more coarse-grained reaction time measures) that do not have the capability of determining such early influences of gesture on speech.

The benefits of ERPs have also been applied to understanding the neural mechanisms involved in FL learning (McLaughlin et al. (2004), Tremblay et al. (2001), Ylinen et al. (2010)). For example, Ylinen and colleagues (2010) showed that phonetic FL training of novel speech sounds improved Finnish learners' ability to perceive vowel contrasts in English, and ERPs revealed that the neural mechanism of this learning was an increase in the pre-attentive "weighting" of spectral cues of those vowels at very early stages of cortical processing.

To our knowledge, there has been only one study using ERPs to study the role of gestures on FL learning. Kelly et al. (2009) found that iconic gestures aided native English speakers in learning Japanese vocabulary compared with speech alone. The researchers also employed ERPs to uncover the specific mechanisms of *how* these gesture facilitated learning. Specifically, they focused on one particular component of the ERP signal: The Late Positive Component. The LPC (sometimes called the "old/new" effect) is a centrally distributed complex that peaks positively in parietal scalp regions approximately 600 ms after stimulus presentation and indexes the ease of recollecting information from long-term memory (Rugg and Curran (2007)). The LPC amplitude is larger for words that have been primed by repetition, and items encoded more deeply and imagistically in long-term memory produce an enhanced LPC during the recollection of a word (Rugg and Curran (2007), Rugg et al. (1998), Schott et al. (2002)). Using this measure, Kelly et al. (2009) showed that words encoded with gesture produced larger LPCs in parietal regions compared to words encoded without gestures, suggesting that one reason *why* people learn novel FL vocabulary better with gesture is that it strengthens imagistic long-term memory traces in the brain.

Following up on the lack of behavioral results for gesture training in Hirata et al. (2014) and Kelly et al. (2014), the present study examined the neural outcomes of four types of increasingly complex gesture instruction: (1) Syllable-Observe (i.e., observing syllable-like hand gesture), (2) Mora-Observe (i.e., observing mora-like gesture), (3) Syllable-Produce (i.e., imitating the syllable gesture with their own hand), and (4) Mora-Produce (i.e., imitating the mora gesture with their own hand). Participants were assigned to one of these four instructional conditions, and after training, ERPs measured LPC differences in discriminating trained from untrained words that only differ in vowel length. Given that our neural measure is more sensitive than previous behavior measures, we predicted that increasing the complexity of the gesture instruction—by making the gestures more "Japanese-like" (i.e., Mora as opposed to Syllable) and more embodied though imitation (i.e., Produce as opposed to Observe)—would improve memory for the newly learned words (i.e., show a larger LPC). If, however, the neural measures do not discriminate among our four types of gesture training—that is, if there are no LPC differences—this would be even stronger evidence that co-speech metaphoric gesture does not facilitate novel FL phoneme learning.

2. Method

2.1. Participants

Seventy monolingual, right-handed English speakers (aged 18-23) participated in the ERP potion of the study.

2.2. Overall Structure of the Experiment

The general structure of the experiment can be found in Hirata et al. (2014) and Kelly et al. (2014), but briefly, the five-day experiment involved an auditory pre-test (not reported in this paper) on Day 1, and four sessions of training over Days 2 and 3. On Day 4, there was a vocabulary test and a behavioral and ERP word identification test (reported here). Finally, there was an auditory generalization post-test on Day 5 (not reported).

2.3. Training Materials

Training stimuli were ten pairs of Japanese words that contrasted in length of vowels [e e: o o: u u:]. A total of 80 audio files (10 word pairs x 2 lengths x 2 repetitions x 2 speakers) were used in the training. In addition, 40 video clips (10 word pairs x 2 lengths x 2 speakers) were created by the same two speakers to provide the visual dimension of our multimodal training. For each video clip presenting short vowel words (e.g., [seki] 'seat' or [joko] 'side'), the speaker spoke words and made the hand gesture of two small downward chopping movements. For words with long vowels (e.g., [se:ki] 'century' or [joko:] 'rehearsal'), two types of clips were made, one for the Syllable condition and the other for the

Mora condition (Figure 1). For the Syllable condition, the speaker's hand made one horizontal sweep for a long vowel (as in Roberge et al. (1996)), followed or preceded by a small downward chopping movement for a short vowel. For the Mora condition, in contrast, the speaker's hand made two small downward chopping movements for a long vowel. Thus, they made three short vertical had movements in long-vowel words (e.g., [se:ki] or [joko:]), and this hand gesture corresponds with the number of moras in those words. Note that gestures for short vowels are identical for the two conditions, with long vowels being the only part where the conditions diverge.

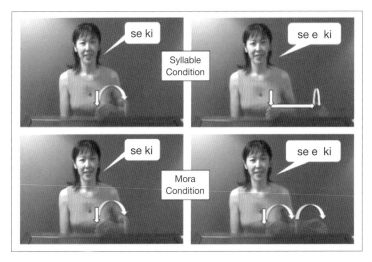

Figure 1. Two types of hand gestures used in the present experiment. The top panel shows the Syllable gesture, in which a word with two short vowels (e.g., [seki]) is represented by two quick downward beats, and a word with one long and one short vowel (e.g., [se:ki]) is represented by a long sweeping gesture and then one quick downward beat. The bottom panel shows the Mora gesture, which is the same as the Syllable gesture for a word with two short vowels, but represents a word with a long and a short vowel with a total of three quick downward beats.

2.4. Training Procedure (Days 2 and 3)

Participants were randomly assigned to one of the four training conditions: Syllable-Observe (SO) (n = 18), Syllable-Produce (SP) (n = 19), Mora-Observe (MO) (n = 17), and Mora-Produce (MP) (n = 16). Four sessions of training were conducted in Days 2 and 3. In all conditions, participants were asked to attend to vowel length differences and remember the meaning of words. For the Observe conditions, participants were instructed to do this while only watching and listening to the training videos, whereas for the Produce conditions, participants were asked to also imitate the gestures (not speech) simultaneously along with the videos they observed.

2.5. Auditory Word Identification ERP Measures (Day 4)

Participants' auditory abilities were measured on a *word identification test* (on Day 4). The purpose was to measure participants' ability to immediately recognize the set of words that they had learned in training and to differentiate them from untrained words that differed in length of the vowels of the trained words. An example of an untrained word would be [seki:](nonsense word), and its trained partner was [se:ki] 'century'. The other half of the pairs consisted of untrained words have a long first vowel, e.g., [go:ke](nonsense word), and the trained word having a short first vowel [goke:] 'word form'. In this way, the untrained and trained words all had the same number of moras, and the location of the long and short vowels was fully counterbalanced. There were a total of 40 words in this test consisting of 20 trained and 20 untrained words.

To measure ERP responses during the above task, these 40 words were each presented five times in a randomized order through a speaker. An automated program was created so that the inter-stimulus intervals were at random intervals between 2 and 3 seconds. The task for participants was a speeded 2-alternative forced identification: Press one button as quickly as possible for words learned during training and another button for new words that were not trained (note that this task requires accurate identification of vowel length). This "old-new" format was chosen because it is well established for measuring the LPC component.

The EEG during sentence presentation was sampled at 250 Hz using a band pass filter of 0.1–30 Hz. The impedances were kept below 40k Ω (the Geonet system uses high-impedance amplifiers). Eye artifacts during data collection were monitored with 4 EOG electrodes. All artifacts were corrected offline, with voltage shifts above 70 µV marked as bad. Non-EOG channels were marked as bad if voltage shifts greater than 200 µV occurred within the electrode for any single trial. If over 20% of the channels were bad, the whole trial was rejected. After rejecting artifacts, the data were re-referenced using an average reference. Individual ERPs were segmented starting 100 ms prior to stimulus onset and continuing 1500 ms post stimulus onset. ERPs were time-locked to the onset of the Japanese word.

There were 88 subjects in the original sample reported in Hirata et al. (2014), but because of excessive motor artifact in twelve subjects and noisy data in six others during the ERP test, the present ERP analysis focused on 70 subjects with clean data (SO = 18; SP = 19; MO = 17; MP = 16).[2] Based on visual inspection of the brainwaves, the time window chosen for the LPC was 450 to 950 ms. The LPC was quantified by taking the average amplitude of that window and subtracting the average amplitude of the 100 ms baseline.

3. Results

3.1. Behavioral

The behavioral results of the present study have been reported in two previous manuscripts published in 2014. In Hirata et al. (2014), we showed that, although all four training conditions significantly improved participants' ability to identify vowel length, there was no difference in the amount of improvement across the four training conditions. Furthermore, this amount of improvement was no different from the improvement

---

[2] The relatively large number of participants rejected due to motor artifacts may be due to the gesture training (on days 2 and 3) creating a residual motor resonance when participants were presented with the auditory words in isolation on the ERP test (day 4).

made after a baseline auditory-only training (Hirata and Kelly (2010)) in terms of their ability to auditorily identify Japanese short and long vowels. Moreover, Kelly et al. (2014) showed that the four training conditions did not produce significant differences in the number of words learned on a vocabulary test in which participants were asked to write down the meaning of words. Thus, on a behavioral level, our gesture training conditions did not yield differential amounts of improvement on the phonetic or semantic levels. The present paper adds to this previous behavioral data by exploring whether more sensitive on-line neural measures might reveal more subtle learning outcomes.

3.2. Electrophysiological

Recall that the LPC reflects strength of memory encoding (Rugg and Curran (2007)), and this was our chosen measure to explore neural learning outcomes. Previous research has shown that when a word has been encoded deeply in long-term memory, it produces a larger LPC than words that are new or encoded more shallowly.

As the first analysis, LPC average amplitudes were analyzed using a mixed ANOVA with four factors: Word Type (trained, untrained), Instruction (SO, SP, MO, MP), Side of Scalp (left, right), and Region (central, frontal, occipital, parietal, temporal; see Kelly et al. (2004), for a map of the scalp locations). Because we predicted a larger LPC to trained as opposed to untrained words—which was our measure of learning—we were interested in effects of Word Type in our primary analysis. The ANOVA, however, revealed no main effects or interactions of Word Type.

This Word Type null result for the LPC fits with behavioral data gathered during the ERP task (Kelly et al. (2014)): Participants across all four conditions were at chance (59%) at identifying untrained ("new") words, so training did not appear to help people discriminate the phoneme contrasts in unfamiliar words. We had hoped that the ERP data would reveal a subtle process beyond these behavioral results, but that was not the case.

Visual inspection of the data showed that the two Mora and two Syllable conditions looked very similar, but the two Observe conditions were very different from the two Produce conditions. Thus, as an exploratory analysis, we collapsed across the Mora and Syllable conditions and performed a post-hoc mixed ANOVA over the LPC window on both word types with two factors: Instruction Modality (observe, produce) and Region (central, frontal, occipital, parietal, temporal). Confirming the visual inspection, there was a significant interaction of the two factors, $F(4, 264) = 9.29$, $p<.001$, $\eta_p^2 = .12$. Focusing on bi-lateral parietal regions—where the effect appeared most prominent—the Produce condition was significantly more negative than the Observe condition, $F(1,68) = 13.38$, $p<.001$, $\eta_p^2 = .16$. Refer to Figure 2.

Note, however, that the above results do not reflect a traditional LPC effect because the brainwaves diverge much earlier in the time course than the LPC window. Therefore, as a third analysis, we analyzed the earliest time window (0 to 100 ms) with the same two factors (Instruction Modality and Region) and found the same pattern as above in the bi-lateral parietal region, $F(1,68) = 5.23$, $p = .025$, $\eta_p^2 = .07$.[3] This significant difference continues through every 100 ms epoch of the brainwave, even well past the LPC window. This suggests that the brainwaves differ not in response to the specific words presented during our ERP test, but instead, might reflect different degrees of motor carry-over between the Produce and Observe conditions from training (which we will discuss in more detail below).

---

[3] In the same 0 to 100 ms time window, the inverse of this pattern was evident in bi-lateral frontal regions, with the Produce condition producing a more positive-going wave than the Observe condition, $F(1, 68) = 7.94$, $p = .006$, use same format as above in text $= .10$.

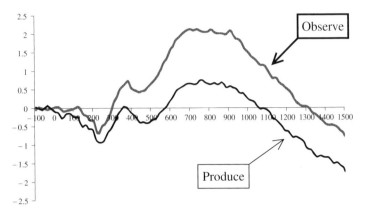

Figure 2. ERPs to all words in bi-lateral parietal regions, collapsed across the Mora and Syllable training conditions. Starting as early as the 0 to 100 ms time window, the Produce condition produced more negative going waves than the Observe condition. Y-axis: Positive microvolts plotted up; X-axis: Zero time-point marks onset of the auditory stimuli.

4. Discussion

Although ERPs are a more sensitive measure of learning than behavioral outcomes, we found no predicted LPC differences across the four training conditions. This pattern corroborates the behavioral results using the same training paradigm (Hirata et al. (2014), Kelly et al. (2014)). Note that the present Syllable-Observe training method yielded a learning effect similar to an "audio-only" training in Hirata and Kelly's (2010). Thus, none of the present training conditions had an effect that is more effective uniquely due to the presence of hand gesture. Together, these behavioral and electrophysiological findings suggest that co-speech hand gestures representing phonemes may play a very limited role in learning novel speech sounds in an FL.

This lack of gesture effect on learning difficult FL phoneme contrasts—and vocabulary items comprised of them—is noteworthy in the context of the collective understanding in the gesture field that gesturing is almost *uniformly* beneficial for comprehension and learning. By now, there are several books and hundreds of journal articles advocating for the communicative and cognitive significance and benefit of co-speech gestures. However, as mentioned above, a growing number of studies have started to reveal that gestures do not always play a positive role in these cognitive and communicative processes (Hirata and Kelly (2010), Hirata et al. (2014), Kelly et al. (2014), Kelly (in press), Post et al. (2013)).

In fact, some research even suggests that gestures may disrupt learning, especially when learners encounter something particularly novel or challenging. For example, researchers have argued that under circumstances in which people are cognitively (Post et al. (2013)) or perceptually (Kelly and Lee (2012)) taxed, gestures may actually detract from learning. Post et al. (2013) found that when "lower ability" children were instructed on complex grammatical structures (in L1), participants who were asked to imitate gestures that accompanied the training performed worse than a control group that neither observed nor imitated gestures during instruction. The explanation was that for "lower ability" children, simultaneously observing and producing gestures for a hard task introduced a cognitive load that detracted from overall learning. A similar explanation was given for how gesture can overload people when perceiving or learning FL vocabulary that is comprised of difficult-to-perceive phoneme contrasts (Hirata and Kelly (2010), Kelly and Lee (2012)). Connecting back to Baddeley's model of FL learning (Baddeley et al. (1998)), it appears that when encountering very unfamiliar speech sounds for the first time, increasingly complex gestures may distract from, or over-tax, the phonological loop, which may weaken the semantic links between words containing those sounds and new meanings.

Although we found no evidence that gestures actually disrupted learning, there is reason to suspect that our training may have actually distracted our participants. For example, note that a relatively large number of subjects—eighteen, in fact—were excluded from the ERPs analyses because of noisy data and motor artifacts. Indeed, the ERP data from this study were generally less clean than is typical when using a strictly auditory FL paradigm. One likely explanation for the prevalence of artifacts and noisy data may be that observing (Borghi et al. (2007), Macedonia and von Kriegstein (2012))—and to a greater extent, producing (Hund-Georgiadis and von Cramon (1999), Krönke et al. (2013), Macedonia et al. (2011))—gestures during training created a residual motor resonance when participants were later presented with the auditory words in isolation on the ERP test. Supporting this possibility, the data showed a difference between our Produce and Observe conditions from very early in the brainwaves, suggesting that motor resonance during training carried over to the ERP session. This residual motor activity during training—from observing, and to a greater extent, producing gestures—could have competed or interfered with the auditory processing of the words in the ERP task (Wulf et al. (2001)). That is, because the learners were complete novices to making auditory length vowel distinctions in Japanese, perhaps the gestures (especially in the Produce conditions) drew too much attention towards the motor component of the task and distracted from auditory cortical processing of the speech sounds, which is actually the most important component to learn. It would be interesting to follow up on this possibility by doing ERP testing with people who speak an L1 that already makes phonemic vowel length distinctions (e.g., Arabic; see Tsukada (2011)). For example, gesture training might actually help more "experienced" or "advanced" learners to perceive those Japanese vowel length distinctions, and such an ability may be reflected on their LPCs.

In conclusion, the novel contribution of the present study is to provide a possible explanation for the earlier behavioral results that co-speech gestures do not uniquely help when teaching vocabulary containing difficult phoneme contrasts in an FL. The previous behavioral results showed that different types of gesture training yielded the same amount of FL learning outcomes, and this amount was no different from auditory-only training (Hirata et al. (2014), Kelly et al. (2014)). We suggest a possible mechanism that observing, and to a greater extent producing, gestures during training interferes with auditory processes that are required to create stable long-term memories (Baddeley et al. (1998)). Thus, one recommendation for beginning FL learners may be not to overwhelm them with multimodal information that is rich as in everyday settings, but rather to control the input to the learners so that they are not distracted about their focus on auditory processing.

Together, these behavioral and electrophysiological findings suggest that gesture and speech may not be a functionally integrated system at the lowest—and perceptually most challenging—level of language comprehension and learning.

References

Baddeley, Alan, Susan Gathercole and Costanza Papagno (1998) "The Phonological Loop as a Language Learning Device," *Psychological Review* 105(1), 158.

Biau, Emmanuel and Salvador Soto-Faraco (2013) "Beat Gestures Modulate Auditory Integration in Speech Perception," *Brain & Language* 124, 143-152.

Borghi, Anna M., Claudia Bonfiglioli, Luisa Lugli, Paola Ricciardelli, Sandro Rubichi and Roberto Nicoletti (2007) "Are Visual Stimuli Sufficient to Evoke Motor Information?: Studies with Hand Primes," *Neuroscience Letters* 411(1), 17-21.

Cook, Susan W., Zachary Mitchell and Susan Goldin-Meadow (2008) "Gesturing Makes Learning Last," *Cognition* 106(2), 1047-1058.

Goldin-Meadow, Susan (2005) *Hearing Gesture: How Our Hands Help Us Think*, Harvard University Press, Cambridge, MA.

Hirata, Yukari and Spencer D. Kelly (2010) "Effects of Lips and Hands on Auditory Learning of Second-language Speech Sounds," *Journal of Speech, Language, and Hearing Research* 53(2), 298-310.

Hirata, Yukari, Spencer D. Kelly, Jessica Huang and Michael Manansala (2014) "Effects of Hand Gestures on Auditory Learning of Second-language Vowel Length Contrasts," *Journal of Speech, Language, and Hearing Research* 57, 2090-2101.

Hirata, Yukari, Elizabeth Whitehurst and Emily Cullings (2007) "Training Native English Speakers to Identify Japanese Vowel Length Contrast with Sentences at Varied Speaking Rates," *Journal of the Acoustical Society of America* 121(6), 3837-3845.

Hostetter, Autumn B. (2011) "When Do Gestures Communicate? A Meta-analysis," *Psychological Bulletin* 137, 297-315.

Hund-Georgiadis, Margret and D. Yves von Cramon (1999) "Motor-learning-related Changes in Piano Players and Non-musicians Revealed by Functional Magnetic-resonance Signals," *Experimental Brain Research* 125(4), 417-425.

Iacoboni, Marco (2009) "Imitation, Empathy, and Mirror Neurons," *Annual Review*

of Psychology 60, 653-670.
Kelly, Spencer D. (in press) "Exploring the Boundaries of Gesture-speech Integration during Language Comprehension," *Why Gesture? How the Hands Function in Speaking, Thinking and Communicating*, ed. by R. B. Church, M. W. Alibali and S. D. Kelly, John Benjamins, Amsterdam.
Kelly, Spencer D., Yukari Hirata, Michael Manansala and Jessica Huang (2014) "Exploring the Role of Hand Gestures in Learning Novel Phoneme Contrasts and Vocabulary in a Second Language," *Frontiers in Psychology* 5, 673.
Kelly, Spencer D., Corinne Kravitz and Michael Hopkins (2004) "Neural Correlates of Bimodal Speech and Gesture Comprehension," *Brain and Language* 89 (1), 253-260.
Kelly, Spencer D. and Angela Lee (2012) "When Actions Speak Too Much Louder than Words: Gesture Disrupts Word Learning when Phonetic Demands Are High," *Language and Cognitive Processes* 27, 793-807.
Kelly, Spencer D., Tara McDevitt and Megan Esch (2009) "Brief Training with Co-speech Gesture Lends a Hand to Word Learning in a Foreign Language," *Language and Cognitive Processes* 24, 313-334.
Kelly, Spencer D., Aslı Özyürek and Eric Maris (2010) "Two Sides of the Same Coin: Speech and Gesture Mutually Interact to Enhance Comprehension," *Psychological Science* 21, 260-267.
Kendon, Adam (2004) *Gesture: Visible Action as Utterance*, Cambridge University Press, Cambridge.
Krönke, K-Martin, Karsten Mueller, Angela D. Friederici and Hellmuth Obrig (2013) "Learning by Doing? The Effect of Gestures on Implicit Retrieval of Newly Acquired Words," *Cortex* 49(9), 2553-2568.
Macedonia, Manuela, Karsten Müller and Angela D. Friederici (2011) "The Impact of Iconic Gestures on Foreign Language Word Learning and Its Neural Substrate," *Human Brain Mapping* 32(6), 982-998.
Macedonia, Manuela and Katharina von Kriegstein (2012) "Gestures Enhance Foreign Language Learning," *Biolinguistics* 6(3-4), 393-416.
McLaughlin, Judith, Lee Osterhout and Albert Kim (2004) "Neural Correlates of Second-language Word Learning: Minimal Instruction Produces Rapid Change," *Nature Neuroscience* 7(7), 703-704.
McNeill, David (1992) *Hand and Mind: What Gestures Reveal about Thought*, University of Chicago Press, Chicago.
McNeill, David (2005) *Gesture and Thought*, University of Chicago Press, Chicago.
Montgomery, Kimberly J., Nancy Isenberg and James V. Haxby (2007) "Commu-

nicative Hand Gestures and Object-directed Hand Movements Activated the Mirror Neuron System," *Social Cognitive and Affective Neuroscience* 2, 114-122.

Özyürek, Aslı, Roel M. Willems, Sotaro Kita and Peter Hagoort (2007) "On-line Integration of Semantic Information from Speech and Gesture: Insights from Event-related Brain Potentials," *Journal of Cognitive Neuroscience* 19(4), 605-616.

Papagno, Costanza, Tim Valentine and Alan Baddeley (1991) "Phonological Short-term Memory and Foreign-language Vocabulary Learning," *Journal of Memory and Language* 30(3), 331-347.

Papagno, Costanza and Giuseppe Vallar (1992) "Phonological Short-term Memory and the Learning of Novel Words: The Effect of Phonological Similarity and Item Length," *The Quarterly Journal of Experimental Psychology* 44(1), 47-67.

Post, Lysanne S., Tamara Van Gog, Fred Paas and Rolf A. Zwaan (2013) "Effects of Simultaneously Observing and Making Gestures while Studying Grammar Animations on Cognitive Load and Learning," *Computers in Human Behavior* 29(4), 1450-1455.

Roberge, Claude, Masayasu Kimura and Yoshikazu Kawaguchi (1996) *Pronunciation Training for Japanese: Theory and Practice of the VT Method* (in Japanese; *Nihongo no Hatsuon Shidoo: VT-hoo no Riron to Jissai*), Bonjinsha, Tokyo.

Rugg, Michael D. and Tim Curran (2007) "Event-related Potentials and Recognition Memory," *Trends in Cognitive Sciences* 11(6), 251-257.

Rugg, Michael, Ruth E. Mark, Peter Walla, Astrid M. Schloerscheidt, Claire S. Birch and Kevin Allan (1998) "Dissociation of the Neural Correlates of Implicit and Explicit Memory," *Nature* 392, 595-598.

Schott, Björn, Alan Richardson-Klavehn, Hans-Jochen Heinze and Emrah Düzel (2002) "Perceptual Priming versus Explicit Memory: Dissociable Neural Correlates at Encoding," *Journal of Cognitive Neuroscience* 14, 578-592.

Strange, Winifred (1995) *Speech Perception and Linguistic Experience: Issues in Cross-Language Speech Research*, York Press, Timonium, MD.

Tremblay, Kelly, Nina Kraus, Therese McGee, Curtis Ponton and Brian Otis (2001) "Central Auditory Plasticity: Changes in the N1-P2 Complex after Speech-sound Training," *Ear and Hearing* 22(2), 79-90.

Tsukada, Kimiko (2011) "The Perception of Arabic and Japanese Short and Long Vowels by Native Speakers of Arabic, Japanese, and Persian," *Journal of the Acoustical Society of America* 129(2), 989-998.

Vance, Timothy J. (1987) *An Introduction to Japanese Phonology*, State University of New York Press, Albany, NY.

Wong, Patrick C. M. and Tyler K. Perrachione (2007) "Learning Pitch Patterns in Lexical Identification by Native English-speaking Adults," *Applied Psycholinguistics* 28, 565–585.

Wulf, Gabriele, Nancy McNevin and Charles H. Shea (2001) "The Automaticity of Complex Motor Skill Learning as a Function of Attentional Focus," *The Quarterly Journal of Experimental Psychology: Section A* 54, 1143–1154.

Ylinen, Sari, Maria Uther, Antti Latvala, Sara Vepsäläinen, Paul Iverson, Reiko Akahane-Yamada and Risto Näätänen (2010) "Training the Brain to Weight Speech Cues Differently: A Study of Finnish Second-language Users of English," *Journal of Cognitive Neuroscience* 22(6), 1319–1332.

Effects of Pitch Height on L2 Learners' Identification of Japanese Phonological Vowel Length*

Izumi Takiguchi

Bunkyo Gakuin University

1. Introduction

Non-native contrasts in the second language (L2) often cause problems to L2 listeners. People agree that L2 listeners' perception and/or perceptual difficulties are attributable to their first language (L1) even if the L1 might not explain all of them. However, it remains unclear what property in the L1 affects L2 speech perception and what does not (McAllister et al. (2002)).

The Feature Hypothesis (McAllister et al. (2002)) claims that phonetic features which are not exploited and less prominent as cues for the L1 phonological contrasts are difficult to discern and use in the L2. This implies that phonetic features which are prominent in the L1 would accordingly be easy to use in the L2. Moreover, L2 listeners might automatically attend to prominent L1 cues, even when the cues are not appropriate in the L2. In fact, L2 listeners are reported to use cues differently than native listeners and to rely on important L1 cues in their L2 (Lippus et al. (2009), Wang (2008)).

Japanese has phonological vowel length contrast. Word meanings can be differentiated by vowel length alone, such as /kado/ (corner) with a phonemic short vowel versus /kado:/ (Japanese flower arrangement) with a phonemic long vowel. Vowel duration is the primary cue for the contrast-

---

* An earlier version of this paper appeared as part of my Ph.D. dissertation submitted to Sophia University in 2014. This study was partly supported by Grant-in-Aid for JSPS research fellow (22-365).

ing length categories (Fujisaki et al. (1975)). In addition to the length contrast, Japanese is known as a lexical pitch accent language, where the presence or absence of an accent on a particular syllable within a word differentiates words.

Much research has pointed out that L2 learners tend to have difficulty identifying Japanese vowel length. Among these, Oguma (2000) and Minagawa-Kawai et al. (2002) showed that pitch affects English and Korean listeners' length identification in a similar manner and length identification is easier for long vowels with a high pitch and for short vowels with a low pitch. They explained this as a psychoacoustic effect. That is, they said that perceived vowel duration is longer for vowels with a high pitch, which seems to deemphasize the influence of L1. However, in Japanese, vowels with a high pitch were found to be acoustically longer than those with a low pitch (Mori (2000, 2003)); therefore, it is necessary to explore effects of pitch height and listeners' L1 on L2 length identification rigorously. Moreover, few studies seem to have examined relation between the role of pitch for L1 phonological contrasts and use of pitch in the L2.

The current study examined how pitch, especially pitch height in the L1 interacts with its use as a cue for Japanese vowel length contrast in the L2. A comprehensive approach for such an investigation should include collecting and comparing data from L2 learners of Japanese whose L1 differs in terms of pitch height as a cue. Accordingly, based on the role of pitch height as a cue, native listeners of Mandarin Chinese, Seoul Korean, American English, and French were selected. Mandarin Chinese uses pitch height for lexical tones. Seoul Korean exploits pitch height for three-way laryngeal contrasts. American English uses pitch height for lexical stress. French, in contrast, does not exploit pitch related cues to differentiate words. This study explored how these differences in the L1 affect listeners' use of pitch height in the L2.

2. Methodology

2.1. Participants

There were a total of 55 participants. Besides native listeners of Tokyo Japanese (NJ) as a control group, there were four groups of nonnative listeners of Japanese: native listeners of Mandarin Chinese (NC), Seoul Korean (NK), American English (NE), and French (NFr). The nonnative listeners of Japanese were all adult L2 learners, who started learning Japanese after the age of 15 years and had previously taken or were taking formal instruction in Japanese. They were residing in Japan when the data were collected. No participants reported any hearing or speaking disorder.

The NJ group consisted of eight participants, one male and seven females and their ages ranged from 20 to 44 years with the mean age being 27.9 years (SD = 9.2). The group of NC had 11 participants, five males and six females. All of them are from mainland China and reported that they spoke Mandarin Chinese as their L1.[1] The participants' ages were between 20 and 28 years with the mean age being 23.5 years (SD = 2.4). There were 12 NK, three males and nine females, who were all born and grew up in Seoul. Their ages ranged from 20 to 32 years with the mean age being 22.9 years (SD = 3.4). There were 12 NE, five males and seven females. They were all born and grew up in the US. Their mean age was 20.7 years (range: 18–25, SD = 1.7). There were 12 NFr, eight males and four females. They were all born and grew up in France.[2] Their mean age was 23.3 years (range: 19–31, SD = 3.6).

2.2. Stimuli

All stimuli were created from a token of a nonsense word /nono:/ produced with an HHH[3] accent pattern in isolation. A female native speaker

---

[1] There were no speakers/listeners of Cantonese, which has vowel length contrast.
[2] French listeners were asked to read seven French words, in which vowel length could contrast in some dialects: *mettre* (to put) vs. *mètre* (meter) vs. *maître* (master), *bal* (ball) vs. *Bâle* (Basel), and *patte* (paw) vs. *pâte* (dough). They made no distinction.
[3] In this study, H and L stand for a high and a low tone, respectively.

of Tokyo Japanese in her twenties pronounced /nono:/ in an HHH accent pattern 20 times and in HLL and LHH patterns 12 times in a random order. The nonsense words were written in Japanese *katakana*, and the intended accent pattern was indicated by using H or L. The tokens were recorded using a linear PCM recorder (SONY PCM-D50) at a 44.1 kHz sampling rate and 16-bit quantization with an electric condenser microphone (SONY ECM-MS957). From the 20 tokens with an HHH pattern, one token which had duration similar to the mean was selected for stimulus manipulation. Table 1 summarizes acoustic characteristics of the selected token.

segment		n	o	n	o:
duration (ms)		26.4	96.3	70.6	339.6
F0(Hz)	onset	235.6	226.4	226.4	227.5
	offset	226.4	226.4	227.5	209.5

Table 1. Segment durations and F0 values of the original token.

F0 and timing information of tonal events were extracted from 12 naturally spoken tokens for the two accent patterns, HLL and LHH. They were used as reference data for manipulation so that it would allow manipulating accent patterns of stimuli as naturally as possible. According to J_ToBI convention, which Venditti (2005) introduced as a prosodic labeling system for the description of Japanese prosodic structure, we can express accented and unaccented Japanese words produced in a citation form as %L (H-) H*+L L% and as %L H- L%, respectively, where %L and L% indicate phrase initial and final boundary tones, H*+L indicates a lexical pitch accent, and H- indicates a phrasal high tone.[4] Based on this model, F0 values of boundary tones, max F0 value and the locus, and F0 values at the onset of each segment were measured for each token using Praat (Boersma and Weenink (2012)). After the measurements, mean F0 values and mean time of the locus of max F0 were calculated, which are summarized in Table 2.

---

[4] The H- and H* are said to correspond to the F0 peak in a word.

	%L	C1 onset	V1 onset	C2 onset	V2 onset	L%	max F0	max loci
		n	o	n	o:			
HLL	152.8	260.1	256.4	268.5	242.0	152.6	275.3	0.09732
LHH	175.2	206.8	182.1	180.8	210.9	209.7	220.5	0.29621

Table 2. Mean F0 values (Hz) and mean time (second (s)) of the location of max F0 in a word.

A total of 30 stimuli were created by manipulating V2 duration and the accent pattern of the original token using the PSOLA function in Praat. First, noise before C1 and after V2 was cut off and 20 ms-silence was inserted instead. Next, the accent pattern was manipulated by removing all pitch points of the original token and setting new pitch points as the F0 values as shown in Table 3. After manipulating pitch contour, V2 duration for each accent pattern was shortened or lengthened from 40 ms to 390 ms in 25 ms steps (15 steps) by adding duration points at V2 onset and offset and setting the duration points in relative form from 0.12 (40 ms) to 1.15 (390 ms) in Praat's manipulation window. V2 duration was manipulated, but the duration of other parts were kept the same as in the original token. This manipulation yielded 30 stimuli (15 steps × 2 accent patterns), which were identical in the durational distribution, but varied in the accent pattern, namely HLL or LHH.[5] The stimuli were checked by two trained phoneticians and were judged as natural Japanese sounds /nono/ or /nono:/. However, by the phoneticians, identification of vowel length was considered more difficult when V2 duration was intermediate than when it was closer to either endpoint. The first syllable was always heard as having a short vowel.

---

[5] HLL and LHH do NOT necessarily mean that they have three moras as often used in the literature. Instead, HLL denotes the stimuli with an accented first syllable and LHH shows the stimuli with unaccented syllables.

	C1 onset	V1 onset	max	C2 onset	V2 onset	max	L%
pitch points[6]	0.019	0.046	0.117	0.142	0.213	0.316	0.552
	962	315	281	616	236	174	823
HLL	260.1	256.4	275.3	268.5	242.0	—	152.6
LHH	206.8	182.1	—	180.8	210.9	220.5	209.7

Table 3. Loci of pitch points (s) and F0 values (Hz) for manipulation.

2.3. Procedure

Each stimulus was presented to participants eight times in a random order, so the test section consisted of 240 trials (15 stimuli × 2 accent patterns: HLL and LHH × 8 times). The trials were divided into 12 blocks. The participants did a practice session containing eight trials (2 endpoints × 2 accent patterns × twice) prior to the test session. It took approximately 8–15 minutes to complete the experiment. All participants read and signed a consent form before the experiment. In addition, L2 learners filled out a questionnaire form for their background information. Participants were all paid.

Each participant used a laptop PC (Panasonic Let's Note CF-S9KYF or Lenovo ThinkPad Edge E430) with headphones (SONY MDR-CD900ST). SuperLab [Cedrus, ver. 4.5] was used to present stimuli to the participants and to collect responses from them. The participants' task was a single-stimulus two-alternative forced-choice identification of word-final vowel length. Participants were asked to identify whether the word was /nono/ or /nono:/. They were told to press one of the two designated keys on the PC, which were labelled as "nono" and "nono:" in Japanese *katakana*, as quickly as possible within three seconds. The next stimulus was presented after participants responded or the 3,000 ms response period had elapsed, whichever came first. They were told to give their best guess even when they were not sure to decrease the number of non-responses.

---

[6] Each value showed time from the beginning, i.e., zero, and it included the duration of a silent interval.

2.4. Statistical Analyses

The current study first analyzed participants' choice between short and long as a function of V2 duration using binary logistic regression with all participants' data, which would be shown as plots of the proportion of "long" responses against V2 duration. The dependent variable was participants' choice, i.e., short or long. The independent variables were participants' L1 (NJ vs. NC vs. NK vs. NE vs. NFr), accent patterns (HLL vs. LHH), and V2 duration (40–390 ms in 25 ms-steps, 15 steps). In addition, the observed proportion of "long" responses for each step of V2 duration for each L1 group for each accent pattern was calculated by dividing the number of "long" responses by the total number of responses for each stimulus using all participants' data in each group.

Second, individual categorization functions were obtained by using binary logistic regression. The perception boundary was estimated as the 50% cross-over point of response rate on the fitted logistic functions. The estimated values on the individual category boundary were subjected to a two-way repeated measures ANOVA with L1 as a between-subjects factor and accent pattern as a within-subjects factor. In the case where the interaction between L1 and accent pattern was found to be significant, a one-way repeated measures ANOVA was conducted for each L1 group with accent pattern as a within-subjects factor.

3. Results

Figure 1 shows the logistic functions for each L1 group for each accent pattern. The lines and the shapes represent the fitted logistic curves and the observed proportion of "long" responses, respectively: the broken lines and circles for HLL and the solid lines and cross marks for LHH. The proportion of "long" responses increased as a function of V2 duration, giving an s-shaped curve for all groups for both accent patterns. NJ, NC, and NE look similar in that their logistic curves for HLL and LHH overlap. Pitch height, high or low does not seem to affect their identification of vowel length. On the other hand, logistic curves of NK and NFr belong to different patterns, suggesting that for these two groups of listeners, length identification may be affected by pitch height. In addition, the effect of pitch height seems to differ for NK and NFr: NK's curve for LHH locates to the left of that for HLL while NFr's curve for LHH locates to the right of that for HLL. This indicates that NK gave more "long" responses to vowels with a high pitch, but NFr gave more "long" responses to vowels with a low pitch. NK's category boundary seems to have occurred at a shorter duration for vowels with a high pitch, but that of NFr occurred at a longer duration for vowels with a high pitch.

Figure 2 shows mean estimates of the category boundary. The category boundary of NJ, NC, and NE seem to be very similar between HLL and LHH. On the other hand, NK show a smaller category boundary for LHH than for HLL while NFr exhibit a slightly smaller value for HLL than for LHH. A two-way repeated measures ANOVA for the data on the category boundary location with L1 (NJ vs. NC vs. NK vs. NE vs. NFr) as a between-subjects factor and accent pattern (HLL vs. LHH) as a within-subjects factor showed no significant main effects of L1 $[F(4, 50) = 2.49, p = 0.055, n.s.]$ and accent pattern $[F(1, 50) = 0.22, p = 0.645, n.s.]$, but the L1-by-accent pattern interaction was significant $[F(4, 50) = 2.63, p<.05]$. Thus, a one-way repeated measures ANOVA was conducted for each L1 group with accent pattern as a within-subjects factor. ANOVAs revealed that there was no main effect of accent pattern for all groups except NK [NJ: $F(1, 7) = 0.12, p = 0.739, n.s.$; NC: $F(1, 10) = 0.599, p = 0.457, n.s.$; NE: $F(1, 11) = 0.167, p = 0.69, n.s.$; NFr: $F(1, 11) = 1.607, p = 0.231, n.s.$]. NK's results displayed that their category boundary of LHH (186.2 ms) was significantly smaller than that of HLL (203.4 ms) $[F(1, 11) = 8.47, p<.05]$. NK's boundary location occurred at a shorter duration for vowels with a high pitch than those with a low pitch. The slight difference shown by NFr did not reach statistical significance.

Effects of Pitch Height on L2 Learners' Identification of Japanese 303

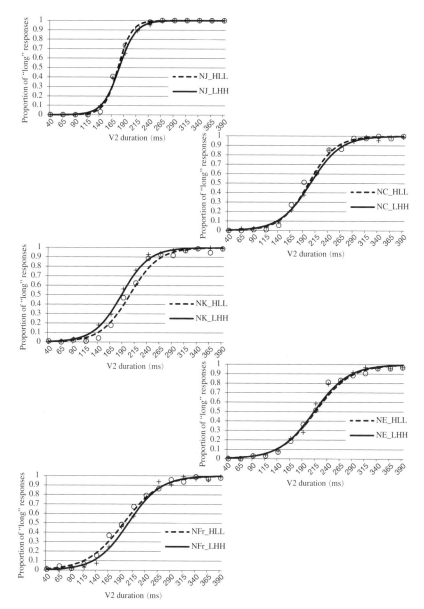

Figure 1. Proportion of "long" responses as a function of V2 duration. From the top to the bottom: NJ, NC, NK, NE, and NFr.

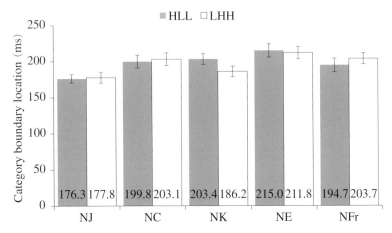

Figure 2. Mean estimates of the category boundary for each L1 group. Gray and white bars for HLL and for LHH, respectively.

4. Discussion

First, it is possible to say that L2 learners, regardless of their non-use of vowel duration for phonological vowel length in the L1, can access vowel duration as a cue when required to use it in the L2. The proportion of "long" responses increased as a function of V2 duration in a rather similar fashion for all groups as shown in Figure 1. These similar s-shaped curves can be interpreted as showing that all groups of listeners identify phonological vowel length primarily based on vowel duration. The four groups of L2 listeners showed no problem in accessing vowel duration as an L2 cue even though none of their L1s employs vowel duration as a cue for vowel length contrast. Non-use of vowel duration for phonological vowel length in the L1 does not result in a loss of ability to access vowel duration as a cue in the L2; however, obviously, this does not necessarily mean that all L2 listeners regardless of the L1 can use vowel duration as NJ do (cf. Takiguchi (2015)).

The fact that the difference in pitch height affected only NK's identification of L2 vowel length does not support a universal pitch height effect on perception of vowel length, such reported as a "psychoacoustic effect" in Minagawa-Kawai et al. (2002) and Oguma (2000). Instead, it suggests that NK's specific experience with pitch height in their L1 relates to their use of pitch height in the L2. If there were a universal pitch height effect on the length identification, the difference in pitch height would have affected all of the groups including NJ group in the same fashion; however, this was not the case. The previous studies proposed the "psychoacoustic effect" based on the results of experiments using natural spoken stimuli. Thus, it is possible that L2 learners were able to identify long vowels with a high pitch and short vowels with a low pitch better than long vowels with a low pitch and short vowels with a high pitch, not because perceived vowel duration was longer for vowels with a high pitch as the studies suggested, but because duration per se actually differed according to pitch height. In fact, durations of vowels with a high pitch are reported to be acoustically longer than those with a low pitch in Japanese (Mori, 2001, 2003). This implies that the universal effect of pitch height on length identification reported in the previous studies could be understood as the effect of physical vowel duration affected by pitch height. The present study using stimuli only differing in accent patterns clearly shows that the effect of pitch height on L2 length identification is not universal, but relates to learner's L1.

Then, what experience in the L1 made NK use pitch height and contrastively led NC, NE, and NFr not to use it when identifying L2 phonological vowel length? We can consider that NK attend to a phonetic difference that is important as a cue in the L1 even when listening to the L2, as implied by the Feature Hypothesis (McAllister et al. (2002)). For NK, whether pitch is high or low is said to be an important cue for the three-way laryngeal contrast among stop consonants, especially between the lenis and aspirated series, where the primary cue, VOT significantly overlaps. In Seoul Korean, in the word-/phrase-initial position the vowel following the lenis series tends to be produced with a lower pitch compared to that following the tense or aspirated series (Silva (2006)). Moreover, the lower pitch on the vowel following a stop/affricate tends to facilitate Korean listeners' perception of the lenis series for the stop/affricate (Kim et al. (2002)). These suggest that the difference in pitch height is connected with a specific category which differentiates words in Seoul Korean and in turn, plays a significant role as a cue to perceive and to produce the contrast. Such L1 experience seems to make NK pay attention to pitch height and use it even in the L2. NK transferred their experience in the L1 with pitch height, which discriminates one category from another which is used to differentiate words, to L2 perception and relied on pitch height as a cue to identify Japanese phonological vowel length, which is also used to differentiate words.

The distributional factor of lexical tones in Mandarin Chinese explains why NC did not rely on pitch height for L2 length identification. Needless to say, pitch is the primary cue for the four distinct lexical tones in Mandarin Chinese. Previous studies agree that Chinese listeners use pitch height as well as pitch contour as a cue for lexical tones (e.g., Lin (2007)). Thus, if we assume that L2 listeners rely on important L1 cues when listening to the L2, NC's use of pitch height for L2 length identification can be expected. However, NC's L1 experience with pitch height did not lead them to use pitch height in the L2. Here we need to look at the distribution of lexical tones, for which pitch height seems to play a less important role as a cue. Mandarin Chinese has only one level tone, high level tone (Tone 1) and the other tones are all contour tones. This indicates that the difference in pitch height per se does not function to distinguish one tone from another and is not associated with any specific category. Consequently, pitch height may not be as important as pitch contour; in turn, NC may be less sensitive to pitch height than to pitch contour, even though they hear both. In fact, Yang and Liu (2012) point out that Chinese listeners' discrimination is categorical between contour tones and level tones, but not between high level tones and low level tones. Qin and Mok (2011), who investigated Mandarin Chinese listeners' discrimination of Cantonese tones, which have three level and three contour tones, showed that pairs of level tones were far more poorly discriminated than pairs of contour tones. These studies support the view that for NC perceiving whether pitch is high or low may not be as crucial as perceiving whether and how pitch moves, and NC are less sensitive to pitch height. Furthermore, contrary to pitch height, pitch fall is reported to be used by Chinese listeners to identify Japanese vowel length in their L2 (Takiguchi (2011, 2014)). This means that they do not completely ignore pitch-related cues when identifying L2 length. Interestingly, pitch fall is the very cue which distinguishes between two lexical tones, Tone 1 (high level) and Tone 4 (high falling). Thus, it is reasonable to think that lack of contrastive level tones (i.e., high level, mid level, low level, etc.) cued only by pitch height is the possible factor behind NC's non-use of pitch height in the L2. Future study should include listeners of languages in which the difference in pitch height plays a crucial role as a cue such as Thai, which has more than two level tones, to add confirming evidence for the above explanation.

Non-use of pitch height for L2 length identification by NE and NFr can also be explained by the insignificance of pitch height as a cue for a specific category distinguishing one word from another in American English and French. It is often claimed that stressed vowels tend to be higher in pitch than unstressed vowels in English (Cutler (2005), Fry (1955, 1958), Lehiste (1970), Ueyama (2000), Zhang and Francis (2010)). In addition, it is reported that English listeners are more likely to perceive lexical stress when vowels carry a high pitch than a low pitch (Cutler (2005), Fry (1955)). These observations suggest that pitch height is used as a cue for lexical stress in the language. However, it is also said that pitch functions as a cue for lexical stress only when lexical stress coincides with sentence stress (Ortega-Llebaria et al. (2013), Shport (2011), Sluijter and van Heuven (1996), Ueyama (2000)). That is, English exploits pitch as a cue for lexical stress in a very limited context. Furthermore, English pitch accent, which stressed syllables carry, can include a low pitch as well as a high pitch (Beckman et al. (2005)). This means that there is no one-to-one relation between pitch height and the presence or absence of lexical stress. Taken together, pitch height is a weaker cue in English than in Korean in that its difference per se is not always associated with a specific category in the former as it is in the latter. As for French, pitch is used as a cue for the obligatory primary stress and the final full syllable of a word often bears a rising pitch movement when it is the last full syllable of a non-sentence final phrase (Jun and Fougeron

(2002)). However, French is known as a fixed stress language and the primary stress always falls on the last full syllable of the final word in a phrase (Di Cristo (1998), Kijak (2009), Tranel (1987)). Thus, in French pitch does not differentiate any words, and pitch height has no lexically distinctive function. The insignificance of pitch height in that it does not specify a category differentiating words in American English and French can account for NE's and NFr's non-use of pitch height for L2 length identification.

Finally, NK's perceived vowel duration is longer for vowels with a high pitch than a low pitch and this bias seems to have stemmed from a psychoacoustic effect. It is difficult to think that NK have acquired it through Japanese learning, because NJ do not show it. Here, two explanations are possible: (1) an effect from some characteristics in the L1, Seoul Korean and (2) a psychoacoustic effect. However, no literature, to my knowledge, reports any interaction between vowel duration and pitch in Seoul Korean. Meanwhile, when perceived vowel duration is longer for vowels which are higher in pitch and intensity, compared to those which are lower, this is known as a psychoacoustic effect (Minagawa-Kawai et al. (2002), Oguma (2000)). Along these lines, Brigner (1988) showed that perceived duration is longer for a high frequency pure tone (4000 Hz) than for a low frequency tone (500 Hz). More recently, Yu (2010) found that perceived duration is longer for syllables with a higher F0 than a lower F0. These findings support the existence of a psychoacoustic effect on perception of duration; NK's results are compatible with the effect. Consequently, it seems more reasonable to consider NK's longer perceived duration for vowels with a high pitch as a psychoacoustic effect, a general auditory mechanism.

5. Conclusion

The current study investigated how pitch height in the L1 interacts with its use as a cue for vowel length in L2 Japanese. The significance of pitch height as a cue differs between Seoul Korean and the other three languages, Mandarin Chinese, American English, and French. This difference in the role of pitch height as a cue was reflected in listeners' use and non-use of pitch height for L2 length identification. As shown by Korean listeners, L2 listeners are likely to attend to a phonetic feature that is important as a cue to perceive a category differentiating L1 words even when listening to the L2, which is implied by the Feature Hypothesis. The role of phonetic features in the L1 determines which acoustic information listeners pay attention to in the L2. A general auditory mechanism then would be activated to interpret phonetic information that they can perceive in the L2 acoustic signals.

References

Beckman, Mary E., Julia Hirschberg and Stefanie Shattuck-Hufnagel (2005) "The Original ToBI System and the Evolution of the ToBI Framework," *Prosodic Typology: The Phonology of Intonation and Phrasing,* ed. by Sun-Ah Jun, 9-54, Oxford University Press, New York.

Boersma, Paul and David Weenink (1992-2016) "Praat: Doing Phonetics by Computer (Version 5.3.11)," [Computer program].

Brigner, Willard (1988) "Perceived Duration as a Function of Pitch," *Perceptual and Motor Skills* 67, 301-302.

Cutler, Anne (2005) "Lexical Stress," *The Handbook of Speech Perception,* ed. by David B. Pisoni and Robert E. Remez, 264-289, Blackwell, Malden, MA.

Di Cristo, Albert (1998) "Intonation in French," *Intonation Systems: A Survey of Twenty Languages,* ed. by Daniel Hirst and Albert Di Cristo, 195-218, Cambridge University Press, Cambridge.

Fry, Dennis Butler (1955) "Duration and Intensity as Physical Correlates of Linguistic Stress," *Journal of the Acoustical Society of America* 27(4), 765-768.

Fry, Dennis Butler (1958) "Experiments in the Perception of Stress," *Language and speech,* 1(2), 126-152.

Fujisaki, Hiroya, Kimie Nakamura, and Toshiaki Imoto (1975) "Auditory Perception of Duration of Speech and Non-speech Stimuli," *Auditory Analysis and Perception Speech,* ed. by Gunnar Fant and M. A. A. Tatham, 197-219, Academic, London.

Jun, Sun-Ah. and Cécile Fougeron (2002) "Realization of Accentual Phrase in French Intonation," *Probus* 14, 147-172.

Kim, Mi-Ryoung, Patrice Speeter Beddor and Julie Horrocks (2002) "The Contribution of Consonantal and Vocalic Information to the Perception of Korean Initial Stops," *Journal of Phonetics* 30(1), 77-100.

Kijak, Anna Magdalena (2009) *How Stressful is L2 Stress?: A Cross-linguistic Study of L2 Perception and Production of Metrical Systems*, Doctoral dissertation, Utrecht University, Netherlands.

Lehiste, Ilse (1970) *Suprasegmentals*, MIT Press, Cambridge, MA.

Lin, Yen-Hwei (2007) *The Sounds of Chinese*, Cambridge University Press, New York.

Lippus, Pärtel, Karl Pajusalu and Jüli Allik (2009) "The Tonal Component of Estonian Quantity in Native and Non-native Perception," *Journal of Phonetics* 37 (4), 388-396.

McAllister, Robert, James Emil Flege and Thorsten Piske (2002) "The Influence of L1 on the Acquisition of Swedish Quantity by Native Speakers of Spanish, English and Estonian," *Journal of Phonetics* 30(2), 229-258.

Minagawa-Kawai, Yasuyo, Kikuo Maekawa and Shigeru Kiritani (2002) "Nihongo Gakushuusha no Chou/Tanboin no Dootei ni Okeru Picchigata to Onsetsuichi no Kouka (Effects of Pitch Accent and Syllable Position in Identifying Japanese Long and Short Vowels: Comparison of English and Korean Speakers)," *Journal of the Phonetic Society of Japan* 6(2), 88-97.

Mori, Yoko (2001) "Akusento no Final Lengthening eno Eikyou (Effect of Accentual Fall on Final Lengthening in Japanese)," *Journal of the Phonetic Society of Japan* 5(1), 92-106.

Mori, Yoko (2003) *Markedness of Prepausal Vowels in Japanese Rhythmic Structure*, Doctoral dissertation, Osaka University of Foreign Studies.

Oguma, Rie (2000) "Eigobogowasha ni yoru Chouon to Tan'on no Chikaku (Perception of Japanese Long Vowels and Short Vowels by English-Speaking Learners)," *Sekai no Nihongokyoiku* 10, 43-55.

Ortega-Llebaria, Marta, Hong Gu and Jieyu Fan (2013) "English Speakers' Perception of Spanish Lexical Stress: Context-driven L2 Stress Perception," *Journal of Phonetics* 41(3-4), 186-197.

Qin, Zhen and Peggy Pik-Ki Mok (2011) "Perception of Cantonese tones by Mandarin, English and French speakers," *Proceedings of the 17th International Congress of Phonetic Sciences*, 1654-1657.

Shport, Irina. A (2011) *Cross-linguistic Perception and Learning of Japanese Lexical Prosody by English Listeners*, Doctoral dissertation, University of Oregon.

Silva, David J. (2006) "Variation in Voice Onset Time for Korean Stops: A Case for Recent Sound Change," *Korean Linguistics* 13, 1-16.

Sluijter, Agaath. M. C. and Vincent. J van Heuven (1996) "Acoustic Correlates of

Linguistic Stress and Accent in Dutch and American English," *Proceedings of the 4th International Conference on Spoken Language Processing*, 630-633.

Takiguchi, Izumi (2011) "Perceptual Development on the Identification of Length in L2 Japanese," *Proceedings of the 17th International Congress on Phonetic Sciences*, 1950-1953.

Takiguchi, Izumi (2014) *Duration and Pitch Cues in L1: Perceptual Effect on Phonological Vowel Length for Learners of Japanese*, Doctoral dissertation, Sophia University.

Takiguchi, Izumi (2015) "The Role of Vowel Duration Cue in L1: Effects on L2 Learners' Identification of Phonological Vowel Length in Japanese," *Proceedings of the 18th International Congress of Phonetic Sciences*, Paper number 0111, 1-5.

Tranel, Bernard (1987) *The Sounds of French: An Introduction*, Cambridge University Press, New York.

Ueyama, Motoko (2000) *Prosodic Transfer: An Acoustic Study of L2 English vs. L2 Japanese*, Doctoral dissertation, UCLA.

Venditti, Jennifer J (2005) "The J_ToBI Model of Japanese Intonation," *Prosodic Typology: The Phonology of Intonation and Phrasing*, ed. by Sun-Ah Jun, 172-200, Oxford University Press, New York.

Wang, Qian (2008) "L2 Stress Perception: The Reliance on Different Acoustic Cues," *Proceedings of the 4th International Conference on Speech Prosody*, 1-4.

Yang, Jie and Chang Liu (2012) "Categorical Perception of Lexical Tone for Monolingual and Bilingual School-aged Children," *International Journal of Asian Language Processing* 22(2), 49-62.

Yu, Alan C. L. (2010) "Tonal Effects on Perceived Vowel Duration," *Laboratory Phonology 10*, ed. by Cécile Fougeron, Barbara Kühnert, Mariapaola D'Imperio and Nathalie Vallé, 151-168, Mouton de Gruyter, Berlin.

Zhang, Yanhong and Alexander L Francis (2010) "The Weighting of Vowel Quality in Native and Non-native Listeners' Perception of English Lexical Stress," *Journal of Phonetics* 38(2), 260-271.

学習者の作文エラーに見る日本語のリズム

権　延姝

神戸大学

1. はじめに

　外国語学習者の作文には様々なエラーが現れる．主に母国語の影響を受けて，または目標言語の特徴に起因して起こる．本研究では日本語を母語とする韓国語学習者（以下学習者）の作文エラーを扱う．

　学習者の発話のエラーとは違って，学習者の作文エラーには音声，音韻的な要因以外にも目標言語の表記（文字）体系が影響を及ぼす．本研究ではまず学習者の作文エラーを音声要因と文字要因から考える．日本人学習者の韓国語の発話エラーについては多数の研究がある．本研究では日本人学習者の発話エラーを紹介している Kwon K. (2011) を参考に，音声エラーを抽出し，外来語の研究（権 (2014)）を参考に文字エラーを抽出する．

(1)

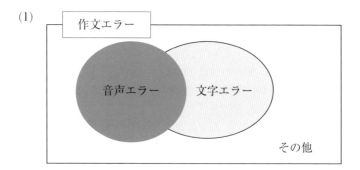

　2節では本研究の資料になった学習者の作文データについて，収集の仕方や分類方法などを紹介する．3節では音声に起因するエラーを母音，子音，音節構造に分けてまとめる．

続く4節では音声と文字に起因しないその他のエラーを紹介する．特に子音挿入のエラーに関しては日本語が好むリズム（窪薗 (2002)，田中 (2008)）での説明を試みる．

2. 学習者データ

本研究で用いるデータは学習者のエラーを集めたものである．関西居住の20代から60代までの学習者によるデータである．データは学習者が書いた韓国語の作文から集めた．学習者のエラー（Error），正しい韓国語の形（Target），エラーの種類（Type）とラベリングした．学習者の韓国語歴は1年から10年以上までで，韓国語のレベルは韓国語の読み書きができる初級レベルから，日常レベルの読み・書き・話しができる上級者までが含まれていた．

同じ形のエラーを1例と数えたType頻度は2613件である．その内，語用論エラーが366件，文法エラーが1139件，発音エラーが703件，文字エラーが381件，その他のエラーが23件あった．

(2) データの分類

	Target		Error		Type
a.	/na.to/	나도	/cə.to/	저도	語用論エラー
b.	/mək.nin.ta/	먹는다	/ək.nin.ta/	억는다	文字エラー
c.	/taŋ.kɨn/	당근	/taŋ.kɨm/	당금	発音エラー
d.	/ye.p'i.ko/	예쁘고	/ye.p'ə.sə/	예뻐서	文法エラー
e.	/yə.heŋ/	여행	/yəŋ.heŋ/	영행	その他エラー

上の表 (2) はエラーをタイプ別に分類した例である．(2a) は敬語の使い方の間違い，(2b) は「ㅁ」を「ㅇ」と書いてしまった間違いであるため，それぞれ語用論エラー，文字エラーと分類した．(2c) は語末子音を間違えた例であるが，発話の時にも起こるエラー（Kwon K. (2011)）であるので発音エラーと分類した．(2d) は連結語尾の使い方の間違いのため文法エラーと分類し，以上に分類できなかった語例 (2e) は，その他と分類した．

3. 音声要因のエラー

3節では，日本語と韓国語の音体系の違いに起因するエラーを考察する．ほかのエラーと区別するために，学習者の発話エラーを扱った先行研究 Kwon K. (2011) を参考にする．以下では学習者の作文エラーの中で音声に起因するエラーを母音，頭子音，尾子音に分けてまとめる．

3.1. 日本語と韓国語の音声の違い

日本語と韓国語は母音の数が異なる．日本語の短母音は5つ，韓国語の短母音は8つある (3)．日本語には /a//i//u//e//o/ があり，韓国語にはそれに加えて /i/, /ə/, /ɛ/ がある．韓国語の /i/ は日本語の /u/ に，/ə/ は /o/ に似ている音であり，日本人学習者には韓国語が2つの /u/ と /o/ を持つ体系のように聞こえる．

(3) 日本語と韓国語の母音

韓	ㅏ /a/	ㅣ /i/	ㅜ /u/	ㅡ /i/	ㅔ /e/, ㅐ /ɛ/	ㅗ /o/	ㅓ /ə/
日	/a/	/i/	/u/		/e/	/o/	

また，日本語と韓国語は子音の体系も異なる．阻害音において，日本語は有声無声の対立を持っている．韓国語は有気・無気，声帯の緊張，トーンの高低などからなる3対立（平音・激音・濃音）を持っている．

韓国語の語頭では平音・激音・濃音の阻害音は無声子音として出現する (4a, b, c)．無声音に後続する平音は，無声として発音される (4d) が，有声音の間では有声子音になる (4e)．しかし，語中でも激音と濃音は無声子音として発音される (4f, g)．したがって，韓国語の3対立は語頭でも語中でも有声無声のみでは区別できない．

(4)　韓国語の阻害音の 3 対立

		語頭			語中	
平音	a. 無声	/kim.cʰi/	김치	d. 無声	/kuk.pap/	국밥
				e. 有声	/kar.pi/	갈비
激音	b. 無声	/pʰa.cən/	파전	f. 無声	/sam.kye.tʰaŋ/	삼계탕
濃音	c. 無声	/k'ak.tu.ki/	깍두기	g. 無声	/t'ək.pok'.i/	떡볶이

　日本語と韓国語は音節構造も異なる．日本語とは違い韓国語には閉音節を有する語彙が多い．日本語で閉音節を作る子音は撥音〈ン〉，促音〈ッ〉がある．韓国語では調音点の異なる，有声の /n//m//ŋ/，無声の /k//t//p/ が尾子音として存在する．また，調音法が異なる有声の /r/ も尾子音として現れる．これらは学習者に〈ン〉や〈ッ〉と知覚される場合もあれば，母音挿入をした〈ム〉，〈ク〉，〈プ〉，〈ル〉などと知覚される場合もある．日本語と韓国語の音声の違いに起因する日本人学習者の作文エラーを，以下ではそれぞれ母音，頭子音，尾子音に分けてみていく．

3.2. 母音

　韓国語の ㅓ /ə/ と ㅡ /i/ は学習者にとって知覚困難な母音である（Kwon K. (2011))．学習者は発話時に韓国語の母音 ㅓ /ə/ を ㅗ /o/ に，ㅗ /o/ を ㅓ /ə/ に間違えて使うことがある（5a, b)．また，母音の ㅜ /u/ と ㅡ /i/ を混同する現象も報告されている（5c, d)．

(5)　発音エラー（Kwon K. (2011))

	韓国語 (Target)		エラー (Error)	
a.	/kə.ur/	거울	/ko.ir/	고을
b.	/tiŋ.kyo/	등교	/tiŋ.kyə/	등겨
c.	/kuk.caŋ/	국장	/kik.caŋ/	극장
d.	/kik.caŋ/	극장	/kuk.caŋ/	국장

　本研究が調査した作文エラーにも同様のエラーが現れる．まず，ㅓ /ə/ を ㅗ /o/ に，ㅗ /o/ を ㅓ /ə/ に間違えて使った例が（6a, b）であり，ㅜ /u/ と ㅡ /i/ を混同した例が（6c, d）である．

(6) 発音エラー：母音

	韓国語		エラー	
a.	/cir.kəp.ke/	즐겁게	/cir.kop.ke/	즐곱게
b.	/yo.to.ka.wa/	요도가와	/yə.to.ka.wa/	여도가와
c.	/tu.si.kan/	두 시간	/ti.si.kan/	드 시간
d.	/kʰe.i.pir/	케이블	/kʰe.i.pur/	케이불

この類の母音のエラーは日本語と韓国語の母音のカテゴリの相違によるものであり，発話のエラーにも報告されているので，音声に起因するエラーとして分類できよう．

3.3. 頭子音

学習者の発話エラー（Kwon K. (2011)）の中では韓国語の子音の3対立が正しく認識できず，平音を激音に（7a），激音を平音に（7b），濃音を激音に（7c）に間違える例が報告されている．

(7) 発音エラー（Kwon K. (2011)）

	韓国語		エラー	
a.	/kur/	굴	/kʰur/	쿨
b.	/kʰur/	쿨	/kur/	굴
c.	/k'ur/	꿀	/kʰur/	쿨

本研究が扱う作文のエラーにも同様の例があった．平音を激音（8a）と濃音（8b）に，激音を平音（8c）と濃音（8d）に，濃音を平音（8e）と激音（8f）にしたエラーが観察された．

(8) 発音エラー：子音

	韓国語		エラー	
a.	/pʰuŋ.ca/	풍자	/pʰun.cʰa/	푼차
b.	/tan.im.ryo/	단음료	/t'an.im.ryo/	딴음료
c.	/kʰɛn/	캔	/kɛn/	갠
d.	/kʰin.sur/	큰술	/k'in.sur/	끈술
e.	/na.p'in/	나쁜	/na.pin/	나븐
f.	/c'i.kɛ/	찌개	/cʰi.ke/	치게

3.4. 尾子音

　学習者の発音エラーとして最後にここでまとめたいのは両言語の音節構造の違いによるエラーである．Kwon. K（2011）でも尾子音のエラーについて言及されている．エラーは尾子音の後に子音が続く場合に起こっており，そのエラーのパターンは尾子音の調音点を間違えるパターン（9a-d）と，母音挿入で開音節を作るパターン（9e）があった．

(9)　発音エラー（Kwon K.（2011））

	韓国語		エラー	
a.	/sik.taŋ/	식당	/sit.t'aŋ/	싣땅
b.	/mit.ko/	믿고	/mit.ko/	믹고
c.	/kap.ca.ki/	갑자기	/kat.c'a.ki/	갇짜기
d.	/toŋ.ne/	동네	/ton.ne/	돈네
e.	/natʰ.mar/	낱말	/nat.ma.ri/	낟마르

　調音点を間違えるエラーは後ろに来る子音に同化する形で現れる．これは日本語の同化（10）と同じ現象である．先行する子音の調音点が変わるという点が共通している．

(10)　日本語の音節末子音の同化現象

a.	神田	/kaNda/	[kanda]
b.	難波	/naNba/	[namba]
c.	漫画	/maNga/	[maŋga]

　以上を踏まえて，(9a-d) の例は，韓国語の子音連続が調音点を共有していなかったためであると解釈できる．本研究の対象である作文のエラーにも調音点の異なる子音連続を調音点を共有するものにさせたエラーが観察できた (11)．

(11)　発音エラー：調音点が一致する例

	韓国語		エラー	
a.	/kən.kaŋ/	건강	/kəŋ.kan/	겅간
b.	/hiŋ.mi/	흥미	/him.mi/	흠미
c.	/toŋ.tɛ.mun/	동대문	/ton.te.mun/	돈데문
d.	/cəŋ.ton/	정돈	/cən.ton/	전돈

(12)　発音エラー：調音点が一致しない例

	韓国語		エラー	
a.	/səŋ.kyək/	성격	/sən.kyək/	선격
b.	/yən.sip/	연습	/yəŋ.sip/	영습
c.	/cəŋ.mar/	정말	/cən.mar/	전말
d.	/kan.caŋ/	간장	/kaŋ.caŋ/	강장
e.	/cun.pi/	준비	/cuŋ.pi/	중비

しかし，作文のエラーでは調音点を共有する子音の連続を作る以外にも，尾子音を間違える語例が観察できた（12）．また，単語末の尾子音についても調音点を間違えるエラーが観察できた（13）．

(13)　発音エラー：単語末の子音

	韓国語		エラー	
a.	/taŋ.kɨn/	당근	/taŋ.kɨm/	당금
b.	/yu.myəŋ/	유명	/yu.myən/	유면
c.	/ma.im/	마음	/ma.in/	마은

Kwon K. (2011) では，その他にも尾子音のエラーは尾子音の ㄹ /r/ と 르 /ri/ を区別できない例を紹介している（9e）．作文のエラーでは ㄹ /r/ 以外の子音に関しても，閉音節と開音節を混同するエラーが観察できた．開音節を閉音節に（14a），閉音節を開音節に間違うパターン（14b, c）があった．

(14) 発音エラー：閉音節と開音節

	韓国語		エラー	
a.	/mo.ri.kesʼ.nɨn.te.yo/	모르겠는데요	/mər.kesʼ.nɨn.te.yo/	멀겠는데요
b.	/ke.im/	게임	/ke.i.mɨ/	게이므
c.	/ir.kuk/	일국	/i.ri.ku.kɨ/	이르구그

4. その他のエラーと日本語のリズム

4.1. その他のエラー

以下では音声，文字以外の例を見ていこう．まず，韓国語母語話者（以下，韓国人）も学習者も間違える正書法のエラーからまとめよう．その1つに，語幹と活用語尾を分けて書く正書法が分からないために生じるエラーがある (15)．韓国語の正書法は用言の場合，語幹の一部と活用語尾は同じ音節として発音されても，異なる音節として書くことになっている．

(15) /ar.da/（알다）- /ar.a.yo/（알아요）*/a.ra.yo/（아라요）
　　　走る―走らない　*走ない

このような正書法は韓国人も，学校教育などを通して学習するものである．その他に，韓国人でも起こすエラーとしてㅔ /e/・ㅐ /ɛ/ の区別と尾子音の表記がある．ㅔ /e/・ㅐ /ɛ/ の綴り間違いは若い世代で2つの母音を区別しなくなったために起こる (16)．

(16) その他のエラー：ㅐ／ㅔ

	韓国語		エラー	
a.	/i.tʰa.mi.e.sə/	이타미에서	/i.tʰa.mi.ɛ.sə/	이타미애서
b.	/he.i.an/	헤이안	/hɛ.i.an/	해이안

(17) その他のエラー

	韓国語		エラー	
a.	/yə.hɛŋ/	여행	/yəŋ.hɛŋ/	영행
b.	/ca.cən.kə/	자전거	/can.cən.ko/	잔전고
c.	/cə.nyək/	저녁	/cən.nyək/	전녁
d.	/se.pən/	세번	/ses.pən/	셋번
e.	/t'a.on/	따온	/t'ak.on/	딱온
f.	/cu.cʰe.cək/	주체적	/cuk.cʰe.cək/	죽체적

　それに比べて，(17) のエラーは韓国人の書き間違いでは発生しないエラーである．このようなエラーは作文だけでなく，学習者の発音でも現れる．[1] 学習者が韓国語の여 [yə] と영 [yəŋ] の区別ができないわけではない．では，(17) は特殊な例であろうか．前述のようにそれは音声に起因するものではない．日本人学習者が여 [yə] と영 [yəŋ] が区別できないと報告している研究もまだない．そして，その原因は文字からも探れない．여 [yə] と영 [yəŋ] を間違える原因は音声や文字という媒体にはないようである．

　日本語の外来語において，脱落は主に子音の脱落で，挿入は主に母音挿入として現れる (18)．このような外来語借用においての戦略は，昔は省略が，現在は挿入が使われる傾向がある (Kwon Y. (2014))．

　昔の日本語の外来語には，日本語に存在しない音が省略される現象が観察できる．尾子音の省略 (18b)，子音群の一部の省略 (18c, d, e) として現れる．これに比べ，最近の日本語は綴り字と一緒に流入されたためか，つづり字の助けを得て，聞こえない音も母音挿入で保存する方向で借用する．

　母音挿入は日本語だけの特殊な現象ではなく，他の言語でも起こる．しかし，(17) で現れる現象は子音挿入は特殊なものである．その子音挿入が母音の音色を補正するものでもないので，音声的な類似性からはその現象の意味を見つけることができない．

---

[1] これは筆者の経験の基に言及したものである．発話エラーにも現れるとしているがKwon K. (2011) で紹介されている例ではない．

(18)

English	Japanese 19th-20th century loan	Contemporary loan
Pocket	a. ポッケ /pokke/	ポケット /poketto/
Lemonade	b. ラムネ /ramune/	レモネード /remone:do/
Crank	c. カラン /karan/	クランク /kuranku/
Cement	d. セメン /semen/	セメント /semento/
Roast	e. ロース /ro:su/	ロースト /ro:suto/

(19) 英語→外来語
 a. スペイン語： stop → estop
 b. 韓国語： strike → [sit^{h}ɨraik^{h}ɨ]

また，日本人に [yə] と [yəŋ] が区別できないということでもないので，聴覚の問題とも思えない．さらに3章で言及した文字のデザインに起因する原因とも考えにくい．

なぜ (17) のようなパターンが繰り返して現れるか．以下ではこのようなエラーの原因が日本語の好むリズムにあることを先行研究（窪薗 (2002)，田中 (2008)）から探る．

4.2. 日本語が好むリズム

本研究では以上の子音挿入の原因を日本語のリズムから検討する．窪薗 (2002)，田中 (2008) は日本語が好むリズムを HL>HH>LL>LH とみて，HL や HH の好まれる例として幼児語，短縮語，語形成のパターンを挙げている．

(20) 幼児語の例
  a. HL 単語：マンマ，ダッコ，クック，オンブ，ネンネ

b. HH 単語：ポンポン，コンコン，ワンワン，ハイハイ

(21) 漢語・和語：LL → HL
    a. しか→しいか（詩歌）
    b. ふき→ふうき（富貴）
    c. みな→みんな（皆）
    d. とび→とんび（鳶）

次に外来語の短縮語の例を見よう．(22a, b) の例だけ見れば，発音が難しいとされる特殊拍を脱落させる現象に見える．しかし，続く語例 (22c, d) から分かるように，特殊拍でも HL を作る特殊拍は脱落しない．

(22) 外来語の短縮： LH/HH/HL → LL/HL
    a. ロケーション→ロケ, *ロケー
    b. デモンストレーション→デモ, *デモン
    c. ローテーション→ローテ
    d. パンフレット→パンフ

また，このような例は野球の声援でも観察できる．(23a) の矢野，(23b) の阿部という LL の音節構造を持つ選手の名前は HL にはするが，LH にはしない．

(23) 野球の声援（窪薗 (2002)，田中 (2008)）
    a. かっとばせえ，やあの　*やのお
    b. かっとばせえ，ああべ　*あべえ

これらは一見すると全く異なる現象のように思われるが，そこに共通のメカニズム (HL>HH>LL>LH) が働いていることは注目に値する．

4.3. LL・LH を HL・HH にする作文のエラー

それでは여행 [yəhɛŋ], 영행 [yəŋhɛŋ] は日本語のリズムがより好む方向で作られた結果であろうか．次の (24) は学習者のエラーの中で韓国語の音声，文字に起因しない子音挿入エラーを集めたものである．

(24) 子音挿入エラー (17) の音節構造

	韓国語		エラー	
a.	/yə.hɛŋ/	여행 (LH)	/yəŋ.hɛŋ/	영행 (HH)
b.	/cə.nyək/	저녁 (LH)	/cən.nyək/	전녁 (HH)
c.	/se.pən/	세번 (LH)	/ses.pən/	셋번 (HH)

　これらは全てLHからHH，またはLLからHLへと日本語が好むリズムに変わっている．また子音脱落エラーの場合にはHH → HLを作る例も観察できた．

(25) 子音脱落エラー (HH → HL)

	韓国語		エラー	
a.	/myəŋ.ryəŋ/	명령	/myəŋ.ryə/	명려
b.	/cir.mun/	질문	/cir.mu/	질무
c.	/tʰoŋ.hɛŋ/	통행	/tʰoŋ.hɛ/	통해

　以上，日本語のリズムという観点から学習者のエラーを考察した．このような現象は日本語母語話者にだけ起こるのかも確認する必要がある．さらに，ほかの言語でも起こるのであれば，その言語が好むリズムがtrochee かiambicかも一緒に見る必要がある．

5. 結び

　本研究では学習者の韓国語作文に見られるエラーを，音声，文字，その他の原因に分けてまとめた．既存の研究にも音声に起因するエラーの分析はあったが，本研究では音声と文字以外の原因として日本語のリズムが学習者のエラーに影響する可能性について考察した．
　学習者のエラーは，学習者の未熟な目標言語学習のためでもある．またその変化は学習者のL1の好むリズムも関与しているようにみえる．本研究ではいくつかの例を挙げて議論を進めたが，さらに数量的な研究を通してどの程度の影響力があるのかについても条件をそろえた知覚実験などを用いて検討する必要もあると思われる．

参考文献

窪薗晴夫（2002）『新語はこうして作られる』岩波書店，東京.
Kwon Kyoung Ae (2011) "A Study on Teaching Natural Korean Pronunciation to Japanese Native Speakers: Focusing on Suprasegmental Units," *Studies in Foreign Language Education*, Vol. 25(1), 1-23.
Kwon Yeonjoo (2014) *The Role of L1 and L2 Orthography on Loanword Phonology*, Doctoral dissertation, Kobe University.
権延姝（2014）「韓国語由来の日本語の外来語と日本人学習者のエラーの比較」韓国日語日文学会，冬季国際学術大会，嘉泉大学，2014.12.20.
田中真一（2008）『リズム・アクセントの「ゆれ」と音韻・形態構造』くろしお出版，東京.

英語および仏語由来の借用語における促音分布

竹村　亜紀子
INALCO（フランス国立東洋言語文化学院）

1. はじめに

　日本語の促音に関しては，これまで様々な側面から研究が行われてきた．たとえば，英語由来の借用語における促音の生起環境（川越・荒井（2002），ほか），英語音声を使った知覚研究（Kawagoe and Takemura (2013), Kawahara (2008), Kubozono et al. (2013)），日本語学習者による促音の生成・知覚（戸田（2003））などの研究が挙げられる．とくに借用語を通して日本語の音韻特徴を明らかにしようという試みでは，促音挿入がなぜ起こるのかということを中心に研究が行われてきた．促音挿入の問題については川越・荒井（2002）に書かれているように，「日本語話者がもつ日本語音韻体系の問題」と「借用語の元の言語の音声の問題」という2つの見方がある．しかし，日本語に取り込まれる借用語の元の言語は英語だけではない．借用元である言語が変われば，英語とは音声が異なるため借用のパタンが英語と同じであるとは言えない．そこで本稿では，(1) 英語・仏語由来の借用語における促音の生起環境に焦点を当て，促音の生起環境をそれぞれ整理する．もし英語・仏語の借用語を通して同じ傾向が見出されれば，それは日本語の音韻論の問題であるということが言えよう．本稿では英語由来の借用語の研究は丸田（2001），川越・荒井（2002）を，仏語を用いた借用語の研究はShinohara（1997）を参考にする．そして (2) 実在する仏語由来の借用語での促音生起の調査結果を提示し，英語・仏語の借用語の傾向と比較する．最後に，まとめとして (3) 実在する英語由来の借用語と仏語由来の借用語で，促音挿入がほぼ同じ傾向を示す部分は日本語の音韻論の問題が大きいことを指摘する．しかし，借用パタンが異なるところもあるため，その部分は借用

元の言語である英語と仏語による音声学的要因が関わることも指摘する．

2. 英語からの借用語──促音に注目して

英語から日本語に取り込まれた借用語研究は様々なものがあるが（Katayama (1998)，北原 (1997)，ほか），ここでは丸田 (2001) を扱った川越・荒井 (2002) を参考に英語由来の借用語について明らかになっている点を，語末の単子音，語末の子音連鎖に分けて整理する．

2.1. 末尾音節が単子音（VC#）で終わる場合

丸田 (2001) および川越・荒井 (2002) では英語の語末単子音を無声阻害音，有声閉鎖音，無声摩擦音，有声摩擦音4種類に分けて促音挿入について調べている．それらを簡略的に整理すると下記のようになる．

(1) 英語の語末単子音の促音挿入
   a. 無声阻害音：促音挿入がほぼ起こる（語例：ヒット，ピック）
   b. 有声閉鎖音：出現が不安定で，促音挿入が起こる場合（語例：ベッド）と起こらない場合（語例：ペリオド）がある．
   c. 無声摩擦音：子音の種類による．摩擦音の /ʃ/ の場合は促音挿入が起こる（語例：キャッシュ）が，/s/ や /f/ の場合は促音挿入が起こらない（語例：キス，タフ）．
   d. 有声摩擦音：出現は不安定で，丸田 (2001) では語末が /z/ で終わる語が6つのみで，促音の出現／非出現の頻度は同等．

上記の通り，英語の語末に現れる子音の種類によって促音挿入が異なることがわかる．3.2.2節の表1は丸田 (2001) をデータもとに表にした川越・荒井 (2002) の再掲である．

2.2. 語末が子音連鎖で終わる場合

続いて，英語の語末が子音連鎖（VC_1C_2#）で終わる場合を簡略的に整理すると下記のようになる．

(2) 英語の語末子音連鎖の促音挿入
  a. 子音連鎖 (C_1C_2) の C_2 が /p/ /t/ /k/ の場合 (-Ct#, -st#, -sk#) は促音挿入が起きない (語例：タクト, マスト, マスク).
  b. 子音連鎖 (C_1C_2) の C_2 が /s/ /r/ /n/ の場合 (-Cs#, -Cr#, -Cn#), 子音連鎖 (C_1C_2) の C_1 の種類によって促音挿入が起こる場合 (語例：タックル) と起きない場合 (語例：ボトル) がある.
    i. 無声阻害音＋流音の子音連鎖：
       語例：タックル, ボトル, ポップス
    ii. 有声阻害音＋流音の子音連鎖：
       語例：パドル
    iii. 無声摩擦音＋流音の子音連鎖：
       語例：リッスン
    iv. 閉鎖音＋/s/ の子音連鎖：
       語例：ミックス, ファックス

これまでの先行研究で言われている通り，英語の語末単子音，子音連鎖によっても，また子音の種類によっても促音挿入が大きく異なることがわかる．同様の傾向は英語以外からの借用語でも観察されるのであろうか．次の3節では Shinohara (1997) の仏語を使った借用語の研究を通して，促音挿入の傾向を整理する．

3. 仏語からの借用語

3.1. 仏語の音節構造と日本語での取り込み方

Shinohara (1997) は仏語由来の借用語のアクセント，子音と母音の長音化（子音の重子音化，および母音の長母音化）を扱った論文である．Shinohara (1997) によるとフランス語の音節構造は母音を中心に，母音の前に3つの子音，母音の後に4つの子音が生起可能であるとしている．

(3) (C) (C) (C) V (C) (C) (C)

Shinohara (1997) では既存の外来語，つまり日本語に取り込まれた形の借用語（仏語由来）は使用していない．その代わりに日本語に取り込まれて

いない仏語を使い，在仏日本語母語話者（女性三名）に日本語で発音した場合の発音を仮名で書いてもらっている．さらに，書いてもらった仮名表記と合致しているのかを確かめるため，同じ調査語彙を日本語で発音してもらっている．[1]

仏語が日本語に取り込まれた際，問題となるのは長音化（仏語 allongement）である．具体的には子音の長音化と母音の長母音化を指す．前者の子音の長音化は子音の持続時間が延びるので促音化を意味する（これ以降，促音挿入と子音の長音化，子音の重子音化は同じ意味とする）．Shinohara (1997) では，この子音の長音化が (1) 必ず起こる場合と (2) 任意的に起こる場合があるとしている．必ず起こる長音化は，日本語で後ろから2番目の音節（次末音節）が仏語の末尾の音節に対応する場合である．例えば archevêque /arʃəvɛk/（大司教）は日本語で /arusjubeQku/ として取り込まれる．この /beQ/ の部分が /arusjubeQku/ で 仏語の末尾の音節 -vêque /vɛk/ に当たる．任意で起こる子音の長音化は話者によって，また同じ話者でも仏語の語彙によって異なる結果が得られたとされる．

3.2. 仏語からの借用語－促音化・母音の長音化について

Shinohara (1997) は三名の女性日本語話者が仏語の単語を日本語で発音した場合，どのように発音されるのかを書いてもらったものをもとに，促音挿入，母音の長音化について述べている．ここでは，Shinohara (1997) で言及されていることを，語末の単子音の場合と語末の子音連鎖の場合と分けて整理する．

3.2.1. (仏語の発音上) 末尾音節が単子音で終わる閉音節の場合　VC#

Shinohara (1997) によると，末尾音節が無声閉鎖音の場合は重子音になる，つまり促音挿入があるとされる．しかし，末尾音節の無声閉鎖音の前の母音が長音化できる母音である場合には母音の長音化が起こるとされる．[2]

---

[1] ここで注意しなければならないのは，三名のインフォーマントが異なる発音をした場合である．三人の内三人が一致する発音であればよいが，そうでない場合（三人が三様に異なる発音をした場合，あるいは三人のうち一対二という形で発音が異なった場合）があることに留意しなければならない．

[2] Shinohara (1997) では，無声閉鎖音の前の母音が（借用形で）長音化できる母音（綴り

(4)　仏語の語末単子音の種類別の促音挿入
　　a.　無声閉鎖音：重子音になる（促音挿入がおこる）[3]
　　　　語例：nappe（テーブルクロス）/naQpu/，patte（動物の脚）/paQto/
　　b.　有声閉鎖音あるいは鼻音：促音挿入および母音の長音化が可能
　　　　語例：robe（ドレス）/roQbu/，/roobu/，aide（援助）/eQdo/，/eedo/
　　c.　摩擦音が /s/ あるいは /f/ で終わる場合：
　　　i.　/s/ の場合：促音が時によって挿入される
　　　　　語例：place（場所）/purasu/ 全ての話者が一致
　　　　　語例：lasse（くたびれた）/rasu/，/raQsu/
　　　ii.　/f/ の場合：様々な取り込み方の可能性がある
　　　　　語例：sportif（スポーツの）/suporutihu/ 全ての話者が一致
　　　　　語例：massif（どっしりした）/masihu/，/masiQhu/
　　d.　有声摩擦音：摩擦音の前の母音が長音化する
　　　　語例：grave（重大な）/guraabu/，rose（バラ）/roozu/

　3.2.2 節の表1，表2はそれぞれ，英語由来の借用語（丸田（2001），川越・荒井（2002）），および仏語を日本語に取り込んだ際の疑似借用語（日本語に実際には存在しない語）における語末の単子音の促音分布を表している．Shinohara（1997）では促音の有無について具体的な数は示されていないため，表2では言及があったところを「T（True）」で示した．表2の空欄は言及がない（そのような調査語彙がなかった）ことを表している．表1，表2を比べると，促音の分布が非常によく似ていることがわかる．

字で au, eu, ou, aî, ay, あるいは綴り字に ê がある場合）が無声閉鎖音の前にくると，借用語では閉鎖音の子音あるいは母音が長音化すると述べられている．しかし，長音化できる母音の定義は曖昧で，綴り字だけできまる訳ではない．
　[3] 母音の長音化が起こる場合は次のような語例が挙げられているが，インフォーマントによって，促音化する人もいるようである．(haute（高い）/ooto/, /oQto/, fête（祭り）/ɸeeto/, /ɸeQto/)

3.2.2. 語末が子音連鎖で終わる場合

英語由来の借用語の場合と同様に，仏語の語末が子音連鎖（VC₁C₂#）で終わる場合を整理する．

(5) 仏語の語末子音連鎖の促音挿入
   a. 子音連鎖（VC₁C₂#）が閉鎖音＋流音，閉鎖音＋/s/ 以外の場合：
      原語の仏語自体の最終音節が閉音節で，閉鎖音＋流音あるいは閉鎖音＋/s/ 以外の子音連鎖の場合，子音・母音の長音化は起きない．
      語例：apte（適した）/aputo/, acte（行為）/akuto/,
   b. 子音連鎖（VC₁C₂#）の C₂ が流音，あるいは /s/ の場合
      英語由来の借用語と同様に，促音挿入が起こる場合と起こらない場合がある．しかし，英語の場合と異なる点は促音挿入が起こらない代わりに，母音の長音化が起こる点が挙げられる．
      i. 無声阻害音＋流音の子音連鎖：促音挿入が起こる場合と直前の母音が長音化する場合がある．
         語例：litre（リットル）/liQtoru/, gaufre（ワッフル）/goQhuru/, /goohuru/,⁴ people（国民）/puQpuru/, /puupuru/
      ii. 有声阻害音＋流音の子音連鎖：阻害音の前の母音が長音化する．
         語例：ivre（(酒）に酔った）/iiburu/, table（テーブル）/taaburu/, cadre（枠）/kaadoru/
      iii. 閉鎖音＋/s/ の子音連鎖：話者によって促音化する場合と，そうでない場合がある．
         語例：fixe（固定の）/ɸiQkusu/ あるいは /ɸikusu/
              index（索引）/aNdeQkusu/ あるいは /aNdekusu/

(5a) の Shinohara (1997) によるこの記述を読むと，英語由来の借用語の場合（例　タクト，マスト，マスク）とほぼ同じであることがわかる．

---

⁴ 阻害音＋流音の音の連鎖の前が au, eu, ou, aî, ay, ê の場合，借用形において阻害音あるいは阻害音の前の母音が長音化する．

	子音	促音有り	促音なし
破裂音	p	67	1
	t	202	1 (2)
	k	188	3
	b (<b)	5	17
	b (<v)	0	25
	d	25	10 (1)
	g	20	16
破擦音	tʃ	39	0
	ts	4	8
	dʒ	18	0
摩擦音	ʃi	1	4
	ʃu	42	0
	s	3	238
	h/ɸ	3	20
	z	3	3
合計		617	355

表1. 借用語（英語由来）の促音分布：語末単子音
丸田（2001: 74），川越・荒井（2002）

	子音	促音有り	促音なし
破裂音	p	T	
	t	T	
	k	T	
	b (<b)	T	T
	b (<v)		T
	d	T	T
	g		T
破擦音	tʃ		
	ts		
	dʒ		
摩擦音	ʃi		
	ʃu		
	s	T	T
	h/ɸ	T	T
	z		T
合計			

表2. 借用語（仏語由来）の促音分布：語末単子音
Shinohara (1997)

表3は丸田（2001）および川越・荒井（2002）の英語の語末子音連鎖における促音分布を表したものである．そして，表4はShinohara (1997)で言及された語末の子音連鎖を表にしたものである．調査語にない子音連鎖，あるいは仏語に存在しない子音連鎖もあるため，その欄は空欄となっている．語末子音連鎖を調べた表3と表4をみると，非常によく似た促音分布であることがわかる．

Cr	子音	促音有り	促音なし
Cr	pr	6	3(3)
Cr	tr	3	5(2)
Cr	kr	5	9(9)
Cr	br	0	22(20)
Cr	dr	0	5(0)
Cr	gr	3	3(0)
Cr	ɸr	6	7(7)
Cr	zr	0	3(0)
Cs	ks	105	25(25)
Cs	krs	0	1(1)
Cs	ps	3	2(2)
Cs	hs	0	1(0)
Cs	brs	0	1(1)
Cn	sn	1	0
Cn	tʃn	1	14(12)
Cn	tn	1	18(14)
Ct	pt	0	5(5)
Ct	kt	0	24(20)
Ct	ht	0	10(3)
Ct	st	0	115(101)
	sp	0	1
	sk	0	14
	合計	135	287

表3. 借用語（英語由来）の促音分布：語末子音連鎖
丸田（2001: 74），川越・荒井（2002）

	子音	促音有り	促音なし
Cr	pr	T	T
Cr	tr	T	T
Cr	kr	T	
Cr	br		T
Cr	dr		T
Cr	gr		T
Cr	hr	T	T
Cr	zr		
Cs	ks	T	T
Cs	krs		
Cs	ps		
Cs	hs		
Cs	brs		
Cn	sn		
Cn	tʃn		
Cn	tn		
Ct	pt		T
Ct	kt		T
Ct	ht		
Ct	st		T
	sp		
	sk		
	合計		

表4. 借用語（仏語由来）の促音分布：語末子音連鎖
Shinohara (1997)

4. フランス語由来の借用語の実在語調査

　3節までは，英語および仏語を借用元とする借用語の先行研究を概観してきた．3節で概観した Shinohara (1997) では，実在する借用語を用いていないため，実在する借用語を用いた丸田（2001: 74），川越・荒井（2002）

の結果と比較することが妥当であるか疑問が残る．そこで，ここでは実在する仏語由来の借用語を用いて，促音挿入の分布をみることにする．

4.1. データベース

小学館の『日本国語大辞典』から借用語のみを取り出した外来語データベース（川越・竹村（2014））を使用した．この外来語データベースには約3万の借用語（複合語を含む）が含まれている（異なり語数 30,640 語，述べ語数 35,940 語）．仏語由来の借用語を抽出するため，借用言語の項目に「フランス語」あるいは「仏語」と書かれている項目（1,562 語）を抽出した．[5] そして，この抽出した語の中からさらに複合語（例　アート＃シアター）を除き 1,194 語を抽出した．

データベース	データの数
外来語データベース （川越・竹村（2014））	述べ語数　35,940 語 （異なり 30,640 語）
仏語由来の外来語（複合語含む）	述べ語数　1,562 語
仏語由来の単純外来語（複合語除く）	述べ語数　1,194 語
仏語データベースと照合して発音が見つかった単純外来語（複合語除く）	述べ語数 883 語（述べ語数　1,194 語のうち）
仏語データベースと照合して発音が見つからなかった単純外来語（複合語除く）	述べ語数 311 語（述べ語数　1,194 語のうち）

表 5. 外来語データベースと仏語の抽出

川越・竹村（2014）のデータベースから抽出した 1,194 語は日本語での借用形である．しかし，この 1,194 語の仏語の綴り字と，日本語の借用形とを単純に比較することはできない．ここには2つの問題がある．1つは，借用元の仏語が1つの単語であっても借用形が複数ある場合と，もう1つは仏語の綴り字と日本語の借用形が異なる場合である．

前者は，借用元が同じ単語であっても日本語での借用形が複数ある場合である．たとえば，croissant という単語は借用形がクロワッサン，クロワサ

---

[5] 借用言語に英語＋フランス語，英語・仏語・ドイツ語と書かれたものも含む．

ン，クロアッサンなど様々な形がある．借用形をどれか1つに絞れば分析は容易になるが，主観的な判断になってしまうため恐れがあるため，全ての借用形を分析に用いた．また，実際にいくつかのバリエーションが存在することも考慮した．

　後者の問題は，たとえば仏語の cabernet が「カベルネ」として借用される場合である．この仏語の綴り字を見ると語末に /t/ があるが，この /t/ は仏語では発音されず，同様に日本語での借用形でも「カベルネ」であり「*カベルネット」ではない．そのため，英語の借用語と違い，綴り字で存在するこの /t/ を単純に語末の単子音の /t/ として扱うことはできない．このように，仏語の綴り字では読まれない子音字が多く存在するため，語末の子音字と借用形が合わないという問題が出てくる．この問題を解決するため，抽出した語（1,194語）と仏語の発音形を照合する必要がある．仏語の発音形を参照するため，ここでは仏語の語彙のデータベース Lexique 3.81 (New et al. (2001)) を利用した．抽出した1,194語と同じ綴り字を仏語のデータベースから抽出し，その発音形も抽出した（883語）．今回ここで扱うのは，この883語である．

4.2. 仏語語末の開音節と閉音節による借用パタン

　ここでは，川越・竹村（2014）のデータベースから抽出した883語を，フランス語の発音上での開音節と閉音節に分けて促音分布を調べてみた．その結果を示したのが4.2節の表6である．

　Shinohara (1997) によると語末が開音節の場合は長音化（母音および子音の化）は起きないとされているが，借用語のデータからは子音の長音化，つまり促音挿入があることが確認された．促音挿入という観点からみると，外来語データベースから抽出したデータ（表6）の結果は Shinohara (1997) の主張（語末が開音節の場合，促音化は起きない）とは異なる．これには恐らく2つの理由があると思われる．1つは今回使った借用語のデータが純粋に仏語から借用されたものと断定できないものが含まれるためであると思われる．そして，もう1つは Shinohara (1997) がフランスに住む日本語母語話者に仏語を日本語で言った場合どのように発音するのかという調査，別の言い方をすれば借用語のオンライン実験という形であったため，辞書に掲載されている実在語とは異なる結果になったと考えられる．

		促音有り	促音なし	合計
開音節	V	35	342	377
閉音節	C	75	431	506
合計		110	773	883

表 6. 促音分布：語末音節別

4.3. 語末の単子音の場合

　語末が閉音節で無声閉鎖音の場合，英語由来の借用語でも（丸田 (2001)，川越・荒井 (2002)），仏語を使った借用語の調査でも (Shinohara 1997) 促音挿入が起こるとされている．川越・竹村 (2014) のデータベースで，同様に語末の閉音節で仏語の発音が単子音で終わる単語の促音挿入について調べた．その結果が表 7 である．表 7 の子音と書かれた列は仏語の綴り字ではなく，仏語の発音に基づいた子音を表している．

　表 7 をみると，語末の無声閉鎖音の場合，確かに促音が多く，英語と同じ分布を示すように見える．だが表 1 の借用語（英語由来）の促音分布と比べてみると，語末の無声閉鎖音の場合，圧倒的に促音有りが多いのに対し（表 1），表 7 の語末無声閉鎖音の場合，促音有りの割合が少し高い程度である．仏語由来の外来語の促音分布は一見すると英語と似ているかもしれないが，精査してみるとその実態は異なる．

　たとえば，各無声閉鎖音の促音挿入の分布をみてみると（表 7），/k/ が語末に生起する場合（43 例（100%）），その内 24 例（55.8%）が促音有りで，19 例（44.2%）が促音なしとなり，英語由来の借用語の /k/ の場合とは異なる．これらの単語を精査してみたところ，促音有り，促音なしの両方に所属する語彙がいくつかある．

	子音	促音有り	促音なし
閉鎖音	p	2	1
	k	24	19
	t	32	12
	b	0	3
	g	0	11
	d	2	18
摩擦音	f	1	20
	s	5	26
	ʃ	5	5
	v	0	7
	z	0	11
	ʒ	1	35
半母音	j	0	8
流音	l	1	49
	R	0	54
鼻音	m	0	16
	n	0	31
	N	0	1
合計		73	327

表7. 川越・竹村（2014）の促音分布：語末単子音

	子音	促音有り	促音なし
Cr	fl	0	1
	fr	0	1
	kl	0	1
	kr	0	3
	tr	1	5
	bl	0	3
	br	0	2
	dr	0	2
	vr	0	3
rC	rg	0	1
	rm	0	4
	rn	1	4
	rs	0	1
	rʒ	0	3
その他	ls	0	1
	sk	0	8
	st	0	16
	str	0	2
	tm	0	1
	zm	0	42
合計		2	104

表8. 川越・竹村（2014）の促音分布：語末子音連鎖

たとえば，avec という単語では，促音有りの形で「アヴェック」「アベック」という2つの語形があり，促音なしの形で「アヴェク」という語形も存在する．この avec のように両方（促音有り，および促音なし）に所属する語は3つしかない．このように語形が複数あるものをひとつにまとめて（つまり「アヴェック」「アベック」を促音有りが1例とみなして）集計すると，促音有りは17例（56.7%），促音なしは13例（43.3%）となるが，その割合は大きく変動はしない．表1の英語由来の借用語（丸田 2001，川越・荒井 2002）では，語末単子音が /k/ の場合（191例（100%）），促音有りが188例（98.4%），促音なしが3例（1.6%）であった．これに比べると，仏語由来の借用語は英語とは異なる借用パタンであるといえる．

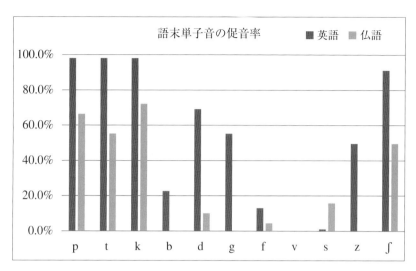

図1. 英語と仏語由来の借用語の語末単子音における促音挿入率

また語末の摩擦音の [s], [ʃ] の場合をみると，英語由来の借用語の [ʃu] は促音が90％近く挿入されるのに対し（表1），仏語由来の借用語の場合 [ʃ] で促音挿入される割合（50％）で促音がない場合が（50％）であることがわかる（表7）．この [ʃ] の促音分布について精査してみると，促音挿入された語は apache（アパッシュ），cloche（クロッシュ），gouache（グワッシュ，グアッシュ，ガッシュ）だけである．最後の gouache の3つの借用形（促音有り）を一つにまとめると，全体としては3例ということになる．語末の [ʃ] で促音挿入がない語例をあげると，cartouche（カルトゥーシュ），cloche（クローシュ），ébauche（エボーシュ），pastiche（パスティーシュ）の4例である．Shinohara (1997) の子音連鎖の場合の借用パタンでは「促音挿入が起こらなければ，母音の長音化が起こる」と言われているが，語末が [ʃ] についても同様の傾向が見られそうである．しかし語末が [ʃ] で終わる仏語由来の語が少ないため，これで一般化することは危険であるが，英語からの借用語とは異なる傾向であることがわかる．

図1は丸田（2001）の表と，この仏語由来の借用語の促音挿入率をグラフにしたものである．[6] これをみると，無声閉鎖音の場合は英語と同じように

---

[6] 英語からの借用語で [ʃi], [ʃu] は1つの [ʃ] として集計して図に掲載した.

促音が挿入される傾向にあるが，仏語で有声阻害音が語末にある場合，そのほとんどが促音なしで取り込まれていることがわかる．表面上，似ているところも観察されるが，細かい点をみてみると英語由来の借用語とは異なる点が観察される．このような点が借用元の言語の音声による違いという可能性も考えられる．

4.3. 仏語の語末が子音連鎖で終わる場合

続いて，仏語の語末が子音連鎖で終わる場合の促音分布を表したものが表8である．この表8の子音と書かれた列は仏語での子音およびその発音を表している．/r/ は口蓋垂摩擦音 [ʁ] として実現する．また左端の列は子音連鎖の種類を表しており，Cr は子音＋流音（r または l）を，rC は流音＋子音を表している．

表8の語末の Cr（子音＋流音）という子音連鎖の場合の促音分布をみてみよう．Shinohara（1997）によると無声阻害音＋流音という場合には，促音挿入が起こる場合と，語末の子音連鎖の前の母音が長音化する場合があるとされている．だが，実在語のデータでは，そのほとんどが促音なしに分布していることがわかる．(litre のみが「リットル」として促音が挿入されている)．その他の語は ancre（アンクル），gaufre（ゴーフル），théâtre（テアトル）のような形で，促音は挿入されていない．この点は Shinohara（1997）のオンラインのような借用語実験の結果とは異なる点である．

同様に，有声阻害音＋流音の場合も，cidre（シードル），livre（リブル，リーブル，リーヴル），poudre（プードル）のように促音は挿入されていない．この点は Shinohara（1997）の記述（阻害音の前の母音が長音化する）とほぼ合致している．

Shinohara（1997）では fixe（固定の）のような，閉鎖音＋/s/ の子音連鎖の例が挙げられていたが，実在語ではそのような子音連鎖は存在しなかったため比較ができなかった．そのほか，実在する借用語で上記以外の子音連鎖をみても促音はほとんど挿入されないことがわかる．

次に英語由来の子音連鎖と比較してみよう．川越・荒井（2002）によると，語末の -Ct#, -st#, -sk# は促音挿入が起きないとされている．仏語由来の借用語をみてみると，川越・荒井（2002）と同様に促音挿入は起きないということがわかる．一方, -Cr#（阻害音＋流音）の場合，英語では促音挿入が起

こる場合と起こらない場合があるとされているが，仏語ではほとんど促音挿入が起こらない．語末の子音連鎖に注目すると，英語由来の借用語と同じ傾向を示す部分（語末の -Ct#, -st#, -sk# は促音挿入が起きない）もあれば，そうでない部分（仏語由来の語では -Cr# という阻害音＋流音の場合は促音挿入が起こらない）もあることがわかる．

5. 考察と展望

　本稿では英語由来の借用語における促音分布（丸田（2001），川越・荒井（2002）），仏語を使った借用語の調査（Shinohara（1997））における促音分布を整理した．そして，外来語データベース（川越・竹村（2014））を使用し，実在する仏語由来の借用語の促音分布を調べた．特にここでは，語末単子音と，語末の子音連鎖を扱った．

　外来語データベース（川越・竹村（2014））を使用した仏語由来の借用語では，語末の単子音も，子音連鎖も促音分布は一見すると英語の促音分布と似た傾向であることが明らかとなったが，語末の単子音を子音別にみると促音分布が全く同じというわけではない．特に，語末の有声阻害音の場合，英語では促音挿入が起こる場合もあるが，仏語では促音挿入がほとんど観察されないことが明らかとなった．また語末の子音連鎖では，英語と仏語で許容される音素配列が異なるため，すべての子音連鎖を比較することはできなかった．しかし，英・仏語の両言語で許容される一部の音素配列を比較すると，促音挿入がほとんど起こらない点は共通する．つまり，促音挿入に関して，英語と仏語由来の借用語の借用パタンで共通する点（語末の特定の子音連鎖では促音挿入が起こらない）は日本語の音韻論で処理しており，その他の異なる借用パタンは原語の英語または仏語の入力音声による違いによるものではないかと考えられる．

　今回は実在する仏語由来の借用語を用いて促音挿入の分布を調べたが，同じ仏語の借用語研究でも，仏語を日本語で読んだ実験を行った Shinohara（1997）の結果とは異なっていた．Shinohara（1997）では仏語自体を日本語に取り込んだときにどのように発音するのかという，いわゆる借用語のオンライン実験の形であったといえる．そのため，今回の実在語の促音分布と Shinohara（1997）の結果とは異なったと考えられる．今回は実在語の調査

であったが，今後は実在語の調査語彙と同じ語彙を用いてオンラインの実験を行い，実在語と同じパタンが現れるのかどうかを確認する必要がある．さらに，借用元の音声による違いから借用形が異なるというのであれば，同じ形の語彙を英語および仏語母語話者にそれぞれ読んでもらい，それを日本語母語話者がどのように聞くのかを調べる必要があるであろう．

　促音挿入が日本語の音韻論に基づく要求で起こるのか，あるいは入力音声による違いに起因するのかを調べるには，一外国語からの借用語の分析では不十分ではないだろうか．Shinohara（2015）は韓国語から日本語への借用語を分析に用いており，借用形は日本語の音韻論的要求で決まるとしている．今後，このようにほかの外国語からの借用語も扱うことで，日本語における借用語音韻論の本質に近づくことができると思われる．

参考文献

Katayama, Motoko (1998) *Optimality Theory and Japanese Loanword Phonology*, Doctoral dissertation, University of California at Santa Cruz.

川越いつえ・荒井雅子（2002）「借用語における促音」『音声研究』第6巻1号，53-66.

Kawagoe, Itsue and Akiko Takemura (2013) "Geminate Judgments of English-like Words by Japanese Native Speakers: Differences in the Borrowed Forms of "Stuff" and "Tough"", *Journal of East Asian Linguistics* 21, 307-337.

川越いつえ・竹村亜紀子（2014）『外来語データベース小学館日本国語大辞典第2版』version 0.1.［非公開］

Kawahara, Shigeto (2008) "Phonetic Naturalness and Unnaturalness in Japanese Loanword Phonology," *Journal of East Asian Linguistics* 17, 317-330.

北原真冬（1997）「1.1 音韻論と文法」．『文法と音声』．音声文法研究会（編），213-231, くろしお出版，東京．

Kubozono, Haruo, Hajime Takeyasu and Mikio Giriko (2013) "On the Positional Aymmetry of Consonant Gemination in Japanese Loanwords," *Journal of East Asian Linguistics* 21, 339-371.

丸田孝治（2001）「英語借用語における促音化：言語音節構造の保持と母語化」『音韻研究』第4号，73-80.

New, Boris, Christophe Pallier, Ludovic Ferrand and Rafael Matos (2001) "Une Base de Données Lexicales du Français Contemporain sur Internet: LEX-IQUE," L'Année Psychologique, 101, 447-462. http://www.lexique.org

Shinohara, Shigeko (1997) *Analyse Phonologique de l'Adaptation Japonais de Mots Etrangers*, Doctoral dissertation, Université de la Sorbonne Nouvelle Paris III.

Shinohara, Shigeko (2015) "Loanword-specific Grammar in Japanese Adaptations of Korean Words and Phrases", *Journal of East Asian Linguistics* 24, 149-191.

戸田貴子 (2003)「外国人学習者の日本語特殊拍の習得」『音声研究』第7巻2号, 70-83.

パドヴァとヴェローナの韻律構造：
イタリア語由来の借用語における音節量・強勢の受入と音韻構造*

田中　真一

神戸大学

1. はじめに

　イタリア北部の都市である Padova と Verona は，ともに子音（C）と母音（V）が交互に繰り返される CVCVCV の音節構造を持つが，日本語化の際，それぞれ「パ'ドヴァ」，「ヴェロ'ーナ」（'：アクセント）のように，少なくとも2つの面で対照的なふるまいを見せる．1つは，アクセントの位置が異なることであり，もう1つは，片方には長母音が生起するのに対し，もう片方にはそれが生起しないことである．このような非対称は，英語由来の借用語においてはほとんど見られない．本稿は，イタリア語から日本語に入った借用語におけるこのような非対称の分析を通して，借用語音韻論における借用元言語（L2）と受入言語（L1）の関係について論じる．

　イタリア語から日本語に入った借用語の分析はいくつかあり，その大半が二重子音の受け入れに関するものである（田中（2007））．音節構造全般やアクセント・強勢構造，および，両者の関係ついては重要性に比してあまり論じられて来なかった．一般に，音節構造とアクセント・強勢との間には関係のあることが知られており（Hayes (1995), Prince and Smolensky (1993/2004), Kager (1999)），そのような観点から見ると，L1 が L2 から語を受け入れる際にも両要素が密接に関係することが予測される．

　また，日本語とイタリア語は，ともに開音節言語で，子音長の対立を持つといった共通点が強調され，相違点を含めた分析は積極的にはなされていな

---

　* 本研究は，日本学術振興会科学研究費補助金基盤研究（B）（課題番号：26284058），基盤研究（C）（課題番号：16K02629）の助成を受けている．

いのが現状である．

　本稿は，このような背景を踏まえ，日本語がイタリア語の強勢や音節構造といった韻律構造をどのように受け入れるかを分析する．

2. 問題の所在

2.1. イタリア語の音韻構造

　イタリア語は母音長の音韻的対立を持たず，長母音は，語末を除く強勢開音節においてのみ生起する．このことは本稿において大きな意味を持つ．

　イタリア語は，開音節性の高い言語として知られている．次語末音節（語末から2音節目）への強勢がデフォルトで，語彙全体の8割前後がその位置に強勢を持つとされる（Borrelli (2002))．それ以外の強勢位置としては，語末3音節目が十数％，語末音節が数％，語末4音節目が僅かに生起するとの報告がある（Krämer (2009))．強勢位置の正確な予測は難しいが，次語末音節が尾子音を伴う重音節の場合，(1) のように，例外なくその音節に強勢の置かれることが知られている（Krämer (2009))．[1]

(1)　イタリア語発音　　　表記　　　　　グロス
　　a.　san.már.ko　　　　San Marco　　サンマルコ
　　　　vi.vál.di　　　　　Vivaldi　　　　ヴィヴァルディ
　　　　skám.pi　　　　　 scampi　　　　手長エビ
　　b.　don.dʒo.ván.ni　　 Don Giovanni　ドン・ジョヴァンニ
　　　　va.po.lét.to　　　　vapoletto　　　水上バス
　　　　bot.ti.tʃél.li　　　　Botticelli　　　ボッティチェリ

他方，次語末が開音節の場合，強勢位置にバリエーションの生じることになる．とくに強勢を伴う開音節内の母音は語末を除き (2) のように伸張し，重音節が形成される（Marotta (1985), Canepari (1992))．

---

[1] 本稿では，議論を単純にするため，便宜上，簡略化した発音記号を用いる．

(2) a. ve.ró:.na　　　Verona　　　ヴェローナ
　　　va.ti.ká:.no　　Vaticano　　ヴァチカン
　　　pa.ra.dí:.zo　　paradiso　　楽園
　　　mi.la.né:.ze　　milanese　　ミラノの
　　b. pá:.do.va　　　Padova　　　パドヴァ
　　　fí:.ga.ro　　　　Figaro　　　フィガロ
　　　bal.sá:.mi.ko　balsamico　　バルサミコ
　　　ba.zí:.li.ko　　basilico　　　バジリコ

それ以外の環境，すなわち非強勢音節，閉音節，語末音節内では，母音は短母音として生起する．(3) に語末強勢開音節の例を示す．[2]

(3)　kaf.fé　caffè　コーヒー　　re.al.tá　realtà　現実
　　　vir.tú　virtù　美質　　　　lu.ne.dí　lunedì　月曜日

(1)(2) のように，語末を除く強勢音節はすべて重音節と対応するわけである．音節量と強勢との間に対応関係を持つという面で，イタリア語は，後述の日本語借用語アクセント規則と共通性が見られる．次語末が閉音節（子音性重音節）の場合，そこに強勢（アクセント）が置かれるという点において，日本語の借用語アクセント規則，とくに (5a) と完全に一致する（そこが開音節の場合，強勢は引きつけないが，強勢の置かれた場合は母音伸長により重音節となり，(5b) と一致することになる）．

　本稿では，イタリア語から日本語に語が借用される際，母音性重音節を形成する長母音や，子音性重音節を形成する二重子音がどのように受け継がれ，原語の強勢がどのように関わるかを分析する．

2.2. 日本語の借用語アクセント規則

　日本語の借用語における原語 (L2) は英語由来が大半であり，また，そこにアクセント規則の存在することが知られている．[3] 英語と異なる L2 において規則とどの程度一致するか検証の必要がある．

---

　[2]（強勢）閉音節内の母音は (1) にあるように伸長しない．また，非強勢開音節の例は，(1)(2) のそれぞれ該当する音節を参照されたい．
　[3] 柴田 (1994) によると，日本語における借用語の 83% が英語由来である．

日本語の借用語において，L2 の強勢は位置に関しては基本的に参照されないとの報告がある (Kubozono (2006)，田中 (2008))．[4]

　東京方言の音節にもとづく借用語アクセント規則として，以下が知られている (Kubozono (1996))．なお，. は音節境界を表す．

(4)　次語末音節にアクセントを置く．ただし，そこが軽音節の場合，もう 1 つ前（語末から 3 音節目）にアクセントを置く．

(5)　a.　ヨー.ロ'ッ.パ，ピ.ラ.ミ'ッ.ド，カ.レ'ン.ダー，
　　 b.　チョ.コ.レ'ー.ト，ア.リ.ゲ'ー.ター，シ.リ'ー.ズ
　　 c.　アルバ'イト，ク.ロ.コ.ダ'イ.ル，プ.ラ'イ.ム

(6)　ド'.ラ.ゴン，エ.ネ'.ル.ギー，ブ.ラ'イ.ダ.ル，ア'.マ.ゾン
　　 シ'ン.フォ.ニー，ク'.ラ.ス，ガ.ラ.パ'.ゴ.ス，ト'.マ.ト

強勢かピッチアクセントかという違いを超えて，各要素の付与される位置に関して，(5) と (6) はイタリア語の強勢付与と大きく関係する．(5) はイタリア語のデフォルト強勢位置における音節量と強勢との関係に対応し，(6) は次語末の非アクセント音節が短母音であるという面で，イタリア語の次語末以外の強勢パターン（とくに語末 3 音節目の強勢）と関係するように見える．

　このような，音節量とその配列に基づくアクセント付与は，一般に次の制約が関与することが知られている．

(7)　Peak Prominence (H' ≫ L') (Prince and Smolensky (1993/2004))
　　 アクセントは卓立性の高い要素（重い音節）に付与される．

なお，後で確認するように，イタリア語において語末に重音節はほとんど生起しないが，このことは (4)–(7) の議論に影響を及ぼさない．アクセント規則では次語末の音節量が問題になるからである．

---

　[4] L2 の強勢・アクセント情報の非参照については，たとえば，日本語から台湾語への借用語の声調付与についても観察される (Tu and Davis (2009))．

2.3. 音節量受け入れとアクセント位置算定

イタリア語は母音長の音韻対立は持たないのに対し，子音長の対立は持つ．この点においては日本語と共通する．しかしながら，イタリア語が子音のほぼすべてに対立（二重子音）を持つのに対し，日本語は一般に流音 /r/ の二重子音（促音）を許容せず，また，/b/, /d/, /g/, /z/ 等の有声二重阻害音の生起に制限が見られる．このことは，イタリア語から日本語が語を借用する際に，音節量，ひいては強勢の受け入れに影響を及ぼすことを予想させる．

イタリア語において，「次語末－語末音節」に跨がり生起する /l/ や /r/ 等の二重流音（例：cam.pa.nel.la（鐘），bur.ro（バター））の前半部分は次語末音節の尾子音に相当し，重音節を形成する．それらが仮にそのまま受け入れられるとすると，(5a) と同じ役割を果たすことになる．日本語において生起し難い二重流音が借用される際，子音そのものの受け入れと強勢（アクセント）との関係が問題になる．

このような観点から，以下では，イタリア語における母音，子音，強勢がどのように引き継がれるかを分析する．

3. 調査

『広辞苑』（第 5 版），『コンサイス・カタカナ語辞典』（第 2 版），『大辞林』（第 2 版）より，イタリア語由来の借用語 1001 例を抽出し，このうち，イタリア語における語末音節，次語末音節，語末第 3 音節（つまり，強勢アクセントの期待される位置にある音節）を分析対象とした．

まず，イタリア語の強勢と日本語のアクセントとの一致度を見る．イタリア語次語末の開音節・閉音節別に分類したのが表1である．

表1. イタリア語次語末音節と強勢・アクセント位置の一致

イタリア語強勢	一致	不一致	合計
全体	828 (83%)	173 (17%)	1001
閉音節	349 (86%)	54 (14%)	402
開音節	479 (80%)	119 (20%)	599

全体値を見ると，83％（828/1001）という高い割合で，イタリア語の強勢位置と日本語のアクセント位置とが一致する．これは，借用語一般における原語アクセントとの一致度を調査した田中（2008）（69％：1659/2415）と比べ，きわめて高い値である．[5] とくに次語末が閉音節の場合にそれが顕著である．ここにおいて，日本語における借用語アクセント規則とイタリア語のデフォルト強勢付与との類似性が浮かび上がる．イタリア語においてデフォルト強勢位置は次語末であり，そこが義務的に重音節として実現されることを考慮に入れれば，一致度の高さは想像に難くない（その前提として，重音節をはじめとするイタリア語のリズム構造が，日本語に正確に受け入れられるということがある）．

興味深いことに，強勢位置受け入れにおける不一致はある程度予測可能であり，その大半は，両言語間における特定のリズム構造に対する処理のずれによって生じるものである．

以下では，このようなリズムの受け入れがアクセントに及ぼす影響について分析する．

4. 分析

4.1. 音節構造の変換と強勢位置の非継承

日本語がイタリア語の強勢と異なるアクセントを示した例の大半は，以下のリズム構造を有している（(9) は具体例を示す）．

(8) a. イタリア語の次語末閉音節（重音節）の尾子音，とくに二重流音が日本語に受け入れられず，軽音節として受け入れられ，アクセントの再計算が行われた．

    b. 次語末の無声二重子音（とくに /tt/）が受け入れられたものの，十分な重さを持つものとして認識されず，軽音節と類似の処理が行われた．[6]

---

[5] 田中（2008）は，『日本語発音アクセント辞典』（1985）に所収の 3〜8 モーラの借用語 2415 例のアクセント調査を行い，上記を報告している．

[6] これは，借用語一般（例：ロ'・ボッ・ト，ト'・リッ・ク，ス'・リッ・パ，ル'ー・レッ・ト）とまったく同様である．田中（2008）は，無声二重子音のソノリティーの低さから，それを尾子

c. イタリア語の語末に /ia/, /ua/, /io/, /uo/ 等の上昇二重母音を含み，日本語との間に音節構造の齟齬が生じた．[7]
d. 4モーラ，かつ，語末が軽音節の連続（-LL#）になることにより，積極的に平板化した．

(9) イタリア語　　　　　表記　　　　　　借用語
 a. ma.kja.vél.li　　　Machiavelli　　マ'.キ.ア'.ヴェ.リ
   kam.pa.nél.la　　campanella　　カン.パ'.ネ.ラ
   taʎ.ʎa.tél.le　　tagliatelle　　タ.リ.ア'.テ.レ
   o.tél.lo　　　　Otello　　　　オ'.テ.ロ（オ'.セ.ロ）
 b. so.nét.to　　　　sonetto　　　　ソ'.ネッ.ト
   ri.zót.to　　　　risotto　　　　リ'.ゾッ.ト
   fal.sét.to　　　falsetto　　　　ファ'.ル.セッ.ト
 c. fan.ta.zí:.a　　　fantasia　　　　ファン.タ'.ジ.ア
   pit.tse.rí:.a　　pizzeri　　　　ピッ.ツェ'.リ.ア
   al.fa.ro.mé:.o　Alfa Romeo　　ア.ル.ファ.ロ'.メ.オ
   san.ta.lu.ʧí:.a　Santa Lucia　　サン.タ.ル'.チ.ア
 d. ve.nét.tsja　　　Venezia　　　　ヴェ.ネ.ツィ.ア⁰
   gón.do.la　　　gondola　　　　ゴン.ド.ラ⁰
   raf.fa.él.lo　　Raffaello　　　ラ.ファ.エ.ロ⁰
   kre.mó:.na　　Cremona　　　ク.レ.モ.ナ⁰

上記（8a-d）の条件の中に，イタリア語とアクセント位置の異なる173例

音として持つ重音節を擬似的な軽音節と再解釈し一般化を提示している．

[7] イタリア語において，語末の上昇二重母音は，強勢の有無により母音長つまり音節構造が異なる（池田他（1999））．強勢を伴う場合，各母音は別の音節に属し，強勢を受けた前半の母音が次語末音節となって長母音化する．その結果，VVの部分がV:.Vとして実現する（例：ma.rí:.a（Maria: マリア））．それに対し，強勢を伴わない場合，前半の母音が渡り音化し，VVがGVの1音節として実現する（例：má:.rjo（Mario: マリオ））．いずれの場合も日本語化の際のモーラ数と対応しない．前者のV:.Vは3モーラが，後者のGVは1モーラが期待されるのに対し，日本語は（9c）のようにそれを2モーラとして受け入れるのが一般的である．興味深いことに，後者の場合，リズムの受け入れ（長さ）は異なるものの，強勢位置はイタリアと結果的に同一になる（例：má:.rjo（Mario）→ ma'.ri.o（マ'.リ.オ））．

(表1）のうちの79%(137/173) が含まれる.[8] このように，リズム構造の受け入れの齟齬により，日本語側でアクセントの計算に違いが生じたと言える.

4.2. 強勢と母音長の受け入れ

ここでは，イタリア語の強勢と母音長受け入れとの関係を分析する．イタリア語において強勢の期待される3つの音節位置，すなわち，語末3音節目（表2），次語末（表3），語末（表4）における開音節／閉音節の別と，強勢の有無に着目して，日本語化の際の母音長受け入れを分析した．ここまでの議論で確認したように，各表の最上行（10a-12a）が，すべてイタリア語の長母音に該当し，各値が日本語の長母音受け入れ率となる（各表下の3行はすべて，イタリア語で短母音の生起する環境である）.

表2. イタリア語の開／閉音節，強勢有無と母音長受け入れ（－3音節）

イタリア語 (L2) ＼日本語 (L1)	①長母音	②短母音	合計
(10a) 開音節, ＋強勢 (＝長母音)	21 (28%)	54 (72%)	75
(10b) 開音節, －強勢 (＝短母音)	0 (0%)	430 (100%)	430
(10c) 閉音節, ＋強勢 (＝短母音)	0 (0%)	25 (100%)	25
(10d) 閉音節, －強勢 (＝短母音)	0 (0%)	291 (100%)	291
合計	21 (3%)	800 (97%)	821

(10) a. ① kó:.mo.do comodo コ'ー.モ.ド
   sí:.mi.le simile シ'ー.ミ.レ
  ② ná:.po.li Napoli ナ'.ポ.リ (*ナ'ー.ポ.リ)
   pá:.do.va Padova パ'.ド.ヴァ (*パ'ー.ド.ヴァ)
   fí:.ga.ro Figaro フィ'.ガ.ロ (*フィ'ー.ガ.ロ)
   mé:.di.tʃi Medici メ'.ディ.チ (*メ'ー.ディ.チ)
   ba.zí:.li.ko basilico バ.ジ'.リ.コ (*バ.ジ'ー.リ.コ)
   bal.sá:.mi.ko balsamico バル.サ'.ミ.コ
               (*バル.サ'ー.ミ.コ)

---

[8] (8a) から (8d) の値は，それぞれ73%（34/47），15%（8/52），35%（29/83），26%（66/254）である.

表3. イタリア語の開／閉音節，強勢有無と母音長受け入れ（次語末）

イタリア語 (L2) ＼日本語 (L1)	①長母音	②短母音	合計
(11a) 開音節, ＋強勢（＝長母音）	322 (63%)	186 (37%)	508
(11b) 開音節, －強勢（＝短母音）	3 (2%)	60 (98%)	63
(11c) 閉音節, ＋強勢（＝短母音）	4 (1%)	398 (99%)	402
(11d) 閉音節, －強勢（＝短母音）	0	0	0[9]
合計	329 (34%)	644 (66%)	973

(11) a. ① ró:.ma　　　　Roma　　　ロ'ー.マ (*ロ'マ)
　　　　 ve.ró:.na　　　Verona　　ヴェ.ロ'ー.ナ
　　　　　　　　　　　　　　　　　（*ヴェロ'ナ,*ヴェ'ロナ）
　　　　 por.tʃí:.ni　　porcini　　ポ.ル.チ'ー.ニ
　　　　　　　　　　　　　　　　　（*ポルチ'ニ,*ポル'チニ）
　　　　 mi.la.né:ze　　milanese　ミ.ラ.ネ'ー.ゼ
　　　　　　　　　　　　　　　　　（*ミラネ'ゼ,*ミラ'ネゼ）
　　　② = (9c, d)

表4. イタリア語の開／閉音節，強勢有無と母音長受け入れ（語末音節）

イタリア語 (L2) ＼日本語 (L1)	①長母音	②短母音	合計
(12a) 開音節, ＋強勢（＝長母音）	1 (9%)	10 (91%)	11
(12b) 開音節, －強勢（＝短母音）	12 (1%)	971 (99%)	983
(12c) 閉音節, ＋強勢（＝短母音）	3 (75%)[10]	1 (25%)	4
(12d) 閉音節, －強勢（＝短母音）	0 (0%)	3 (100%)	3
合計	16 (2%)	985 (98%)	1001

(12) a. ① pó　　　　　　Po　　　　　ポー
　　　② pje.tá　　　　Pietà　　　ピ'.エ.タ
　　　　 ti.ra.mi.sú　　tiramisù　ティ'.ラ.ミ.ス

---

[9] イタリア語において，次語末位置の閉音節は必ず強勢を引きつける（＋強勢となる）ため，体系上「閉音節,－強勢」の組み合わせは生起しない．

[10] (12c ①) の具体例のように，語末に /r/ を伴い，日本語化の際，末尾に /u/ が挿入され再音節化した例がすべてである．再音節化後の次語末を長母音化することで重くし, (11a ①) と同じ構造にするための操作と解釈できる．

b. ①　gét.to　　　ghetto　　　ゲ'ッ.トー
　　　　　brá:.vo　　　bravo　　　ブ.ラ'.ボー
　　　　　gráf.fi.ti　　graffiti　　グ.ラ'.フィ.ティー
　　c. ①　bár　　　　bar　　　　バ'ー.ル
　　　　　ka.vúr　　　Cavour　　カ.ヴ'ー.ル, カ.ブ'ー.ル
　　d. ②　ín.ter　　　Inter　　　イ'ン.テ.ル
　　　　　ju.vén.tus　Juventus　ユ.ヴェ'ン.ト.ス

　データの面からも，日本語化の際の長母音は，基本的にイタリア語における（語末以外の）強勢開音節のみに生じることが確認できる（94%: 344/366）．全体の長母音受け入れ率は58%（344/594）であり，また，二重子音の受け入れ率との間に，強勢が関与するという面においても平行性が見られる（田中（2007），Tanaka (2015)）．

　重要な点として，長母音の生起する強勢開音節において，語末3音節目と次語末とで，受け入れに非対称が見られることである．次語末では，強勢開音節は基本的にL2と同じ長母音として受け入れられるのに対し，語末3音節目においては，それが長母音ではなく，むしろ短母音として受け入れられる（イタリア語の長母音が受け入れられにくい）．これは，日本語の借用語アクセント規則が関与する．なお，表3（11a ②）の大半が，(8c) あるいは (8d) の構造を持つ例である．

　日本語においてL2と同じく次語末にアクセントが付与される場合，必ず重音節（開音節では長母音）が生起しなければならないのに対し，語末3音節目は軽音節（短母音）でもアクセントの付与は可能である．このように，日本語側（L1）の要請により，長母音の受け入れに非対称が生じると解釈できる．

4.3.　強勢の受入と母音長

　ここでは，イタリア語借用語の強勢位置の保持率が高い要因について音節量との関係から考察する．

　これを明らかにするための手がかりとして，イタリア語におけるCV連続の語の，日本語への受け入れを分析する．

　これまでに確認したように，イタリア語においては，次語末が開音節の場

合，そこが閉音節の場合とは異なり，強勢位置の正確な予測が困難であり，強勢付与後に次語末あるいは語末3音節目の母音が長母音として生起する．日本語化の際，イタリア語の強勢・母音長がどのように参照されたのかが問題となる．

このことを検証するため，すべてが開音節であり，強勢を直接は引き付けない CV 連続の語における韻律の受け入れを分析する．

表5は，イタリア語で2～5音節 CV 連続の語における強勢位置とそれに対応する日本語における長母音およびアクセントの生起との関係を，とくに（強勢の期待される）語末3音節に着目して示したものである．

表5．イタリア語 CV 連続語における強勢位置と日本語の母音長受入

伊語＼日本語	a.-CV:.CV.CV	b.-CV.CV:.CV	c.-CV.CV.CV	計
(13)-CV:.CV.CV#	4 (21%)	0 (0%)	15 (79%)	19
(14)-CV.CV:.CV#	0 (0%)	73 (80%)	18 (20%)*	91
(15)-CV.CV.CV#	0 (0%)	0 (0%)	2 (100%)*	2
合計	4 (4%)	73 (66%)	33 (30%)	110

※下線：イタリア語強勢音節，波線：日本語デフォルトアクセント音節

(13)　　イタリア語　　表記　　日本語
　　a.　kó:.mo.do　　comodo　　コ'ー.モ.ド　　（*コ.モー.ド）
　　　　sí:.mi.le　　 simile　　シ'ー.ミ.レ　　（*シ.ミー.レ）
　　　　a.má:.bi.le　amabile　　ア.マ'ー.ビ.レ　（*ア.マ.ビー.レ）
　　c.　pá:.do.va　　Padova　　パ'.ド.ヴァ　　（*パ.ドー.ヴァ）
　　　　ná:.po.li　　Napoli　　ナ'.ポ.リ　　　（*ナ.ポー.リ）
　　　　ó:.pe.ra　　 opera　　 オ'.ペ.ラ　　　（*オ.ペー.ラ）
　　　　lí:.be.ro　　libero　　リ'.ベ.ロ　　　（*リ.ベー.ロ）
　　　　ba.zí:.li.ko basilico　バ.ジ'.リ.コ　　（*バ.ジ.リー.コ）
(14) b.　ve.ró:.na　 Verona　　ヴェ.ロ'ー.ナ
　　　　　　　　　　　　　　　（*ヴェ.ロ'.ナ, *ヴェ'.ロ.ナ）
　　　　dʒe.lá:.to　 gelato　　ジェ.ラ'ー.ト
　　　　　　　　　　　　　　　（*ジェ.ラ'.ト, *ジェ'.ラ.ト）
　　　　fi.ná:.le　　finale　　フィ.ナ'ー.レ
　　　　　　　　　　　　　　　（*フィ.ナ'.レ, *フィ'.ナ.レ）

		pa.ní:.ni	panini	パ.ニ'ー.ニ
				(*パ.ニ'.ニ, *パ'.ニ.ニ)
	c.	o.ka.rí:.na	ocarina	オ.カ.リ.ナ⁰
		so.na.tí:.ne	sonatine	ソ.ナ.チ.ネ⁰
		ka.za.nó:.va	Casanova	カ.ザ.ノ.ヴァ⁰
(15)	c.	u.ni.tá	unità	ウ'.ニ.タ
				(*ウ.ニ'ー.タ, *ウ.ニ.タ')
		ti.ra.mi.sú	tiramisù	ティ'.ラ.ミ.ス
				(*ティ.ラ.ミ'ー.ス, *ティ.ラ.ミ.ス')

表5は，日本語がイタリア語から語を借用する際の方策について，いくつかの事実を端的に示している．まず，日本語の長母音がイタリア語において長母音の生起する環境においてのみ生起することが確認できる．イタリア語の長母音を日本語が短母音として受け入れることはあっても，その逆，つまり短母音を長母音として受け入れることは，基本的にないということである．[11]

イタリア語の強勢位置との一致率は(表中 * の数を除いた) 83% (90/110)であり，とくに，日本語において長母音として受け入れられたすべての例において，原語の強勢がピッチアクセントとして実現されている ((13a) と (14b) とで 100% (77/77) であり，逆は真ならず)．

さらに，重要な点として，長母音受け入れには原語の母音長をもとに，日本語の調整が行われることがわかる．このことは (13) と (14b) との非対称を見れば明白である．つまり，どの位置に長母音を生起させるか，あるいはさせないかは，原語の強勢による母音長を参照した上で，借用語アクセント規制の要請により，日本語の音韻構造にとってふさわしい長さとアクセントが選択されることになる．

CV 連続の3音節語に焦点を絞ると，このことが明確に浮かび上がる．表6は表5の例のうち，とくに3音節語の強勢・アクセントと母音長との関係を示したものである．

---

[11] 例外としては (12b ①) がこれに当たる．イタリア語における語末 (-HL#) が，日本語化の際に (-LH#) となるケースが多く (例：spa.ghet.ti → su.pa.ge.tii)，かつ，そのまま受け入れられた (-HL#) の例を併せ持つ場合が多い (例：su.pa.get.ti)．

表6. イタリア語3音節語（CVCVCV）の強勢と借用語の韻律構造

伊語＼日本語	a.CV:.CV.CV	b.CV.CV:.CV	c.CV.CV.CV	計
(16) CV:.CV.CV	2 (14%)	0 (0%)	14 (86%)	16
(17) CV.CV:.CV	0 (0%)	37 (84%)	7 (16%)*	44
(18) CV.CV.CV	0 (0%)	0 (0%)	1 (100%)*	1
合計	2 (3%)	37 (61%)	22 (36%)	61

(16a), (16c), (17b), (18c) の具体例は, それぞれ (13a), (13c), (14b), (15c) の3音節語の部分と同一である. (17c) に, イタリア語強勢が保持されず, 日本語のデフォルトアクセントの付与された例を挙げる.

(17) c. mi.lá:.no   Milano   ミ'.ラ.ノ   (*ミ.ラ'ー.ノ)
         to.rí:.no   Torino   ト'.リ.ノ   (*ト.リ'ー.ノ)
         sa.lá:.me   salame   サ'.ラ.ミ   (*サ.ラ'ー.ミ)
         ka.pó:.ne   capone   カ'.ポ.ネ   (*カ.ポ'ー.ネ)
         ka.dʒí:.no   casino   カ'.ジ.ノ   (*カ.ジ'ー.ノ)
         du.bí:.ni   Dubini   ズ'.ビ.ニ   (*ズ.ビ'ー.ニ)
         so.ná:.ta   sonata   ソ'.ナ.タ   (*ソ.ナ'ー.タ)

(17c) の生起要因として考えられることとして, 英語経由で日本語に借用された可能性のあることである. また, 文字列CVCVCVの情報のみにより, 日本語のデフォルトアクセント規則が選択された可能性も考えられる. いずれの要因が関わるか検証の必要があるが, 重要な点として, (17c) は例外であり, (17b) が無標の型であることである.

以上をまとめると, 日本語は原語（イタリア語）の強勢にもとづき母音長（子音長）を入力情報として音節構造を確定し, それをもとに, 借用語アクセント規則 (4) を適用するといえる.

5. まとめと課題

本稿は, イタリア語由来の借用語における強勢と音節構造の受け入れ, および, その相互作用について分析し, 次の知見を得た.

第一に, 借用語はイタリア語の強勢と高い割合で一致し, 両言語の類似の

方策による可能性を確認した．同時に，（とくに開音節語において）日本語がイタリア語の強勢位置を母音長知覚の手がかりとして参照することが明らかになった．日本語化の際の長母音は，イタリア語の（語末を除く）強勢開音節を受け入れた結果，生起するということを，データによって確認した．さらに同じ長母音でも，原語の強勢位置によって受け入れ方策に非対称が見られ，イタリア語における次語末音節の長母音は，そのまま受け入れられるのが基本であるのに対し，語末3音節目の長母音はむしろ短母音として受け入れられること，そこには日本語（L1）のアクセント規則が作用することが明らかになった．さらに，このことが子音長受け入れ（Tanaka (2015)）と平行的であることを指摘した．

今後の課題としては，他言語，とくに，母音長の対立を持つ言語におけるイタリア語からの借用語受け入れについて分析することである．日本語では受け入れられなかった語末3音節目の長母音がどのように受け入れられるか確認の必要がある．

関連して，知覚との関連を検証する必要がある．イタリア語の強勢開音節内の母音は，次語末，語末3音節目ともに長母音として実現されるが，持続時間は，語末3音節目の方がわずかに短いとの報告がある（郡 (1993))．

イタリア語話者が長母音として認識する語末3音節目の母音を，日本語話者がじっさいにどのように知覚するのか検証するのも，今後の課題である．

参考文献

Borrelli, Doris (2002) *Raddoppiamento Sintattico in Italian: A Synchronic and Diachronic Cross-Dialectal Study*, Routledge, New York/London.

Canepari, Luciano (1992) *Manuale di pronuncia italiana* (Manual of Italian Pronunciation), Zanichelli, Bologna.

Hayes, Bruce (1995) *Metrical Stress Theory: Principe and Case Studies*, University of Chicago Press, Chicago.

池田廉・西村暢夫・郡史郎・在里寛司・米山喜晟 (編) (1999)『伊和中辞典』(第2版)，小学館，東京．

Kager, René (1999) *Optimality Theory*, Cambridge University Press, Cambridge.

Kang, Yoonjung (2011) "Loanword Phonology," *The Blackwell Companion to Pho-*

nology IV, 2258-2282, Wiley-Blackwell, Oxford.
郡史郎（1993）「イタリア語の韻律的特徴：音の長さを規定する要因について」『池田廉教授退官記念論文集』，185-210，大阪外国語大学，大阪．
Krämer, Martin (2009) *Phonology of Italian*, Oxford University Press, Oxford.
Kubozono, Haruo (1996) "Syllable and Accent in Japanese: Evidence from Loanword Accentuation," *The Bulletin* (*Phonetic Society of Japan*) 211, 71-82.
Kubozono, Haruo (2006) "Where Does Loanword Prosody Come from?: A Case Study of Japanese Loanword Accent," *Lingua* 116, 1140-1170.
Marotta, Giovanna (1985) *Modelli e Misure Ritmiche: la Durata Vocalica in Italiano*, Zanichelli, Bologna.
松村明（編）（1995）『大辞林』（第2版），三省堂，東京．
Prince, Alan and Paul Smolensky (1993/2004) *Optimality Theory: Constraint Interaction in Generative Grammar*, Blackwell, Oxford.
三省堂編修所（編）（2000）『コンサイス・カタカナ語辞典』（第2版），三省堂，東京．
柴田武（1994）「外来語におけるアクセント核の位置」『現代語・方言の研究』佐藤喜代治（編），388-418，明治書院，東京．
新村出（編）（1998）『広辞苑』（第5版），岩波書店，東京．
田中真一（2007）「イタリア語の重子音と促音形成：位置と種類に着目して」『日本言語学会第134回大会発表論文集』252-257．
田中真一（2008）『リズム・アクセントの「ゆれ」と音韻・形態構造』くろしお出版，東京．
Tanaka, Shin'ichi (2015) "The adaptation of Italian Geminates and Vowels in Japanese and Its Relation to Perception," A paper presented at GemCon 2015, ICPhS 2015 (International Congress of Phonetic Sciences 2015), Scottish Exhibition and Conference Centre, Glasgow.
田中真一（2016a）「日本語・イタリア語の借用語における相手言語からの母音長受け入れと音韻構造」『神戸言語学論叢』第10号，37-50，神戸大学言語学研究室．
田中真一（2016b）「イタリア語における日本語由来の借用語と韻律構造」『現代音韻論の動向：日本音韻論学会の歩みと展望』，日本音韻論学会（編），84-87，開拓社，東京．
Tu, Jung-yueh and Stuart Davis (2009) "Japanese Loanwords into Taiwanese Southern Min," *Proceedings of the Second International Conference on East Asian Linguistics*, Simon Fraser University.

執筆者紹介
(アルファベット順)

儀利古幹雄（ぎりこ・みきお）　大阪大学・講師
【主要業績】　Kubozono, H., Takeyasu, H. and Giriko, M. (2013) "On the positional asymmetry of consonant germination in Japanese loanwords," *Journal of East Asian Linguiostics* 22(4), 339-371.
(2011)「日本語における疑似複合構造と平板型アクセント——語末が /Cin/ である外来語のアクセント分析——」『音韻研究』14, 73-84.

Hashimoto, Daiki（橋本大樹）　University of Canterbury・Doctoral Candidate（カンタベリー大学・博士候補）
【主要業績】　(2016) "Recursive feet in Japanese: Avoidance of LH structure,"『音韻研究』19, 3-10.
(2015)「単純語短縮語形成に関する第3の解釈」西原哲雄・田中真一（編）『現代の形態論と音声学・音韻論の視点と論点』294-312, 開拓社.
(2015) "Hypocoristic word formation in Māori,"『音韻研究』18, 11-18.

Hayashi, Akiko（林安紀子）　Tokyo Gakugei University・Professor（東京学芸大学・教授）
【主要業績】　Hayashi, A. and Mazuka, R. (in press). "Emergence of Japanese infants's preferences in infant-directed vocabulary," *Developmental Psychology*.
大伴潔・林安紀子・橋本創一・菅野敦（編著）(2013)『LCSA 学齢版　言語・コミュニケーション発達スケール（増補版）』学苑社.
Hayashi, A., Tamekawa, Y. and Kiritani, S. (2001) "Developmental changes in auditory preferences for speech stimuli in Japanese infants," *Journal of Speech, Language, and Hearing Research* 44, 1189-1200.

Hirata, Yukari（平田由香里）　Colgate University・Professor（コルゲート大学・教授）
【主要業績】　(2015) "L2 phonetics and phonology," H. Kubozono (ed.) *Phonetics and Phonology* (The Handbook of Japanese Language and Linguistics), 719-762. De Gruyter Mouton.

Hirata, Y., Kelly, S. D., Huang, J., and Manansala, M. (2014) "Effects of hand gestures on auditory learning of second-language vowel length contrasts,"*Journal of Speech, Language, and Hearing Research* 57, 2090-2101.

Hirata, Y. and Amano, S. (2012) "Production of single and geminate stops in Japanese three- and four-mora Japanese words," *Journal of the Acoustical Society of America* 132(3), 1614-1625.

本間猛（ほんま・たける）　首都大学東京・教授
【主要業績】　(2013) "Trochaic Clusters in English,"『音声研究』17(1), 38-45.

(2004) "The CodaMax approach to the English stress," in Honma, T., Okazaki M., Tabata, T. and Tanaka, S. (eds.), *A New Century of Phonology and Phonological Theory: A Festschrift for Prof. Shosuke Haraguchi on the Occasion of His Sixtieth Birthday*. Kaitakusha.

窪薗晴夫・本間猛（2002）『音節とモーラ』研究社.

Ito, Junko（伊藤順子）　University of California, Santa Cruz・Professor（カリフォルニア大学サンタクルーズ校・教授）
【主要業績】　Ito, J. and Mester, A. (2013) "Prosodic subcategories in Japanese," *Lingua* 124, 20-40.

Ito, J. and Mester, A. (2003) *Japanese Morphophonemics: Markedness and Word Structure*. Linguistic Inquiry Monograph Series 43. MIT Press.

(1989) "A Prosodic theory of epenthesis," *Natural Language and Linguistic Theory* 7, 217-260.

Kelly, Spencer D.（ケリー・スペンサー）　Colgate University・Professor（コルゲート大学・教授）
【主要業績】　Siciliano, R., Hirata, Y., and Kelly, S. D. (2016) "Electrical stimulation over left inferior frontal gyrus disrupts hand gesture's role in foreign vocabulary learning,"*Educational Neuroscience* 1, 1-12.

Kelly, S., Hirata, Y., Manansala, M. and Huang, J. (2014) "Exploring the role of hand gestures in learning novel phoneme contrasts and vocabulary in a second language," *Frontiers in Psychology* 5, 673.

Kelly, S. D., Ozyurek, A., and Maris, E. (2010) "Two sides of the same coin: Speech and gesture mutually interact to enhance comprehension,"

Psychological Science 21, 260-267.

北原真冬（きたはら・まふゆ）　上智大学・教授
【主要業績】　Tajima, K., Kitahara, M. and Yoneyama, K. (2015) "Production of an Allophonic Variant in a Second Language: The Case of Intervocalic Alveolar Flapping," *JELS* 32, 139-145.
Kitahara, M. and Yoneyama, K. (2014) "Voicing Effect on Vowel Duration: Corpus Analyses of Japanese Infants and Adults, and Production Data of English Learners," *Journal of the Phonetic Society of Japan* 18(1), 30-39.
北原真冬（2008）「最小対立における音韻システムの歪みと不均衡」児玉一宏・小山哲春（編）山梨正明教授還暦記念論文集『言葉と認知のメカニズム』545-556, ひつじ書房.

Kondo, Tadahisa（近藤公久）　Kogakuin University・Professor（工学院大学・教授）
【主要業績】　Wydell, T. and Kondo, T. (2015) "Behavioral and neuroimaging research of reading: A case of Japanese," *Current Developmental Disorders Report*, 1-7.
Mochida, T., Kimura, T., Hiroya, S., Kitagawa, N., Gomi, H., and Kondo, T. (2013) "Speech misperception: speaking and seeing interfer differently with hearing," PLOS One 8, 1-8.
天野成昭・近藤公久（1999）『日本語の語彙特性』第1巻〜6巻, 三省堂.

権延姝（こん・よんじゅ）　神戸大学・研究員
【主要業績】　(2016)「韓国語の濃音の促音としての知覚」『音韻研究』19, 35-42.
(2014)「韓国語外来語の英語 schwa の借用」『音韻研究』17, 27-34.
(2008)「英語からの韓国語外来語の音節末母音挿入」『音韻研究』11, 47-54.

松井理直（まつい・みちなお）　大阪保健医療大学・教授
【主要業績】　(2016)「C/D モデルの特徴と課題」『現代音韻論の動向：日本音韻論学会20周年記念論文集』208-211, 開拓社.
(2016)「日本語における無声摩擦音の特性と摩擦母音──知覚的母音挿入の再検討──」『KLS』36, 147-158.
(2015)「日本語の母音無声化に関する C/D モデルの入力情報について」『音声研究』19(2), 55-69.

Mazuka, Reiko（馬塚れい子）　RIKEN Brain Science Institute・Laboratory Head（理化学研究所・チームリーダー）
【主要業績】　Martin, A., Igarashi, Y., Jincho, N., and Mazuka, R. (2016) "Utterances in infant-directed speech are shorter, not slower," *Cognition* 156, 52-59.
(2015) "Learning to become a native listener of Japanese," in Nakayama, M. (ed.) *Handbook of Japanese Psycholinguistics, Berlin/Boston: De Gruyter Mouton*. Chapter 2, 19-47.
(1998) *The Development of Language Processing Strategies: A Cross-linguistic Study between Japanese and English*. Lawrence Erlbaum Associates.

Mester, Armin（メスター・アーミン）　University of California, Santa Cruz・Professor（カリフォルニア大学サンタクルーズ校・教授）
【主要業績】　Ito, J. and Mester, A. (2016) "Unaccentedness in Japanese," *Linguistic Inquiry* 47, 471-526.
Ito, J. and Mester, A. (2009) "Lexical classes in phonology," Miyagawa, S. and Saito, M. (eds.) *Handbook of Japanese Linguistics*, 84-106. Oxford University Press.
(1994) "The quantitative trochee in Latin," *Natural Language and Linguistic Theory* 12. 1-61.

那須昭夫（なす・あきお）　筑波大学・准教授
【主要業績】　(2015) "The phonological lexicon and mimetic phonology," Kubozono, H. (ed.) *The Handbook of Japanese Phonetics and Phonology*, 253-288. De Gruyter Mouton.
(2008) "Phonological markedness and asymmetries in Japanese mimetics," Kubozono, H. (ed.) *Asymmetries in Phonology: An East-Asian Perspective*, 49-76. Kurosio.
(2007)「オノマトペの語末促音」『音声研究』11(1), 47-57.

小川晋史（おがわ・しんじ）　熊本県立大学・准教授
【主要業績】　(編) (2015)『琉球のことばの書き方──琉球諸語統一的表記法』くろしお出版.
(2012)『今帰仁方言アクセントの諸相』ココ出版.
(2004) "Sino-Japanese word accent and syllable structure,"『音韻研究』7,

41-48.

太田聡（おおた・さとし）　山口大学・教授
【主要業績】　(2013) "On the Relationship between Rendaku and Accent: Evidence from the *-kawa/-gawa* Alternation in Japanese Surnames," *Current Issues in Japanese Phonology: Segmental Variation in Japanese*, van de Weijer, J. and Nishihara, T. (eds.) 63-87. Kaitakusha.
(2003)「混成語制約再考」『音韻研究』6, 59-68.
窪薗晴夫・太田聡 (1998)『音韻構造とアクセント』研究社.

Poppe, Clemens（ポッペ・クレメンス）　National Institute for Japanese Language and Linguistics・JSPS Postdoctral Fellow（国立国語研究所 日本学術振興会・特別研究員）
【主要業績】　(2016) "Iambic feet in Japanese: Evidence from the Maisaka dialect,"『言語研究』150, 117-135.
van de Weijer, J., Poppe, C. and Sloos, M. (2013) "Family Matters: Lexical Aspects of Japanese Rendaku," *Current Issues in Japanese Phonology: Segmental Variation in Japanese*, van de Weijer, J. and Nishihara, T. (eds.), 129-148. Kaitakusha.
(2012) "Accent and domain structure in Tokyo Japanese: Generalizing across lexical classes,"『音韻研究』15, 43-50.

薛晋陽（せつ・しんよう）　山西大学・講師
【主要業績】　(2014)「シュワー借用のメカニズム」*Proceedings of the 38th Annual Meeting of The Kansai Linguistic Society*, 145-156.
(2012)「日本語における外来語語末長母音の短母音化」『音韻研究』15, 51-58.
(2011)「日本語における音節量の中和」*Proceedings of the 35th Annual Meeting of The Kansai Linguistic Society*, 228-239.

田端敏幸（たばた・としゆき）　千葉大学・教授
【主要業績】　(2010)「借用語音韻論の諸相」岸本秀樹（編）『ことばの対照』297-308. くろしお出版.
(2010)「数詞「三」と「四」について」大島弘子・中島晶子・ブラン・ラウル（編）『漢語の言語学』91-106. くろしお出版.
(2006)「鏡像関係をなすアクセントシステム——古典ギリシャ語とラテン語——」

『実験音声学と一般言語学』(城生佰太郎博士還暦記念論文集) 194-205. 東京堂出版.

高山知明(たかやま・ともあき) 金沢大学・教授
【主要業績】 (2016)「ハ行子音の脱唇音化 個別言語の特色と音韻史」大木一夫・多門靖容(編)『日本語史叙述の方法』ひつじ書房.
(2015) "Historical phonology," Kubozono, H. (ed.) *Handbook of Japanese Phonetics and Phonology* (*Handbooks of Japanese Language and Linguistics 2*). De Gruyter Mouton.
(2014)『日本語音韻史の動的諸相と蜆縮涼鼓集』笠間書院.

竹村亜紀子(たけむら・あきこ) フランス国立東洋言語文化学院・講師
【主要業績】 Kawagoe, I. and Takemura, A. (2013) "Geminate judgments of English-like words by Japanese native speakers: Differences in the borrowed forms of 'stuff' and 'tough'," *Journal of East Asian Linguistics* 21 (4), 307-337.
(2012) "Parental influence on dialect acquisition: The case of the tone system of Kagoshima Japanese," *NINJAL Research Papers* 3, 103-116.

竹安大(たけやす・はじめ) 福岡大学・講師
【主要業績】 Kubozono, H., Takeyasu, H. and Giriko, M. (2013) "On the positional asymmetry of consonant gemination in Japanese loanwords," *Journal of East Asian Linguistics* 22(4), 339-371.
(2012)「促音の知覚に対する先行音節子音・母音の持続時間の影響」『音韻研究』15, 67-78.
(2009)「摩擦音の促音知覚における摩擦周波数特性の影響」『音韻研究』12, 43-50.

Takiguchi, Izumi(瀧口いずみ) Bunkyo Gakuin University・Assistant Professor(文京学院大学・助教)
【主要業績】 (2015) "The role of vowel duration cue in L1: Effects on L2 learners' identification of phonological vowel length in Japanese," *Proceedings of the 18th International Congress of Phonetic Sciences*, Paper number 0111, 1-5.
(2011) "Perceptual development on the identification of length in L2 Japanese," *Proceedings of the 17th International Congress on Phonetic Scienc-*

es, 1950-1953.

田中真一（たなか・しんいち）　神戸大学・准教授
【主要業績】　（2016）「大阪方言複合語におけるアクセント回避と位置算定」『音韻研究』19, 81-88.
（2008）『リズム・アクセントの「ゆれ」と音韻・形態構造』くろしお出版.
田中真一・窪薗晴夫（1999）『日本語の発音教室――理論と練習』くろしお出版.

Tanaka, Shin-ichi（田中伸一）　University of Tokyo・Professor（東京大学・教授）
【主要業績】　日本音韻論学会（編）（2016）『現代音韻論の動向：日本音韻論学会 20 周年記念論文集』開拓社.
（2009）『日常言語に潜む音法則の世界』開拓社.
（2005）『アクセントとリズム』研究社.

上田功（うえだ・いさお）　大阪大学・教授
【主要業績】　（2013）"Retention of an irregular feature specification as a source of functional Misarticulation," *Philologia* 11, 1-10.
（2013）"The phonetic similarity in transliterated trademarks―A preliminary case study in Japanese," Cubrović, B. and Paunović, T. (eds.) *Focus on English Phonetics*, 237-250. Cambridge Scholars Publishing.
（2005）"Some formal and functional typological properties in developing phonologies,"『言語研究』127, 115-135.

Vance, Timothy J.（バンス・ティモシー）　National Institute for Japanese Language and Linguistics・Professor（国立国語研究所・教授）
【主要業績】　（2008）*The Sounds of Japanese*. Cambridge University Press.
（1987）*An Introduction to Japanese Phonology*, State University of New York Press.

山本武史（やまもと・たけし）　近畿大学・准教授
【主要業績】　（2016）「英語における子音の重さについて」日本音韻論学会（編）『現代音韻論の動向：日本音韻論学会 20 周年記念論文集』52-55．開拓社.
（2012）「ソノリティーによる言語現象の一般化」米倉綽（編）『ことばが語るもの――文学と言語学の試み』179-211．英宝社.
（2011）「一般米語における母音体系のクラスター分析と音声教育への応用」

『音声研究』15(1), 63-72.

吉田優子（よしだ・ゆうこ）　同志社大学・教授
【主要業績】　(2003) "Licensing constraint to let," S. Ploch (ed.) *Living on the Edge: Festschrift for Jonathan Kaye*, 449-464. Mouton de Gruyter.

(2000) "Nature of phonological representation (Review article of J. Coleman, Phonological representations: Their names, forms and powers)," *English Linguistics* 17(1), 220-242.

(1999) *On Pitch Accent Phenomena in Standard Japanese*, Holland Academic Graphics.

音韻研究の新展開：
窪薗晴夫教授還暦記念論文集

ISBN978-4-7589-2237-1　C3080

編　者	田中真一・ピンテール=ガーボル・小川晋史・儀利古幹雄・竹安大
発行者	武村哲司
印刷所	日之出印刷株式会社

2017 年 3 月 25 日　第 1 版第 1 刷発行©

発行所　株式会社　開拓社

〒113-0023 東京都文京区向丘 1-5-2
電話　(03) 5842-8900（代表）
振替　00160-8-39587
http://www.kaitakusha.co.jp

JCOPY ＜(社)出版者著作権管理機構　委託出版物＞

本書の無断複写は，著作権法上での例外を除き禁じられています．複写される場合は，そのつど事前に，(社)出版者著作権管理機構（電話 03-3513-6969, FAX 03-3513-6979, e-mail: info@jcopy.or.jp）の許諾を得てください．